THE BUSINESS OF FASHION
Designing, Manufacturing, and Marketing

Leslie Davis Burns

Nancy O. Bryant

Oregon State University

Fairchild Publications
New York

Text and Cover Design: Jeanne Calabrese
Cover Illustration: Sharon Watts
Photo Research: Gabrielle Heitler
Production Editor: Martin Schwabacher

Library of Congress Catalog Card Number: 96-085747

ISBN: 1-56367-073-9

GST R 133004424

Printed in the United States of America

The Business of Fashion: Designing, Manufacturing, and Marketing focuses on the organization and operation of the U.S. fashion industry—how fashion apparel is designed, manufactured, marketed, and distributed. This book captures the dynamics of the fashion industry, with its various components, by emphasizing the changing nature of the industries—technological changes, organizational changes, and changes in the global dimension of the industries involved.

As we investigate this ever-changing industry, it is important to set current strategies within their historical context. Thus, Chapter 1 begins with a history of the U.S. textile and apparel industry, from its inception in the late 1700s to the development and implementation of Quick Response. Once this historical context is set, we turn to current organizational structures of companies within the fashion industry. Chapter 2 discusses types of company ownership, including sole proprietorships, partnerships, and corporations, and forms of competition evident within the industry. Because of the prevalence of licensing agreements within the textile and apparel industry, the types of licensing, licensing contracts, and the advantages and disadvantages of licensing are discussed. The chapter ends with an explanation of the laws affecting the textile apparel industry, including laws protecting personal property and laws related to business practices.

Chapter 3 outlines the organization and operation of the U.S. textile industry—that is, the designing, manufacturing, and marketing of textiles. We follow textile production from fiber processing through the marketing of seasonal lines of fabrics. Recent developments and issues within the industry, including Quick Response strategies and environmental issues, provide a basis for our understanding of future trends in the industry.

Chapter 4 focuses on the general classifications and organizational structures of apparel companies that produce men's, women's, and children's apparel. Comparisons between ready-to-wear and couture, among types of producers, among types of apparel brand names, and among wholesale price zones reinforce the complexities of the apparel industry. The major divisions within apparel organizations (merchandising; fashion/product development; production, planning, and control; marketing and sales; and advertising and promotion) are introduced in this chapter.

Chapter 5 begins a four-chapter sequence on the creation and marketing of fashion apparel. This sequence follows an apparel line/collection through the various stages of research, design development and style selection, and marketing. Chapter 5 focuses on the various forms of research conducted prior to the development of a line/collection. Chapter 6 highlights the design stage—design planning, design inspirations, design sketches, and writing garment specification sheets. The creation of an apparel line continues in Chapter 7, which discusses how first patterns are developed, prototypes are sewn, cost analyses are conducted, and styles are selected for the final line. This chapter also analyzes and compares other ways in which apparel lines are created, including private label and specification buying. The final line is then marketed to retail buyers. Chapter 8 describes locations of and roles played by marts and trade shows in facilitating the marketing of apparel. How apparel is sold through corporate selling and through sales representatives is described next. The chapter ends with an overview of marketing strategies used by apparel companies in the distribution and promotion of their lines. Throughout this sequence of events in the creation and marketing of an apparel line, the chapters highlight new technological developments, global perspectives, and organizational changes within the industry.

Chapter 9 begins a four-chapter sequence on the production and distribution of apparel. Preproduction processes, including production orders, pattern finalization, pattern grading, and making the production marker are described. Chapter 10 outlines the sourcing options for apparel production, and the criteria used by apparel companies in making sourcing decisions. Issues surrounding domestic and foreign production of apparel, such as sweatshops and human rights, are also discussed. Chapter 11 explores the various methods by which apparel is produced, focusing on new technological advancements in these methods. Once produced, the apparel is distributed (often through distribution centers) to retailers. Chapter 12 summarizes distribution strategies and processes used by apparel companies. A description of the various types of store and nonstore retailers ends the chapter. Quick Response strategies are also highlighted throughout this discussion of production and distribution.

Our focus turns to home fashions and accessories in Chapters 13 and 14. A strong relationship exists between these industries and the apparel industry. Thus an overview of the organization and operation of the primary accessory industries is included in Chapter 13. Chapter 14 introduces the various facets of the home fashion industry, including the use of textiles for home furnishings such as sheets, towels, and draperies.

The book describes the dynamic nature of the textile, apparel, and retailing industries. Wherever possible, examples from the industry itself have been incorporated. Career profiles are also included at the end of each chapter to allow readers to better understand the job functions of careers throughout the fashion industry.

Many people have assisted with the development of this book, and we thank them for their time, effort, and support. Leslie Burns would like to thank her students, former students, and colleagues at Oregon State University, who have shared ideas and resources in the development of the book. She would also like to thank her husband, Chris, for his patience and infinite support throughout the project. Leslie Burns particularly appreciates her coauthor, Nancy Bryant, who brought extensive technical expertise and knowledge of the apparel industry to this work.

Nancy Bryant would like to express her appreciation first to her co-author, Leslie Burns, whose initial concept and direction for this text brought it into existence. Her knowledge of marketing and merchandising provided this text with the breadth necessary to reflect the industry as it operates now and will operate in the future. Her leadership through the publication process was invaluable. She would also like to thank her former students for their continual sharing of information about the apparel industry and expecially Tammy Wilson Sutter for her comments. Many other professional contacts in the apparel industry have also most willingly shared their expertise. The support of her colleagues at Oregon State University, her family, and most especially her husband, Dick, is deeply appreciated.

We wish to thank the following readers and reviewers: Ardis Koester, Cheryl Jordan, Carol Caughey, and Elaine Pedersen, Oregon State University; and Pamela Ulrich, Auburn University. Readers selected by the publisher were also very helpful. They include Nancy Rudd, Ohio State University; Stella Warnick, Seattle Pacific University; Pam Norum, University of Missouri–Columbia; Harriet Swedlund, South Dakota State University; Teresa Robinson, Middle Tennessee State University; Mary Boni, Kwantlen College; Fay Gibson, University of North Carolina–Greensboro; Kathleen Rees, University of Nebraska–Lincoln; Jo Kallal, University of Delaware; Ann Beth Presley, Auburn University; Bonnie Johnson, Fashion Institute of Technology; Jacqueline Robeck, University of Wisconsin–Stout.

Leslie Davis Burns
Oregon State University

Nancy O. Bryant
Oregon State University

CONTENTS

EXTENDED CONTENTS

Part Three

APPAREL PRODUCTION AND DISTRIBUTION   243

Part Four

ORGANIZATION AND
OPERATION OF THE
ACCESSORIES AND HOME
FASHIONS INDUSTRIES   355

Part One

ORGANIZATION OF THE U.S. TEXTILE AND APPAREL INDUSTRIES

1

From Spinning Machine
to Quick Response

Objectives

▌ To describe the technological developments in the textile and apparel industries.

▌ To describe the transition of the apparel industry from a craft industry to a factory-based industry.

▌ To describe the historical basis for the emergence of the Quick Response program.

▌ To discuss the forms of interindustry cooperation needed for the success of Quick Response strategies.

THE U.S. TEXTILE and apparel industries consist of companies that produce fibers, textiles, and apparel products for consumers in the United States as well as around the world. These industries are among the largest and most productive in the world. Textile and apparel companies can be found in every state, employing nearly two million people. When apparel distribution through retailers is included, these industries contribute to the economy of virtually every town in the nation. But how did it all begin? How did these industries develop and grow into the dynamic industries they are today? To fully understand the modern textile and apparel industries, a brief review of how they began, grew, and changed over the past two hundred years is important.

3

1789-1890: MECHANIZATION OF SPINNING, WEAVING, AND SEWING

For thousands of years, the spinning and weaving of fabrics were labor-intensive hand processes. Then, in England, in the mid-1700s, the spinning of yarn and weaving of cloth began to be mechanized. Indeed, at this time, England's cotton and wool textile industries were the most technologically developed in the western world. In response to a growing demand for textiles both in England and abroad, a series of advancements in spinning and weaving fabrics by such English inventors as John Kay (1733, invention of the flying shuttle loom), James Hargreaves (1764, invention of the spinning jenny), Sir Richard Arkwright (1769, invention of a water-powered spinning machine), and Edmund Cartwright (1785-1787, invention of the mechanized power loom) brought the British industry to world prominence. In addition, the process for printing fabrics was also being mechanized. England was protective of its technological developments, and severe penalties existed for attempting to take blueprints and/or machines or their parts out of the country. Even the mechanics themselves were restricted from leaving the country.

In the United States, a fledgling cotton industry was taking root, but America lacked England's advanced technology for spinning and weaving cotton fibers. Then, in 1789, Samuel Slater, a skilled mechanic, brought English textile technology to the United States by memorizing the blueprints of the Arkwright water-powered spinning machine. He declared himself a farmer (farmers were permitted to leave England) and came to the United States, settling in New England where a ready supply of water

Figure 1.1
Early spinning mill, including carding, drawing, roving, and spinning, as introduced by Samuel Slater.

existed. Hired by Moses Brown, a merchant, Slater set up a spinning mill. Who would have thought that this small **spinning mill** in Pawtucket, Rhode Island, would prove that cotton yarn could be spun profitably in the United States? This mill, opened in 1791, sparked the textile industry in the United States. Within a few years, spinning mills had sprung up all over New England. By the mid-1800s, towns such as Waltham, Lowell, Lawrence, and New Bedford, Massachusetts, and Biddeford, Maine, became centers of the newly emerging textile industry. A reliance on British inventions still existed; any technological changes were based on reproducing and improving textile machinery used in England.

Although the spinning process was becoming mechanized, the weaving process continued to be contracted out to individual handweavers. Then, in 1813, Francis Cabot Lowell originated a functional **power loom.** He set the stage for vertical integration within the industry; his factory was the first in the United States to mechanically perform all processes from yarn spinning to producing finished cloth under one roof. As early as 1817, power looms were being installed in textile mills all over New England. However, despite the technological developments in weaving, contracting out the weaving process to handweavers for complex fabrics continued to exist until the late 1800s.

The mechanization of spinning and weaving made these processes so much faster that fiber producers were pressured to supply a greater amount of cotton and wool. Cotton growers in the South were limited, however, by the time needed to hand pick seeds from cotton. Then, in 1794, Eli Whitney patented the **cotton gin** ("gin" for "engine"), which could clean as much cotton in one day as 50 men. As a result of this invention, the cotton growers soon were able to supply New England's spinning and weaving mills with the needed amount of fibers. By 1847, more people were employed in textile mills

Figure 1.2
The Whitney Cotton Gin, constructed by Eli Whitney, increased the speed of the cotton-cleaning process.

Figure 1.3
Sewing machine inventions provided increased speed in the production of apparel.

than in any other industry in the United States. To be closer to this very important source of cotton, manufacturers built textile mills in the Southern states.

The **ready-to-wear** (RTW) industry had its beginnings in the early eighteenth century. To meet the demand for ready-made clothing, tailors would make less expensive clothes from scrap material left over from sewing custom-made suits. Sailors, miners, and slaves were the primary target market for these early ready-made clothes, which were cut in "slop shops" and sewed by women at home. The term "slops" later became standard for cheap ready-made clothing.

In the early nineteenth century, the demand for ready-to-wear clothing grew. The expanding number of middle-class consumers wanted good-quality apparel but did not want to pay the high prices associated with custom-made clothing. It was not until the sewing process of apparel production became mechanized, however, that ready-to-wear apparel became available to the majority of consumers. **Sewing machine** inventions by Walter Hunt (1832), Elias Howe (1845), and Isaac Singer (1846) made it possible for apparel to be produced by machine, thereby speeding the process by which clothing could be made. From 1842 to 1895, 7,339 patents for sewing machines and accessories were issued in the United States. The invention of the sewing machine allowed relatively unskilled immigrant workers to sew garments in their homes. In addition, sewing factories were established; some of the first men's clothing factories appeared as early as 1831. Singer's sewing machine, patented in 1851, was indeed designed for factory use.

The development of men's wear size standards and their use in sewing uniforms during the Civil War allowed further advancements in the industry. By 1860, a variety of ready-made men's clothing was available. Indeed, between 1822 and 1860, the ready-to-wear segment of the men's wear tailoring industry grew larger than the custom-made segment. Because of this increased demand, sewing factories also grew.

One reason why the men's RTW industry developed before the women's or children's in the United States is that men's size standards existed for apparel producers to use. The term **size standards** relates to the proportional increase or decrease in garment measurements for each size produced. Patterns could be made for a range of men's sizes. Thus, multiple sizes could be cut and sewed using mass production methods. In addition, in the late nineteenth century, the styling of men's apparel was less complicated than that of women. Thus, men's RTW developed first, then children's (boys' apparel before girls' apparel), and finally women's.

A number of other advancements contributed to the growth of the industry at this time. During the late 1800s, motorized cutting knives and

Figure 1.4

Left: Distribution of ready-to-wear apparel was facilitated by retail stores, such as R.H. Macy's Dry Goods.

Right: By the turn of the century, RTW apparel and accessories were available in retail stores, such as Rike's Department Store in Dayton, Ohio.

TABLE 1-1

Supply and Demand Needs for the Emergence and Growth of Textile and Apparel Industries in the United States.

SUPPLY

Need plenty of inexpensive fabric and means to sew it quickly

spinning jenny	1764
power loom	1785–1787
cotton gin	1794
sewing machine	1832, 1845, 1846

Need supply of labor
▌ immigrant workers (began production sewing in their homes)

DEMAND

Need customers, a demand for mass-produced apparel
▌ sailors, miners, slaves needed cheap ready-made clothing (slops)
▌ expanding number of middle-class consumers wanted good quality apparel at "reasonable" prices

Need distribution system
▌ mail order catalogs: Wards, 1872; Sears, 1886
▌ department stores: mid-1800s

pressing equipment were developed. Mass production of apparel was also facilitated by the invention of paper patterns. Ebenezer Butterick started a pattern business in 1863; James McCall started a similar one in 1870. Thus, by the end of the nineteenth century, mechanization of the textile and apparel production processes had led to a growing number of companies.

With the availability of ready-made clothing, distribution methods to consumers in both cities and rural areas increased. Brooks Brothers, the first men's apparel store, opened in New York City in 1818 and catered primarily to sailors and working-class men who could not afford custom-tailored clothing. The mid-1800s saw the development of the department store in cities. In New York City's Greenwich Village, Lord & Taylor opened in 1826 (and in 1903 moved to Fifth Avenue); in Haverhill, Massachusetts, Macy's Wholesale and Retail Dry Goods House opened in 1851; in Chicago, Marshall Field's opened in 1852 and Carson Pirie Scott & Co. in 1854; and in Philadelphia, Wanamaker's opened in 1862. Although these stores initially offered a limited range of products, by the end of the Civil War, the range of merchandise expanded and included apparel.

To those consumers unable to shop in the cities, illustrated catalogs offered a wide variety of goods by the latter part of the nineteenth century. With expansion of the U.S. postal service (parcel post was introduced in 1913), railroads, and rural free delivery (RFD, introduced in 1893), a growing mail-order business for ready-made clothing was created by such companies as Montgomery Ward (established in 1872) and Sears, Roebuck & Co. (established in 1886). Table 1-1 summarizes these supply and demand needs for the emergence and growth of the textile and apparel industries in the United States.

1890-1950: GROWTH OF THE READY-TO-WEAR INDUSTRY

Figure 1.5
The popularity of separates for women, epitomized by the "Gibson Girl," led to a growth in RTW production.

Although most men's apparel was available ready-made by the mid-nineteenth century, the women's RTW industry did not expand until the late nineteenth century. The first types of RTW apparel produced for women were outerwear capes, cloaks, and coats. Because these garments fit more loosely than fashionable dresses, sizing was not a critical problem. Manufactured corsets, petticoats, and other underwear items were also accepted by consumers, perhaps because these clothing items were hidden from public view. But, by the beginning of the twentieth century, RTW skirts and shirtwaists (blouses) were offered for sale. The popularity of the shirtwaist, made fashionable by Charles Dana Gibson's "Gibson girls," shifted women's apparel production away from a craft to a factory-based industry. It was the shirtwaist and the popularity of "separates," that is, coat, blouse (shirtwaist), and skirt worn by young working women in the cities, that provided the basis for the development of the women's RTW industry.

The production of RTW apparel was labor intensive. Production was divided into two segments: (1) a large number of contract sewing operations located in the homes of immigrants producing lower-priced garments, and (2) a relatively small number of large, modern sewing factories engaged in the production of better quality garments. A ready supply of immigrant workers spurred the growth of the **mass production** of apparel. By 1900, approximately 500 shops in New York City were producing shirtwaists. The contracting system of production grew in popularity, as it was estimated that a $50 investment was all that was necessary to start a business with a few workers and a bundle of cut garments obtained from a manufacturer or wholesaler. These sewing factories, primarily on the Lower East Side of New York City, were notorious for their poor working conditions. The term "sweatshop" became associated with the long hours, unclean and unsafe working conditions, and low pay of these

Figure 1.6
By the 1890s, most men's apparel and some women's apparel was available RTW.

sewing factories, and with the dismal conditions of "home factories" where contract workers sewed clothing. In an effort to improve working conditions for the employees in these factories, most of whom were young immigrant women, the **International Ladies' Garment Workers' Union** (ILGWU) was formed in 1900. The tragic fire in the Triangle Shirtwaist factory on March 25, 1911, in which 146 young women died, brought public attention to the horrid working conditions and increased support for the ILGWU. In the 1920s, the women's fashion industry in New York moved from the Lower East Side to Seventh Avenue. This area of midtown Manhattan became known as New York's "garment district" and has remained the hub for women's fashions. The manufacturing of men's wear was less centralized, with Chicago, Baltimore, and New York emerging as manufacturing centers.

At the beginning of the twentieth century, the majority of RTW clothing was made from cotton and wool. Silk fabric, imported from France and Italy, was highly desired for its luxurious qualities. However, it was very expensive and the supply was limited. Therefore, when synthetic substitutes for natural fibers were first explored, "artificial silk" (rayon, made from wood pulp) was the first to be developed and patented in the United States. The first American rayon plant was opened in 1910. Synthetic dyestuffs for textile dyeing were developed and available by the beginning of the twentieth century.

Other inventions made during this time became staples in the RTW industry. An invention called the "locker" was demonstrated at the Chicago World's Fair in 1893. Named the zipper in 1926, it was to have a major

Figure 1.7
Boys' apparel was also available RTW by the 1890s.

impact on the apparel industry. However, not until the 1930s was the zipper generally used in fashion apparel.

Fashion magazines, such as *Vogue,* first published in the United States in 1892, provided consumers with up-to-date fashion information and helped spur the desire for new fashions. Between 1910 and 1920, a variety of communication channels helped unite the fledgling RTW industry. Trade publications, such as the *Daily Trade Record* (men's wear), established in 1892, and *Women's Wear Daily,* established in 1910, provided a great impetus to the RTW industry. Wannamaker's department store in Philadelphia held the first in-store fashion show in the country. This event marked the beginning of a new era in fashion promotion.

Another step in the developmental progress of the RTW industry was the result of wartime manufacturing. World War I spurred the need for the manufacture of war uniforms, and, in turn, helped streamline apparel production methods. Also important to the U.S. textile and apparel industries was the closing of French and British fashion houses during the war, which allowed American fashion to develop on its own from 1914 to 1918.

Although most items of women's clothing were available ready-made by the early 1900s, growth in the garment industry came about with the simplification of garment styles in the 1920s. Who knows which came first? Indeed, the simpler styles may have spurred the growth of the industry, but industry methods also affected the styles of apparel that could be produced for, and thus adopted by, consumers. By the 1920s mass-produced clothing was available to the majority of individuals. The era of inexpensive fashion had begun. New styles and variety became more valued than costly one-of-a-kind apparel by the majority of consumers. Retail stores increased their inventory ratio of moderately priced clothing compared to more expensive goods. A new development in retailing during this decade was the country's first outdoor shopping mall. The Country Club Plaza was built in 1922 in Kansas City, Kansas. It remains a gem among shopping malls, with its Spanish style architecture and fountains reminiscent of Seville, Spain.

The boyish chemise style dresses of the 1920s were easy to manufacture because there were few contours to shape and fit. This loose, boxy style also fit a wider variety of figures than did previous styles. However, this style was not favored by the textile manufacturers because it utilized approximately one-third less yardage per garment than the styles of the previous decade. With the growing popularity of movies, movie stars began to influence the fashion preferences of consumers. Fashion news also became available over a new invention—radio. Fortunately for the textile manufacturers, the women's garment styles of the 1930s used more fabric.

New York City emerged as the center of the women's fashion industry, and Seventh Avenue was becoming synonymous with women's fashion. Indeed, by 1923 New York City was producing nearly 80 percent of U.S. women's apparel in the city's growing garment district. Also during the 1920s, specialized sewing machines, such as overlockers (sergers) and power-driven cutting equipment were developed.

Figure 1.8
The loose styles of the 1920s were ideal for mass production.

As mass communications expanded in the 1920s, so did the flow of fashion information. A new generation of high-fashion designers, including Patou, Chanel, Vionnet, and Schiaparelli, was rising in Paris. France dominated the fashion scene. Covering the fashion shows in Paris and bringing this news to American consumers was a huge undertaking. In 1926, more than 100 reporters covered the Paris couture openings for newspapers and magazines. When the stock market crashed in 1929, it devastated all aspects of the American economy. Repercussions were felt in Paris, as retail stores and private clients canceled orders overnight.

The Depression of the 1930s, which resulted from the stock market crash, caused a severe blow to the textile and apparel industries. These and other industries did not recover until the start of World War II. In 1929, it was estimated that New York had 3,500 dress companies; by 1933 there were only 2,300. However, the 1930s brought about the development of the first "synthetic" fibers. Because most manufactured fibers were developed as substitutes for natural fibers, their properties were intended to emulate those of silk, wool, and cotton. Nylon, the first synthetic fiber, was first conceptualized by the Du Pont de Nemours Company in 1928, successfully synthesized in 1935, marketed in 1938, and introduced in nylon stockings in 1939. However, nylon production for consumer use was interrupted by World War II, so that its widespread use for consumer products did not come until after the war.

It also became more common for manufacturers to subcontract some of the sewing operations. Some subcontractors specialized in specific processes, such as fabric pleating. For example, the manufacturer would ship the needed quantity of yard goods to the contractor for pleating. The contractor would return the pleated goods to the apparel manufacturer, who would proceed with cutting and sewing operations.

During the 1930s, a number of large dress and sportswear companies emerged and grew in New York. In addition, the sportswear industry in California and other Western states began to expand. The California sportswear industry actually began in the 1850s, when Levi Strauss & Co. began production of jeans. It was not until the 1930s that sportswear made by other companies, such as White Stag, Jantzen, Cole of California, Pendleton Woolen Mills, and Catalina, became popular. The sportswear trend was further legitimized by American designers such as Claire McCardell and Vera Maxwell who, in the late 1930s, introduced informal casual "designer" clothing.

A number of fashion magazines also debuted in the 1930s, each catering to a particular segment of consumers. *Mademoiselle,* established in 1935, and *Glamour* magazine, first published in 1939 as *Glamour of Hollywood,* catered to fashionable college coeds and young working women. *Esquire,* established in 1933, was designed to enlighten men about the world of fashion and elegance. Movies of the era also served as a source of fashion information for consumers, and movie stars became the fashion leaders of the day.

Brand names of manufacturers gained strong consumer recognition during the 1930s. One of the first to gain national recognition was the Arrow

Figure 1.9
The 1930s brought a growth in the sportswear industry and the influence of California (particularly Hollywood) on fashion.

shirt. It remains a classic example of lifestyle advertising. Launched in 1905, the Arrow shirt campaign continued for many years. The ads featured color fashion illustrations of a very sophisticated male, wearing Arrow shirts, of course, engaged in a variety of activities suitable to a man of taste and leisure. By the 1930s, consumers were familiar with a variety of national brand names. The college student and young working woman were clearly identified as target customers for the fashion industry; special markets included junior and large-size customers. Size standards were widely adopted by the industry after the U.S. Department of Agriculture published size measurements in 1941. The demand for good quality RTW was strong, and fashion news spread quickly.

A number of changes in the 1940s had profound influences on the U.S. apparel industry. Although World War II devastated the fashion industry in France, Paris emerged after the War as a prominent player in the international fashion industry. However, the war did allow American designers, such as Claire McCardell, to become well known among consumers. The United States became known as the sportswear capital and held onto this lead even after the Paris fashion houses reopened.

The U.S. fashion industry founded several organizations during the 1930s and 1940s, including The Fashion Group International, the New York Couture Group, and the California Fashion Creators, to strengthen and promote the industry. The Coty American Fashion Critics Award was founded in 1942 to recognize outstanding fashion designers.

By the 1940s, the production of ready-to-wear clothing was primarily in modern factories. However, because of rising costs in New York City, factories had been built in New Jersey, Connecticut, and upstate New York. Apparel manufacturing factories also were springing up in other parts of the country. The apparel industry in California, centered in Los Angeles, emerged as the hub for the growing active and casual sportswear industry in the west. Dallas, Texas, also gained prominence in apparel manufacturing.

1950-1980: DIVERSIFICATION AND INCORPORATION

The 1950s saw not only a general growth in consumer demand for apparel, but also a shift in the product mix demanded by consumers. Because of lifestyle changes, casual clothing and sportswear were an expanding segment of the fashion industry. In fact, between 1947 and 1961, wholesale shipments of casual apparel and sportswear increased approximately 160 percent. During the same time period, suit sales decreased by approximately 40 percent. Teenage fashion, which developed as a special category during the 1950s, reached its peak during the youth explosion of the 1960s, when "mass fashion" became affordable to the majority of the population. In 1965, half of the U.S. population was under 25, and teenagers spent $3.5 million annually on apparel.

Figure 1.10
Ozzie and Harriet Nelson, with sons David and Ricky. Spurred by the popularity of television and pop music, teenage fashion became a separate category in the 1950s.

Spurred by increased orders from the military in the early 1950s, the textile industry also grew. In 1950, Burlington ranked as the largest Fortune 500 textile manufacturer, with annual sales just over $1 billion. Developed in the 1940s, acrylic and polyester were available on the U.S. market by the early 1950s. Triacetate, introduced in 1954, provided a less heat-sensitive alternative to acetate, a previously developed synthetic fiber. The use of synthetic fibers in apparel provided consumers with easy-care, wrinkle-free, and "drip-dry" clothing that freed them from the high demands of caring for cotton and wool clothing. These new fibers provided lower-cost and lighter-weight alternatives. Textile mills developed new texturizing processes, such as stretch yarn. Nylon stretch socks became available in 1952. Later in the decade, nylon stretch pants became a fashion sensation. In the 1960s, manufactured fibers began to overtake natural fibers in popularity. Apparel designers such as Pierre Cardin experimented with space-age materials. Plastic was used extensively, and heat-fusing was developed. The natural fiber industry fought back with strong organizations, such as the Cotton Council and the International Wool Secretariat. Eventually, natural fibers would again gain public favor, but not until after the decade of America's love affair with polyester—the 1970s.

After World War II came Dior's "New Look," and consumer attention turned again to Paris. During the 1950s and 1960s, Parisian haute couture continued to set fashion trends worldwide. However, increased productivity in mass-produced clothing now made it possible for designer fashions to be copied and reproduced at a fraction of the cost of haute couture. During this time period, ready-to-wear fashions became the standard worldwide; and "Chanel" suits, once the realm of the very rich, were available to everyone. Since the 1970s, haute couture has been overshadowed by mass-market apparel. Indeed, currently all haute couture designers also create ready-to-wear collections.

One of the most apparent changes in the apparel industry during the late 1950s and throughout the 1960s was the increase in large, publicly owned apparel corporations. In 1959, only 22 public apparel companies existed, but by the end of the 1960s more than 100 apparel companies had become public corporations. Some of the early companies to "go public" were Jonathan Logan, Bobbie Brooks, and Leslie Fay.

Because of the growth of suburbia in the United States, consumers wanted shopping outlets closer to their homes. Thus emerged the shopping mall. In 1956, Southdale, the first enclosed shopping mall was built in a suburb of Minneapolis. During the 1960s, shopping malls

Figure 1.11
Mass produced apparel, such as the clothing worn by these UCLA students in 1958, copied the couture designers of the time.

Figure 1.12
Discount retailers, such as Kmart, grew from an attempt to keep merchandise costs down for consumers.

appeared in virtually every suburb, typically with regional or national department stores as anchors.

During the 1960s and 1970s, the American designer name also saw increased prominence. Although American designers were first promoted by the Lord & Taylor department store in New York in the 1930s, it was not until the late 1960s that stores such as Saks Fifth Avenue featured specific American designers. Aware of the broad appeal of their names, designers such as Halston and Bill Blass ventured into licensing their names for a variety of products.

However, rising labor costs in the United States led to increased prices for consumers. In an attempt to keep costs down, retailers explored the idea of low overhead, self-service, and volume for apparel and other products. The strategy was successful, and retailers such as Kmart, Target, Wal-Mart, and Woolco, known as discounters, flourished. In addition, as labor costs continued to rise, companies searched for a cheaper workforce, first within the United States (particularly in the South) and then outside the United States (particularly in Hong Kong and Southeast Asia). Textile technology, once the domain of American companies, was increasingly imported from abroad. In 1967, for the first time in its history, the United States ran a trade deficit in textile machinery.

The 1970s saw the beginning of trends in which companies became vertically integrated and large publicly owned conglomerates bought apparel companies. For example, General Mills acquired Izod, David Crystal, and Monet Jewelers; Consolidated Foods purchased Hanes Hosiery and Aris Gloves; and Gulf & Western bought Kayser-Roth.

Technological advances in the textile industry included a new generation of photographic printing and dyeing processes. Computer technology entered the textile and apparel manufacturing areas. The popularity of polyester double knit and denim fabrics sparked sales in the textile industry. However, increased competition from textile companies outside the United States cut into profits, and textile imports rose 581 percent from 1961 to 1976.

1980-PRESENT: THE ERA OF QUICK RESPONSE

In the 1970s and early 1980s, the U.S. textile and apparel industries saw a decline in consumer demand for their products and an increase in labor, energy, and materials costs. During the 1980s, several of the largest department store groups (Associated Dry Goods, Federated, Allied, and Macy's) were leveraged by management or as part of takeovers. Consumer demands for lower prices, quality merchandise, and better service were reflected in business strategies. By 1990 many well-known New York retailers were out of business, including B. Altman & Co., Bonwit Teller, Korvette, and Peck & Peck. However, stores such as Nordstrom, the Limited, the Gap, and Wal-Mart were thriving.

At the same time, certain segments of the industry were being affected by the continued growth of textile and apparel imports. Companies such as Liz Claiborne, founded in 1976, were producing apparel worldwide in order to obtain the best labor price for production. Concern about these rising costs and the continued surge of imports led industry executives to join forces in examining ways to improve the productivity of the U.S. textile and apparel industries. Analyses indicated that apparel manufacturers and retailers were working with a 66-week cycle (1 1/4 years) to go from raw fiber to a garment on the retail selling floor. It was estimated that for 55 weeks (83 percent) of this cycle, products were in inventory. Thus, products were actually being processed for only 11 weeks (Quick Response, 1988). Industry executives recognized that this represented a huge inefficiency.

In 1984-1985, the Crafted with Pride in U.S.A. Council engaged Kurt Salmon Associates, textile and apparel industry analysts, to analyze industry inefficiencies. This project developed the idea of **Quick Response (QR)** to describe potential ways to increase efficiencies. The following year, the Crafted with Pride in U.S.A. Council sponsored pilot projects linking fabric producers, apparel manufacturers, and retailers to determine if QR was feasible and to identify obstacles and difficulties in implementing QR strategies. Results from these pilot projects, in terms of increases in sales, stock turnover (the number of times during a specific time period that the average inventory on hand has been sold), and return on investment (relationship between company profits and investment in capital items), were positive, and a few mass merchants and department stores as well as top-name branded manufacturers ventured to implement new technologies (Hasty, 1994). Because investments in technology led to higher productivity, companies found their investments quickly paid off. Pioneers in QR included textile companies such as Milliken and Burlington; apparel manufacturers such as Haggar, Levi Strauss, and Arrow; and retailers such as Dillard's, JCPenney, and Belk, among others.

WHAT IS QUICK RESPONSE?

The phrase Quick Response is an umbrella term used to describe various management systems and business strategies in the textile and apparel industries that reduce the time between fiber production and sale to the ultimate consumer. Specific definitions of QR vary, depending on the industry division. For textile producers, QR focuses on connections between fiber producers, fabric producers, and apparel manufacturers; for apparel manufacturers, QR focuses on increased use of technology and connections between fabric producers, apparel producers, and retailers. As defined by the Quick Response Leadership Committee of the American Leadership Committee (1995), Quick Response is:

> A comprehensive business strategy to continually meet changing requirements of a competitive marketplace which promotes responsiveness to consumer demand, encourages business partnerships, makes effective use of resources and shortens the business cycle throughout the chain from raw materials to the consumer.

In general, these strategies include increasing the speed of design and production through the use of computers, increasing the efficiency with which companies communicate and conduct business with one another, reducing the amount of time goods are in warehouses or in transit, and decreasing the amount of time needed to replenish stock on the retail floor. QR is a change from the "push system" (supply side) strategies of the past, in which products were produced and then "pushed" on the consumer. In contrast, QR can be referred to as a "pull system" (demand side) strategy, because timely and accurate information on consumers' wants and needs flows from consumers to the manufacturers.

QR strategies are implemented at all stages of the textile and apparel manufacturing and distribution marketing channel or pipeline, from fiber production to retail sale to the ultimate consumer. As such, QR strategies will be discussed throughout this text. Business strategies under the heading of QR include the use of computer aided design/manufacturing systems, the use of bar codes on merchandise and shipping cartons, sending orders and other forms electronically, and the use of the most efficient fabric and apparel production systems. In other words, any business strategy that reduces the amount of time used in the production and distribution of fabrics and apparel can be considered part of QR.

It soon became apparent that the key barrier in the nationwide implementation of QR was the use of a variety of computer systems by manufacturers and retailers and the lack of standards within the industry. Thus, in the mid-1980s, interindustry councils were formed to establish voluntary communications standards. Once these standards were instituted and adopted, companies that had embraced QR saw growth in sales and market share. Although Kurt Salmon Associates predicted that virtually all firms would become QR companies by 1996 (Hasty, 1994), industry analysts disagree as to the rate of implementation among small companies. Even though the phrase Quick Response is used in conjunction with Made in U.S.A. and Crafted with Pride in U.S.A., QR strategies have also been adopted by overseas apparel manufacturers, especially those manufacturers that work with large retailers in the United States (Douglas-David, 1989).

INDUSTRY COOPERATION AND PARTNERSHIPS

Figure 1.13
In 1995, the Amalgamated Clothing and Textile Workers Union (ACTWU) and the International Ladies' Garment Workers' Union (ILGWU) merged to become the Union of Needletrades, Industrial and Textile Employees (UNITE).

For Quick Response strategies to be successful, cooperation among the various components of the textile, apparel, and retailing industries is essential. A level of trust also must exist between companies for many of the strategies to be effective. For example, with QR, because fabric is inspected for flaws at the mill, apparel producers do not have to reinspect it at the apparel plant. However, the apparel producers must trust that the fabric producers, in fact, adequately inspected the fabric. A number of the partnerships have been "formalized" to focus on ways in which companies within the various industries could best cooperate in achieving increased productivity. These "formalized" partnerships include (TC)², industry "linkage" councils, and the Crafted with Pride in U.S.A. Council.

(TC)². In the late 1970s Harvard professors John T. Dunlop and Frederick H. Abernathy assessed the productivity of the U.S. apparel industry within the global economy. They argued that new approaches were needed to reduce labor costs if the apparel industry was to maintain its market share. This study led to a two-day conference of industry, union, government, and university representatives to plan a joint research and development program. This 1979 conference led to much industry speculation about the viability of a joint R&D program. In October 1980, the Tailored Clothing Technology Corporation, commonly known as (TC)², was established by the Amalgamated Clothing and Textiles Workers Union (ACTWU), three men's suits manufacturers (Hartmarx, Palm Beach, and Greif), and the menswear division of fabric producer Burlington Industries (Kazis, 1989). Later, the name was changed to the **Textile/Clothing Technology Corporation** to better reflect its broader focus. Currently, (TC)² remains a nonprofit corporation supported by membership dues paid by fiber, textile, and apparel manufacturers; the U.S. Department of Commerce; and union funds from the

Figure 1.14

Left: Established in 1980, (TC)² conducts research and development for the apparel industry.

Right: The Apparel Technology Center provides technology tranfer to apparel companies.

ACTWU, which is now included in the Union of Needletrades, Industrial, and Textile Employees (UNITE). Although the focus of (TC)² has been to reduce labor costs by increasing computer automation within the industry, ACTWU has been an active participant from its beginning. According to Murray Finley, former president of the ACTWU, "by improving the technology, you reduce the labor content and thereby you reduce the advantage that low-wage areas around the world have. You involve fewer person-hours in the manufacturing, of course, but our idea is that we can be more competitive, and that means more consistency of employment in the domestic industry" (Fortess, 1988, p. 104).

Since its beginning, (TC)² has focused on developing, testing, and teaching advanced apparel technology that could contribute to the reduction of direct labor costs involved in the production of apparel made in the United States. Initially, its work focused on automating the men's tailored clothing industry, but the group's current work is much broader in nature and represents needs throughout the entire fiber-textile-apparel industry (Kazis, 1989).

One of the biggest challenges for (TC)² was to gain the support of small and midsize apparel companies through technology transfer. Therefore, in 1988, the Apparel Technology Center was opened. Located in Cary, North Carolina, the purpose of the Center is to demonstrate, educate, and carry out short-term development of state-of-the-art equipment for apparel production. The mission statement for the Apparel Technology Center states three objectives:

▮ To *demonstrate* in a credible manner the latest state-of-the-art machinery, computer systems, and methodology for apparel manufacturing.

▮ To foster the utilization of these systems by *educating* apparel manufacturing management, engineers, and technicians on the benefits, capabilities, operations, and financial ramifications of these systems.

▮ To carry out *short-term development* activities that will enhance the performance and product quality of existing production equipment (Fortess, 1988, p. 108).

These objectives are carried out by: (1) operating a complete apparel production line that compares the progressive bundle system, unit production system, and modular manufacturing; (2) evaluating computer simulation modeling systems for design and manufacturing modification analysis; (3) testing development systems under controlled production conditions; (4) sponsoring research projects with institutions of higher education; (5) performing in-house short-term development activities; and (6) conducting seminars and short courses as well as long-term, hands-on management development programs for managers, engineers, technicians, and students (Fortess, 1988). (TC)^2 also works in alliance with the American Apparel Manufacturers Association (AAMA) to facilitate the communication of industry needs to researchers and the transfer of technology and research from the center to the apparel industry (Fortess, 1988).

Members of (TC)^2 receive a number of benefits, including:

- The opportunity to view apparel production demonstrations three days a week, learning the practicality, profitability, and productivity of new equipment and manufacturing systems;

- hands-on use of (TC)^2 facilities two days a week to run experiments and evaluations, including the measurement of potential gains in increased productivity, improved quality, reduced throughput, and decreased in-process inventories;

- use of the center's machine shop and library, including its videotape equipment; and

- access to the computer modeling simulation system to evaluate new designs, consider new production lines, or even experiment with product changes (Smarr, 1988, p. 127).

INTER-INDUSTRY LINKAGE COUNCILS. In the mid-1980s a number of councils were formed to develop and encourage the use of voluntary standards to facilitate faster, more accurate information flow between producers and suppliers (Figure 1-15). **The Voluntary Inter-Industry Communications Standards Committee (VICS)** was formed in 1986 by a group of industry executives who believed that "a more timely and accurate flow of product information between distributors and manufacturers of apparel, textiles and fabrics can significantly improve the competitive position of domestic participants in these industries" (VICS Mission Statement). Initial efforts of VICS focused on several goals:

1. to gain agreement among retailers and producers on the use of the Universal Product Code (UPC) system to identify products and to accurately acquire information on consumers' purchases on an individual Stock Keeping Unit (SKU) basis;

2. to encourage the creation of common item-identification standards for yarn and fabric products used in the production of consumer apparel and textile items;

Figure 1.15
The role of interindustry linkage councils in the Quick Response chain.

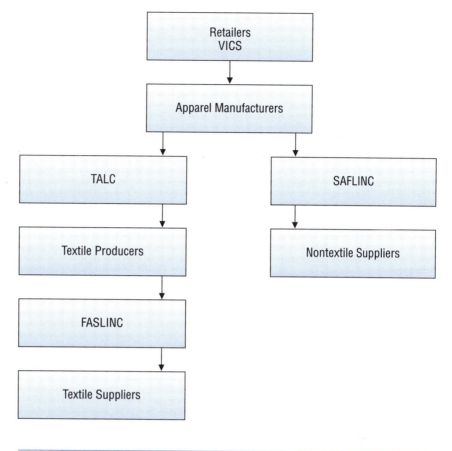

3. to gain agreement on a single set of communication formats and electronic data interchange (EDI); and

4. to encourage the development of equipment to record and make available to producers information concerning consumer purchases of these products.

VICS has been very successful in meeting these objectives. In 1987, the UPC-A bar code was recommended for branded general merchandise, including apparel. This voluntary standard was later endorsed by the National Retail Merchants Association (now called the National Retail Federation) and the International Mass Retailer Association. Shipping container marking (SCM) standards have also been established. These marking standards support the flow of merchandise through distribution centers. In terms of EDI, a retail-specific version of the ANSI X.12 standard was published and made available through the Uniform Code Council. This standard was developed

TABLE 1-2

A Brief History of the U.S. Textile, Apparel, and Retailing Industries

1770	Lemuel Cox invents a machine for cutting card wires used in the fiber carding process, thus reducing the cost of textile production.
1793	The same year her husband, Samuel, opens his first U.S. cotton mill, Hannah Slater invents the two-ply cotton sewing thread.
1794	Eli Whitney's cotton gin is patented.
1818	Brooks Brothers opens in New York City.
1853	Levi Strauss joins the family business founded by his brother-in-law, David Stern, which will come to be known as Levi Strauss & Co.
Mid-1880s	Peddlers open dry-goods stores (forerunners to today's department stores):
	Lord & Taylor (1826), Gimbel's (1842), Famous-Barr (1849), Jordan Marsh (1851), Marshall Field's (1852), Macy's (1858), Stewart's (1862), Rich's (1867),
1854	The first U.S. trade association, the Hampden County Cotton Manufacturers Association, is founded in Hampden County, Massachusetts.
1860	Census data on the women's clothing industry indicated 96 manufacturers manufacturing apparel worth $2,261,546 annually.
1865	William Carter begins knitting cardigan jackets in the kitchen of his house in Needham Heights, Massachusetts. The William Carter Company will grow to be one of the nations largest children's underwear companies.
1892	American *Vogue* magazine begins publication.
1892	*Daily Trade Record*, the trade newspaper for the RTW men's wear industry begins publication. It becomes the *Daily News Record* in 1916.
1900	The International Ladies' Garment Workers' Union (ILGWU) is founded, representing 2,000 workers.
1901	Walin & Nordstrom Shoe Store opens in downtown Seattle.
1902	James Cash Penney, age 26, opens a dry goods and clothing store in Kemmerer, Wyoming. Opening day receipts totaled $466.59.
1904	New York seamstress Lena Bryant introduces ready-to-wear maternity wear. Her company, named Lane Bryant, becomes the first manufacturer of large-size ready-to-wear apparel.
1907	Herbert Marcus Sr., his sister Carrie, and brother-in-law A. L. Neiman, start Neiman Marcus department store in Dallas.
1908	Filene's opens its Automatic Bargain Basement in Boston. Merchandise carried in the basement was automatically marked down 25 percent every week. This was the beginning of the off-price store.
1909	In November, 20,000 New York shirtwaist makers staged the largest strike by American women to that time.
1910	*Women's Wear Daily,* trade newspaper for the women's wear industry, begins publication.
1911	John Wanamaker opens Wanamaker's department store in Philadelphia. It is the first large store to offer a one-price, no-haggle policy, and a money-back guarantee.
1911	146 garment workers die in a fire at the Triangle Shirtwaist factory in New York's Lower East Side. The tragedy stimulates a movement to end sweatshop conditions.
1914	The Amalgamated Clothing Workers of America union is formed as the primary union for the men's wear industry.
1920	Membership in the ILGWU grows to 200,000.
1922	Country Club Plaza, the country's first outdoor shopping mall, opens in Kansas City, Kansas.
1923	Pushed by the growing demand among women for ready-to-wear clothing, New York leads the growing industry, manufacturing 80 percent of all women's apparel.
1927	The average price for women's full-fashioned silk stockings was $11.50 per dozen; by 1933 the price had plummeted to a low of $5.10 per dozen.
1928	Sanford Cluett develops a process to compress fabric under tension to reduce shrinkage; this "Sanforized" trademark is licensed to cotton finishers.
1932	Sales at Sears Roebuck & Co retail outlets surpass catalog sales.

1934	Membership in the ILGWU grows to 217,000.
1939	Nylon stockings are introduced.
1941	Congress fixes Thanksgiving day, which had previously been a floating holiday in November, at the fourth Thursday in November. Fred Lazarus Jr., is credited with the idea as a way to expand the Christmas shopping season.
1941	Employment in the textile industry peaks at approximately 1.4 million people.
1944	The Fashion Institute of Technology is founded to support New York's fashion industry.
1947	Leslie Fay is established—and becomes one of the largest women's apparel companies.
1949	Bloomingdale's opens its first branch store in Fresh Meadows, New Jersey.
1951	Employment in the apparel and knitwear industries in New York City peaks at 380,000.
1952	Stilleto heels are introduced by Christian Dior.
1952	*Orlon®* acrylic is introduced; and by 1956, more than 70 million *Orlon®* sweaters had been sold.
1955	Mary Quant opens her boutique, Bazaar, in London.
1956	Southdale, the first enclosed shopping mall, is built in a Minneapolis suburb.
1957	*Gentlemen's Quarterly* is first published and distributed through men's wear stores.
1957	Christian Dior passes away and Yves Saint Laurent takes over as head designer of the House of Dior.
1958	*Supp-hose*, a 100 percent nylon stocking designed for women suffering from leg fatigue is patented by the Chester H. Roth Co., Inc.
1958–59	To the benefit of intimate apparel, hosiery, and swimwear companies, DuPont introduces its first Spandex fiber.
1960	Hanes-Millis Sales Corp. becomes the first national brand of socks to distribute through wholesalers.
1968	Calvin Klein Ltd. is established.
1968	"Polo by Ralph Lauren" is created.
1969	The Gap opens in San Francisco, selling records, cassettes, and Levi's. The store drew its name from the phrase, "the generation gap."
1970s	The Amalgamated Clothing Workers of America union merges with the Textile Workers of America and the United Shoe Workers of America unions to form the Amalgamated Clothing and Textile Workers Union.
1970	*L'eggs®* Products Inc. introduces egg-shaped packaging and self-service distribution for hosiery.
1971	First introduced in Europe, hot pants become a short-lived fad in America.
1971	Diane Von Furstenberg introduces her jersey wrapdress, which is an immediate success.
1973	No Nonsense hosiery is first distributed by Kayser Roth.
1975	Giorgio Armani Company is founded.
1975	Geoffrey Beene becomes the first American designer to show his collections during Milan (Italy's) fashion openings.
1976	Liz Claiborne, Inc., is created and grows to become the largest U.S. women's apparel company.
1976	The nation's first major warehouse retailer, the Price Club, opens in San Diego.
1978	Ralph Lauren designs the costumes for the movie *Annie Hall*.
1980	(TC)² begins operation to research and demonstrate new computer technology in the textile and apparel industries.
1984	Donna Karan New York is founded by Donna Karan and her husband Stephan Weiss.
1984	Crafted with Pride in U.S.A. Council is formed.
1987	Christian Lacroix opens a new couture house in Paris.
1987	Isaac Mizrahi forms his own business.
1991	Donna Karan launches her men's wear line.
1995	The two primary labor unions in the textile and apparel industries, the Amalgamated Clothing and Textile Workers Union (ACTWU) and the International Ladies' Garment Workers' Union (ILGWU), merge to become the Union of Needletrades, Industrial, and Textile Employees (UNITE).

Figure 1.16
Crafted with Pride in
U.S.A. logo.

by the American National Standards Institute (ANSI), a national voluntary organization of companies and individuals who develop standardized business practices. The ANSI X.12 committee is responsible for EDI standards. The retail-specific version of the ANSI X.12 standard focuses on electronic transmission of data for business transactions, such as purchase orders and invoices. Currently, ANSI X.12 has published standards for more than twenty commonly traded documents. Once these standards were put in place, VICS refocused its mission to feature cost/benefit analyses of using VICS' voluntary standards for UPC marking, EDI, and shipping container marking.

The **Textile/Apparel Linkage Council (TALC)** and **Sundries and Apparel Findings Linkage Council (SAFLINC)** were originally formed (in 1986 and 1987, respectively) to establish voluntary electronic data interchange (EDI) standards between apparel manufacturers and their suppliers. Since that time, the councils have completed and published all of the required standards. In 1992 they were merged to form TALC/SAFLINC and in 1994 they were integrated into the Quick Response Committee of the American Apparel Manufacturers Association. The **Fabric and Suppliers Linkage Council (FASLINC),** also organized in 1987, focused on communications standards between textile manufacturers and their suppliers. After completing its goals, the FASLINC disbanded in 1991, leaving the implementation of future programs to the American Textile Manufacturers Institute.

CRAFTED WITH PRIDE IN U.S.A. COUNCIL. The **Crafted with Pride in U.S.A. Council** is a "one-industry" approach to marketing textiles and apparel made in the United States. Formed in 1984, the council is made up of representatives from fiber producers, apparel manufacturers, and retailers. As indicated in its mission statement, "The Crafted with Pride in U.S.A. Council, Inc. is a committed force of U.S. cotton growers and shippers, labor organizations, fabric distributors and manufacturers of man-made fibers, fabric, apparel and home fashion whose mission is to convince consumers, retailers and apparel manufacturers of the value of purchasing and promoting U.S.-made products" (Crafted with Pride in U.S.A. mission statement). From its conception, The Crafted with Pride in U.S.A. Council has played a major role in coordinating unified efforts among the various segments of the industry to communicate to consumers that "buying American" matters, for them and for the U.S. economy. This has been accomplished by the use of TV spots, magazine supplements, labels and hang-tags, in-store displays, and other promotions (Figure 1-16).

SUMMARY

With its beginnings in the Industrial Revolution of the nineteenth century, the textile and apparel industries have maintained an important place in the American economy. Spurred by mechanization of spinning, weaving, and sewing processes, the textile and apparel industries moved from craft industries to factory-based industries. Immigrants provided the necessary labor force for these growing industries.

By the 1920s, ready-made apparel was available to most consumers. Two types of apparel production were developed—modern, large factories and small contractors who sewed piecework at home. The textile and apparel industries emerged from the Depression of the 1930s with the need to address growing and changing demands from consumers. Technological advancements in synthetic fibers provided a new source of materials for apparel. However, it was not until after World War II that these easy-care fibers hit the American market.

The 1950s saw growth and expansion of apparel companies, many becoming large publicly owned corporations. This growth continued through the 1960s. However, as labor costs in the United States increased and consumer demand for lower-cost clothing also increased, companies began moving production outside the United States. As imports of textiles and apparel surged, the American industry examined how it could increase productivity and global competitiveness. The result of this analysis was "Quick Response," an industry-wide program made up of a number of strategies to shorten the time from raw fiber to product sale to the ultimate consumer. Quick Response strategies are seen in all segments of the textile, apparel, and retailing industries. Interindustry cooperation through joint research ventures, $(TC)^2$, interindustry linkage councils, and the Crafted with Pride in U.S.A. Council have increased the effectiveness of Quick Response strategies.

REFERENCES

Abend, Jules. (1995, October). Textiles making all the right moves. *Bobbin*, pp. 40–45.

American Apparel Manufacturing Association. (1995, January). *Quick Response Handout* [online]. Available HTTP: http://www.tc2.com/qrlc/qrhand.htm [December 6, 1995].

American Textile Manufacturers Institute. (1978). *Textiles: Our First Great Industry.* Charlotte, NC: Author.

Bedell, Thomas. (1994, March). Innocents lost: The great Triangle fire. *Destination Discovery*, pp. 24–31.

Bicentennial of U.S. Textiles. (1990, October). *Textile World.*

Brill, Eileen B. (1985). From immigrants to imports. In *WWD/75 Years in Fashion, 1910–1985.* Supplement to *WWD*, pp. 10–14. New York: Fairchild Publications.

Davis-Meyers, Mary L. (1992). The development of American menswear pattern drafting technology, 1822 to 1860. *Clothing and Textiles Research Journal, 10* (3), 12–20.

Douglas-David, Lynn. (1989, October). EDI: Fiction or reality? *Bobbin*, pp. 86–90.

Ewing, Elizabeth. (1992). *History of Twentieth Century Fashion.* (3rd ed.). Lanham, MD: Barnes & Noble Books.

Fortess, Fred. (1988, May). Squaring off with the competition. *Bobbin*, pp. 104–110.

Fraser, Steven. (1983). Combined and uneven development in the men's clothing industry. *Business History Review, 57*, 522–547.

Hasty, Susan E. (Ed.). (1994, March). *The Quick Response Handbook.* Supplement to *Apparel Industry Magazine.*

Hohanty, Gail F. (1990). From craft to industry: Textile production in the United States. *Material History Bulletin, 31*, 23–31.

Hosiery and Underwear. (1976, July). Issue devoted to the history of hosiery and underwear. NY: Harcourt Brace Jovanovich.

Kazis, Richard. (1989, August/September). Rags to riches? *Technology Review*, pp. 42–53.

Kidwell, Claudia B., and Christman, Margaret C. (1974). *Suiting Everyone: The Democratization of Clothing in America.* Washington, DC: Smithsonian Institution.

Kramer, William M. and Stern, Norton B. (1987). Levi Strauss: The man behind the myth. *Western States Jewish Historical Quarterly, 19* (3), 257–263.

Melinkoff, Ellen. (1984). *What We Wore.* New York: Quill.

Quick Response: America's Competitive Advantage [slide set program guide] (1988). Washington, D.C.: American Textile Manufacturer's Institute.

Richards, Florence S. (1951). *The Ready-to-Wear Industry 1900–1950.* New York: Fairchild Publications.

Smarr, Susan L. (1988, December). (TC)²'s call to action. *Bobbin*, pp. 127–135.

Steele, Valerie. (1988). *Paris Fashion: A Cultural History.* New York: Oxford University Press.

Stegemeyer, Anne. (1996). *Who's Who in Fashion* (3rd ed.). New York: Fairchild Publications.

KEY TERMS

spinning mill
power loom
cotton gin
ready-to-wear (RTW)
sewing machine
size standards
mass production
International Ladies' Garment Workers' Union

Quick Response
Textile/Clothing Technology Corporation (TC)²

Voluntary Inter-Industry Communications Standards Committee (VICS)

Textile/Apparel Linkage Council (TALC)

Sundries and Apparel Findings Linkage Council (SAFLINC)

Fabric and Suppliers Linkage Council (FASLINC)

Crafted with Pride in U.S.A. Council

DISCUSSION QUESTIONS

1. What technological developments were imperative for the development and growth of the textile and apparel industries in the United States?

2. Look in a historic costume book and select a fashion from at least 15 years ago. What social and technological developments were necessary for the production and distribution of the fashion?

3. In your own words, define Quick Response. Why would a textile or apparel manufacturer want to adopt QR strategies?

THESE YOU CAN BORROW.

THESE YOU CAN'T.

Only Levi Strauss & Co. is entitled by the U.S. Patent and Trademark office to use the Arcuate Stitching Design®, Tab Device® or the Two Horse Design® trademarks. Our lawyers agressively pursue every legal means at their disposal to protect our trademarks. So if you're thinking of borrowing something, it's probably best to stick with tools and stuff.

Business and Legal Framework of Textile and Apparel Companies

---

Objectives

▐ To survey the forms of ownership a business can take—sole proprietorships, partnerships, and corporations.

▐ To define terminology related to business organization.

▐ To examine the forms of competition among businesses within the textile and apparel complex.

▐ To explore the concept of licensing and how textile and apparel companies use licensing agreements.

▐ To identify and describe the federal laws that can affect textile and apparel companies.

BUSINESS ORGANIZATION AND COMPANY OWNERSHIP

TEXTILE AND APPAREL COMPANIES come in all sizes and types. Some are large corporations that employ thousands of people; others are small companies with one or two employees. Regardless of size and organizational structure, every company in the textile and apparel pipeline is in business to make a profit while providing consumers with the products and services they

TABLE 2-1

Comparisons Among Sole Proprietorships, Partnerships, and Corporations

BUSINESS ORGANIZATIONAL FORM	SOLE PROPRIETORSHIP	PARTNERSHIP	CORPORATION
Ease of formation	Easy to form. Business licenses required.	Easy to form. Business licenses required and written contract advisable.	Difficult to form. Charter required. Registration with the SEC required for public corporations.
Operational strategies	Owner also runs the business.	Partners can bring range of expertise to running the business.	Board hires individuals with specific expertise to run the business.
Liability	Unlimited personal liability.	Unlimited personal liability for each partner.	Limited liability; stock-holders not personally liable for corporate debt.
Tax considerations	Sole proprietor's income is taxed.	Partnership income taxed at individual tax rates.	Double taxation. Corporation's income taxed and dividends taxed as personal income.
Potential for employee advancement	Limited, depending on size of company.	Some incentive for employees to become partners.	Employees can move up the ranks.
Examples	Small companies. Freelance designer, independent sales representative	Small- or medium-sized companies. Designer and marketer who join forces to form an apparel company.	Large companies. May be private or public, e.g., Liz Claiborne, Monsanto, VF Corp.

desire. Because many people planning careers in the textile and apparel industries hope to own their own businesses someday, an understanding of the variety of business organizations among textile and apparel companies in the United States is an important starting point for our further examination of the operation of these companies. In addition, information about business organizations is meaningful for individuals in planning their careers and assessing companies for employment and advancement. Depending on their objectives, needs, and size, textile and apparel companies can be owned and organized in a number of ways. The three most common legal forms of business ownership are sole proprietorships, partnerships, and corporations; they are compared in Table 2-1. Each can be found among textile and apparel companies.

SOLE PROPRIETORSHIPS

Sole proprietorships are a very common form of business ownership, in which an individual owns the business and its property. The sole proprietor typically runs the day-to-day operations of the company but may have employees to help in running the business. Any profit from the business is considered personal income and taxed accordingly; the owner is personally liable for any debt the business may incur.

ADVANTAGES OF SOLE PROPRIETORSHIPS. This type of business ownership has a number of advantages. For one thing, only a few business licenses are needed. For example, in Los Angeles the following licenses are needed to open an apparel manufacturing business: (1) City of Los Angeles business license, (2) Garment license, (3) Resale license, (4) Public health license, (5) Federal employer identification number (if there are employees), (6) State employer identification number (if there are employees), and (7) Registration number (for labeling purposes; in lieu of putting the company name on labels). Sole proprietorships are also easy to dissolve. When the sole proprietor decides to stop doing business, the sole proprietorship is essentially ended.

Another advantage of a sole proprietorship is the control and flexibility given the sole proprietor, who often finds personal satisfaction in being the boss and making the decisions regarding the direction the business will take. This personal satisfaction is the characteristic of this form of business owner-ship that individuals most often desire.

DISADVANTAGES OF SOLE PROPRIETORSHIPS. This type of business ownership also has a number of disadvantages. The biggest is that sole proprietors are personally liable for any business debts. This means that if the business owes money, creditors can take all business and personal assets (such as the owner's home) to pay the debts of the business. This **unlimited liability** is one of the largest risks a sole proprietor takes in start-ing the business.

Another disadvantage of sole proprietorships is that because there are no partners, the sole proprietor needs to have expertise in all areas of run-ning the business. For example, an apparel designer who wants to start his/her own business must handle not only the design aspect of the business, but may also need to work with fabric suppliers, contractors, and retailers; deal with accounting; manage personnel; and market the product. The diffi-culty in running all aspects of the business is often overwhelming for new sole proprietors. In some cases, sole proprietors will hire employees who have expertise in specific areas in which the owner is not expert.

In a sole proprietorship, raising capital (funds or resources) for business initiation or expansion can be difficult. Capital needed to start or expand the business may be obtained by tapping the owner's personal funds, by purchasing goods and services on credit, or by the sole proprietor personally borrowing money. As with other forms of business ownership, sole proprietorships must keep books of account for federal, state, and municipal income tax and other regulatory purposes. Profits are taxed as personal income.

EXAMPLES OF SOLE PROPRIETORSHIPS. Sole proprietorships tend to be small companies whose resources and complexities can be handled by one owner. Individuals may start companies as sole proprietorships and then, as the company grows, change the business ownership to a partnership or corporation. Examples of sole proprietorships within textile and apparel industries might include a freelance textile or apparel designer who sells his/her work to larger textile or apparel companies, an independent sales representative who sells apparel lines to retailers, or an apparel retailer who owns a small specialty store.

PARTNERSHIPS

There are times when two or more people want to join forces in owning a business. In these cases a **partnership** is formed. According to the Uniform Partnership Act (UPA), a partnership is an "association of two or more persons to carry on as co-owners of a business for profit." A partnership may be formed between two individuals or among three or more individuals through a written contract or "articles of partnership." Although contracts will vary, they typically include:

1. the partnership's name,
2. the partners' names and officers,
3. the intentions or purpose of the partnership,
4. the amount and form of contributions of each partner (e.g., money, real estate),
5. the length of the partnership,
6. procedures to add and eliminate partners,
7. how any profit or losses will be divided between/among the partners,
8. the degree of management authority each partner will have,
9. who, if anyone, is entitled to a salary, and
10. the way to handle partnership affairs if a partner dies or is disabled.

Profits are shared among the partners, known as **general partners,** according to the conditions of the partnership contract. Profit from a partnership is taxed as part of each partner's personal income. Like sole proprietorships, partnerships have unlimited liability in that each partner is liable for all debt of the partnership as outlined in the partnership contract. Dissolution of a partnership can result from a partner's withdrawal, entry of new partners, a partner's death, a partner's bankruptcy, a partner's incapacity or misconduct, or the goals of the business becoming obsolete.

LIMITED PARTNERSHIPS. Sometimes individuals want to join or invest in a partnership, but do not want to have the unlimited liability for partnership claims that may be larger than their investment. This can be achieved through a limited partnership. In this type of partnership, a **limited partner** is liable only for the amount of capital invested in the business, and any profits are shared according to the conditions of the limited partnership contract. Establishing limited partnerships can be an attractive way for general partners to raise capital to initiate or expand their business. Typically the limited partner does not take an active role in managing the business, which is handled by the general partners.

ADVANTAGES OF PARTNERSHIPS. Partnerships have some advantages over sole proprietorships. Like sole proprietorships, partnerships are relatively easy to establish; the same business licenses are required to start a partnership as a sole proprietorship. Unlike sole proprietorships, however, where only one person owns the business, partners can pool their range of expertise and resources in running the company. For example, one partner in an apparel company may have expertise in design and another partner may have expertise in business and accounting. Raising capital for partnerships is also somewhat easier than for sole proprietors, because the resources of more than one person can be tapped and the combined resources of partners can be used as collateral when borrowing money. Through the use of limited partnerships, resources can also be raised for business initiation or expansion.

Another advantage of partnerships is that advancement opportunities within the organization can exist for employees. Employees may be given the opportunity to become partners in the business. This type of incentive is important when recruiting and hiring employees.

DISADVANTAGES OF PARTNERSHIPS. Partnerships also have a number of disadvantages. As with sole proprietorships, the primary disadvantage of partnerships is liability exposure. This means that each partner is personally liable for any debt of the partnership, regardless of which partner was responsible for incurring the debt. In addition to books of account, the UPA also requires that partnerships keep minutes and business records.

Another disadvantage of a partnership is the potential for disagreement between/among partners in running the business or setting the future direction of the business. Partnerships often dissolve because of such disagreements. As with sole proprietorships, a partnership is dependent on its owners, and dissolution is presumed when a partner leaves the partnership. Although ease of dissolution of a partnership can be viewed as an advantage, it can also lead to a lack of continuity in the organization.

EXAMPLES OF PARTNERSHIPS. Partnerships are typically small-to-medium-sized companies that require a combination of specialized skills to be successful. For example, two or more individuals may start an apparel company, each bringing unique skills (e.g., design, marketing, operations, etc.) to the business. A number of large apparel manufacturers, such as Calvin Klein Inc., Esprit de Corp., and Liz Claiborne, started as partnerships. For example, Calvin Klein borrowed money from his friend Barry Schwartz to start his design company, and the two have remained partners in the business (now a private corporation). In the 1960s and 1970s, Doug Tompkins, Susie Tompkins, and Jane Tise owned an apparel company called Plain Jane. In 1979, the Tompkins bought out Tise and renamed the company Esprit de Corp. Since the Tompkins divorced in the early 1990s, Susie Tompkins runs Esprit (now a private corporation). Elisabeth "Liz" Claiborne started her business in 1976 with her husband, Arthur Ortenberg, and a manufacturing expert, Leonard Boxer, as partners. Later, Jerome Chazen joined as a partner. Within a year the company was making a profit, and in 1981 it became a public corporation.

CORPORATIONS

The **corporation** is the most complex form of business ownership, because corporations are considered legal entities that exist regardless of who owns them. Although assets owned by the corporation, such as buildings or equipment, are tangible, the corporation itself is considered intangible. Unlike a sole proprietorship or partnership, ownership of a corporation is held by **stockholders** (or shareholders), who own shares of stock in the corporation. Each share of stock represents a percentage of the company, so that if someone owns 50 percent of the stock in a company, he/she owns 50 percent of the company. Stockholders in a corporation are only liable for the amount they paid for their stock. Thus, if the company fails, stockholders are not liable for the corporation's debts beyond their initial investment.

The **board of directors** of the corporation is elected by the stockholders. Each stockholder has a percentage of votes in electing the board that reflects the percentage of stock owned by the stockholder. The board is the chief governing body of the corporation. It plans the direction the company will take and sets policy for the corporation. The board of directors also hires the officers of the corporation (e.g., the president, chief executive officer, chief financial officer, etc.) who run the business. Stockholders may participate in the management of the business, but many stockholders in corporations have very little or no participation in the day-to-day operations of the business. Profit is paid to stockholders in the form of **dividends** that are taxed as personal income. Stockholders may also receive dividends in the form of additional stock in the company.

TYPES OF CORPORATIONS. The two basic types of corporations are public and private. Differences between public and private corporations are primarily in terms of the ownership and transferability of shares of stock. In **public corporations,** at least some of the shares of stock are owned by the general public. Public corporations usually have a large number of stockholders who buy and sell their stock on the public market either through an

Figure 2.1

Examples of corporations in the textile, apparel, and retailing industries.

exchange (New York Stock Exchange, American Stock Exchange, or National Association of Securities Dealers Automatic Quotation System [NASDAQ]) or through brokers "over the counter." Public corporations must submit financial information to the Securities and Exchange Commission (SEC), which regulates the securities markets. Table 2-2 lists top public corporations in the textile industry; Table 2-3 lists top public corporations in the apparel industry.

Private corporations are those in which the shares are owned by a small number of individuals. There is no public market for the stock, and stock has not been issued for public purchase. Typically, the stockholders of a private corporation are highly involved in the operations of the company. Calvin Klein Inc. and Pendleton Woolen Mills are examples of private corporations in the apparel industry.

ADVANTAGES OF CORPORATIONS. Corporations have a number of advantages over other forms of business ownership. First of all, "going public" (becoming a public corporation) can be a benefit to businesses in raising capital to expand or diversify. When going public, investors will buy shares of stock based upon how well they believe the company will perform in the future. These investments can then be used to expand or improve the company. For example, Liz Claiborne "went public" in 1981 and grew to become one of the largest apparel companies in the world.

For both public and private corporations, the main advantage is the **limited liability** for the owners (stockholders). If the corporation fails, creditors cannot seize personal assets of the stockholders to pay the corporate debt. Another advantage of corporations is the flexibility and ease with which ownership can be transferred. Unlike a sole proprietorship or partnership, a corporation does not cease to exist if one of its owners withdraws or dies. Shares are simply sold or transferred to heirs. In most cases, stockholders are free to sell their stock at any time. Thus, because of this ease in transfer in ownership, corporations seldom dissolve because of ownership issues.

TABLE 2-2

Top U.S. and Canadian Public Fiber and Textile Manufacturers by Annual Sales

COMPANY	1994 SALES ($ MILLIONS)
Monsanto	8,272.0
DuPont (fibers division)	6,767.0
Hoechst Celanese	3,389.0
Owens-Corning	3,351.0
Burlington Industries	2,127.1
Springs Industries	2,068.9
WestPoint Stevens	1,596.8
Collins & Aikman	1,536.0
Unifi	1,384.8
Dominion Textile	1,332.8
Fieldcrest Cannon	1,063.7
Triarc	1,011.4
Cone Mills	806.2
Guilford Mills	703.7
Dixie Yarns	688.5
Delta Woodside	613.8
Galey & Lord	451.1
Texfi	282.9
Thomaston	279.5
Culp	245.0
U.S. Industries	237.0
Concord Fabrics	197.8
Carolina Mills	190.3
Fab	189.8
Dyersburg	180.5

Unlike the management of a sole proprietorship or partnership, management of a corporation is not dependent on ownership. The management group runs the day-to-day operations of the company regardless of who owns the business that day. This allows the board of directors to hire the best qualified individuals to manage the specialized areas of the company.

In addition, because corporations are generally large companies, there is potential for employee advancement within the organization. Employees may work in specialized areas of the company and advance through the ranks. Such potential for advancement can serve as an incentive for employees within the organization.

TABLE 2-3

Top U.S. and Canadian Public Apparel Corporations by Annual Sales

COMPANY	1994 SALES ($ MILLIONS)
VF Corporation	4,971.7
Fruit of the Loom	2,297.8
Liz Claiborne	2,162.9
WestPoint Stevens	1,596.8
Kellwood	1,364.8
Phillips-Van Heusen	1,255.5
Russell Corporation	1,098.3
Warnaco Group	788.8
Hartmarx Corporation	717.7
NIKE	697.3
Jones Apparel	633.3
Oxford Industries	624.6
Delta Woodside	613.8
Tultex	565.4
Leslie Fay	535.3
Cygne Designs	516.1
Haggar	491.2
Salant	419.3
Starter Corp.	379.5
OshKosh	363.4
Chic By H.I.S.	354.2
Tommy Hilfiger	321.0
Nautica	247.6
Farah	242.8
Oneita	193.5

DISADVANTAGES OF CORPORATIONS. With all of these advantages, why are not all businesses corporations? Despite the apparent advantages, a number of disadvantages exist. It is much more complicated to establish a corporation than a sole proprietorship or partnership. A corporation is organized around a legal charter that outlines its scope and activity. Because of this, legal fees and other costs involved in incorporation are much higher than in other forms of business ownership. This is especially true if a company wants to go public. It is estimated that out-of-pocket expenses in going public can exceed $250,000 (Alterbaum, 1987). This formal charter also restricts the type of business performed by the corporation. In other words, the board of directors or officers of a public apparel company cannot shift from producing apparel to producing automobiles without filing a new charter. Corporations are organized under the laws of specific states, and each state has a statute that governs corporations. There are also federal laws (i.e., Securities Act of 1933, Securities Exchange Act of 1934) that regulate public corporations in issuing and selling their shares of stock. Other federal laws that govern businesses, including corporations, are described later in this chapter.

Another disadvantage to corporations are corporate taxes. Because they are legal entities, corporations are taxed on their income at a tax rate higher than that on personal income. In addition, dividends paid to stockholders are considered personal income and therefore subject to personal income tax.

Corporations are typically large companies that can have thousands of employees. Because of this, employees sometimes view corporations as impersonal and bureaucratic. In addition, unlike other forms of business ownership, owners of the corporation (especially public corporations) may not be involved in the day-to-day operations of the business. Thus employees who are not stockholders may not have the same commitment to the corporation as owners may have.

Despite these disadvantages, the limited liability associated with corporations and ease in transferring ownership makes them very attractive for investors wanting to own part of specific companies. Thus, private and public corporations are the most powerful forms of business in the textile and apparel industries.

TERMS ASSOCIATED WITH COMPANY EXPANSION AND DIVERSIFICATION

As one reads trade and consumer literature about companies' organizations and operations, the reader will come across a number of terms (e.g., merger, consolidation, takeover, leveraged buyout, and conglomerate) related to the company's organization. In interpreting the literature, it is important to have a basic understanding of these terms. A **merger** is the blending of one company into another company. For example, if company A and company B merge, the result will be company A, which will assume ownership of company B's assets and liability for all of company B's debts. On the other hand, a **consolidation** is the combining of two companies, with the result being a new company. For example, if company A and company B consolidate, the result is company C. A **takeover** results when one company or individual gains control of another company by buying a large enough portion of its shares. Takeovers can be either mergers or consolidations; "friendly," in that the companies agree with the association, or "hostile," in that the company being taken over does not agree with the association. Being informed about possible mergers and consolidations within the industry is important for management-level textile and apparel executives in their strategic decision making.

In a **leveraged buyout (LBO),** a public corporation's stock is purchased by a group of investors who borrow money from an investment firm using the corporation's assets as collateral. A leveraged buyout is often used in changing a public corporation into a private corporation. For example, in 1985 Levi Strauss and Co. went through a $1.6 billion leveraged buyout led by its chief executive officer, Robert D. Haas, that resulted in the then public corporation becoming a private corporation.

Conglomerates are diversified companies (typically corporations) that are involved with significantly different lines of business. For example, the Sara Lee Corporation is considered a conglomerate because it not only produces food products, but is also the parent company for a number of businesses that produce other products, including pantyhose (e.g., Hanes, L'eggs), intimate apparel (e.g., Bali), sportswear (e.g., Champion), and accessories and small leather goods (e.g., Coach).

FORMS OF COMPETITION

The goal of every sole proprietorship, partnership, and corporation in the textile and apparel industries is to provide products or services that are desired by the ultimate consumer. However, many companies are vying for the consumer's dollar. Thus companies, whether they be sole proprietorships, partnerships, or corporations, compete with one another. Companies that successfully compete will make a profit that will either be reinvested in the company or paid to the company's owners and stockholders.

COMPETITIVE STRATEGIES

Companies compete in a number of ways that in part determine their business strategies. Companies typically compete on the basis of:

- the price of the merchandise to the retailer or consumer;
- the quality of the design, fabrics, and construction;
- innovation—how unique or fashionable the merchandise is;
- services offered to the retailer or consumer; and
- a combination of these factors

For example, a company that produces children's wear may have lower prices than its competition; another may provide better quality merchandise; another may produce children's wear that is more fashionable; and still another company may provide consumers with catalogs or other services. Thus a company's business practices are based on competitive strategies. For example, Hanna Andersson, a children's apparel manufacturer headquartered in Portland, Oregon, is known for its socially responsible business practices. As part of this corporate philosophy, Hanna Andersson offers its customers the opportunity to recycle their Hanna Andersson clothing through the "Hannadowns" program. Used Hanna Andersson children's clothing can be returned to the company, which donates the clothing to

Figure 2.2
Hanna Andersson's competitive strategies focus on quality of merchandise, service, and social responsibilty.

charities across the country. In return, the customers receive a credit of 20 percent of the purchase price on their Hanna Andersson accounts.

COMPETITIVE SITUATIONS

Within American society, four primary competitive situations can exist: (1) monopoly, (2) oligopoly, (3) monopolistic competition, and (4) pure competition. In a **monopoly,** there is typically one company that dominates the market and can thus price its goods and/or services at whatever scale it wishes. Because a monopoly essentially eliminates or drastically reduces competition, federal laws prohibit companies from buying out their competition and, in effect, becoming a monopoly. Only essential services, such as utilities, can be considered monopolies in today's market, and the prices they charge are heavily regulated by the government. In an **oligopoly,** a few companies dominate and essentially have control of the market, thereby making it very difficult for other companies to enter. The dominant companies compete among themselves through product and service differentiation and advertising. Although oligopolies are not illegal, it is illegal for the domi-

Two years ago we were a newcomer to the men's jean market.

Today, H·I·S can be found in every Target and K-Mart in the United States.

Figure 2.3
Apparel companies strive to create a unique image to gain a competitive advantage.

nant companies to set artificial prices among themselves. In many ways, the athletic shoe industry can be considered an oligopoly because it is dominated by a few companies (e.g., NIKE Inc. and Reebok). Thus the companies have some control over the price they charge for their goods.

In **pure competition,** there are many producers and consumers of similar products, so price is determined by market demand. The market for agricultural commodities, such as cotton or wool, is the closest to pure competition that can be found in the textile and apparel industries. In these cases price for the product—raw cotton or wool—is determined by supply and demand of the commodity. For example, in the early 1990s the price for raw cotton skyrocketed because of high consumer demand and worldwide shortages (low supply).

The most common form of competition in the textile and apparel industries is **monopolistic competition,** in which many companies compete in terms of product type, but the specific products of any one company are perceived as unique by consumers. For example, many companies, including Levi Strauss, Lee, Wrangler, Guess?, Girbaud, Chic by H.I.S., Liz Claiborne, and Calvin Klein, produce denim jeans. However, through product differentiation, advertising, and pricing, each company has created a unique image. Thus by creating this unique image in consumers' minds, they have, in some respect, a monopoly in terms of their specific product and therefore have some control over price. A consumer who wants only Guess? jeans and seeks out that particular brand may be willing to pay a premium for that brand.

Within monopolistic competition, companies must create a perceived difference between their product and the competition. This can be achieved in a number of ways. The company may use advertising to create public awareness of its brand name or trademark; the company may buy the use of a well-established brand name, trademark, or other image through licensing programs; a retailer may create **private label** merchandise which is unique to its store; or a company may expand its services to consumers including opening retail stores or offering goods through catalogs and other home shopping forums. In these ways, consumers associate a company's goods with a particular unique image.

LICENSING

One of the methods used by textile and apparel companies to create a perceived difference in their product is licensing. Because of the widespread use of licensing within the textile and apparel industries, an understanding of the role played by licensing in textile and apparel production is important. **Licensing** is an agreement whereby the owner (licensor) of a particular image or design sells the right to use the image or design to another party, typically a manufacturer (licensee), for payment of royalties to the licensor. The licensee buys the right to use the image or design, referred to as the property, on merchandise to add value to the merchandise. Examples of licensed products include sunglasses manufactured by Bausch and Lomb with the Donna Karan label on them, sweatshirts manufactured by Champion with the San Francisco 49ers football team logo on the front, infant and toddler apparel produced by Franco Apparel under the name Starter Baby and Starter Kids, athletic activewear produced by Fruit of the Loom under the Wilson label, or sheets and pillowcases manufactured by Dundee Mills with Disney Babies characters printed on the fabric. According to Murray Altchuler, executive director of the Licensing Industry Merchandisers' Association, "licensed merchandise well marketed creates excitement and uniqueness by adding an extra dimension to a product line" (1988, p. 5). This extra dimension is the image of the property transferred to the product. Some companies are entirely licensed (e.g., J.G. Hook, Hang Ten) in that all of their products are licensed; other companies license certain product lines (e.g., Liz Claiborne fragrance, Donna Karan sunglasses).

TYPES OF LICENSED GOODS

Licensed goods vary widely although the majority fall into these categories:

▪ *Character licensing,* such as cartoon characters, movie or television characters, and fictional images. Examples include Disney characters, Peanuts cartoon characters, Barbie Doll, Superman, or Indiana Jones. In recent years licensed merchandise relating to movies and movie characters has been extremely popular.

Figure 2.4

Left: Character licensing is an important competitive strategy among infant and children's apparel companies.

Right: Designer name licensing of fragrances adds immediate image and glamour to the fragrance.

▌ *Corporate licensing*, including brand names and trademarks of corporations such as IBM, Harley-Davidson, or Coca-Cola. This includes brand extension licensing such as Porsche, a name associated with expensive cars, being used on sunglasses; or L.A. Gear, a brand name associated with athletic shoes, being used on hair accessories.

▌ *Designer name licensing*, including Pierre Cardin, Chanel, Yves St. Laurent, Ralph Lauren, or Donna Karan, just to name a few designers who license their names.

▌ *Celebrity name licensing*, including celebrities such as Stephanie Powers, who has licensed her name to Sears; Jaclyn Smith, who has licensed her name to Kmart; and Kathie Lee Gifford, who has licensed her name to Wal-Mart for lines of private label apparel.

▌ *Nostalgia licensing*, including licensing of legends such as Marilyn Monroe, James Dean, or Babe Ruth.

▌ *Sports and collegiate licensing*, such as professional sports teams or university logos.

▌ *Event and festival licensing*, such as the Kentucky Derby, the Indianapolis 500, Wimbledon, or the Olympics.

▌ *Licensing of the arts* for merchandise featuring replications of great works of art.

The diversity of types of licensed goods attests to its effectiveness in creating a favorable perceived difference in the eyes of consumers.

DEVELOPMENT OF LICENSED PRODUCTS

The success of licensing depends on consumers' desire for goods whose perceived difference is based on brand name, trademark, or image. Development of licensed products involves a number of steps, but a well-established image-oriented property is a must for the success of any licensed product. The stages of development of licensed products (Altchuler, 1988) are as follows:

1. The image or design, commonly referred to as the property, is created. For example, the triangular trademark of Liz Claiborne is created.
2. Consumers are exposed to the property through the media. The Liz Claiborne name and trademark are used in advertising, hangtags, publications, and so on.
3. The property is marketed by the licensor to build name or image recognition. Liz Claiborne builds a reputation among consumers for fashion, quality, versatility, and value. The name and trademark are associated with these characteristics in consumers' minds.
4. Merchandise with the property added is produced by a variety of manufacturers. Liz Claiborne licenses the name and trademark to manufacturers of accessories (e.g., belts, shoes, handbags), hosiery, and fragrances.
5. Merchandise is distributed by retailers. Retailers who have been successful with Liz Claiborne apparel also will want to carry licensed Liz Claiborne merchandise, such as accessories, hosiery, and fragrances.
6. Merchandise is demanded by consumers. Consumers have learned to respect the Liz Claiborne name and perceive the licensed products as having an added value because the Liz Claiborne name and trademark are attached to the merchandise.

THE LICENSING CONTRACT

The terms of the agreement between the licensee and licensor is outlined in a contract. Typically a licensing agreement will include the following elements:

- *Time limit.* For many licensed products timing is everything. For example, the image of a currently popular movie character may be part of a shorter contract than a classic designer name.
- *Royalty payment.* Typically royalties are 6 to 8 percent of the wholesale price of the goods sold.
- *Clauses specifying control* of graphics, colors, and other design details. For example, OP controls the design of all graphics on its licensed merchandise.
- *Clauses specifying marketing and distribution control.* For example, licensors often want to control the consistency of marketing their licensed mer-

chandise. Many designers also do not want their licensed merchandise distributed through discount or off-price retailers.

- *Clauses focusing on quality control* of merchandise and submission of samples of merchandise for approval by the licensor.
- *Advance or up-front money* that would be applied to the royalties.
- *Guarantee of minimum* dollar amount of royalties that will be paid.
- *Notification of agreements to customs department* so that if goods are being manufactured offshore (outside the United States), they will clear customs inspections for counterfeit goods.

ADVANTAGES OF LICENSING

Licensing agreements have a number of advantages for both the licensor and licensee. For the licensee, the value added to the merchandise by a licensed image or design comes in many interrelated forms. The licensee gets automatic brand identification. For example, a children's T-shirt with a picture of Pocahontas from the 1995 Disney movie received automatic recognition from children and parent-consumers. Many times the licensed product is trusted for qualities that stem from the licensor. For example, a designer name attached to a silk scarf adds fashion credibility to the scarf. For manufacturers, a licensed product can also be a marketing shortcut for launching new products. For example, by purchasing the rights to a designer or celebrity name, a fragrance company can launch a new fragrance with immediate brand name recognition.

The licensor also gains from licensing agreements. Such arrangements allow companies to expand their product lines by taking advantage of the manufacturing expertise and facilities of other companies. For example, when NIKE Inc. decided to expand its product line into women's swimwear, rather than spending the resources to develop the expertise in this area, they licensed their name to Jantzen, one of the world's largest women's swimwear manufacturers. By such an agreement, NIKE was able to take advantage of the expertise at Jantzen, and Jantzen had the opportunity to expand its business by producing a new line of women's swimwear for a new target market. As another example of this cooperation between corporations in licensing, Hartmarx Corporation, a well-known and well-respected producer of men's tailored clothing, is one of Tommy Hilfiger's licensees handling all tailored clothing and slacks for Tommy Hilfiger. Hilfiger controls the design, distribution, and visual presentation of the products, and Hartmarx handles the production. Designer-manufacturer licensing collaborations are common in intimate apparel. Sara Lee Personal Products produces a line of intimate apparel under the label Ralph Lauren Underwear collection. Warnaco Group produces Calvin Klein women's underwear, and Maidenform Worldwide produces Oscar de la Renta foundation lines.

For well-established names or images, licensing arrangements can also be very lucrative. It is estimated that designers such as Pierre Cardin, Calvin

Klein, and Ralph Lauren make millions of dollars each year in royalties from licensed merchandise. In the 1980s and early 1990s, licensed merchandise based on cartoon and movie characters were extremely lucrative. For example, in the 1990s, sales of Teenage Mutant Ninja Turtles goods were more than $650 million.

DISADVANTAGES OF LICENSING

There are also a number of disadvantages for the licensor and licensee. For the licensor, overuse of licensing arrangements may result in a saturation of the property in the marketplace. This can lead to consumers who do not perceive a distinct image with the property. For example, with hundreds of licensing agreements, Pierre Cardin's name can be seen on everything from luggage to cookware to children's apparel. Because of this, in recent years, the name has lost some of its prestige. Depending on the licensing contract, licensors also risk a loss of control over quality or distribution of licensed merchandise. The loss of control of the use of his name by the designer Halston is a tragic example of this disadvantage. In the 1960s and 1970s, Halston became a well-known designer of expensive apparel worn by celebrities. This status was lost when in 1973, he sold the use of his name to JCPenney for a line of affordable mass-merchandised clothing. With this arrangement he also lost control over the use of his name. Although he received some royalties until his death in 1990, he never regained control over the use of the Halston name, which changed ownership six times during the 1980s.

For the licensee, there is a risk associated with licensed goods. Timing is extremely important for the success of many licensed products, and licensees must be experts in understanding and predicting consumer demand. However, despite these disadvantages, licensing will continue to be an important business strategy for many companies.

LAWS AFFECTING THE TEXTILE AND APPAREL INDUSTRIES

A number of federal laws that affect the textile and apparel industries will be briefly reviewed in this section. Obviously, not all of these laws will affect all companies, but it is important to note the variety of areas that are covered by federal laws—everything from protecting personal property to protecting consumers to protecting fair trade. In addition to these federal laws, a number of state and municipal laws may apply to companies. Professionals in the industries must be aware of and abide by these laws, the details of which can be found in federal, state, and municipal government documents.

LAWS PROTECTING PERSONAL PROPERTY

Many companies dealing in textiles and apparel are involved with creating, inventing, or designing new processes and products. Therefore, laws related to patents, trademarks, and copyrights were established to protect these inventions and creations.

PATENTS. A **patent** is a "publicly given, exclusive right to an idea, product, or process" (Fisher & Jennings, 1991, p. 595). A patent allows the inventor or producer the exclusive right to use, make, or sell a product for a period of seventeen years. For processes, patents can run for three and one-half to fourteen years. From a legal perspective, products must be new inventions or technological advancements in product design. In the textile and apparel industries, patents can be acquired for technological advancements in textile processing, apparel production, or in products themselves. For example, NIKE recently acquired a patent (#5,396,675) for a "method of manufacturing a midsole for a shoe and construction therefor." If someone else uses a patented product or process, the owner of the patent has the right to sue the party for patent infringement. For example, in the early 1990s, NIKE sued L.A. Gear and Etonic Inc. for patent infringement. NIKE claimed that these companies' athletic shoes infringed on NIKE's patents for shoe technology. Patents cannot be acquired for garment *designs* per se.

TRADEMARKS. A **trademark** is a "distinctive name, word, mark, design, or picture used by a company to identify its product" (Fisher & Jennings, 1991, p. 595). The Lanham Act (Federal Trademark Act) provides for federal registration and protection of trademarks. Trademarks and tradenames can be registered for a period of ten years and can be renewed. Once they have been registered, others cannot use the trademark or tradename without permission or they can be sued for trademark infringement. Trademark and patent searches are conducted by attorneys who specialize in ensuring that a trademark, tradename, patent, or business name is available for use. Trademarks and tradenames may not be generic terms such as "wonderful" or "exciting," or, in the apparel industry, such generic terms as "trouser" or "dress." In the early 1990s, Fruit of the Loom claimed to have ownership of

Figure 2.5
Tradenames and trademarks provide immediate consumer recognition of products.

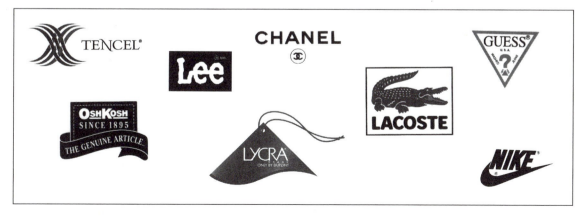

THESE YOU CAN BORROW.

THESE YOU CAN'T.

Only Levi Strauss & Co. is entitled by the U.S. Patent and Trademark office to use the Arcuate Stitching Design®, Tab Device® or the Two Horse Design® trademarks. Our lawyers aggressively pursue every legal means at their disposal to protect our trademarks. So if you're thinking of borrowing something, it's probably best to stick with tools and stuff.

Figure 2.6
Trademark infringe-
ment—the unauthorized
use of a registered
trademark—is illegal.

the word "fruit" and sued another company for trademark infringement for using the word "fruit" as a trademark on apparel goods. Fruit of the Loom did not win the case. Sometimes even similar names can be considered trademark infringement. For example in the 1980s, when a northern California company, Blue Puma, wanted to expand its distribution nationally, the athletic shoe company, Puma, protested. The courts upheld Puma's protest and required Blue Puma to change its name because of trademark infringement.

In the textile and apparel industry, registered trademarks and tradenames are widespread and include tradenames of manufactured fibers (e.g., *Dacron®* polyester), apparel manufacturers' tradenames (e.g., Levi's *Dockers*), trademarks of trade associations (e.g., the Woolmark of the Wool Bureau), and trademarks of apparel manufacturers (e.g., NIKE's swoosh, the stitching on the back pocket of Levi's jeans). Well-known and well-respected tradenames and trademarks take years to establish through concentrated efforts in designing goods that meet the needs of consumers, quality control, and advertising. Consumers become confident that goods with a well-known tradename or trademark will meet certain standards in terms of quality and/or image, and thus desire these goods.

Consumers' desire for apparel with well-known and visible tradenames and trademarks has led to problems in trademark infringement and a proliferation of **counterfeit goods** (those with unauthorized use of registered tradenames or trademarks). Typically, counterfeit goods are of a much lower

Figure 2.7
Companies often use special sewn-in labels, hangtags, and logos on authentic licensed goods.

quality than the authentic merchandise and are sold at a fraction of the genuine merchandise's price. The International Anti-Counterfeiting Coalition estimates that more than $200 billion worth of counterfeit goods are sold every year to knowing or unknowing consumers. The Trademark Counterfeiting Act of 1984 created criminal sanctions against domestic manufacturing of counterfeit goods. Retailers who knowingly traffic in counterfeit goods can also be criminally charged. Companies also discourage trademark infringement by monitoring the production of their goods, using coded labels to identify real goods from imitations, and working with the U.S. Customs Service to catch counterfeit goods being imported into the United States. To establish trademark infringement in court, the plaintiff must prove: (1) his/her trademark has achieved a secondary meaning (i.e., the consumer associates the trademark with the company or product), (2) the trademark is nonfunctional (i.e., the trademark is ornamental or does not contribute to the function of the product), and (3) there would be a likelihood of public confusion if the trademark were copied (Gerber, 1984).

"I Hate Copycats"

Figure 2.8
The U.S. Customs Service can provide information to companies in obtaining copyright, trademark, and patent protection.

COPYRIGHTS. Copyrights protect a number of written, pictorial, and performed work including literature, music, films, television shows, art work, dramatic works, and advertisements. Under the Copyright Act of 1947 (amended in 1976), the copyright holder has the exclusive right to use, perform, or reproduce the material. Under "fair use" amendments, copyrighted work can be used on a limited basis for educational or research purposes. Reproduction of copyrighted material without permission is considered infringement. In the textile and apparel industries, although the cut of a garment cannot be copyrighted, original textile prints, patterns, and graphic designs (even when incorporated into a garment) can be copyrighted by registering the work with the U.S. Copyright Office of the Library of Congress. A textile designer may also put a copyright notice © in the selvage of the fabric, although this notice is not necessary (Hughes, 1991). A designer owns the copyright unless the designer is a salaried employee of a company; then the design copyright is held by the employer. If a textile print or design is copyrighted, any unauthorized reproduction of the textile print or design is considered copyright infringement and the copyright holder can take the infringer to court. Examples of copyright infringement in the textile industry include when dishonest textile converters buy apparel at retail in order to then copy the textile print, when an unscrupulous apparel manufacturer works with a converter in developing a new print and then take the samples to another converter to have them reproduced more cheaply, or when a fraudulent retailer copies textile prints for use in their private label merchandise (Ellis, 1995). U.S. copyrights are partially protected in the international market under the Berne Convention, an international treaty designed to help fight infringement of U.S. copyrights in other countries.

FEDERAL LAWS RELATED TO BUSINESS PRACTICES

Many federal laws relate to how a company must run its business, including requirements concerning competition, international trade, protecting consumers, protecting the environment, and employment practices.

FAIR COMPETITION. A number of federal laws have been established to assure fair competition. Table 2-4 describes the primary laws that prohibit monopolies and unfair or deceptive practices in interstate commerce. Any textile and apparel company whose products or services cross state lines are governed by these laws. These laws are all administered by the Federal Trade Commission (FTC).

INTERNATIONAL TRADE. Federal regulations also exist concerning the international trade of products, including textiles and apparel (see Table 2-5). The primary objective of these laws is to establish fair trade among countries. Because of shifts in international relations, these laws are regularly reviewed and amended. Any textile and apparel company that imports

TABLE 2-4

Federal Laws Related to Competition

▪ **The Sherman Antitrust Act (1890):** outlaws monopolies or attempts to form monopolies.

▪ **The Clayton Act (1914):** amended the Sherman Act by forbidding a seller from discriminating in price between and among different purchases of the same commodity, outlawing exclusive dealing and tie-in arrangements, forbidding corporate asset or stock mergers where the effect may be to create a monopoly, and forbidding persons from serving on boards of directors of competing corporations.

▪ **The Federal Trade Commission Act (1914):** declares unlawful unfair methods of competition in or affecting commerce and unfair or deceptive acts or practices in interstate commerce.

▪ **The Robinson-Patman Act (1936):** amended the Clayton Act by preventing large firms from exerting excessive economic pressure to drive out small competitors in local markets.

▪ **The Cellar-Kefauver Amendment (1950):** made it illegal to create a monopoly by eliminating competition through company mergers and acquisitions.

▪ **The Wheeler-Lea Act:** amended the Federal Trade Commission Act by allowing the FTC to stop unfair competition even if a competitor was not shown to be harmed by a business practice, but a consumer was injured by deceptive acts or practices.

goods into or exports goods from the United States is affected by these laws. Except for the Export Trade Act, which is administered by the FTC, these laws are administered by the U.S. Customs Service of the Department of the Treasury.

ENVIRONMENTAL PRACTICES. Federal environmental laws regulate business practices related to environmental pollution. The goal of these laws is to protect the environment from toxic pollutants. These laws particularly affect chemical companies (that may produce manufactured fibers) that produce or work with toxic substances or factories that may emit toxic substances considered pollutants. A listing of the primary environmental laws are in Table 2-6. These laws are administered by the Environmental Protection Agency.

CONSUMER PROTECTION. In the 1930s and 1940s a number of laws were enacted to protect the health and safety of consumers (see Table 2-7). These laws require companies to truthfully label the fiber content and care procedures of products and prohibit companies from selling flammable products. They are either administered by the Federal Trade Commission or the Consumer Product Safety Commission.

TABLE 2-5

Laws Related to International Trade Practices

▮ **The General Agreement on Tariffs and Trade (GATT, 1947):** a multinational agreement regarding global trade policies. In international trade of textiles and apparel, GATT allows for the use of tariffs (taxes on imports) to protect domestic industries and for quantitative limits (quotas) on the entry of certain textile and apparel merchandise into the United States from specified countries during a specified period of time. By the year 2005, GATT will reduce tariffs and eliminate quotas on imports in most countries. Under GATT, country-of-origin marking on apparel must include where the garment was sewed.

▮ **Multifiber Agreement (MFA I: 1947–1997, MFA II: 1977–1981, MFA III: 1981–1986, MFA IV: 1986–1991, extensions to MFA IV, 1991, 1992, 1993):** general framework for international textile trade that operates under the authority of GATT and allows for the establishment of bilateral agreements between trading partners. The MFA will be phased out by the year 2005 and will bring the textile and apparel industry under the jurisdiction of the newly formed World Trade Organization. Quotas on textiles and apparel will be phased out and tariffs reduced.

▮ **North American Free Trade Agreement (NAFTA, 1994):** authorizes duty-free trade among the United States, Canada, and Mexico for goods manufactured in these three countries.

▮ **The Export Trade Act:** authorizes FTC supervision of the registration and operation of associations of U.S. exporters.

▮ **The World Trade Organization (WTO, 1995):** According to the Office of Textiles and Apparel, "The World Trade Organization (WTO) Agreement on Textiles and Clothing (the Agreement) provides for the phased liberalization and elimination over the transition period of quotas on textiles and apparel imported from WTO member countries. The Agreement was approved as part of the Uruguay Round Agreements Act by the U.S. Congress in December 1994. The Agreement went into effect on January 1, 1995. Article 2 of the Agreement states that product integration, including the phase out of Multifiber Arrangement (MFA) quotas and acceleration of quota growth rates for products not yet integrated into the WTO, is to occur over 10 years [to 2005], in three stages."

TABLE 2-6

Federal Laws Related to Practices to Protect the Environment

▮ **The Clean Water Act:** controls water pollution by keeping pollutants out of lakes, rivers, and streams.

▮ **The Clean Air Act (1963):** controls air pollution through air-quality standards to protect public health.

▮ **The Resource Conservation and Recovery Act of 1976:** controls the management of solid waste problems and encourages resource conservation and recovery.

▮ **The Toxic Substances Control Act (1976):** allows regulation of the manufacturing, use, and disposal of toxic substances.

EMPLOYMENT PRACTICES. To assure fair hiring and employment practices among companies, a number of laws have been established to regulate child labor and homework and to prohibit discrimination based on such characteristics as race, sex, age, or physical disability. Any company with employees is regulated by these laws (see Table 2-8).

TABLE 2-7

Federal Laws Associated with Practices for Consumer Protection

- **The Wool Products Labeling Act (1939), the Fur Products Labeling Act (1952), the Textile Fiber Products Identification Act (1958, became effective 1960):** require specified information be on textile and fur product labels; require the advertising of country-of-origin in mail order catalogs and promotional materials. Administered by the FTC.

- **Flammable Fabrics Act (1954, amended 1971):** prohibits interstate commerce of wearing apparel and fabrics that are so highly flammable as to be dangerous when worn. Sets standards of flammability and test methods. Sets standards for flammability of children's sleepwear. Administered by the Consumer Products Safety Commission (CPSC).

- **Care Labeling of Textile Wearing Apparel and Certain Piece Goods (effective 1972):** requires that care labels be affixed to most apparel and be dispensed with retail piece goods. Administered by the FTC.

- **Federal Hazardous Substance Act:** addresses choking, ingestion, aspiration, and sharp point or edge hazards of articles intended for use by children by requiring that decorative buttons or other decorative items on children's clothing pass use and abuse testing procedures. Prohibits the use of lead paint on children's articles including clothing. Administered by CPSC.

TABLE 2-8

Federal Laws Related to Employment Practices

- **Fair Labor Standards Act (1938):** guarantees fair employment status by establishing minimum wage standards, child labor restrictions, and other employment regulations.

- **Equal Pay Act of 1963:** amended the Fair Labor Standards Act by requiring employers to provide equal pay to men and women for doing equal work.

- **Age Discrimination in Employment Act (1967):** prohibits an employer from discriminating in hiring or other aspects of employment because of age. Administered by the Equal Employment Opportunity Commission (EEOC).

- **Occupational Safety and Health Act of 1970:** assures safe and healthful working conditions for men and women by setting general occupational safety and health standards and requiring that employers prepare and maintain records of occupational injuries and illnesses. Administered by the Department of Labor.

- **Equal Employment Opportunity Act of 1972:** prohibits discrimination by employers in hiring, promotions, discharge, and conditions of employment if such discrimination is based on race, color, religion, sex, or national origin.

- **Worker Adjustment and Retraining Notification Act (1988):** provides protection to workers, their families, and communities by requiring employers to

Continued

TABLE 2-8 (*continued*)

provide notification sixty calendar days in advance of plant closings and mass lay-offs. Administered by the Department of Labor.

▌ **Americans with Disabilities Act of 1990:** prohibits discrimination against qualified individuals with disabilities in all aspects of employment; prohibits discrimination on the basis of disability by requiring that public accommodations and commercial facilities be designed, constructed, and altered in compliance with accessibility standards. Administered by the Office of the ADA, Department of Justice.

SUMMARY

Depending on the objectives, needs, and size of textile and apparel companies, they are owned as sole proprietorships, partnerships, or corporations. The advantages and disadvantages of each form of business ownership are based on the ease of formation and dissolution (advantage of sole proprietorship and partnership and disadvantage of corporations), the degree of liability owners have for business debts (advantage of corporations and disadvantage for sole proprietorship and partnerships), and operational strategies (can be advantages or disadvantages of each form).

Each company, whether a sole proprietorship, partnership, or corporation, competes with other companies on the basis of price, quality, innovation, service, or a combination of these factors. Within the textile and apparel industries the competitive strategies include pure competition (e.g., textile commodities), oligopolies (e.g., athletic shoe industry), and monopolistic competition, the most common of the three. In monopolistic competition, although companies compete in terms of product type (denim jeans), the specific product attributes of any one company (Levi's jeans) are perceived as different from the product attributes of other companies (Guess? jeans, Calvin Klein jeans).

Companies create this perceived difference through product differentiation, advertising, licensing programs, private label merchandise, or services offered. In licensing programs, the owner (licensor) of a particular image or design (property) sells the right to use the image or design to another party, typically a manufacturer (licensee), for payment of royalties. For example Hartmarx pays Tommy Hilfiger Inc. royalties for the use of the Tommy Hilfiger name on a line of men's tailored clothing. Tommy Hilfiger controls the design, distribution, and presentation of the products; Hartmarx controls the production. A licensing contract outlines the terms of the licensing agreement. Licensing programs can be advantageous to both licensors and licensees in terms of expanding product lines and exposure. Disadvantages can be expressed in terms of market saturation and timing of the release of the product.

A number of federal laws affect businesses in the textile and apparel industries. Laws related to patents, trademarks, and copyrights protect the personal property of designers and companies. For example, a textile designer can copyright a fabric design so that others cannot copy it. Laws have also been established that relate to how companies must run their businesses, including requirements regarding competition, international trade, protecting consumers, protecting the environment, and employment practices.

REFERENCES

Altchuler, Murray. (1988). Welcome to your share of $13 million an hour! In F. Ash (Ed.) *The International Licensing Directory*, p.5. East Sussex, England: A4 Publications Ltd.

Alterbaum, James. (1987, January). What to look for in going public. *Apparel Industry Magazine*, pp. 30–31.

American Apparel Manufacturers Association. (1992). *Federal Standards and Regulations for the Apparel Industry*. Arlington, VA: Author.

Cohen, Gordon S. (1995, April). Hartmarx and Hilfiger team up for success. *Bobbin*, pp. 54–62.

Dickerson, Kitty G. (1995). *Textiles and Apparel in the Global Economy* (2nd ed.). Englewood Cliffs, NJ: Prentice-Hall.

Ellis, Kristi. (1995, June 2–8). Imitation has its price. *California Apparel News*, pp. 18, 20.

Fisher, Bruce D., and Jennings, Marianne M. (1991). *Law for Business* (2nd ed.). St. Paul, MN: West Publishing Co.

Gerber, David A. (1984, September 14). Protecting apparel designs: Tough, but there are ways. *California Apparel News*, p. 24.

Hughes, John. (1991, January 4–10). Getting it in writing. *California Apparel News*, pp. 16–17.

Office of Textiles and Apparel, U.S. Department of Commerce. *WTO* (*World Trade Organization*) [online]. Available HTTP: http://www.ita.cod.gov/industry/textiles/wto/html [February 29, 1996].

KEY TERMS

sole proprietorship	**board of directors**
unlimited liability	**dividends**
partnership	**public corporation**
general partner	**private corporation**
limited partner	**limited liability**
corporation	**merger**
stockholder	**consolidation**

takeover	private label
leveraged buyout (LBO)	licensing
conglomerate	patent
monopoly	trademark
oligopoly	counterfeit goods
pure competition	copyright
monopolistic competition	

DISCUSSION QUESTIONS

1. Interview a small business owner in your community. Find out whether the business is a sole proprietorship, partnership, or corporation. Ask the owner why this form of business ownership was chosen and what he/she views as the primary advantages and disadvantages to the ownership form. What business licenses were required of the owner to start the company? Compare the information you find with others in class.

2. Suppose you wanted to invest (buy stock) in a public corporation. Where can you find information about the corporation? Select a public corporation in the textile and apparel industry and find information about the company in the library. You might want to refer to *Fairchild's Textile and Apparel Financial Directory, Standard and Poor's Register of Corporations,* or other directories in your library.

3. What are some examples of licensed textile and apparel products that you own? Which category of licensed goods does each fall into? What characteristic of the property or product was appealing to you as a consumer? Why?

4. Currently copyrighted textile designs and prints are protected from illegal copying, but apparel designs (designs of the garment itself) are not protected. Do you think that apparel designs should also be covered under copyright law? Why or why not? Justify your response.

CAREER PROFILES

OWNER, SOLE PROPRIETOR, *Women's Specialty Store*

Job Description
Do all the purchasing (buying); advertising; supervising of personnel (hiring, training, scheduling); special events (in-store and community); in-store selling; visual merchandising.

Typical Tasks
▮ write orders
▮ handle special orders

- promotions
- pricing
- making decisions regarding merchandise returns
- customer contact and selling
- remerchandising the store

What Do You Like Best About Your Job?

Constant change, travel, relationships with the customers. I like to make my own decisions as opposed to group decision making process. I like having control (in a way) over charting my success or failure.

CORPORATE EXECUTIVE OFFICER, CHAIRMAN OF THE BOARD, *Private Corporation, Children's Apparel Manufacturer and Retailer*

Job Description

Responsible for everything from finance to cleaning bathrooms. Conceive, create all new products sold wholesale by our company. Run the retail stores. Work with all management people who report to me, as well as with 300 employees. Supervision at all levels. Knowledge of latest trends and ideas in our market. Sell all products to customers at wholesale and retail.

Typical Tasks

- After being in business for 28 years, my main job is the design and sales of new products; after that all the other things fall into place
- Keep my company as professional and polished as possible
- Make sure everyone remembers that the customer is always right and makes our business possible

What Do You Like About Your Job?

I love my job and the creativity that goes along with what I do. I love the fact I have made it work for 28 years. I love to conceive and create new designs and ideas.

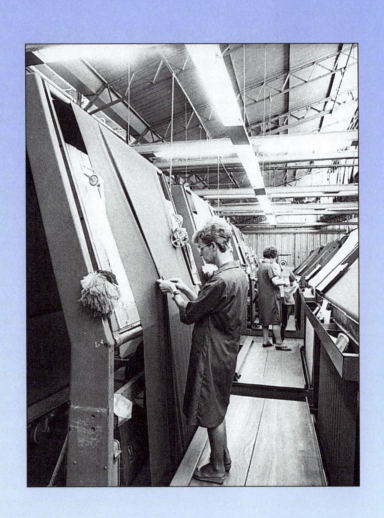

3

Structure of the U.S. Textile Industry

Objectives

▮ To understand the importance of knowledge of textiles for successful design, production, and marketing of apparel and home furnishings.

▮ To define the terms used in describing textiles and textile manufacturing.

▮ To understand the organization and operation of the domestic textile industry.

▮ To examine the processing and marketing of natural and manufactured fibers, yarns, and fabrics.

▮ To explore current developments in the textile industry including textile trade, Quick Response strategies, and environmental issues.

CONSIDER THE FOLLOWING scenarios: an apparel designer is starting a new line of apparel, but before she begins she examines the newest textiles shown by textile companies; or, a retail buyer decides to attend a textile trade show in order to become familiar with the newest trends in colors and fabrics. These scenarios highlight the integrated nature of the textile, apparel, and retailing industries. As textiles are the foundation of the soft-goods industries, an understanding of the organization and operation of the textile industry is important for all professionals. Therefore, this chapter describes the organization and operation of the U.S. textile industry, the marketing of fibers and fabrics, and new developments.

WHAT ARE TEXTILES?

Before we review the organization and operation of the U.S. textile industry, let us first reexamine the basic terminology used to describe textiles. This terminology forms the basis for an understanding of the fabrics used in apparel and home fashions. First, what are textiles? The term **textile** is used to describe "any product made from fibers" (Joseph, 1988, p. 347). The four basic components of textile production are fiber processing, yarn spinning, fabric production, and fabric finishing.

Fibers are the basic unit used in making textile yarns and fabrics. Fibers are classified into **generic families** according to their chemical composition, and can be divided into two primary divisions: natural fibers and manufactured (man-made) fibers. Natural fibers include those made from natural protein fibers of animal origin (e.g., wool, cashmere, camel, mohair, angora, and silk) and natural cellulose fibers of plant origin (e.g., cotton, flax, jute, ramie, and sisal). Leather and fur are considered natural fiber products manufactured from the pelts, skins, and hides of various animals. Leather and fur are unique textiles in that the fibers are not spun into yarns and then constructed into fabrics. Instead the pelts are tawned or tanned to create supple and durable "fabrics."

Whereas natural fibers have been used in making textiles for thousands of years, manufactured fibers have been around for just over 100 years. In the mid-1800s scientists became interested in duplicating natural fibers. In 1891 "artificial silk," made from a solution of cellulose, was commercially produced in France. In 1924, the name of this fiber was changed to rayon. In 1939, the first synthetic fiber, nylon, was introduced by DuPont. Since then many more manufactured fibers have been developed, including cellulose-based (e.g., acetate) synthetic (e.g., acrylic, aramid, modacrylic, olefin, polyester, and spandex), and mineral-based (e.g., glass, metallic).

Yarns refer to the collection of fibers or filaments laid or twisted together to form a continuous strand strong enough for use in fabrics. Yarns are classified as **spun yarns** made from shorter staple fibers or **filament yarns** made from long continuous fibers. Filament yarns can be either plain or textured. The type of yarn selected will affect the performance, tactile qualities, and appearance of the fabric.

Fabric construction processes include methods used to make fabrics from solutions (e.g., films, foam), directly from fibers (e.g., felt, nonwoven fabrics), and from yarns (e.g., braid, knitted fabrics, woven fabrics, and lace).

The fabric construction process used often determines the name of the fabric (e.g., satin, jersey, lace, or felt).

Dyeing and finishing the fabric complete the textile production process. A **finish** refers to "anything that is done to fiber, yarn, or fabric either before or after weaving or knitting to change the *appearance* (what you see), the *hand* (what you feel), and the *performance* (what the fabric does)" (Hollen, Sadler, Langford & Kadolph, 1988, p. 300). **Greige goods** (also referred to as grey, gray, or loom state goods) are fabrics that have not received finishing treatments, such as bleaching, shearing, brushing, embossing, or dyeing. Dyeing can also be applied at the fiber or yarn stage of processing. Once finished, the fabrics are then referred to as **converted or finished goods.** Finishes can be classified as general or functional, mechanical or chemical, and durable (permanent) or renewable (nonpermanent). Both greige goods and finished fabrics are used in a variety of end uses.

ORGANIZATION OF THE TEXTILE INDUSTRY

OVERVIEW OF THE INDUSTRY

The textile industry is one of the oldest manufacturing industries in the United States. With its beginnings during the Industrial Revolution, the textile industry has been an important part of the U.S. manufacturing industry for 200 years. A $63 billion industry in 1994, the U.S. textile industry encompasses approximately 5,000 companies. In 1994, the textile industry employed on the average, 672,000 workers, down from a high in 1984 when there were, on the average, 760,000 workers in this industry. In the United States, the majority of textiles are produced in the southeastern states. In 1994, North Carolina had the largest number of workers (220,633) in the textile industry (including employment in textile mills and manufactured fiber processing, wool growers, and cotton growers), followed by Georgia (120,210), South Carolina (106,159), Texas (74,699), Alabama (50,733), and Virginia (50,680).

Until the 1930s fiber production in the United States focused entirely on natural fibers. By the end of the 1940s, natural fiber production accounted for 85 percent and manufactured fiber production accounted for only 15 percent of the nation's textile mill fiber consumption. By 1965, manufactured fibers accounted for more than 42 percent of total fiber consumption by U.S. textile mills. In 1994, 16.2 billion pounds of fibers were consumed by textile mills with manufactured fibers accounting for 67 percent, cotton accounting for 32 percent and wool accounting for 1 percent.

STRUCTURE OF THE INDUSTRY

Companies within the textile industry take part in one or more of the four basic components of textile production: fiber processing, yarn spinning, fab-

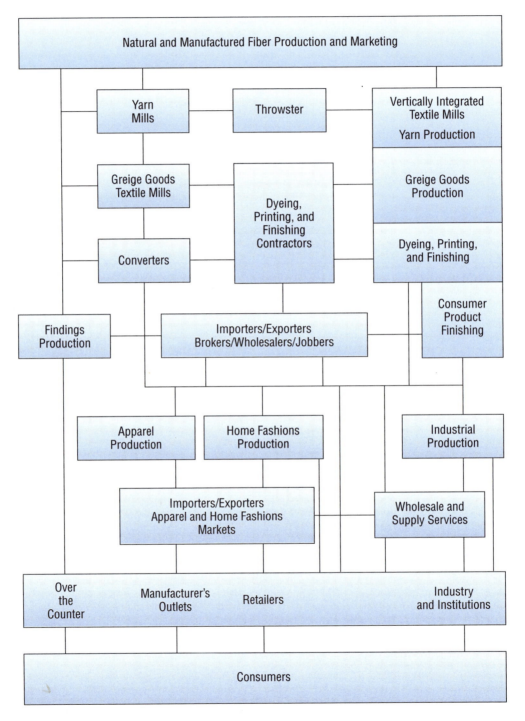

Figure 3.1
Structure of the textile industry.

ric production, and fabric finishing. The structure of the textile industry is diagrammed in Figure 3-1. Some companies specialize in certain aspects of textile production. For example, **throwsters** modify filament yarns for specific end uses. **Textile mills** concentrate on the fabric construction stage of production (e.g., weaving, knitting, nonwoven, lace). Companies that specialize in finishing fabrics are called **converters.** Finished fabrics are sold to apparel and home fashions manufacturers, to retailers who sell fabrics, or to jobbers who sell surplus goods. Retailers who sell private label merchandise may also work directly with converters and/or textile mills.

Within the textile industry are a number of large corporations that are **vertically integrated.** This means that a company handles all four steps, from processing the fiber to finishing the fabric, within its own departments. Some vertically integrated companies are also involved with production of the end-use product. Vertically integrated companies include companies that produce textile products made from both natural and manufactured fibers. Although vertically integrated companies may process fibers, they might not actually produce their own fibers. For example, a vertically integrated company that produces cotton knit fabrics might not be involved in growing the cotton, but will purchase raw cotton from cotton growers. Some companies are partially integrated, in that they focus on several steps of production. For example, some knitting operations (e.g., hosiery, sweaters) not only knit, dye, and cut the fabrics but also construct the knitted garments to be sold to retailers.

One of the oldest vertically integrated textile companies in the United States is Pendleton Woolen Mills, headquartered in Portland, Oregon. Pendleton was started by Clarence and Roy Bishop in Pendleton, Oregon, in 1909. Led by a fourth generation of Bishops, the company now manufactures wool men's wear, women's wear, and blankets; nonwool apparel; and over-the-counter fabrics. It is involved with the selection and processing of wool, the designing and weaving of fabrics, garment development, and shipment and sale of garments, over-the-counter piece goods, and blankets. Such vertical integration allows for coordination among each production step and increased control of quality throughout the production of the textiles and end-use products. For example, Pendleton textile designers work closely with the apparel designers in engineering plaid fabrics that will work best for pleated skirt designs.

END USES OF TEXTILES

According to the American Textile Manufacturers Institute, end uses for U.S. textiles vary widely:

▌ 38 percent of the square meters of textiles produced in the United States goes into apparel, such as fabrics for men's, women's, and children's apparel and hosiery; over-the-counter retail piece goods; and craft fabric (some estimate this category to be as high as 40 to 45 percent),

Figure 3.2
Textiles are used for a variety of end-use products, including apparel, hosiery, and home fashions.

- 27 percent goes into home fashions, such as drapery and upholstery fabrics; sheets, pillowcases, and mattresses; blankets; bedspreads; table cloths; and towels,
- 8 percent goes into floor coverings, such as carpets, rugs, and paddings,
- 23 percent goes into industrial and other uses, such as tires, ropes and cordage, tents, belting, bags, shoes and slippers, and medical and surgical supplies, and
- 4 percent is exported.

According to the American Fiber Manufacturers Association, of the manufactured fibers produced in the United States:

- 45 percent is used in home fashions (providing 80 percent of U.S. carpets, sheets, drapery fabric, and upholstery),
- 30 percent is used in apparel, and
- 25 percent is used in industrial products.

Thus, although apparel and home fashions are the primary end uses for textiles made in the United States, it is important to note the variety of goods made from natural and manufactured fibers.

FIBER PROCESSING AND YARN SPINNING

The development and marketing of fibers varies greatly between natural and manufactured fibers. In general, natural fibers, as part of the larger agricultural industry, are the product of a crop that is grown and harvested or of an animal that is raised. Manufactured fibers, on the other hand, are created by large nonagricultural corporations through research and development efforts.

NATURAL FIBER PROCESSING

Of the natural fibers produced in the United States, cotton has the largest production and wool the second largest production. In 1994, 5.19 billion pounds of cotton and 153.1 million pounds of wool were used by textile mills. On a much smaller level, specialty fibers, such as mohair and cashmere, are also produced. Almost all linen and silk are imported into the United States.

Cotton is obtained from the hairs surrounding the seeds of the cotton plant. The plant is grown most satisfactorily in warm climates where irrigation water is available. In 1994, Texas had the largest number of cotton growers in the United States (63,299), followed by Mississippi (18,793) and California (16,079). The cotton industry has been criticized in recent years for its significant use of chemical pesticides, fertilizers, and water. It is estimated that 800 million pounds of pesticides are used each year to produce cotton (Yates, 1994). The growing of cotton also requires large amounts of water

Figure 3.3
In the United States, cotton production and processing facilities are found primarily in southern and southwestern states.

per acre. It is estimated that nearly 1,000 gallons of water are needed to grow enough cotton for a pair of denim jeans (Robbins, 1994). However, efforts to reduce the environmental impact of cotton production are being studied and implemented. These recent developments will be discussed later in this chapter.

In traditional cotton production, after the cotton is picked, a cotton gin is used to separate the fiber, called cotton lint, from the seed. The seeds are a valuable by-product of the cotton industry and are used to produce cattle feed and cottonseed oil. The cotton lint is then packed into large bales and shipped to yarn and textile mills. The spinning process of cotton yarns is highly automated; cotton fibers are cleaned, carded, combed, and drawn and spun to create yarns. For blended yarns, other fibers such as polyester, nylon, or wool are blended with the cotton during the spinning process.

Wool fibers are derived from the shearing of sheep, goats, alpacas, and llamas. In the United States, most wool comes from a number of specific breeds of sheep, including Delaine-Merino, Rambouillet, Hampshire, and Suffolk. Wool production is often a secondary industry for sheep producers, who raise sheep primarily for food. Sheep production occurs in every state, with the largest number of wool growers found in Texas (7,600), Iowa (6,500), Ohio (5,200), and California (5,000). Some breeds of sheep can graze in areas of the country with extreme climates that are unsuitable for other livestock. Farm flock production (animals raised in a more confined area) is best suited for other breeds.

The first step in wool processing is shearing the sheep. Shearing usually takes place once a year in the spring, just before lambing. Using electric clippers, a skilled shearer can remove the fleece from a sheep in five minutes. Some shearers can shear more than 100 sheep per day. A chemical shearing process is used on a limited basis. Bags of wool fleece are inspected, graded, and sorted according to the diameter and length of the wool fibers. Then, they are scoured to remove grease (unrefined lanolin) and impurities. The lanolin is separated from the wash water, purified, and used in soaps, creams, cosmetics, and other products. Next, clean wool fibers from different batches are blended to achieve uniform color and quality. Fibers are then carded, which straightens the fibers and removes any remaining vegetable matter. Wool to be used in worsted fabrics undergoes a combing process in which the fibers are further straightened. The fibers are then drawn and spun into yarns.

Wool fibers and fabrics are often dyed and finished by the same company that processes the fiber. Wool, like other fibers, can be dyed at several stages in the production process: immediately after it is washed and blended (stock dyed), after it has been spun into yarns (yarn dyed), or after it has been woven or knitted into fabric (piece dyed). Wool absorbs uniformly many different dyes. Some wool producers are starting to market wools that, rather than being dyed, are sorted and sold in natural sheep colors, ranging from cream to a broad spectrum of browns and grays.

Mohair comes from the wool of the Angora goat. The United States accounts for 45 percent of world mohair production. There are more than 10,000 growers of Angora goats in 47 states, although approximately 90 percent of U.S. production is in southwest Texas. More than 90 percent of the raw mohair fiber produced is exported for processing because mohair fibers are often 4 to 6 inches in length. Because cotton and wool are much larger industries in the United States than mohair, most U.S. textile mills have equipment only for the shorter fibers of cotton and wool, which measure two inches or less.

LEATHER PRODUCTION

Leather is obtained from the skins and hides of cattle, goats, and sheep, as well as from a variety of reptiles, fish, and birds. Most skins and hides are a by-product of animals raised primarily for their meat or fiber. Thus, "the leather industry is a bridge between production of the hide, a by-product of the meat industry, and manufacture of basic raw material into non-durable goods, such as shoes and wearing apparel" (Eberspacher, 1993, p. 26). The term **skins** refers to pelts weighing 15 pounds or less when shipped to the tannery; the term **kips** refers to pelts weighing from 15 to 25 pounds; and the term **hides** refers to pelts weighing more than 25 pounds. Animal pelts go through a number of processes that transform them into leather. They are first cleaned to remove hair, tanned, colored or dyed, and finished (e.g., glazed, embossed, napped, or buffed).

Tanning is the process used to make skins and hides pliable and water resistant. The tanning process can use a number of agents, including vegetable materials, oils, chemicals, and minerals, or a combination of more than one type of agent. With vegetable tanning, natural tannic acids found in extracts from tree bark are used. Because vegetable tanning is extremely slow and labor intensive, it is seldom used in commercial tanning. Oil tanning uses a fish oil (usually codfish) as a tanning agent. Oil tanning is used to make chamois, doeskin, and buckskin. One of the quickest tanning methods is through the use of chemicals, typically formaldehyde.

Two tanning methods use minerals—alum tanning and chrome tanning. Alum tanning is rarely used today. Chrome tanning, the least expensive and most commonly used method, requires the use of heavy metals and acids, which are toxic. The chrome tanning process also produces acidic waste water with a pH of 4.5 to 5.

Figure 3.4
To create varying surface grain effects, leather is embossed during the finishing process.

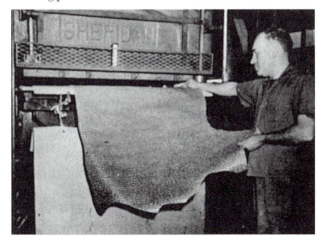

This explains why there are few leather tanneries remaining in the United States (approximately 200) and a proliferation of them in countries where environmental standards are not as strict.

U.S. tanneries are typically small companies. **Regular tanneries,** the most common type of tannery, buy skins and hides and sell finished leather. Converters buy skins and hides, contract with a tannery to tan them according to specifications, and then sell the finished leather. The number of tanneries with 20 or more employees declined by 82 percent between 1968 and 1988 (Eberspacher, 1993).

Footwear accounts for approximately half of all U.S. leather production. Compared to other textiles, leather production is a relatively slow process. Because of the longer lead time needed to go from hide to finished product, leather producers often must make styling and color decisions before other textile producers. Therefore, they are keenly involved with trend forecasting and market research.

FUR PRODUCTION

Fur fibers are considered luxury products that come from animals valued for their pelts, such as mink, rabbit, beaver, and muskrat. **Pelts** are the unshorn skins of these and other animals. The United States is the largest consumer market for fur products in the world and the third largest producer of raw fur.

Fur is divided into two categories—farm-raised and wild. Farm-raised fur is derived from reproducing, rearing, and harvesting domestic fur-bearing animals in captivity. Mink comprises 80 percent of the farm-raised fur-bearing animals. The United States has approximately 2,000 mink and fox farms and produces approximately 10 percent of the world's mink supply. Wild fur is the selective and regulated harvesting of surplus fur bearing animals (nonendangered or nonthreatened) that do not live in captivity. Most fur processors are located in New York City.

The raising and processing of mink, sable, and fox can be considered more "environmentally safe" than the processing of other textiles. One mink consumes 120 pounds of by-products from the food industry that are not suitable for or graded for human consumption by government agencies. Very low water consumption is needed—2 to 3 ounces per day per pelt. Sable, farm-raised fox, and other animals raised for fur (e.g., rabbits, chinchillas, lambs, nutrias, and raccoons) also consume food-industry by-products not fit for human consumption. Manure produced by fur-bearing animals is organically natural and is used as fertilizer for crops. All of the animal is used; the carcass is rendered for its fats and oils, then cooled to create meal and fertilizer. All parts of the fur pelt are used to make garments. Euthanasia techniques practiced in fur farms are recognized as humane and recommended by the Farm Animal Welfare Coalition.

The tanning process for fur, known as **tawning,** differs from the tanning of hides for leather. To tan fur pelts, salt, water, alum, soda ash, sawdust, cornstarch, and lanolin are used. Each ingredient is natural and nontoxic, and the tanning process produces neutral waste water with a pH of 7. Many furs are also bleached or dyed to improve their natural color or to give them a nonnatural color (e.g., blue, green). Pelts are also glazed to add beauty and luster to the fur.

In recent years, animal rights organizations have organized antifur campaigns creating an intense and widespread debate over the humane treatment of animals used for fur production. According to the Fur Farm Animal Welfare Coalition, Ltd., "North American mink and fox farmers are strongly committed to the ethic of humane care." In their "Statement of Environmental Principles," the coalition resolved to support the international treaties that prohibit the trade of pelts of endangered species, to adhere to humane care of animals in fur farms, to use safe and efficient systems for harvesting animals in the wild which minimize injury and/or stress to the animal, to endorse principles regarding proper natural resource conservation, and to support efforts to ensure clean air and water.

PROCESSING OF MANUFACTURED FIBERS

The U.S. manufactured fiber industry is the largest in the world, employing approximately 50,000 people primarily in North Carolina, South Carolina, Virginia, Tennessee, Georgia, and Massachusetts. The most widely produced synthetic fibers in the United States are nylon, polyester, acrylic, and spandex. Because of the high capital investment needed, manufactured fiber producers are typically owned by or are part of a large chemical company, such as E.I. du Pont de Nemours and Company (DuPont), Hoechst Celanese Corporation, BASF Corporation, Monsanto Chemical Company, Allied Signal Inc., and Courtaulds North America Inc. This connection between manufactured fiber production and chemical companies is evident in the U.S. Standard Industrial Classification (SIC) system, whereby manufactured fiber production is grouped with chemical and allied products rather than with textile mill products. Table 3-1 lists selected U.S. manufactured fiber producers. These companies are said to be **horizontally integrated,** in that integration of production is at essentially the same stages in the process (i.e., fiber processing). For example, Hoechst Celanese Corporation is involved in the production of several manufactured fibers including acrylic and polyester.

Manufactured fibers are developed through research efforts that take up to five years before the fiber is available on the market. According to the Textile Products Identification Act, when a fiber belonging to a new generic family is invented, the U.S. Federal Trade Commission assigns it a new generic name. Currently there are more than 20 generic fiber names.

The first step of manufactured fiber production is the conversion of the raw material into a group of related chemical compounds that are treated with intense steam heat, chemicals, and pressure. During this process, which

TABLE 3-1

Selected U.S. Manufactured Fiber Producers

AlliedSignal Inc.
Corporate sales: $11.8 billion
Sales from fibers: $1.1 billion
Key fibers: nylon and polyester

BASF Corporation, a subsidiary of BASF AG
Corporate sales: $5.3 billion
Sales from fibers: $967.5 million
Key fibers: nylon and bicomponent. BASF also makes polyester chip

Courtaulds Fibers Inc.
Corporate sales: $2.93 billion
Sales from fibers: $1.09 billion (includes chemicals)
Key fibers: rayon and *Tencel*

Cytec Industries
Corporate sales: $970.7 million
Sales from fibers: $107 million
Key fibers: acrylic

DuPont
Corporate sales: $37.1 billion
Sales from fibers: $6.2 billion

Key fibers: *Dacron* polyester, *Lycra* spandex, nylon

Globe Manufacturing Co.
Corporate sales: N/A
Sales from fibers: N/A
Key fibers: spandex

Hoechst Celanese Corp.
Corporate sales: $6.9 billion
Sales from fibers: $3.1 billion
Key fibers: *ESP* stretch polyester, *Polar Guard* and *Trevira* polyester, *Microsafe AM* and *Celebrate!* acetate fibers

Lenzing Fibers Corp.
Corporate sales: $150 million
Sales from fibers: $150 million
Key fibers: rayon

Martin Color-Fi Inc.
Corporate sales: N/A
Sales from fibers: N/A
Key fibers: nylon, polyester (both virgin and recycled), polypropylene

Miles Inc.
Corporate sales: $6.46 billion
Sales from fibers: N/A
Key fibers: *Dralon* acrylic, *Dorlastan* spandex, type 6 nylon, type 6.6 nylon

Monsanto Co.
Corporate sales: $7.9 billion
Sales from fibers: $1.1 billion
Key fibers: *Acrilan* acrylic, nylon

Nan Ya Plastics Corp.
Corporate sales: N/A
Sales from fibers: N/A
Key fibers: polyester

Wellman Inc.
Corporate sales: $842.1 million
Sales from fibers: $655.2 million
Key fibers: *Fortrel* polyester (virgin fiber), *Fortrel EcoSpun* (recycled polyester fiber), nylon, wool processing

is called polymerization, the molecules become long-chain synthetic polymers. The molten resin is then converted into flakes or chips.

Next the flakes or chips are melted and extruded to form filaments. Variations in the appearance of the filaments may be obtained at this stage by changing the shape of the fiber or adding chemicals to modify the fiber characteristics. In the last step, the cold-drawing process winds and stretches the filaments from one rotating wheel to a second faster-rotating one. This straightens the molecules and permanently introduces strength, elasticity, flexibility, and pliability to the yarn. Manufactured fibers can be modified in terms of shape (cross section), molecular structure, chemical additives, or spinning procedures to create better quality or more versatile fibers. Generic fibers are also combined within a single fiber or yarn to take advantage of specific fiber characteristics. Yarn variations include monofila-

TABLE 3-2

Selected U.S. Yarn Producers

Amicale Industries Inc.
Yarn sales: N/A
Key products: acrylic, angora, camel hair, cashmere, lambswool, and various blends of natural and manufactured fibers

Amital Spinning Corp.
Yarn sales: N/A
Key products: acrylic high-bulk yarns and acrylic open-end yarns, in both dyed and natural form

Burlington Madison Yarn Co., *a division of Burlington Industries*
Sales: $1.36 billion
Key products: textured polyester, air-texture and spun yarns of rayon, rayon blends, polyester, polyester blends, and acrylic; ring-spun and open-end yarns, and plied yarns

Commonwealth Yarn Sales Inc.
Yarn sales: N/A
Key products: acrylic and acrylic blends, cotton, polyester, wool, and worsted wool

Dixie Yarns Inc.
Yarn sales: $594.6 million
Key products: cotton, nylon, rayon, acrylic, polyester and various blends of manufactured and natural fibers

Dominion Yarn Group
Yarn sales: $220 million
Key products: aramid; blended, carded, combed cotton; knitting; manufactured; novelty; open-end spun; roving

Doran Textiles Inc.
Yarn sales: $215 million
Key products: ring-spun and open-end cotton

heathers, packaged-dyed yarns including linen and wool and polyester/cotton heather blends

Glen Raven Mills
Yarn sales: N/A
Key products: open-end spinner acrylic yarns, rayon and acrylic blends, ring-spun and package-dyed acrylic yarns, textured nylon yarns, microdeniers

National Spinning Co.
Yarn sales: N/A
Key products: acrylic; polyester; rayon; wool blends; acrylic, polyester and rayon blends; microdeniers; various specialty yarns

Pharr Yarns Inc.
Yarn sales: N/A
Key products: dyed-cotton, acrylic, polyester, rayon and worsted wool

SCT Yarns Inc.
Yarn sales: N/A
Key products: mercerized, thread yarns, package-dyed yarns, ring spun and combed. Key fibers: spandex and cotton

Spectrum Dyed Yarns Inc.
Yarn sales: N/A
Key products: cotton, filament polyester, polyester/cotton blends, spun polyester, rayon, acrylic, and various novelty yarns

Unifi
Yarn sales: $1.38 billion
Key products: dyed, hosiery, industrial, knitting, textured and weaving. Key fibers: nylon and polyester

ment and multifilament yarns, stretch yarns, textured yarns, and spun yarns. Table 3-2 lists selected U.S. yarn producers of both natural and manufactured fibers.

FIBER MARKETING AND DISTRIBUTION

MARKETING NATURAL FIBERS

Natural fibers are considered commodities; they are bought and sold on global markets, with prices based upon market demand. For example, in the mid-1990s, cotton prices soared as consumer demand went up and cotton supplies dwindled because of devastating weather and insect-related crop failures in China (the world's largest producer of cotton) and other major producing countries such as India and Pakistan. The largest commodity markets for cotton in the United States are Dallas, Houston, Memphis, and New Orleans; for wool Boston; and for mohair, a warehouse system throughout Texas. These natural fibers are sold to mills for yarn spinning and fabric construction stages. Furs are sold at public auction. In the United States, the largest fur markets (where furs are auctioned) are St. Louis and New York.

Not until the late 1940s and early 1950s, when the popularity of manufactured fibers was growing, were marketing efforts for natural fibers initiated by the **trade associations** that represent a specific fiber. These trade associations, such as Cotton Incorporated, the Wool Council, or the Mohair Council of America, are supported by natural fiber producers and promote the use of the natural fibers through activities such as research, educational programs, and advertising on television and in trade and consumer publications. Through these activities, fiber trade associations have become an important support arm for the apparel and home fashions industries, and strong relationships have developed between the trade associations and the apparel and home fashions companies who use the natural fibers. Table 3-3 lists the primary trade associations in the textile industry. A number of trade publications cater to the textile industry by providing timely information about trends in the industry, new products, company success stories, and technological advancements. Table 3-4 lists the primary trade publications in the textile industry.

Covering both natural and manufactured fibers, the American Textile Manufacturers Institute (ATMI) "is the national trade association representing the domestic mill products industry. ATMI members operate in 30 states and use about 75 percent of all textile fibers consumed in the United States. ATMI provides international trade, government relations, economic information, communications and product services in support of the U.S. textile industry." Among other activities, ATMI publishes a quarterly periodical, *Textile HiLights*, which covers economic developments in textiles, textile markets, international trade, mill consumption, production, financial information, end use markets, and employment information.

Founded in 1961, Cotton Incorporated is a research and promotional organization supported by more than 30,000 U.S. cotton growers. Cotton Incorporated's members receive technical services, color and trend forecasting services, and promotional services. Cotton Incorporated's "Cotton Seal" registered trademark is used on hangtags and in advertisements along with the association's slogan "The Fabric of Our Lives." In recent years, Cotton Incorporated has sponsored collections of new designers during the spring shows in New York City. Cotton Incorporated is also involved in market research such as its ongoing "Lifestyle Monitor" (McNamara, 1995, p. 11), a national survey of 3,600 consumers, which is used to "track behavioral attitudes behind purchasing in both apparel and home furnishings." In 1995, the monitor indicated that most people wanted to dress casually, with denim being the favored casual type of fabric. Among the consumers surveyed, function and comfort were more important than fashion in selecting apparel.

Several trade associations are involved with marketing wool. These include Wool Bureau Inc., the American Wool Council, Woolknit Associates, and the National Woolgrowers Association. The Wool Bureau Inc., which is

Figure 3.5
Cotton Incorporated's registered trademark for products made of 100% (U.S. upland) cotton.

TABLE 3-3

Textile Trade Associations

Acrylic Council
1285 Avenue of the
Americas
New York, NY 10016
(212) 554-4040
Fax: (212) 554-4042

**American Association
for Textile Technology,
Inc.**
347 Fifth Avenue
New York, NY 10016
(212) 481-7792
Fax: (212) 481-7969

**American Association of
Textile Chemists and
Colorists**
P.O. Box 12215
Research Triangle Park,
NC 27709
(919) 549-8141

**American Fiber
Manufacturers
Association**
1150 17th Street NW
Washington, D.C. 20036
(202) 296-6508
Fax: (202) 296-3052

American Fur Industry
363 7th Avenue
New York, NY 10001

**American Printed
Fabrics Council**
45 West 36th Street
New York, NY 10018
(212) 695-2254
Fax: (212) 947-0115

**American Textile
Machinery Association**
7297 N. Lee Highway,
Suite N
Falls Church, VA 22042
(703) 533-9251

**American Textile
Manufacturers Institute**
1801 K Street NW
Suite 1200
Washington, D.C. 20006
(202) 862-0550
Fax: (202) 862-0570

American Wool Council
6911 S. Yosemite Street
Denver, CO 80112
(303) 771-3500
Fax: (303) 771-8200

50 Rockefeller Plaza
Suite 830
New York, NY 10020
(212) 245-6710
Fax: (212) 333-560

**American Yarn Spinners
Association**
P.O. Box 99
Gastonia, NC 28053
(704) 824-3522

**Camel Hair and
Cashmere Institute
of America**
230 Congress Street
Boston, MA 02110
(617) 542-8220
Fax: (617) 542-2199

Carpet and Rug Institute
P.O. Box 2048
Dalton, GA 30722
(706) 226-3877

Cotton Incorporated
1370 Avenue of the
Americas
34th Floor
New York, NY 10019
(212) 586-1070
Fax: (212) 265-5386

**Eastern Mink Breeders
Association**
151 West 30th Street
New York, NY 10001

**Fur Farm Animal
Welfare Coalition, Ltd.**
405 Sibley Street
St. Paul, MN 55101
(612) 293-0349

**International Linen
Promotion Commission**
200 Lexington Avenue
New York, NY 10016
(212) 685-0424
Fax: (212) 725-0438

**International Silk
Association**
c/o American Silk Mills
41 Madison Avenue
New York, NY 10010
(212) 213-1919
Fax: (212) 683-2370

**Knitted Textile
Association**
386 Park Avenue South
New York, NY 10016
(212) 689-3807
Fax: (212) 889-6160

**Leather Industries
of America**
1000 Thomas Jefferson
Street NW
Suite 515
Washington, D.C. 20007
(202) 342-8086
Fax: (202) 342-9063

**Mohair Council of
America**
36 W. Beauregard Street
Room 516, FNB Bldg.
San Angelo, TX 76903
(915) 655-3161
Fax: (915) 655-4761

**National Cotton Council
of America**
P.O. Box 12285
Memphis, TN 38182
(901) 274-9030

Polyester Council
1675 Broadway
33rd Floor
New York, NY 10019
(212) 527-8941
Fax: (212) 527-8989

Wool Bureau Inc.
330 Madison Avenue
19th Floor
New York, NY 10017
(212) 986-6222
Fax: (212) 557-5985

Woolknit Associates
267 Fifth Avenue
New York, NY 10016
(212) 683-7785
Fax: (212) 683-2682

a branch of the International Wool Secretariat headquartered in London, was established in 1949. Companies purchasing the use of the Woolmark receive services of the Wool Bureau, including fabric testing services; color, yarn and fabric trend forecasting; global sourcing and product development services; retail training programs; market research; and participation in

TABLE 3-4

Selected Trade Publications in the Textile Industry

America's Textiles International: published monthly; for managers in the textile industry; includes information concerning textile business, finances, and manufacturing.

American Dyestuff Reporter: published monthly; covers textile wet processing.

Daily News Record (DNR): published three times per week (except holidays).

Fiber World: published quarterly; provides information for fiber producers.

Knitting Times: published weekly; covers business conditions, technical developments, and forecasts for knitted fabrics and apparel.

Nonwovens Industry: published monthly; covers manufacturing processes, distribution and end-use applications of nonwoven textile products.

Textile Hi-Lights: published quarterly by the American Textile Manufacturers Institute; statistical study of all aspects of the textile industry.

Textile Organon: published monthly; market data for natural and manufactured fibers.

Textile Technology Digest: published monthly; abstracts of periodicals, books, and patents related to the textile industry.

Textile World: published monthly; covers technical developments in the textile industry.

PURE NEW WOOL

Figure 3.6
The Woolmark, a registered trademark of the Wool Bureau, is used on hangtags and in advertising.

Figure 3.7
Registered trademark of the Mohair Council of America.

advertising campaigns. Established in 1954, the American Wool Council is a division of the American Sheep Industry Association. The headquarters for the council are in Denver, with a marketing office in New York City. The American Wool Council has been involved in standardizing quality levels of wool and promoting wool applications with spinners, weavers, knitters, designers, manufacturers, and retailers.

Established in 1966, the Mohair Council of America is "dedicated to promoting the general welfare of the mohair industry" (Mohair Council of America). The council has offices in San Angelo, Texas, and New York. The council's programs focus on market surveys, research, and development activities including advertising, workshops, and seminars. Because 90 percent of the mohair produced in the United States is exported, the council conducts foreign as well as domestic market research and promotion. The Cashmere and Camel Hair Manufacturers Institute (CCMI) is "an international trade association representing the interests of producers and manufacturers of camel hair and cashmere fiber, yarn, fabric and garments throughout the world." Established in 1984, the goal of the institute is to "promote and protect the image and integrity of camel hair and cashmere textile products. This is accomplished through government relations, product testing, public and industry relations." Other trade associations focusing

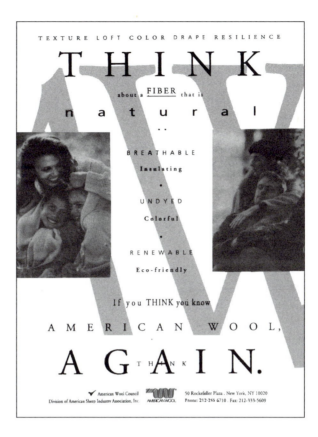

Figure 3.8
Natural fiber trade associations promote the use of natural fibers through advertising.

on natural fibers include the International Linen Promotion Commission, National Cotton Council, and International Silk Association.

Trade associations also play an important part in marketing leather and fur. Associations, such as the Leather Industries of America and the American Fur Information and Industry Council, are involved with promotional and consumer educational programs. The mink industry also has a number of breeder associations, such as the Eastern Mink Breeders Association (EMBA) and the Great Lakes Mink Association (GLMA), involved in promotional efforts.

MARKETING MANUFACTURED FIBERS

Manufactured fibers are most often produced by vertically integrated companies. Prices are set primarily by the cost of developing and producing the fiber. Manufactured fibers are sold either as commodity fibers or brand-name fibers. Commodity fibers are generic manufactured fibers ("parent fibers") sold without a brand name attached. For example, a carpet labeled 100 per-

A **big success**, this
Micromattique™ Small
wonder / It's a real
innovation in softness, in
luster / In how clothes
drape / At once more
graceful, more dramatic /
Creating clothes that are
more popular / Up to

This is why Micromattique™ is taking off.

Then again, so is this.

93% sell through / Bergdorf
Goodman, Bloomingdale's
and Macy's have ordered,
then **reordered** / Sportswear
to eveningwear is just the
start / With more **diverse**
fabrics to choose from, the
end uses are endless / Which
brings us back to where we
started / Tiny fiber, **big**

success / Micromattique™

DUPONT
MICROMATTIQUE
A FINER FEEL FOR LIFE
See Us At The Bobbin Show. Booth #5738

Figure 3.9
Brand name manufac-
tured fibers are adver-
tised to increase name
recognition among
customers.

cent nylon is probably manufactured with commodity nylon fibers. Manufactured fibers are
also sold under **brand names or trade names**
(trademarks) given to the fibers by manufacturers. Brand names distinguish one fiber from
another in the same generic family. Modified
manufactured fibers with special characteristics
are typically sold under brand names. Examples include *Lycra*® spandex fiber (DuPont),
Dacron® polyester fiber (DuPont), *Fortrel*®
polyester fiber (Celanese), *Acrilan*® acrylic
fiber (Monsanto Chemical Company), and
Antron® nylon fiber (DuPont). To establish
consumer recognition of brand-name fibers,
promotional activities focus on the company,
the brand name, and the specific qualities of
the fiber. Chemical companies spend a great
deal of money establishing brand name identification among consumers, and brand-name
fibers are generally higher in price than commodity fibers. Advertisements also connect
brand-name fibers with specific end uses.
Therefore cooperative advertising between
manufactured fiber companies and apparel
manufacturers is common.

Licensed or controlled brand-name
programs set minimum standards of fabric performance for the trademarked fibers. Determined through regular textile testing, these standards
are established as a form of quality assurance and relate to a specific end use.
For example, the *Trevira*® polyester program (Hoechst Celanese Corporation) establishes minimum standards for fabric quality, and the *Zepel*® program (DuPont) establishes standards for fabric water and stain repellency
quality. These standards can be especially beneficial to apparel and home
fashions manufacturers in quality assurance and marketing of the end-use
products.

Trade associations are also important to the manufactured fiber industry. The American Fiber Manufacturers Association (AFMA) began in 1933,
first as the Rayon Institute and then as the Man-Made Fiber Producers
Association. The current name was adopted in 1988. AFMA members
include companies such as BASF Corporation, E.I. du Pont de Nemours
and Company, Inc., Hoechst Celanese Corporation, Monsanto Chemical
Company, and Wellman, Inc. The AFMA focuses on domestic production of
manufactured fibers. Programs include government relations, international
trade policy, the environment, technical issues, and educational services. In
1982, AFMA established the Polyester Council to "inform the trade and

consumers about the fashionability and performance benefits of today's polyester." The Polyester Council, supported by U.S. polyester producers and suppliers, promotes the use of polyester in apparel and home fashions industries through activities such as press releases, cosponsoring fashion shows, and promotional events with retailers.

COLOR FORECASTING

Color is an important criterion used by consumers in the selection of textile products, including apparel and home fashions. Therefore an understanding of color preferences by consumers is crucial to successfully marketing a particular textile product. Whereas some "classic" colors remain popular over many years, "fashion" colors have a shorter fashion life cycle. Because color is typically applied at the textile production stage, textile companies are often involved in determining which colors are to be used in the end-use products. Through the process of **color forecasting,** color palettes or **color stories** are selected and translated into fabrics produced by a company for a specific fashion season. Color forecasting is also conducted by apparel manufacturers (see Chapter 5).

The Color Association of the United States (CAUS) is a nonprofit service organization that has been involved in color forecasting since 1915. More than 700 companies, including fiber producers, textile companies, apparel manufacturers, and home fashions producers, belong to CAUS. A committee of volunteers from these companies determines general color palettes for the coming 18 to 24 months. Twice a year (in March and Sep-

Figure 3.10
Swatch cards from color forecasting services assist textile companies in their color decisions.

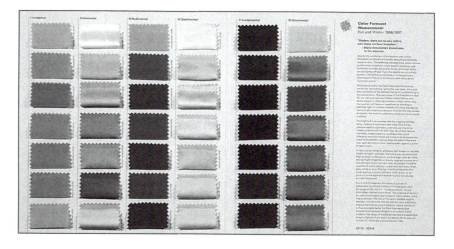

tember), swatch cards are sent to member companies for their use in determining color palettes for their own products.

Intercolor and the International Color Authority are two international color forecasting services. Representatives from member companies meet biannually to determine general color palettes approximately 24 months before the products they produce would be available to the consumer. Forecasts are then sent to member companies for their use.

A number of private color forecasting services also sell color forecasts to companies. These forecasts may be specific to a particular target market and product (e.g., women's apparel, children's apparel). Often the services will also include style and fabrication forecasting. For example, Promostyl is an international color, fabric, and style forecasting service that provides trend analyses for men's, women's, and children's apparel 12 to 18 months ahead of the fashion season. Color forecasts may also be conducted by trade associations for their member companies. For example, Cotton, Incorporated provides color forecasting services to its members.

Companies also conduct their own color forecasting, which is more specific to their product and target market than the information provided by color forecasting services. This type of color forecasting is accomplished by reviewing color predictions from color forecasting services, tracking color trends by examining the colors that were the best and worst selling from previous seasons, observing general trends that may affect color preferences of the target market, and looking at what colors have been missing from the color palettes in order to select colors that may be viewed as "new."

FABRIC PRODUCTION

TEXTILE MILLS

Textile mills focus on the fabric construction stage of textiles. The two most common methods are weaving and knitting. Except for vertically integrated companies that produce both woven and knitted goods, textile mills typically specialize in the production of one type of fabric. In addition to fabric production, woven textile mills often spin their own yarn, whereas knitters typically purchase their yarn. All textile mills sell greige goods (unfinished fabrics). Greige goods may be used "as is" or bought by converters who finish the goods. In addition to selling greige goods, vertically integrated companies also finish the goods themselves and may produce end-use products, such as home textiles (e.g., sheets and towels). Some large vertically integrated textile mills include Burlington Industries, Inc., Cone Mills Corporation, Dan River, Inc., Milliken and Company, Springs Industries, Inc., and Swift Textiles (see Table 3-5).

Mills sell either staple or specialty (novelty) fabrics. Staple fabrics, such as denim or tricot, are produced continually each year with little change in construction or finish. Novelty fabrics have special design features that are

TABLE 3-5

Selected U.S. Apparel Fabric Weaving Mills

ALICE MILLS

Headquarters: Easley, SC

Marketing Headquarters: New York, NY

Ownership: Private

Main Fabrics: gray polyester/cotton print cloths, broadcloths and sheetings, gray 100% cotton print cloths and sheetings, widths ranging from 48 inches to 140 inches

ARKWRIGHT MILLS

Headquarters: Spartanburg, SC

Marketing Headquarters: Hoboken, NJ

Ownership: Private

Trade Names: Nashua

Main Fabrics: Canton flannel, Canton fleece, dobby fabrics, soft-filled sheetings, drills, ducks, twills, double-faced flannels

Volume: 30 million linear yards annually

AVONDALE MILLS

Headquarters: Monroe, GA

Marketing Headquarters: Sylacauga, AL

Ownership: subsidiary of Avondale, Inc., a privately held company

Trade Names and Marks: Fast Times, Bermuda Blue, Bermuda Triangle, Ancient Age Colors, Homebrew, Oldye Tymes, Pioneer, Ranch Denim, Green Card Collection(eco-products), Avonspun yarns, Softspun yarns, Nature's Collection (organically grown, naturally colored cotton)

Main Fabrics: All-cotton indigo denim, polyester/cotton indigo denim, yarn-dyed stripes and plaids, piece-dyed all-cotton and polyester/cotton bottomweight and flannel, open-end and ring-spun yarns, yarns made from organically grown, naturally colored cotton

Volume: approximately $600 million annual sales volume, produces 340 million pounds of yarn and fabric annually

BURLINGTON INDUSTRIES

Headquarters: Greensboro, NC

Marketing Headquarters: New York, NY

Ownership: Public

Trade Names and Marks: Plateau, Pyramid Ultra, Resillia, Esenzia, Ultrex, Versatech, Durepel, UltraWeaves, Fluid Attitudes, M.C.S., Washable Weaves, Reused, Stonefree, Crystal, Black Nova, Profile, Goldrush, Tenderskin, Iron Horse

Main Fabrics: wool worsted and wool worsted blends; denim; polyester and polyblend sportswear fabrics; 100% nylon; nylon and polyester blends, and waterproof, breathable fabrics for activewear

Volume: approximately $2.1 billion sales annually

CARLETON WOOLEN MILLS

Headquarters: New York, NY

Marketing Headquarters: New York, NY

Ownership: Allied Textile Cos.

Trade Names and Marks: Carlana, Carlana Wool Brilliance, Carlana 5

Main Fabrics: 100% wool and high-percentage-wool-content blends, billiard- and gaming-table fabrics

Volume: approximately $55 million annual sales

CMI INDUSTRIES

Headquarters: Columbia, SC

Marketing Headquarters: New York, NY

Ownership: private

Main Fabrics: unbleached polyester and cotton, and 100% cotton print cloths, poplins, twills

CONE MILLS CORPORATION

Headquarters: Greensboro, NC

Ownership: public

Trade Names and Marks: Cone Deeptone Denim, Conesport, Cone XX Denim, Cone North Pointe Specialty Sportswear Fabrics, Splashdown, Brawny, Cone XXX Denim

Main Fabrics: denim, flannel, synthetics, specialty sportswear fabrics

Volume: over $800 million annual sales

DAN RIVER

Headquarters: Danville, VA

Marketing Headquarters: New York, NY

Ownership: private

Trade Names and Marks: Dan River, Criterion, Bed-in-Bag

Main Fabrics: yarn-dyed and piece dyed fabrics of cotton and cotton blends, velour and fashion circular knits, sheets, pillowcases, pillow shams, comforters, drapes and other bedroom accessories

Volume: over $300 million annual sales, produces over 240 million square yards of fabric annually

DELTA MILLS MARKETING CO.

Headquarters: Greenville, SC

Sales Headquarters: New York, NY

Ownership: public—Delta Woodside Industries

Trade Names and Marks: Suncatcher, Trinidad-Twister, Triblend, Irish Linen

Main Fabrics: polyester and rayon linens, polyester and wool blends, polyester, rayon, and acrylic, 100% cotton

Volume: $370 million annual sales

Continued

TABLE 3-5 (continued)

EASTLAND WOOLEN MILLS

Headquarters: Corinna, Maine

Marketing Headquarters: New York, NY

Ownership: private

Trade Names and Marks: Wool Denim, Eco-Wool, Cazju-wool, Bangor Flannel, Corinna Fabrics, Itchless Collection, Mellanna

Main Fabrics: wool and wool-blend flannel, melton, velour, piece-dyed solids, stock-dyed heathers, and fancies

Volume: $25 million annual sales

GALEY & LORD

Headquarters: New York, NY

Ownership: public

Main Fabrics: Woven cotton and polyester/cotton sportswear fabrics, corduroy, printed fabrics, home furnishings fabrics

Volume: $500 million annual sales

GREENWOOD MILLS

Headquarters: Greenwood, SC

Sales Office: New York, NY

Ownership: private

Trade Names and Marks: Clipper, Winchester, Silverdust, Elite Denim

Main Fabrics: denim and chambray, gray goods in print cloth, batiste, broadcloth, twill, poplin

Volume: n/a

HAMRICK MILLS

Headquarters: Gaffney, SC

Marketing Headquarters: New York, NY

Ownership: private

Main Fabrics: gray fabrics, polyester/cotton blended and textured-fill print cloths, 48 inches to 135 inches

Volume: n/a

INMAN MILLS

Headquarters: Inman, SC

Marketing Headquarters: New York, NY

Ownership: private

Main Fabrics: all-cotton twills, oxfords, and sailcloths; polyester/cotton poplins, broadcloths, twills, sailcloths and sheetings; dobbies and other specialty weaves; all fabrics are sold in loom/gray state

Volume: over 100 million linear yards annually

JOHNSTON INDUSTRIES

Headquarters: Columbus, GA

Marketing Headquarters: New York, NY

Ownership: public

Main Fabrics: home furnishings, industrial, apparel, drills, twills, denims, osnaburgs, dobby, jacquard, polyester, poly/cotton blends and 100% cotton

Volume: $162 million annual sales

JPS TEXTILE GROUP

Headquarters: Greenville, SC

Marketing Headquarters: New York, NY

Ownership: private

Main Fabrics: high-twist filament and spun novelties, satins, crepes, linens, challis, acetate linings

Volume: $750 million annual sales

MAYFAIR MILLS

Headquarters: Arcadia, SC

Marketing Headquarters: Hoboken, NJ

Ownership: private

Trade Names and Marks: American Premium Quality

Main Fabrics: wide-print cloth, broadcloth, sheetings, twills, medium and bottom-weight fabrics, poplins, chamois cloth

Volume: 200 million linear yards annually

MILLIKEN & CO.

Headquarters: Spartanburg, SC

Marketing Headquarters: New York, NY

Ownership: private

Trade Names and Marks: Visa, Capture, Millitorn, Blazon, Agilon, Worsterlon, Virtuoso, Weathermark, Soft-Trek, Barrier

Main Fabrics: cotton, cotton blend and manufactured fiber fabrics for apparel, industrial, home furnishings, and automotive use

Volume: over $1 billion annual sales

MISSION VALLEY TEXTILES INC.

Headquarters: New Braunfels, TX

Marketing Headquarters: New York, NY

Ownership: private

Trade Names: Mission Valley Textiles and Creative Textiles

Main Fabrics: yarn-dyed woven fabrics; indigo chambray and denims; 100% cotton, organic cotton, poly/cotton, and linen/cotton fabrics

Volume: $61 million annual sales

MOUNT VERNON MILLS INC.

Headquarters: Greenville, SC

Ownership: private

Trade Names and Marks: Mount Vernon, Riegel, LaFrance, Brentex

Main Fabrics: velvet, denim, print cloth, piece-dyed bottom weights, infant bedding, napery

Volume: over $750 million annual sales

NEW CHEROKEE

Headquarters: Spindale, NC

Marketing Headquarters: New York, NY

Ownership: 78% employee-owned

Trade Names and Marks: Phoenix wrinkle-resistant fabrics

Main Fabrics: dress shirting, sportswear, Tencel fabrics, military and career fabrics

Volume: n/a

RAMTEX INC.

Headquarters: Ramseur, NC

Marketing Headquarters: New York, NY

Ownership: private

Main Fabrics: dress shirting, pocketing, bed sheeting, lightweight home furnishings, workwear poplin

Volume: n/a

REEVES BROTHERS INC.

Headquarters: Spartanburg, SC

Marketing Headquarters: New York, NY

Ownership: private

Trade Names and Marks: Caliber Cloth, Reeveset, Mountain Cloth, Glengary, New Generation, So Easy

Main Fabrics: wrinkle-resistant cottons and blends, flax blends, poly/cottons, synthetic blends, greige sales (rayon and poly/rayon crinkles, flax blends, character yarns and dobbies and patterns in all blends

Volume: $180 million annual sales

SPARTAN MILLS (WOVEN APPAREL BUSINESS)

Headquarters: Spartanburg, SC

Marketing Headquarters: New York, NY

Ownership: closely held public company

Trade Names and Marks: Ranger, Edisto, Comanche, Skipper, King, Renegade, True Blues, Midnight Blues

Main Fabrics: all cotton indigo and colored chambray, denims, piece-dyed bottomweight fabrics, gray apparel and institutional fabrics in 100% cotton and blends

Volume: $400 million annual sales

SPRINGS INDUSTRIES

Headquarters: Fort Mill, SC

Marketing Headquarters: New York, NY

Ownership: public

Trade Names and Marks: Springmaid, Wamsutta, UltraSuede, Dundee, Dawson, Skinner, Pacific, Fashion Pleat, Custom Designs, Pacific Silvercloth

Main Fabrics: broadcloth, batiste, poplin, twill, polyester/cotton blends, 100% cotton, linens, and Ultrasuede

Volume: $2.1 billion annual sales

STONECUTTER MILLS CORP.

Headquarters: Spindale, NC

Marketing Headquarters: New York, NY

Ownership: public

Main Fabrics: woven novelty fabrics using blends of manufactured and natural fibers

Volume: n/a

SWIFT TEXTILES

Headquarters: Atlanta and Columbus, GA

Ownership: wholly owned subsidiary of Canada-based Dominion Textile Company

Trade Names: Swiflex, Colors to Go, Soda Pop Denim, Monaco, Peach Blues

Main Fabrics: black, yarn-dyed colors and valued-added indigo denims; open-end ringlike and ringspun products in a variety of blends and finishes

Volume: more than $500 million annual sales

TEXFI INDUSTRIES

Headquarters: Raleigh, NC

Marketing Headquarters: New York, NY

Ownership: public

Trade Names and Marks: Texfi Blends, Special T., Kingstree, Fashion Knits, Texfi Elastics

Main Fabrics: rayon and polyester; plains and novelties and piece-dyed fancies; 100% filament polyester, and poly/wool blends; flame retardant fabrics; woven and knitted elastics

Volume: $260 million annual sales

THOMASTON MILLS INC.

Headquarters: Thomaston, GA

Marketing Headquarters: New York, NY

Ownership: public

Trade Names and Marks: Thomaston Fabrics

Main Fabrics: indigo denim and bottomweight piece-dyed fabrics in rigid, stretch and brushed finishes

Volume: $276.5 million annual sales

THE WORCESTER CO.

Headquarters: N. Providence, RI

Marketing Headquarters: New York, NY

Ownership: private

Trade Names and Marks: Greystone Fabrics, Worcestervision, Century Collection, Hi-Tex

Main Fabrics: wovens, worsted and worsted blends; rayon and rayon blends; silk; linen; mohair

Volume: n/a

Figure 3.11
Fabric production is highly automated. These machines are used at Pendleton Mills for carding, or straightening the tangled wool fibres (upper left); spinning the wool into yarn (upper right); and producing woolen fabric (lower right).

"fashion-based" and therefore change with fashion cycles. Because of this, fashion fabrics require shorter production runs and greater flexibility.

The knitting industry has two main divisions: (1) the knitted products industry, which manufactures end use products such as T-shirts, hosiery, and sweaters, and (2) the knitted fabrics industry, which manufactures knitted yard goods sold to apparel and home fashions manufacturers and retailers.

TEXTILE DESIGN

Textile design involves the interrelationships among color (e.g., dyeing, printing), fabric structure (e.g., woven, knitted), and finishes (e.g., napping, embossing). In addition, textile designers must have expertise in computer-aided design and an understanding of the technology used in producing textiles. The use of computer-aided design allows the textile designer to experiment with color and fabric construction, and then to print and prepare exact instructions to replicate the fabric design. Textile designers specialize according to printing method and fabric structure; they may be freelance designers or work for textile design studios, textile mills, or converters. For example, one textile designer may work for a textile mill and specialize in direct roller printing processes; another may be a freelance designer of

Figure 3.12
Computer aided design
facilitates the work of textile designers in creating
new fabrics.

graphics for T-shirts and specialize in screen printing processes. Under U.S.
copyright law, graphic designs on fabric are protected, even if incorporated
into an apparel item. The term textile stylist is currently used to describe
individuals who have expertise in the design and manufacturing of textiles as
well as an understanding of the textile market. The stylists' combination of
design, technical, and consumer/business expertise is particularly important
in reflecting consumer preferences in the textiles being designed. Designers
and stylists may work directly with apparel and home fashions manufacturers to create special prints or with retailers in creating prints to be used for
private label merchandise.

TEXTILE CONVERTERS

Textile converters buy greige (unfinished) goods from mills, have the fabrics dyed, printed, or finished, and then sell the finished fabrics. Converters
focus on aesthetic finishes (e.g., glazing, crinkling), performance finishes
(e.g., colorfast, stain resistant, water resistant, durable pressed), and dyeing or
printing fabrics. Most converters are headquartered in New York City,
although they can also be found in other major apparel markets (e.g., Los
Angeles, Dallas, Atlanta). Converters are experts in color forecasting and
understanding consumer preferences in fiber content, fabric construction,
and various aesthetic and performance fabric finishes. Often converters will
contract with dyers, printers, and finishers to create fabrics which they market to apparel and home fashions manufacturers, jobbers, and retailers. Some
converters specialize in a certain type of fabric; others may design several

types of fabrics. Because the fabric is finished closer to the time when consumers will be purchasing the end use product, converters play an important role in analyzing and responding to changing consumer preferences.

Although converters are the primary means by which fabrics are finished for end use specifications, not all finishing operations are handled by converters. For example, apparel and home fashions manufacturers and retailers are fulfilling the converter's functions to some extent when they specify to a textile mill the color they want a fabric dyed. Woolen and worsted wool fabrics are seldom sold through converters, as they are generally sold finished by mills. In addition, industrial fabrics are typically sold directly from mills because of the performance tests and specifications necessary for these fabrics. Converters are also not used much in the manufacturing of sweaters and other knitwear, which is typically knitted and then constructed into garments by the same company.

OTHER FABRIC RESOURCES

Textile jobbers and fabric retail stores buy and sell fabric without any involvement in producing or finishing the fabric. Textile jobbers buy from textile mills, converters, and large manufacturers, and then sell to smaller manufacturers and retailers. Typically jobbers will buy mill overruns (when a textile mill produces more fabric than was ordered) or discontinued fabric colors, designs, or prints. For example, a textile jobber may buy extra discontinued fabric from a textile mill and sell it to a small apparel manufacturer who does not need a large volume of fabric. Retail fabric stores sell over-the-counter piece goods primarily to home sewers. Fabric stores may purchase their bolt yardage from fabric wholesalers who have purchased large rolls from textile mills. Textile brokers serve as a liaison between textile sellers and textile buyers. For example, a broker may connect a small textile mill wanting to sell greige good fabrics to a small converter who wants to buy the greige goods. Textile brokers differ from jobbers in that brokers never own the fabric.

TEXTILE TESTING AND QUALITY ASSURANCE

The textile industry is highly involved in quality assurance programs and **textile testing.** "Textile testing is the process of inspecting, measuring and evaluating characteristics and properties of textile materials" (Cohen, 1989, p. 165). Standard test methods developed by the American Society for Testing and Materials (ASTM) and the American Association of Textile Chemists and Colorists (AATCC) are used by companies in testing the quality and specific performance requirements of the textile materials they use. Although the terms quality control and quality assurance are sometimes used interchangeably, there are distinct differences. The term **quality control** focuses on inspecting finished textiles and making sure they adhere to specific quality standards as measured by a variety of textile testing methods. The term

Figure 3.13
Fabrics are inspected by trained experts to assure quality standards.

quality assurance is broader than the term quality control and takes into consideration not only the general functional performance (quality) of the material, but also the satisfaction of consumer needs for a specific end use. For example, a textile to be used in children's apparel must not only meet minimum standards of functional performance, but must also meet specifications such as color fastness that are important to the consumer of children's apparel. Whereas a textile mill may test for general functional performance of the fabric, often the apparel or home fashions manufacturer or retailer must determine if the fabric meets the specifications of importance to their consumers. This is why textile testing of fabrics is often conducted by apparel and home fashions manufacturers (e.g., NIKE, Jantzen), by retailers (e.g., JCPenney, Target) of these goods, or by independent textile testing companies contracted by manufacturers or retailers.

MARKETING AND DISTRIBUTION OF FABRICS

MARKETING SEASONAL LINES

Fiber producers, textile mills, and converters take part in the marketing of textile fabrics. Most manufactured fiber producers have showrooms in New York City exhibiting fabrics and end-use products made from their fibers. Hoechst Celanese uses a home in New York City, known as the Hoechst Celanese House, as a showroom for fibers used in home textiles. Interior designers are commissioned to design individual rooms with products—fabrics, floor coverings, and furniture—that are all available to the consumer. This unique

Figure 3.14
The Hoechst Celanese
House in New York City
is used as a showroom
for upholstery, pillow,
curtain, and wall fabrics.

merchandising tool exhibits drapery fabric, upholstery fabrics, bed linens, tablecloths, and carpeting, all made from Hoechst Celanese fibers.

Textile mills and converters market their textile fabrics as fall/winter and spring/summer seasonal lines. Each fabric line includes a grouping of fabrics with a similar "theme" or "color story." It is the responsibility of the merchandising/marketing staff of textile companies to show fabric samples to prospective buyers in their showrooms or at textile trade shows. Samples of fall/winter lines of fabrics are shown to prospective fabric buyers in October or November, approximately 6 to 9 months before the end use product (e.g., apparel) hits the stores. Spring/summer lines of fabrics are shown in March or April. For large accounts, fabric samples can be "confined," which means that the textile company will not sell the fabric to other end-use companies. During these shows, apparel and home fashions companies will purchase yardage for their samples. Some large manufacturers may order their end use fabrics at this time, but most will wait until their own orders from retailers are known.

Textile showrooms are located in most major U.S. cities (e.g., Los Angeles, Dallas, Atlanta, Chicago), although New York is the primary market center for textile mills, converters, and textile product manufacturers. Showrooms house the fabric samples to be marketed by textile mills or converters to designers and apparel or home fashions manufacturers.

Fabric companies are also promoting their lines through sites on the Internet and through other on-line services. Such on-line marketing of fabrics offers an efficient method for companies to advertise their products to prospective fabric buyers (Greco, 1996).

Figure 3.15
Textile trade shows
provide opportunities
for textiles companies
to promote their lines
to manufacturers.

TEXTILE TRADE SHOWS

Textile **trade shows** exhibit textile mills' newest fabrics for the coming fashion seasons. Typically held twice per year, in spring (March) and fall (October/November), textile trade shows offer visitors a look at general trends in color, textures, prints, and fabrications. For example, a textile trade show held in March 1997 would exhibit spring/summer 1998 fabrics. Because every apparel line or collection begins with fabrics, textile shows provide designers and manufacturers with inspirations for their next line or collection. "A designer's creativity is limited by what a fabric can be made to do, so in a sense a collection doesn't really start with the designer but with the fabric mill" (Schiro, 1995, p. L16).

Interstoff, held in Frankfurt, Germany, is considered one of the most important and one of the largest international textile trade shows. It features more than 1,000 exhibitors from over 40 countries and attracts more than 25,000 visitors. Interstoff is attended by designers, manufacturers, and retailers from around the world who wish to purchase fabrics or become familiar with fabric trends. Since 1996, Interstoff has consisted of six textile fairs held each year, three per fashion season—Take Off, Interstoff World, and Interstoff Season—each catering to a slightly different group of buyers.

Another important European textile trade show is Premiere Vision, held twice a year in Villepinte, near Paris. At the March 1995 show, more than 800 European textile mills exhibited their textiles for spring/summer 1996. The show attracted more than 44,000 attendees from around the world including designers, apparel manufacturers, retailers, and representatives from cosmetic companies (Schiro, 1995). Designers often get inspirations for apparel designs from the textiles shown at Premiere Vision. Cosmetic companies are also interested in general color trends and textures in fabrics.

Other textile trade shows are Ideacomo held in Como, Italy (near Milan); Texitalia held in Milan, Italy, and New York City; Interstoff/Asia in Hong Kong; the International Fashion Fabric Exhibition (with more than 450 exhibitors held in conjunction with the Boutique Show) in New York City; the L.A. International Textile Show; and Textile Association of Los Angeles (TALA) Show. Leather producers also use trade shows to market their products. Two of the best-known are Semaine du Cuir, held in Paris in September, and the Tanner's Apparel and Garment (TAG) Show, held in New York City in October.

DEVELOPMENTS IN THE TEXTILE INDUSTRY

TEXTILE TRADE AND "QUICK RESPONSE"

As part of a global economy, textiles are traded among countries throughout the world. Until 1981, the United States exported more textiles than it imported. Since that time, however, a trade deficit has existed. This means that the United States imports more textiles than it exports. In recent years, increased productivity in the industry because of capital investments has resulted in an increase of textile exports. According to U.S. Department of Commerce data, textile exports have risen every year since 1986. In 1994, textile exports reached an all-time high of $6.4 billion. The largest market for U.S. textiles is Canada; Mexico is the second largest, the United Kingdom is third, and Japan is fourth. Even with this growth in exports, however, textile imports have risen steadily over the past 15 years; they set a record in 1994 at $9.7 billion. This is primarily the result of lower labor costs in other countries. For example, in 1993, labor costs in the U.S. textile industry averaged $11.61 per hour, while China averaged $.36 per hour, India $.56 per hour, Thailand $1.04 per hour, Malaysia $1.18 per hour, and Singapore $3.56 per hour.

In order to successfully compete in a global economy, the U.S. textile industry has invested in new technology to increase productivity in textile mills and improve communication among textile mills, their suppliers, and their customers. These investments in technology are part of a soft-goods industry program called **Quick Response.** As discussed in Chapter 1, Quick Response is an umbrella term that refers to any strategy that shortens the time from fiber to sale to the ultimate consumer. In the textile industry, Quick Response strategies include such technological advancements such as computer-aided textile design, computerized knitting machines, and communication links between textile companies, their suppliers, and their customers. However, the textile industry has also played an important role in the research, development, and implementation of new strategies to increase productivity and competitiveness. During the past decade, the tex-

Figure 3.16
Computer-controlled robots are used to transport packages in textile mills. Such investments in technology have increased the textile industry's productivity.

tile industry has spent on the average $2 billion per year (3 to 4 percent of sales of the entire industry) on capital expenditures (plants and equipment); in 1994, the amount spent was $2.4 billion. For example, in the woven fabric industry, companies have invested in shuttleless looms (e.g., rapier, projectile, air-jet, water-jet) that have the capability to weave more than twice as many yards per hour as shuttle looms. In addition, greater flexibility and a willingness to manufacture shorter runs of fabrics have also increased the competitiveness of U.S. textile mills. Mills also have become more specialized, building on areas of strength (Abend, 1994).

ENVIRONMENTAL ISSUES

According to some analysts, the demand for environmentally friendly products, particularly among younger consumers and consumers who have a sense of social responsibility, appears significant. In an effort to show they are environmentally conscious, companies (including textile producers) are manufacturing and making available to consumers products that include organic or recycled materials, are produced with less toxic materials such as low-impact dyes, use less water in production, or have incorporated other environmentally friendly processes. Apparel manufacturers are also pressuring textile producers to supply environmentally friendly textiles. Some companies, such as L.L. Bean, have indicated that they will not work with suppliers that are not environmentally sound. L.L. Bean has pressured denim companies to eliminate the use of pumice stones (they become sand and grit) in the manufacture of stonewashed products (Maycumber, 1994). Therefore, in the last few years a number of environmentally safe textile manufacturing processes have been introduced, including organically grown cotton, cleaner dyeing and finishing processes, and waste reduction.

According to the American Textile Manufacturers Institute (ATMI), the textile industry has invested $1.3 billion on environmental controls since the mid-1980s. Trade associations have played an important role in research and implementation of environmentally safe processes. In 1992, ATMI launched its Encouraging Environmental Excellence (E3) program. According to ATMI, "the E3 program calls for textile companies to implement a 10-point plan that starts with a corporate environmental policy and includes a detailed environmental audit of facilities, an outreach program to suppliers and customers that encourages recycling, establishment of corporate envi-

TABLE 3-6

E3 Program Guidelines

The program's guidelines provide the framework for a company's application and retention in the program. Each member company must:

▌ Formulate and submit to ATMI a company environmental policy;

▌ Describe in detail senior management's commitment toward environmental excellence and how greater environmental awareness is encouraged throughout the company;

▌ Submit a copy of its audit form describing how it ensures that officers and employees are in full compliance with existing laws;

▌ Describe how it has worked with suppliers as well as customers to address environmental concerns;

▌ List environmental goals and targeted achievement dates;

▌ Describe its employee education program;

▌ Identify and describe its emergency response plans;

▌ Describe how it has related its environmental interests and concerns to the surrounding community, residents, and policy makers;

▌ Describe how it has been able to offer environmental assistance and insights to citizens, interest groups, other companies, and local government agencies;

▌ Describe its interaction with federal, state, and local policy makers.

Figure 3.17
ATMI's Encouraging Environmental Excellence (E3) program challenges textile companies to implement environmentally safe processes.

ronmental goals and the development of employee education, and community awareness programs." In 1994, 58 members of ATMI had qualified for membership in the E3 program (see Table 3-6), representing 42 percent of the industry's fiber consumption and 34 percent of the industry's employees (Abend, 1994).

In 1993 the American Fiber Manufacturers Association sponsored an impact assessment of the overall environmental impact of a 100 percent polyester fiber knit fabric woman's blouse (Franklin Associates, 1993). The study examined all energy requirements, atmospheric emissions, waterborne wastes, and solid wastes (both industrial and postconsumer). Results of this study indicated that all operations in manufacturing and caring for the apparel product had some impact on the environment and energy consumption. Approximately 82 percent of the total energy requirements were related to consumer use. Fabric production and apparel manufacture (packaging of product for retailer and consumer) created most of the solid waste from manufacturing operations. In addition to this research, the Council for Textile Recycling was created to increase recycling efforts to prevent textiles from ending up in landfills.

Figure 3.18
Fabrics made with environmentally friendly processes are targeted at consumers who share environmental concerns.

A number of "environmentally cleaner" processes have been tried in the cotton industry. These include naturally colored cotton, "cleaner" dyeing methods, and reduced water use. For example, one cotton producer, Sally Fox, grows naturally colored cotton in various shades of green and brown. Natural colors had been bred out of modern cotton because the colored fibers were too short and weak for automated textile manufacturing. Fox began crossing the longer, stronger white cotton fibers with colored cotton to create *Foxfibre®* cotton, the first naturally colored cotton that can be processed with modern textile equipment (Robbins, 1994). The natural colors do more than eliminate the need for dyeing the cotton; instead of fading, naturally colored cotton actually deepens in color when washed. In addition, Foxfibre cotton has a silky feel and a wool-like elasticity.

Fox is also committed to organic cotton production, in which synthetic chemical fertilizers and pesticides are used minimally or not used at all. In 1993, approximately 80 percent of the three million pounds of Foxfibre were grown organically. Fox is not the only cotton producer interested in organic cotton. In 1993 an estimated 20,000 to 40,000 acres (out of a total of 17 million acres in U.S. cotton production) was devoted to growing certified organic cotton (Yates, 1994). Most of this production was in California and Texas.

Rather than using synthetic chemical fertilizers and pesticides, natural fertilizers (manure, which biodegrades) are used with organic techniques, crops are rotated for disease control, and beneficial insects that consume destructive insects are introduced. Once harvested, certified organic cotton is stored without the use of chemical rodenticides and fungicides. Mission Valley Textiles Inc. was the first woven apparel and home furnishings fabrics mill in the United States to receive the government's Organic Fiber processing certification (Rudie, 1994). This certification is used in advertising end-use products to the consumer. A few apparel companies are using organic cotton for at least some of their production. In 1996 Patagonia Inc. (the Ventura, California, manufacturer of sportswear and outdoor clothing), shifted its entire line of cotton apparel to organic cotton fabrics. Although the goods cost slightly more than if regular cotton fabrics were used, the company believed its customers would respond positively to the change.

Because the majority of textiles are colored using chemical dyes to create bright, colorfast characteristics, some manufacturers are attempting to lessen the environmental impact of cotton production through the use of "cleaner" dyeing processes, including new forms of synthetic "low-impact" dyes, natural dyes, and undyed, unbleached cottons. In an effort to reduce the amount of effluence during denim laundering, Burlington Industries has developed Stone Free, a dyeing process that allows indigo shades to break down 50 percent faster in the laundering cycle, without the use of stones or chemicals. However, using a cleaner dyeing process does not necessarily mean that the entire manufacturing process is totally clean.

Natural dyes are extracted from a variety of leaves, barks, flowers, berries, lichens, mushrooms, roots, wood, peels, nutshells, minerals, shellfish, and insects. However, many of these sources do not produce stable dyes for textiles. The most common natural dyes currently used are cochineal (red), which is derived from the body of an insect; osage orange (yellow), which is extracted from the osage orange tree; madder root (red), which is extracted from the woody root of the madder plant; and indigo (blue), which is extracted from a number of plants. It is estimated, however, that in current production, natural dyes add 10 to 40 percent to the cost of the goods. This is primarily the result of the cost of the dyestuffs themselves, since most natural dye producers are small operations (McManus & Wipplinger, 1994).

A number of manufactured-fiber companies have explored the use of recycling as a means of creating more environmentally friendly processes. *Tencel®* is Courtaulds Fibers' new cellulosic fiber made from harvested wood pulp that is processed with recycled chemicals. In its production, virtually all the dissolving agent is recycled. The resulting fiber is machine washable and is stronger than cotton or wool—as well as having a silkier touch. Fabrics can be made from 100 percent Tencel or in a variety of blends. Often companies will combine the use of Tencel with other environmentally friendly processes. For example, Esprit's ecollection uses Tencel, organically grown cotton and linen, natural and low-impact dyes, and reconstituted glass buttons.

Currently, polyester staple fibers are also being recycled from plastic soda bottles, which are made of polyethylene teraphthalate, or PET. In the process of making recycled polyester fibers, all caps, labels, and bases made of other materials are removed from the bottles. The bottles are sorted by color (clear and green), then chopped, and the pieces are washed and dried. Next, the pieces are heated, purified, and formed into pellets. The purified polyester is extruded as fine fibers that can be spun into thread, yarn, or other materials. It takes an average of 25 plastic soda bottles to make one garment. Wellman, Inc.'s fibers division produces *Fortrel EcoSpun®*, recycled polyester that contains 100 percent recycled fiber. It is estimated that 2.4 billion bottles are kept out of landfills per year through the manufacturing of Fortrel EcoSpun fibers. Hoechst Celanese's recycled polyester fiber is marketed under the name *Trevira®II.* It is a blend of 50 percent postconsumer waste (plastic bottles) and 50 percent virgin polyester. Malden Mills Industries, a leading fleece fabric producer, is promoting Trevira II for collections of lightweight outerwear fabrics. Dixie Yarns manufactures recycled 100 percent cotton or cotton/polyester blend yarn made from waste fibers that were collected during the yarn spinning process, baled, and sold in bulk as a waste product. Joma International is producing sweaters from recycled cotton for their Waste Knot line. The process combines waste fabric from new cotton garments with virgin cotton yarn creating an 85 percent recycled and 15 percent virgin cotton fabric. Burlington Industries Denim Division recently came out with Reused Denim, made from 50 percent virgin cotton and 50 percent recycled denim yarns ("Scrap denim," 1995). Swift Textiles's Soda Pop denim blends 20 percent recycled polyester (from soda bottles) with 80 percent cotton.

Although consumers say that environmental aspects of textiles are important to them, some retailers are finding it more difficult to sell organic and recycled textile products because of their higher prices. Many companies are asking the question, "How much can we afford to do for the environment and still be competitive?" For example, Dixie Yarns introduced Earthwise, a collection of naturally dyed cotton yarns in 1992. Although initially well received, colorfastness problems forced Dixie to take them off the market in 1994. Some analysts note that environmentally friendly products are best suited to a niche market of environmentally aware consumers.

SUMMARY

The textile industry includes companies that contribute to the four basic stages of textile production: fiber processing, yarn spinning, fabric production, and fabric finishing. Some companies specialize in one or more of the production processes; vertically integrated companies handle all four. Both natural and manufactured fibers are processed in the United States. Natural fibers produced in the United States include cotton, wool, mohair and other specialty fibers. Leather and fur, also produced in the United States, are considered natural fiber products. Natural fibers are commodities bought and sold on international markets and are generally promoted by trade associations that focus on a specific fiber. These trade associations encourage the use of the various natural fibers through such activities as market research, advertising, and consumer education programs. Manufactured fibers are typically produced by large chemical companies. They are marketed either as commodity fibers or brand-name (trademarked) fibers, such as *Lycra*® spandex fiber or *Dacron*® polyester fiber. Brand-name fibers are advertised by companies in order to create consumer awareness and preference for the specific fibers. Trade associations are also involved in promoting manufactured fibers.

Textile companies are often involved in determining the colors to be used in end-use products. Through the process of color forecasting, color palettes are selected and translated into fabrics produced by a company for a specific fashion season. Color forecasts are available from nonprofit service organizations, such as the Color Association of the United States, or from private color forecasting services. Companies may also conduct their own color forecasting.

Textile mills focus on fabric production and sell greige goods (unfinished fabrics); some textile mills will finish the fabric as well. Textile design involves the interrelationships among color (e.g., dyeing, printing), fabric structure (e.g., woven, knitted), and finishes (e.g., napping, embossing). Converters specialize in fabric finishing. They buy greige goods and finish the fabric according to textile mills', apparel manufacturers', or retailers' specifications. Other fabric resources include textile jobbers, textile brokers, and fabric retail stores. Through quality assurance programs, textile mills, apparel manufacturers, and retailers test textiles according to standards for end-use products. Textile mills and converters market their textile fabrics as fall/winter and spring/summer seasonal lines in showrooms and at textile trade shows held throughout the world.

In order to successfully compete in a global economy, the U.S. textile industry has invested in new technology to increase productivity in textile mills and improve communication among textile mills, their suppliers, and their customers. These investments in technology are part of a soft-goods industry program called Quick Response, whose strategies are designed to shorten the time from fiber to finished product.

The textile industry is addressing environmental concerns through manufacturing and by making available to consumers products that include organic or recycled materials, are produced with less toxic materials such as low-impact dyes, use less water in production, or have incorporated other environmentally friendly processes.

REFERENCES

Abend, Jules. (1994, November). The green wave swells. *Bobbin*, pp. 92–98.

American Fiber Manufacturers Association. *The American Manufactured Fiber Industry*. Washington, D.C.: Author

American Textile Manufacturers Institute. (1995, June). *Textile HiLights.* Washington, D.C.: Author.

American Textile Manufacturers Institute. *America's Textiles.* Washington, D.C.: Author.

Eberspacher, Jinger J. (1993). The declining domestic leather industry: Implications and opportunities. *Clothing and Textiles Research Journal, 12* (1), 26–30.

Cohen, Allen C. (1989). *Marketing Textiles: From Fiber to Retail.* New York: Fairchild Publications.

Franklin Associates, LTD. (1993, June). Resource and environmental profile analysis of a manufactured apparel product. Report prepared for the American Fiber Manufacturers Association.

Greco, M. (1996, February). Is on-line fabric sourcing next? *Apparel Industry Magazine*, pp. 32–34.

Hollen, Norma, Sadler, Jane, Langford, Anna L., and Kadolph, Sara J. (1988). *Textiles.* (6th ed.). New York: Macmillan.

Joseph, Marjory L. (1988). *Essentials of Textiles* (4th ed.). New York: Holt, Rinehart and Winston.

Maycumber, S. Gray. (1994, April 26). L.L. Bean to ATMI: Environment key factor. *WWD*, p. 14.

McManus, Fred, and Wipplinger, Michele. (1994, February/March). Nature shows her true colors. *Green Alternatives*, pp. 26–31.

McNamara, Michael. (1995, February 9). Cotton Inc. lifestyle monitor, to survey consumer attitude. *WWD*, p. 11.

Patagonia switches to organic cotton. (1995, October). *Bobbin*, p. 24.

Robbins, Jim. (1994, December). Undying devotion. *Destination Discovery*, pp. 18–21.

Rudie, Raye. (1994, February). How green is the future? *Bobbin*, pp. 16–20.

Schiro, Anne-Marie. (1995, May 7). Mills weave trends in fabric of fashion. *The Oregonian*, p. L16.

Scrap denim spun into "Green" jeans. (1995, February). *Apparel Industry Magazine*, p. 16.

Yates, Dorian (1994, February/March). Organic cotton. *Green Alternatives,* pp. 33–36.

KEY TERMS

textile	**finish**
fiber	**greige goods**
generic families	**converted or finished goods**
yarns	**throwsters**
spun yarns	**textile mills**
filament yarns	**converters**
fabric construction	**vertically integrated**

cotton	trade association
wool	brand name or trade name
mohair	licensed or controlled brand-name program
skins	color forecasting
kips	color stories
hides	textile converter
tanning	textile testing
regular tanneries	quality control
pelts	quality assurance
tawning	trade show
horizontally integrated	Quick Response

DISCUSSION QUESTIONS

1. What are the advantages and disadvantages if a textile company is horizontally or vertically integrated? How are these advantages and disadvantages reflected in the types of textile companies that are horizontally or vertically integrated?

2. Follow a cotton/polyester blend woven fabric from the fiber production to the marketing of the fabric to apparel manufacturers. What are the primary stages of production and marketing? Give the approximate time frame for this process.

3. What are the differences between the production and marketing of natural fibers and manufactured fibers? Why do these differences exist?

4. What role do trade associations play in the promotion of natural and manufactured fibers? Give examples of the activities performed by trade associations. Bring in examples of coop advertising between trade associations and end use producers.

5. What are greige goods? Why are converters important in creating end use products that can best meet the needs of consumers?

CAREER PROFILE

Careers in the textile industry are as varied as the industry itself. Textile chemist, textile designer, textile production supervisor, and textile marketer are just a few of the many careers available in this industry.

INDEPENDENT SALES REPRESENTATIVE,
Fabrics and Trims

Job Description
Show lines of fabrics and trims to designers and merchandisers, send samples, help design products, follow up with vendors to see that goods are

delivered through production, negotiate prices, make presentation books and boards.

Typical Tasks

- Drive to accounts in three states and Canada—traveling 2 to 3 days per week minimum
- Pack and unpack sample bags
- Keep price lists organized
- Manage office and finances; purchase supplies and office equipment
- Work with purchasing agents
- Write orders, follow-up letters, price quotes
- File, update files and materials, keep office clean

What Do You Like Best About Your Job?
Showing the latest products; the people I work with.

4

Ready-to-Wear: Company Organization

Objectives

▮ To compare the ready-to-wear industry with haute couture.

▮ To describe the various types of ready-to-wear companies.

▮ To discuss the organizational structure of apparel companies.

▮ To examine the merchandising philosophies of apparel companies.

▮ To describe trade associations and trade publications in the apparel industry.

LIZ CLAIBORNE, Levi Strauss, Russell, Osh Kosh B'Gosh, Ralph Lauren—all are examples of successful U.S. apparel companies. Although each of these companies creates merchandise recognized by consumers around the world, they vary in the way they are organized and in the way they operate. This chapter focuses on the general organization and operation of companies that produce men's, women's, and children's apparel. Apparel companies are classified by the categories of apparel products they produce, such as size range, styling, price zone, type of product (suits, active sportswear), age, and gender. These classifications, in turn, relate to the organizational structure of the producers and retailers of fashion goods.

READY-TO-WEAR: WHAT DOES IT MEAN?

The majority of apparel produced and sold is called **ready-to-wear (RTW).** As the term implies, the apparel is completely made and ready to be worn (except for finishing details such as pant hemming in tailored clothing) at the time it is purchased. In England, this merchandise is called "off-the peg," in France it is called *"prêt-à-porter,"* and in Italy it is called *"moda pronto."* RTW apparel is made in large quantities using mass manufacturing processes that require little or no hand sewing.

Sizing in RTW is a combination of standardized body dimensions, company sizing, and wearing and design ease. As discussed in Chapter 1, the standardization of sizing was necessary for the development of the ready-to-wear industry. Clothing sizes were developed by grouping computed average circumference measurements of a large group of people (of average height) into specific size categories. For example, the men's size 42 relates to an "average height" (5' 10") male with a chest circumference of 42 inches, waist of 36 inches, and hip measurement of 43 inches. These body measurements or dimensions are what are referred to as the standardized size.

As catalog sales of apparel have increased, direct marketing apparel companies have worked to develop consistent body measurements and related size measurements. A fit that can be determined accurately from body measurement charts can reduce returns and thus increase customer satisfaction with the product and the company. Standardized tables of body dimensions are being developed by the American Society for Testing and Materials (ASTM) for various figure types.

The apparel industry does not adhere strictly to the "set" standardized sizes. A company may develop its "company size" based on a target customer with a smaller waist compared to hip circumference, or a larger chest compared to waist circumference. The term, "athletic fit" is used to refer to a men's suit built to fit the male body with a larger chest compared to waist ratio than the standardized size. This is why many consumers say that one brand of apparel fits them better than other brands.

Wearing ease and design ease are added to the body measurements to create the garment measurements. Each company decides how much wearing and design ease to add to create the "look" for the company. Some styles are designed to fit looser than other styles. The company sizing will reflect these style aspects.

Each company's size range is based on its predetermined body measurements, plus ease. The size measurements increase and decrease in specified increments from the base or sample size to create the size range. The size increments used to create the various sizes will be discussed in more detail in Chapter 9.

Apparel companies produce seasonal **lines** or **collections** of merchandise. Lines or collections refer to groups of styles designed for a particular **fashion season.** The primary difference between a line and a collection is the cost of the merchandise—collections typically refer to groups of merchandise that are more expensive. Often "name designers" will create and offer collections; other apparel companies will offer lines.

Apparel companies typically produce four to six new collections or lines per year, corresponding to the fashion seasons: spring, summer, fall I, fall II, holiday, and resort. These fashion seasons coincide with the time consumers would most likely *wear* the merchandise, not to when companies design or manufacture the merchandise or when the merchandise is delivered to stores. For example, a company may start creating a fall season line in December, actually manufacture it from March through June, and deliver the merchandise to the stores in July.

Not all companies will produce lines for all six fashion seasons. How many lines will be produced depends on both the product category and the target market. For example, a company that produces men's tailored suits may only create two lines per year (fall and spring), whereas a men's sportswear company may create five lines per year (fall I, fall II, holiday, spring, and summer).

READY-TO-WEAR VERSUS COUTURE

Designer names, such as Coco Chanel, Christian Dior, and Yves St. Laurent, first became famous in the realm of French *haute couture* (high fashion) and later became associated with expensive ready-to-wear. Because of the continued prominence and importance of these designers, it is important to understand the distinction and the relationship between couture and ready-to-wear. "Couture" is a French term that literally means "sewing." In general, **couture** apparel is produced in smaller quantities, utilizes considerable hand sewing techniques, and is sized to fit an individual's body measurements. Generally, more expensive fabrics are used in couture apparel than in RTW.

The term couture is derived from **haute couture** (pronounced oat cootur), literally meaning "high sewing." As discussed in Chapter 1, the haute couture industry developed in Paris during the nineteenth century. At that time, apparel was produced by dressmakers and tailors who custom fit each garment to the client. The garment style and fabric were selected for or by each client, the client's body measurements were taken, and the garment was completed after one or more fittings during the construction process. For persons who did not have personal dressmakers or tailors, apparel was produced in the home, by whomever had the necessary skills.

Selecting a fabric and creating a garment prior to an order from a client was a new concept, attributed to Charles Frederick Worth, the founder of the haute couture business. He created several gowns which were modeled by his wife. Clients came into his shop and selected a style to have copied for them, custom fit to their body measurements. Soon he had a clientele of wealthy and noble patrons. He used exquisite fabrics and trims and

Figure 4.1
Haute couture shows
are huge events in the
fashion world and are
covered in detail by the
press. Christian Lacroix,
Spring 1996.

employed a bevy of seamstresses to complete the intricate handwork. In time other designers followed Worth's lead, and the haute couture business was formed. These designers "created" new fashions, while the rest of the western fashion world followed their lead.

During the early twentieth century, the *Chambre Syndicale de la Couture Parisienne* was formed to provide an organizational structure and to offer protection for designers against designs being copied. Currently, the *Chambre Syndicale* organizes and manages the collections which are shown twice per year, arranges the calendar for the showings, organizes accreditation for press and buyers who want to attend the showings, and assists the couture houses so each gains the maximum press coverage possible. Today, there are fewer than thirty haute couture designers in Paris. To be a member of the Paris haute couture requires specific qualifications, including the use of one's own "house" seamstresses, the presentation of fall and spring collections each year in one's own salon using live models, adherence to the dates of showings set by the *Chambre Syndicale*, and registration of the original designs.

Each designer's business is called a "house." Thus, there is the House of Dior, the House of St. Laurent, and the House of Chanel. The haute couture designer is called the **couturier(ière)** or the Head of the House. While some couturiers control their own businesses, many couture houses are owned by corporations that finance the house. In recent years, some financial backers have been known to hire and fire head designers.

A Paris haute couture designer typically has a store, or "boutique," located on one of several "fashion avenues" in Paris. Located on the main floor, the boutique sells the designer's licensed products, such as perfume, scarfs, jewelry, and other accessories, and home furnishings. Some designers sell a boutique collection of apparel and shoes on the main floor as well.

The term **salon de couture** is used to indicate the showroom of the couture designer. It is typically on the second floor of the building that houses the designer's boutique. Entry to the second level, the salon, is limited to those with invitations to a collection show. The **atelier de couture** (ah-tal-lee-aye), or workrooms, may be on the floors above the salon or in a separate building.

The twice-per-year Paris haute couture collection openings continue to be huge events in the fashion world and are covered in detail by the fashion press. Fall fashion season haute couture collections are typically shown in July, and spring fashion season haute couture collections are typically shown in January. The press, buyers, other designers, celebrities, and wealthy clients are in attendance. While the fashion influence of the couturiers waxes and wanes, the designs presented are considered to represent "a laboratory of design creativity." Currently, all Paris haute couture houses also produce a RTW collection, called *prêt-à-porter*. These RTW collections may be sold in the house boutique, in free-standing boutiques (e.g., YSL's *Rive Gauche* boutiques), or in up-scale department or specialty stores.

In addition to the couturiers who are members of the *Chambre Syndicale,* other designers consider themselves to be couture designers. Generally, a couture designer uses elegant fabrics, creates original designs (as opposed to copying another's designs), uses high-quality hand-finishing details, and custom fits the garment to a client's body measurements. Couture designers may produce all custom work (ordered by a specific client), or they may present a seasonal collection and then take custom orders for the collection. There are couture designers in New York, Los Angeles, and in other cities around the world.

The term "couture" is sometimes used in the apparel industry to impart an "upper class" ambience to an apparel line. For example, an apparel company might produce a high-priced line and call it a "couture" line. Indeed, some stores even have departments called "couture." However, if mass-production techniques are used in producing the apparel, the line is considered RTW and *not* couture.

TYPES OF RTW APPAREL PRODUCERS

From large corporations to small companies, from those that produce innovative trendy merchandise to those that produce classics, RTW companies come in all shapes and sizes and vary tremendously in their organization.

Because of the diversity found in RTW apparel company organization, any attempt to classify types of apparel producers is difficult. However, according to industry analysts, the major types of apparel suppliers can be grouped into the categories that follow (Kurt Salmon Associates, 1989).

Conventional manufacturers perform all functions of creating, marketing, and distributing an apparel line on a continual basis. These companies typically make products in their own plant(s) or factories, but might also use outside companies (contractors) to make their products. Manufacturers include multidivision companies that produce several product lines of nationally advertised merchandise (e.g., Levi Strauss, Jantzen) as well as companies that specialize in one product category, such as infants' and children's wear (e.g., Carter's) or fleecewear (e.g., Tultex, Russell). Manufacturers may produce brands of merchandise distributed nationally or regionally, licensed products, or private label merchandise for a specific store. Retail distribution of products will vary depending on the manufacturer.

Jobber is the traditional name given to companies that buy fabrics and acquire styles from independent designers or by copying or designing lines themselves, but use outside companies (contractors) to make their products. This type of company became popular in the early 1900s with New York (Seventh Avenue) men's and women's wear companies serving as intermediaries. They carried huge inventories of merchandise and could make prompt deliveries to retailers. As retailers started sending their own buyers to New York and as resident buyers became more popular, the need for jobbers declined. Today, because so many apparel producers contract out the manufacturing functions, the use of the term "jobber" is not as widespread as it used to be. Instead, most apparel producers are referred to as "manufacturers" regardless of whether or not they use contractors. In fact, this recent definition of "manufacturer" offered by industry analysts suggests a broader perspective—"manufacturers in the apparel industry are the main contractors of apparel production. Some have internal production capabilities, but most contract out a substantial portion of actual production to contractors" (Southern California Edison Company, 1995, Appendix A).

Contractors are companies that specialize in the sewing and finishing of goods. Contractors are used by full-function manufacturers who lack sufficient capacity in their own plants, by jobbers, and by retailers for private label merchandise. According to the industry definition, "contractors in the apparel industry are the many, usually small factories in which most apparel production actually takes place. Several different types of industry entities source apparel goods from contractors, including manufacturers, retailers, buyers, importers, and trading companies" (Southern California Edison Company, 1995, Appendix A). Most contractors specialize in a product category (e.g., knit tops) or have specialized equipment and skilled workers (e.g., embroidery machines). The term **item house** is used to describe contractors that specialize in the production of one product. For example, item houses are used in the production of baseball caps. Contractors also offer their customers fast turn around. Some contractors, in working with retailers, have begun to also offer fabric procurement and apparel design services that were traditionally part of the manufacturers' role.

Importers/Packagers develop full lines of apparel with contractors in other countries and sell them to retailers as complete packages for their use as private label merchandise (items carry the retailer's name).

Licensors are companies that have developed a well-known designer name (e.g., Calvin Klein, Liz Claiborne), brand name (e.g., Guess?, Hang Ten), or character (e.g., Mickey Mouse, Indiana Jones) and sell the use of these names or characters to companies to put on merchandise. As discussed in Chapter 2, successful licensing depends on a well-known name or image (property).

It should be noted that these categories are not mutually exclusive. For example, a manufacturer may use a contractor when its own plant's capacity is exceeded, or may license its brand name to a company that produces product categories different from its own. The details of these various types of apparel production will be discussed in later chapters.

CLASSIFYING APPAREL ORGANIZATIONS

Apparel producers are classified in a number of ways—by the type of merchandise they produce, by the wholesale prices of the products or brands, and by the standard industry classification system. An examination of these classification systems is in order to better understand the diversity of apparel organizations.

GENDER/AGE, SIZE RANGE, PRODUCT CATEGORY

The apparel industry is divided into the primary categories of men's, women's and children's wear manufacturers. Some companies produce apparel in only one of these categories; others produce apparel for more than one. In some cases, companies began as producers of one category of apparel, then branched out into one or more other categories as the company grew. For example, Levi Strauss began as a producer of men's apparel and then expanded into women's and children's wear; Liz Claiborne began as a producer of women's apparel and then developed men's and children's divisions.

The separate gender/age categories have their roots in the early history of the U.S. apparel industry. Apparel producers specialized in one category because of a variety of factors. The types of machinery used for producing men's apparel was often different than the machinery needed for women's apparel. The sizing standards developed differently for men's, women's and children's wear. The number of seasonal lines produced per year differs for each category; therefore the production cycle varies.

The organizational structure of retail stores is related to these categories of apparel and is another reason why the apparel industry remains divided into the three primary categories. Retail buyers are often assigned responsibilities in one of the three categories of apparel. For example, a men's wear buyer buys apparel for the retail store from men's apparel producers. This allows for the producers and retailer to establish and maintain profitable working relationships.

Within each of the three primary categories, the apparel producers are subdivided into additional categories. Apparel producers generally specialize in one or several subcategories. These subcategories relate to a term called the **classification** of apparel. These classifications are by type of garment produced (product type), and they correspond to the departments of most retail stores. Traditional classifications for women's apparel include:

- outerwear—coats, suits, jackets, and rainwear
- dresses
- blouses
- sportswear and active sportswear—separates such as pants, sweaters, and skirts, and active sportswear such as swimwear, skiwear, and tennis wear
- eveningwear
- bridal and bridesmaid dresses
- maternity wear
- uniforms
- furs
- intimate apparel

    Categories of intimate apparel include:
    - foundations, including girdles (body-shapers), bras, and other shapewear
    - lingerie, including petticoats, slips, panties, camisoles, nightgowns, and pajamas
    - loungewear, including robes, bed jackets, and housecoats

Foundations and lingerie worn under other clothing is sometimes referred to as innerwear. In addition, lingerie and loungewear are sometimes divided into daywear and nightwear.

From four to six seasonal lines per year are typically produced in the women's apparel category. The various subcategories are organized by size range and clothing classification (see Table 4-1). For example, some apparel companies manufacture apparel only in missy or only in junior sizes. Some companies produce apparel in missy and women's (large) sizes, while other companies manufacture missy, women's, petite, and tall sizes. Within one size range, an apparel producer may manufacture clothing in one or more of the classifications previously listed.

TABLE 4-1

Men's, Women's and Children's Wear Categories

MEN'S WEAR	WOMEN'S WEAR	CHILDREN'S WEAR
Subcategories: (organized by classification of apparel)	*Subcategories:* (organized by size, then classification)	*Subcategories:* (organized by gender and size)
Tailored clothing	(not all companies produce entire size range)	Infants—sizes by weight/height or 3 months, 6 months, 12 months, 18 months
suits, sport coats, evening wear (tuxedos), overcoats	Missy—sizes 4 to 18 or S-M-L	Toddler—sizes 2T to 3T
sizes: 36 to 44 (chest circumference) and portly sizes 46 to 50, Regular, Short, Long	Women's (large size, Queen, Custom)—sizes 16W to 26W or 1X to 4X	Children's—sizes 3 to 6X
separate trousers, sizes: waist/hemmed at retailer's	Petite—sizes 2P to 16P, under 5'4"	Boys—sizes 8 to 18 or 20 and Husky or Chubby
Examples: manufacturers (e.g., Hart-Marx, Christian Dior) and private labels (e.g., Nordstrom, Stafford)	Tall—sizes 10T to 18T, over 5'9"	Girls—sizes 7 to 14
	Junior—sizes 3 to 15	Subteen (girls)—sizes 6 to 14
Sportswear	Classifications: dresses, blouses, sportswear, active sportswear, outerwear, furs, maternity, evening/bridal, uniforms, intimate apparel	Young junior—sizes 3 to 13
sport shirts (S-M-L-XL sizes), pants (waist/inseam of S-M-L), casual jackets (36 to 44 or S-M-L-XL sizes)		
Examples: Levi's Dockers, Claiborne, private/store label (e.g., The Gap)		
Furnishings		
shirts (neck/sleeve length or S-M-L-XL sizes), neckwear, sweaters, underwear (waist size), socks, robes, pajamas		
Examples: John Henry, Arrow, Pendleton		
Active sportswear		
swimwear, athletic wear, windbreakers		
sizes: S-M-L-XL-XXL		
Examples: Nike, Speedo-Authentic Fitness		
Uniforms and work wear		
overalls, work pants (waist/inseam or S-M-L-XL sizes), work shirts (S-M-L-XL)		
Examples: Levi's, OshKosh B'Gosh		

In addition to the difference between size range categories of missy and junior apparel, there are styling differences as well. The junior size range is designed for a customer who is approximately 16 to 22 years old, whereas the missy size range is designed for a target customer who is approximately 22 years and older. The styling, fabrics, and trims of missy apparel have a more mature fashion look than the style of junior apparel.

Traditional men's wear classifications include:

- tailored clothing—structured or semistructured suits, coats, and separates, such as sportsjackets and dress slacks
- sportswear—casual pants, including jeans
- furnishings—dress shirts and casual shirts; sweaters; neckties, handkerchiefs, and other accessory items; underwear and nightwear; hosiery; and hats and caps
- active sportswear—athletic clothing, golf wear, tennis wear, swimwear
- uniforms and work wear—work shirts and pants, overalls

Figure 4.2
Women's apparel includes size ranges such as misses (missy), junior, and women's. The base size is used to create the style prototypes.

SWIM BODY SIZES   AUG 1995

MISSES SWIM

SIZE	6	8	**10	12	14	16	18
BUST	34 1/2	35 1/2	36 1/2	38	39 1/2	41	43
RIBCAGE	28	29	30	31 1/2	33	34 1/2	36 1/2
WAIST	25 1/2	26 1/2	27 1/2	29	30 1/2	32	34
HIP	36 1/2	37 1/2	38 1/2	40	42	44	46
TORSO	59	60 1/2	62	63 1/2	65	66 1/2	68
LONG TORSO	62	63 1/2	65	66 1/2	68	69 1/2	71

JUNIOR SWIM

SIZE	3	5	7	**9	11	13
BUST	32 1/2	33 1/2	34 1/2	35 1/2	36 3/4	38 1/4
RIBCAGE	26 1/2	27 1/2	28 1/2	29 1/2	30 3/4	32 1/4
WAIST	23 1/2	24 1/2	25 1/2	26 1/2	27 3/4	29 1/4
HIP	34 1/2	35 1/2	36 1/2	37 1/2	38 3/4	40 1/4
TORSO	57	58 1/2	60	61 1/2	63	64 1/2

WOMEN SWIM   [18W]

SIZE	16W	**18W	20W	22W	24W	26W	28W
BUST	40	42	44	46	48	50	52
RIBCAGE	33 1/2	35 1/2	37 1/2	39 1/2	41 1/2	43 1/2	45 1/2
WAIST	32	34	36	38	40	42	44
HIP	41 1/2	43 1/2	45 1/2	47 1/2	49 1/2	51 1/2	53 1/2
TORSO	65	66 1/2	68	69 1/2	69 1/2	69 1/2	69 1/2

** = BASE SIZE

Table 4-1 lists these classifications, typical sizes offered, and examples of producers. The number of seasonal lines produced per year varies with the classification of apparel. Tailored clothing producers tend to develop a large fall line and a somewhat smaller spring line, while sportswear producers develop four to six seasonal lines per year.

In children's wear, the subcategories are organized by size range (age-related) and by gender (see Table 4-1). Many children's wear manufacturers produce apparel in both infants and toddlers sizes. In the older size ranges, apparel companies usually specialize in either boys' wear or girls' wear. Seasonal lines produced in children's wear typically include Back to School (largest line), holiday, spring and summer.

WHOLESALE PRICE ZONES

Ready-to-wear apparel companies typically specialize in one or more **wholesale price zones** which are categories based on the approximate wholesale cost of the merchandise. These categories include:

▌ **Designer.** The designer price zone is the most expensive of the wholesale price zones. It includes collections of name designers such as Calvin Klein, Donna Karan, Yves St. Laurent, Bill Blass, Armani, and Chanel, as well as collections of brands such as St. John Knits. Although this category is sometimes referred to as "couture," it should not be confused with couture apparel that is made to the size specifications of an individual.

▌ **Bridge.** Bridge lines traditionally fall in between designer and better price zones. These may include designers' less expensive lines, sometimes called **diffusion lines** (e.g., Armani X, DKNY), or those brands that are situated between designer and better price zones (e.g., Ellen Tracy, Adrienne Vittadini).

▌ **Better.** Better lines are generally nationally known brand names, such as Liz Claiborne, Jones New York, and Evan Picone in women's wear, or Nautica, Claiborne, and Re-union in men's wear. Private label merchandise (goods that carry the retailer's name) are sometimes in this price zone as well (e.g., Nordstrom's Classiques Entier line).

▌ **Moderate.** Moderate lines include nationally known sportswear brand names (e.g., Jantzen, Dockers, Levis, Guess?) and other reasonably priced lines (e.g., Kaspar suits). Moderate lines also include less expensive lines of companies that also produce better merchandise (e.g., Lizwear). Private label merchandise may also be in this price zone (e.g., Macy's Charter Club line).

▌ **Budget** or **Mass.** Found primarily in mass merchandisers and discount stores, budget lines are the least expensive of the wholesale price zones. Private label merchandise for discount stores is also considered to be in the budget price zone category (e.g., Kmart's Jaclyn Smith line).

It is important to note that the wholesale price zones can be considered a continuum for classification purposes. For example, some lines may be considered in between budget and moderate, while others may be considered in between moderate and better.

BRAND NAME CLASSIFICATIONS

Companies also vary in the brands they produce. Brand names fall into one of the following categories (Lewis, 1995, p. 3):

- **National/designer brands:** "a label that is distributed nationally, to which consumers attach a specific meaning. Typically a national brand represents a certain image, quality level and price-point range to consumers." Examples include Hanes, Fruit of the Loom, Calvin Klein, Wrangler.

TABLE 4-2

The 25 Most Recognizable Brands in Women's Apparel and Accessories

1. **L'eggs**
Product: Legwear
Volume: $700 million (estimate)
Owner: Sara Lee Corp., Chicago

2. **Timex**
Product: Watches
Volume: $700 million
Owner: Timex Corp., Middlebury, CT

3. **Lee**
Product: Jeans and sportswear
Volume: $1 billion
Owner: VF Corp., Wyomissing, PA

4. **Hanes**
Product: Hosiery and activewear
Volume: $350 million
Owner: Sara Lee Corp., Chicago

5. **Levi Strauss**
Product: Jeans and sportswear
Volume: $6.1 billion
Owner: Levi Strauss & Co., San Francisco

6. **Hanes Her Way**
Product: Underwear, daywear, bras, casual wear, socks, casual shoes
Volume: $400 million (innerwear only)
Owner: Sara Lee Corp., Chicago

7. **Fruit of the Loom**
Product: Underwear, daywear, activewear
Volume: $2.3 billion (corporate), $70 million (women's FTL inner wear)
Owner: Fruit of the Loom Inc., Chicago

8. **Reebok**
Product: Athletic shoes, activewear
Volume: $3.3 billion
Owner: Reebok International Ltd., Stoughton, MA

9. **Calvin Klein**
Product: Designer apparel, jeans, fragrances, licensing, retail
Volume: $210 million (Collection and CK), $500 million (fragrance), $100 million (underwear)
Owner: Calvin Klein Inc., New York

10. **No Nonsense**
Product: Hosiery
Volume: $200 million
Owner: Grupo Synkro, Mexico City

11. **Nike**
Product: Athletic shoes, activewear
Volume: $3.8 billion
Owner: Nike Inc., Beaverton, OR

12. **Dockers**
Product: Sportswear
Volume: $1 billion
Owner: Levi Strauss & Co., San Francisco

▌ **Private label brands:** "a label that is owned and marketed by a specific retailer for use in their stores." Examples include JCPenney's Worthington label and Target's Greatland label.

▌ **Retail store/Direct market brands:** "a name of a retail chain that is, in most cases, used as the exclusive label on the items in the store." Examples include The Gap, Victoria's Secret, and L.L. Bean.

▌ **All other brands:** "miscellaneous labels that are not included in the categories above. Includes licensed brands." Examples include Wilson, Mickey & Co., Looney Tunes.

▌ **Nonbrands:** "a label to which consumers attach no significant identity, awareness, or meaning."

See Table 4-2 for a listing of the twenty-five most recognizable brands in women's apparel and accessories.

13. **Seiko**
Product: Watches
Volume: $360 million (U.S. only)
Owner: Seiko Corp., Tokyo

14. **Playtex**
Product: Bras, shapewear
Volume: $375 million
Owner: Sara Lee Corp., Chicago

15. **Wrangler**
Product: Jeans, denim sportswear
Volume: $1 billion
Owner: VF Corp., Wyomissing, PA

16. **Jordache**
Product: Jeans, sportswear
Volume: $250 million
Owner: Jordache Enterprises Inc., New York

17. **London Fog**
Product: Rainwear, outerwear
Volume: $300 million
Owner: Londontown Corp., Eldersberg, MD

18. **Guess**
Product: Jeans, sportswear, licensing
Volume: $600 million
Owner: Guess Inc., Beverly Hills, CA

19. **LA Gear**
Product: Athletic shoes, activewear
Volume: $430 million
Owner: LA Gear, Santa Monica, CA

20. **Bugle Boy**
Product: Jeans, sportswear
Volume: $481 million
Owner: Bugle Boy Industries, Simi Valley, CA

21. **Liz Claiborne**
Product: Sportswear, accessories, fragrances
Volume: $2.2 billion
Owner: Liz Claiborne Inc., New York

22. **Rolex**
Product: Watches
Volume: $1.8 billion (worldwide)
Owner: Rolex, Geneva

23. **Adidas**
Product: Athletic shoes, activewear
Volume: $445 million
Owner: Adidas America, Portland, OR

25. **The Gap**
Product: Jeans, casual sportswear
Volume: $3.7 billion
Owner: The Gap Inc., San Francisco

TABLE 4-3

Standard Industrial Classification (SIC) Codes for Textiles and Apparel

SIC 22 TEXTILE MILL PRODUCTS

2211	Broad woven fabric mills, cotton
2221	Broad woven fabric mills, man-made fiber and silk
2231	Broad woven fabric mills (including dyeing and finishing)
2241	Narrow fabrics and other smallwares mills: cotton, wool, silk, and man-made fiber
2251	Women's full-length and knee-length hosiery
2252	Hosiery, except women's full-length and knee-length hosiery
2253a	Knit outerwear mills
2254a	Knit underwear and nightwear mills
2257	Circular knit fabric mills
2258	Lace and warpknit fabric mills
2259	Knitting mills, not elsewhere classified
2261	Finishers of broad woven fabrics of cotton
2262	Finishers of broad woven fabrics of man-made fiber and silk
2269	Finishers of textiles, not elsewhere classified
2273	Carpets and rugs
2281	Yarn spinning mills
2282	Throwing and winding mills
2284	Thread mills
2295	Coated fabrics, not rubberized
2296	Tire cord and fabric
2297	Nonwoven fabrics
2298	Cordage and twine
2299	Textile goods, not elsewhere classified

SIC 23 APPAREL AND OTHER FINISHED PRODUCTS MADE FROM FABRICS AND SIMILAR MATERIALS

2311	Men's and boys' suits, coats, and overcoats
2321	Men's and boys' shirts
2322	Men's and boys' underwear and nightwear
2323	Men's and boys' neckwear
2325	Men's and boys' trousers and slacks
2326	Men's and boys' work clothing
2329	Men's and boys' clothing, not elsewhere classified
2331b	Women's misses', and juniors' dresses

SIC CODES

The federal government categorizes companies according to **Standard Industrial Classification (SIC)** numbers. These numbers group companies based on their chief industrial activity. Industry data is often compiled according to the SIC. Table 4-3 shows the SIC codes for the textile industry and the apparel industry. The primary groups are:

2337b Women's, misses', and juniors' suits, skirts, and coats
2339b Women's, misses', and juniors' outerwear, not elsewhere classified
2341b Women's, misses', children's, and infants' underwear and nightwear
2342b Brassieres, girdles, and allied garments
2353   Hats, caps, and millinery
2361b Girls', children's, and infants' dresses, blouses, and shirts
2369b Girls', children's, and infants' outerwear, not elsewhere classified
2371   Fur goods
2381a Dress and work gloves, except knit and all-leather
2384a Robes and dressing gowns
2385a Raincoats and other water-proof outerwear
2386a Leather and sheep-lined clothing
2387a Apparel belts
2389a Apparel and accessories, not elsewhere classified
2391   Curtains and draperies
2392   Housefurnishings, except curtains and draperies
2393   Textile bags
2394   Canvas and related products
2395b Pleating, decorative and novelty stitching, and tucking for the trade
2396   Automotive trimmings, apparel findings, and related products
2397a Schiffli machine embroideries
2399   Fabricated textile products, not elsewhere classified

OTHER

2823   Artificial (cellulosic) fibers
2824   Synthetic (noncellulosic), organic fibers
3552   Textile machinery
3069a Fabricated rubber products, not elsewhere classified (insofar as it includes vulcanized rubber clothing)
3079a Miscellaneous plastic products (insofar as it includes plastic clothing)
3151a Leather gloves and mittens
3842a Orthopedic, prosthetic, and surgical appliances and supplies (insofar as it includes surgical corsets, belts, trusses, and similar articles)
3962b Feathers, plumes, and artificial flowers (insofar as it includes artificial flowers)

a Branch of industry specializing in producing articles of apparel for both sexes.
b Branch of industry specializing in producing women's and children's apparel.

▌ SIC 22: textile mill products
▌ SIC 23: apparel
▌ SIC 28: chemical and allied products including manufactured fibers

Within these major groups, additional numbers are used to designate more specific products.

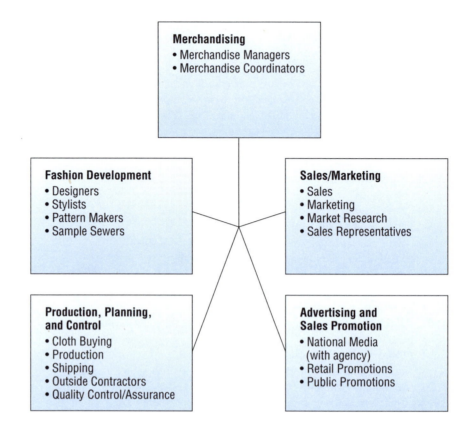

Figure 4.3
Apparel company
organization.

ORGANIZATIONAL STRUCTURE OF APPAREL COMPANIES

Figure 4-3 outlines the organizational structure of a typical apparel company. Although companies will vary in terms of their exact organizational structure, the activities often included in the organizational structure are: merchandising; fashion/product development; sales/marketing; production, planning and control; and advertising and sales promotion. Very large companies may have separate departments or divisions with dozens of employees which handle each of these activities. On the other hand, in very small companies a few employees may handle several of these activities.

MERCHANDISING

The term **merchandising** generally refers to "a management process of collecting and assimilating information from a variety of sources and drawing conclusions from that information regarding the product offering" (Brown &

Brauth, 1989, p. 78). This process includes developing strategies to have the right merchandise, at the right price, at the right time, in the right amount, at the right locations to meet the wants and needs of the target customer. The merchandising area of apparel companies includes merchandise managers, merchandise coordinators, and fashion directors. These individuals research and forecast fashion trends and trends in consumer purchasing behavior in order to develop color, fabric, and garment silhouette directions for the company's merchandise. When making these forecasts, merchandisers interpret these trends for the company's target market, which is determined by their customer's age, sex, income, and lifestyle. The role of merchandisers in an apparel company can vary. In some companies they facilitate the creation of lines; in other companies they oversee the fashion direction of the company. The merchandising function of the apparel company will be discussed in greater detail later in this chapter and in Chapter 5.

FASHION/PRODUCT DEVELOPMENT

The merchandisers work closely with those in the **fashion/product development** area who will interpret the trend forecasts and create designs to be manufactured by the company. Those in the fashion development area include designers, stylists, pattern makers, and sample sewers. The fashion development area may also include the management and operation of company-owned factories, including the employment and training of sewing operators (for companies that own their own factories). Chapters 5 through 7 will focus on the product development activities of an apparel company.

Figure 4.4
A sales representative sells the apparel manufacturer's merchandise to retail store buyers.

SALES/MARKETING

The sales/marketing area of the apparel company works to sell the company's merchandise to the retail buyers. This includes the regional sales managers and sales representatives, as well as those who conduct marketing research for the company. The sales and marketing staff show the company's merchandise to retail buyers in their showrooms during market weeks and at trade shows. Some companies will employ their own sales staff, others will contract with independent sales representatives to handle their merchandise. Chapter 8 will discuss the marketing and sales activities of an apparel company.

PRODUCTION, PLANNING, AND CONTROL

The preproduction, production, planning, and control area of the apparel company includes those people involved with

Figure 4.5
The production, planning, and control area includes management of production facilities.

Figure 4.6
Advertising and sales promotion departments create promotional and advertising strategies and tools to sell the merchandise to retail buyers and to the ultimate consumer.

material buying, production, quality control, and shipping of the merchandise. It also includes those who work with domestic and foreign contractors to sew the garments, if the company contracts out these services. Some companies refer to these activities as product engineering. Chapters 9 through 11 will focus on production, planning, and control.

ADVERTISING/SALES PROMOTION

Working with the fashion development staff and the sales and marketing staff, those in the advertising and sales promotion area focus on creating promotional and advertising strategies and tools to sell the merchandise to the retail buyers and to the ultimate consumer. Often these services are contracted to an outside advertising agency, which specializes in these activities.

In reviewing Figure 4-3, it is important to note the connections among all of the areas or divisions. Communication among the various activities is imperative for the success of the company. Merchandisers must communicate with designers; designers must communicate with marketers. This can be a challenge for large companies. In recent years, computers have facilitated the communication links among the various areas of apparel companies.

MERCHANDISING PHILOSOPHIES OF APPAREL COMPANIES

According to industry analysts the overall goal of the merchandising area is to "make a profit by developing an assortment of products that reflects the company's market strategy and that can be delivered and sold on time" (Brauth & Brown, 1989, p. 110). To meet this goal, apparel merchandisers set the overall direction for the merchandise assortment and work closely with the other areas of the apparel company that carry out the designing, production, marketing, and distribution of the goods. Effective merchandising and product development depends on the company's product category (e.g., men's sportswear, women's dresses, children's outerwear), the whole-sale price zone, and its marketing strategy. Companies can be classified according to their merchandising philosophy on the following continuum (Brown & Brauth, 1989)—from a true design-driven company on one end to a real-time merchandiser at the other end (see Figure 4-7).

A true design-driven company depends upon its innovative designs to attract its target market, which is generally composed of fashion innovators. Because their target market represents a very small number of customers, competition among design-driven companies is intense and the odds of a company succeeding are probably less than 1 in 100. Designers for design-driven companies rely on their skill, reputation, and advertising to lure customers. Examples of design-driven companies are Calvin Klein, Donna Karan, Isaac Mizrahi, and Anna Sui.

Rather than creating their own design innovations, a number of companies "interpret" successful innovative trends of design-driven companies for their own target market. Although design skills and reputation are often key

Figure 4.7
Merchandising philosophies of apparel companies range from design-driven companies, at one end of the continuum, to real-time merchandisers at the other.

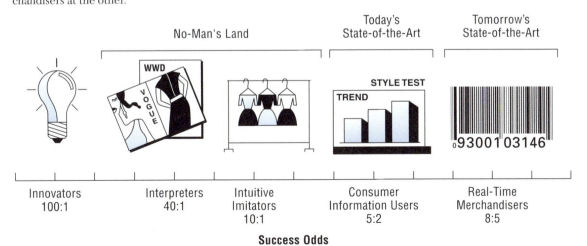

factors in the success of these companies, the risk of creating unsuccessful innovations is reduced.

Next along the continuum are the imitators who develop their product lines based on unsystematic "research," including trade information, observations as to what's selling at market and in the stores, and gut-level feelings about what will sell. The success of imitators often depends on their ability to produce affordable "knock-offs." Timing is crucial for the imitators, who must react immediately to new trends in the market.

Beyond interpreters and imitators are companies who base their merchandising decisions on systematic research. Consumer information users conduct market research and obtain direct feedback from consumers on the product line through style testing. Although they may interpret and imitate, they often research and conduct their own fashion forecasts and therefore tend to be more accurate in their predictions.

At the far end of the continuum, opposite from design-driven companies, are the real-time merchandisers. These companies assess consumer preferences based on style testing and analyses of trends in retail sales. Real-time merchandisers get sales information directly from retailers and can produce and ship goods within weeks. Their focus is to produce only the merchandise wanted by consumers and to assure retailers that they will have the appropriate stock on hand at all times. These companies are highly involved with Quick Response strategies.

TRADE ASSOCIATIONS AND TRADE PUBLICATIONS IN THE APPAREL INDUSTRY

A number of trade associations in the apparel industry promote, conduct market research, sponsor trade shows, and develop and distribute educational materials related to various segments of the apparel industry. The largest of these associations is the American Apparel Manufacturers Association (AAMA), which serves as an umbrella trade association for apparel companies. Representatives of member companies and other professionals in the industry are active in AAMA's many committees. Activities of the AAMA include compilation of statistical information related to apparel manufacturing, industry forecasts, trend forecasts, publication of educational materials, publication of information for use by industry analysts and company executives, and sponsorship of the Bobbin Show/AAMA Convention. Started in 1960, the Bobbin Show/AAMA Convention is currently the largest annual trade show for the apparel/sewn products industry. Other trade associations (see Table 4-4 for a listing of selected trade associations in the apparel industry) focus their efforts on specific divisions of the RTW industry such as intimate apparel, men's sportswear, or knitwear, to name just a few.

TABLE 4-4

Selected Trade Associations in the Apparel Industry

AMERICAN APPAREL MANUFACTURERS ASSOCIATION
2500 Wilson Blvd.
Arlington, VA 22201
(705) 524-1864

ASSOCIATED CORSET & BRASSIERE MANUFACTURERS INC
1430 Broadway, Suite 1603
New York, NY 10018
(212) 354-0707

CLOTHING MANUFACTURERS ASSOCIATION
1290 Avenue of the Americas
New York, NY 10104
(212) 757-6664

COUNCIL OF FASHION DESIGNERS OF AMERICA
1412 Broadway
New York, NY 10018
(212) 302-1821

CRAFTED WITH PRIDE IN THE USA
1045 Avenue of the Americas
New York, NY 10018
(212) 819-4397

THE FASHION GROUP INTERNATIONAL INC
597 Fifth Avenue
New York, NY 10017
(212) 593-1715

INFANT'S, CHILDREN'S & GIRL'S SPORTSWEAR & COAT ASSOCIATION, INC
225 W. 39 Street
5th Floor

New York, NY 10018
(212) 398-2982

INTERNATIONAL ASSOCIATION OF CLOTHING DESIGNERS
475 Park Avenue
17th Floor
New York, NY 10016
(212) 685-6602

INTERNATIONAL SWIMWEAR & ACTIVEWEAR MARKET AND THE SWIM ASSOCIATION
110 East 9 Street
Los Angeles, CA 99079
(213) 239-9347

THE INTIMATE APPAREL COUNCIL
150 Fifth Avenue
Fifth Floor
New York, NY 10011
(212) 807-0878

MEN'S APPAREL GUILD IN CALIFORNIA (MAGIC)
100 Wilshire Blvd.
Santa Monica, CA 90401
(310) 393-7757

NATIONAL ASSOCIATION OF HOSIERY MANUFACTURERS
200 N. Sharon Amity Road
Charlotte, NC 28211
(704) 365-0913

NATIONAL ASSOCIATION OF MEN'S SPORTSWEAR BUYERS (NAMSB)
500 Fifth Avenue
New York, NY 10110
(212) 391-8580

NATIONAL KNITWEAR & SPORTSWEAR ASSOCIATION
386 Park Avenue South
New York, NY 10016
(212) 447-1234

NATIONAL WOMEN'S NECKWEAR AND SCARF ASSOCIATION
1350 Avenue of the Americas
New York, NY 10019
(212) 708-0316

NECKWEAR ASSOCIATION OF AMERICA
151 Lexington Ave., #2F
New York, NY 10016
(212) 967-3002

UNDERFASHION CLUB INC
347 Fifth Avenue
New York, NY 10016
(212) 481-7792

UNITED INFANT'S & CHILDREN'S WEAR ASSOCIATION
1328 Broadway
New York, NY 10001
(212) 244-2953

YOUNG MENSWEAR ASSOCIATION
47 West 34th Street
New York, NY 10001
(212) 594-6422

TABLE 4-5

Selected Trade Publications in the Apparel Industry

NEWSPAPERS

Women's Wear Daily (WWD): Published Monday through Friday by Fairchild Publications. Covers national and international news in the fashion industry. Focus is on women's and children's apparel and fabrics.

Daily News Record (DNR): Published Monday, Wednesday, and Friday by Fairchild Publications. Covers national and international news in the men's wear and textile industries.

California Apparel News, Dallas Apparel News, Atlanta Apparel News, Chicago Apparel News: Published weekly. Covers fashion industry news with a focus on regional companies and markets. Includes classified advertisements.

MAGAZINES

Apparel Industry Magazine: Published monthly by Shore-Varrone, Inc. Covers all facets of the apparel manufacturing industry.

Bobbin: Published monthly by Bobbin Blenheim Media. Bobbin is the "premier news and information source of the global sewn products industry."

Earnshaw's Infants, Girls, and Boys Wear Review: Published monthly by Earnshaw Publications. Earnshaw's is the "business/fashion magazine of the children's wear industry."

A number of trade publications focus on the apparel industry and are of use to professionals in the RTW industry. These publications (see Table 4-5 for a listing of selected trade publications in the apparel industry) range from daily newspapers to monthly magazines.

SUMMARY

Most of the apparel produced and sold is considered ready-to-wear (RTW); that is, the apparel is completely made and ready to be worn at the time of purchase. RTW apparel is possible because of standardized sizing and mass production techniques evident in today's apparel industry. Apparel companies typically produce four to six lines or collections corresponding to the fashion seasons: spring, summer, fall I, fall II, holiday, and resort. It is important to note the distinctions between RTW and couture. In couture, garments are made to the size specifications of an individual rather than to standardized sizes as is found in RTW. In addition, couture garments are generally made with more hand techniques and from more expensive materials than RTW. Haute couture collections are shown twice per year, in July and January, to the press, others in the fashion industry, and wealthy clients.

Based on their organizations and operations, RTW apparel companies fall into the following categories: conventional manufacturers, jobbers, con-

Figure 4.8
Trade publications
provide important
information for people
employed in the apparel
industry.

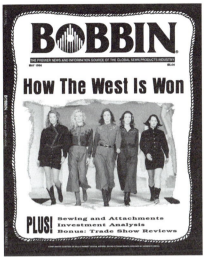

tractors, importers/packagers, or licensors. Apparel companies are also classified according to the type of merchandise they produce, the wholesale price zones of their products or brands, and by the standard industrial classification (SIC) system established by the government.

A typical apparel company includes areas or divisions that focus on the following activities: merchandising; fashion/product development; sales and marketing; production, planning, and control; and advertising and sales promotion. Apparel merchandisers set the overall direction for the merchandise assortment and work closely with the other divisions of the company that carry out the design, production, marketing, and distribution of the goods.

Companies vary in their merchandising philosophies from design-driven companies to real-time merchandisers. A number of trade associations in the apparel industry promote, conduct market research, sponsor trade shows, and develop and distribute educational materials related to various segments of the apparel industry. Examples include the American Apparel Manufacturers Association (AAMA), Men's Apparel Guild in California (MAGIC), and the Underfashion Club. A number of trade publications focus on the apparel industry and are of use by professionals in the RTW industry. Examples include *Women's Wear Daily, Daily News Record, Bobbin Magazine,* and *Apparel Industry Magazine.*

REFERENCES

Brown, Peter, and Brauth, Bonnie. (1989, August). Merchandising methods. *Apparel Industry Magazine,* pp. 78–82.

Brauth, Bonnie, and Brown, Peter. (1989, June). Merchandising malpractice. *Apparel Industry Magazine,* pp. 108–110.

Kurt Salmon Associates. (1989, January). The changing lineup. *Bobbin,* pp. 56–57.

Lewis, Robin. (1995, November). What's in a Name? *DNR Infotracs: Supplement to DNR.* New York: Fairchild Publications.

Southern California Edison Company (1995, February). *Southern California's Apparel Industry: Building a Path to Prosperity.* Rosemead, CA: Author.

KEY TERMS

ready-to-wear (RTW)	**item house**
line	**importers/packagers**
collection	**licensor**
fashion season	**classification**
couture	**wholesale price zone**
haute couture	**diffusion line**
couturier(ière)	**national/designer brand**
salon de couture	**private label brand**
atelier de couture	**retail store/direct market brand**
conventional manufacturer	**Standard Industrial Classification (SIC)**
jobber	**merchandising**
contractor	**fashion/product development**

DISCUSSION QUESTIONS

1. Name your three favorite apparel brands. What companies manufacture these brands? How would you classify these brands in terms of product category, wholesale price zone, and type of brand name?

2. Examine copies of trade publications in the apparel industry. To whom does each of the trade publications cater (i.e., what are the publications' target markets)? What types of information are included in the trade publications? How might this information be used by professionals in the industry?

CAREER PROFILE

Careers within apparel companies include positions in merchandising; product/fashion development; sales and marketing; preproduction, production, control, and quality assurance; and advertising and promotion.

WOMEN'S MERCHANDISE MANAGER,
Better Men's and Women's Apparel Company

Job Description
Manage and control the development of merchandise from color, fabric, and style selection to presentation and sales marketing. The Merchandise Manager works with the development team, which consists of a designer, pattern maker, and product engineer. The Merchandise Manager is ultimately responsible for the line.

Typical Tasks
▮ Analyze wholesale and retail performance of the product
▮ Read trade and fashion publications to keep current on market direction
▮ Communicate with retail accounts to gain sales information
▮ Estimate units per style/color for a designated season. Design produces patterns; merchandising decides in which fabrics each style will be available
▮ Write and deliver presentations to sales representatives, five sales meetings held a year
▮ Travel domestically to meet with sales reps and retail accounts—approximately three to four times a year
▮ Travel to New York twice a year for major development trips
▮ Work with Fabric Design Department to develop fabrics and patterns for future seasons
▮ Work with contractors to develop garments not produced by our own factories
▮ Work with quality control on production problems
▮ Work with design to develop a style plan, design follows up with prototype development. Merchandise Manager attends fit sessions, signs off on all garments

What Do You Like Best About Your Job?
The ability to work with numbers, but also to be creative.

Part Two   CREATING AND MARKETING
            AN APPAREL LINE

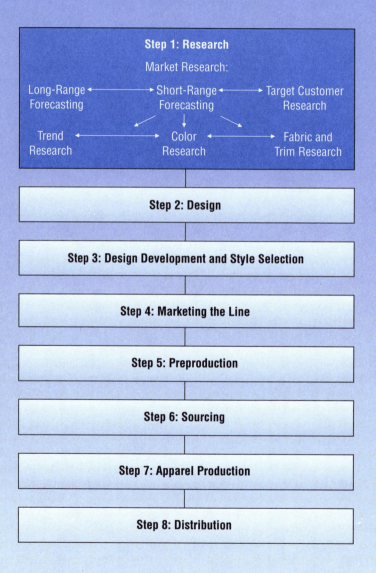

Step 1: Research

Market Research:

Long-Range ◄──────► Short-Range ──────► Target Customer
Forecasting   Forecasting   Research

Trend ◄──────► Color ◄──────► Fabric and
Research   Research   Trim Research

Step 2: Design

Step 3: Design Development and Style Selection

Step 4: Marketing the Line

Step 5: Preproduction

Step 6: Sourcing

Step 7: Apparel Production

Step 8: Distribution

5

The Creation Stage: Research

Objectives

▌ To describe various types of market research used to understand target customers' characteristics and preferences.

▌ To explain the concept of an apparel line.

▌ To identify the scope of the job responsibilities of the apparel designer and merchandiser in conducting research.

▌ To identify resources for fashion trend, color trend, and fabric trend forecasting.

CREATING AN APPAREL LINE

THE CREATION OF a group of apparel pieces into a collection or a line involves a series of steps. Each step is closely related to and influenced by all other steps in the process. The next several chapters will discuss these steps sequentially. The first step, research, is discussed in this chapter. The flow chart shown in Figure 5-1 will help acquaint you with the "big picture" before each stage in the design process is explored in greater detail. It is important to keep in mind that the flow chart is a "generic" model. Some apparel companies deviate from this sequence for many reasons. The industry is constantly changing in areas such as computer integration, speed of

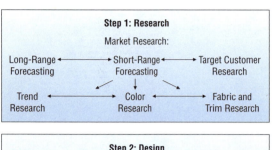

Step 1: Research

Market Research:

Long-Range Forecasting ↔ Short-Range Forecasting ↔ Target Customer Research

Trend Research ↔ Color Research ↔ Fabric and Trim Research

Step 2: Design

Design Inspiration
↓
Plan the Line
↓
Design Sketch (or Technical Drawing) with Fabric and Trim Swatches
↓
Design Team Selects Styles
↓
Write Preliminary Garment Specifications

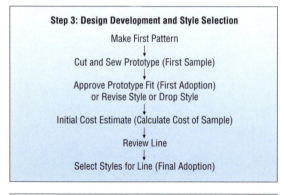

Step 3: Design Development and Style Selection

Make First Pattern
↓
Cut and Sew Prototype (First Sample)
↓
Approve Prototype Fit (First Adoption) or Revise Style or Drop Style
↓
Initial Cost Estimate (Calculate Cost of Sample)
↓
Review Line
↓
Select Styles for Line (Final Adoption)

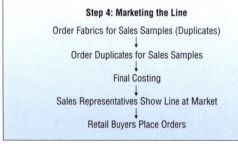

Step 4: Marketing the Line

Order Fabrics for Sales Samples (Duplicates)
↓
Order Duplicates for Sales Samples
↓
Final Costing
↓
Sales Representatives Show Line at Market
↓
Retail Buyers Place Orders

Step 5: Preproduction

Finalize Production Pattern
↓
Order Production Fabrics, Trims, and Sundries Based on Sales Orders
↓
Finalize Garment Spec and Size Spec Sheets
↓
Grade Production Pattern into Size Range
↓
Make Production Marker

Step 6: Sourcing

Select Production Facility

Step 7: Apparel Production

Cut and Sew (CMT) Sewing Sample (contractor's sew by)
↓
Inspect Production Fabric
↓
Cut Production Order
↓
Sew Production Order
↓
Inspect, Press, Tag, and Bag Order

Step 8: Distribution

Send Order to Manufacturer's Distribution Center or Retailer's DC or Directly to Retailer
↓
Quality Assurance Check
↓
Pick Orders and Send to Retail Store Distribution Center
↓
Review Season's Sales Figures

Figure 5.1
Flow chart shows steps in the Design/Manufacture process.

Figure 5.2
A group of products is developed with a theme for a seasonal line.

production, geographic location for production, quota limits on goods manufactured outside the United States, number of new lines introduced each year, and distribution channels. These changes affect the sequence of events. A company may also follow one sequence for some lines and use a modified sequence for other lines. Also, several activities may occur simultaneously during the progress of a style's development.

The terms "line," "group," and "collection" are used to designate a combination of apparel items presented together to the buying public for a particular season. The term **collection** is used generally to refer to the apparel presented each fall and spring by the high fashion designers in Paris, Milan, New York, London, and other locations. The designer collections often include a wide range of apparel, including swimwear, dresses, suits, sportswear, evening wear, and, of course, bridal wear as the finale. The designer collections may include approximately 100 to 150 apparel items.

An apparel **line** consists of one large group or several small groups of apparel items, or "styles," developed with a theme, such as color, fabric, and design details or to meet a purpose (such as golf or tennis) that links the items together. For example, NIKE develops a line for each of a variety of sports, including men's cycling, men's running, men's tennis, women's aerobics, and women's running. A line is composed of coordinated items or styles, such as shirts, pants, jackets, vests, and sweaters, that can be worn together in various combinations. Each line is developed for a specific target customer and could consist of as many as 50 or 60 apparel items. Each line will have a designer assigned to create the line; some designers will have responsibility for several lines. Sometimes within a line, several small groups will be developed, each with its own theme. A **group** might use three to five fabrics in varying combinations and include a dozen apparel items, all carefully coordinated.

The stereotypical image of a fashion designer is that (s)he sits at a drawing table, sketching garment idea after idea. The sketches are handed to a staff who turn the sketches into garments. Is this what really happens in the apparel industry? In actuality, the creation of an apparel line is a carefully orchestrated series of processes—a team effort, involving many people.

Just as fashion, in general, follows an evolutionary pattern, apparel designers who work for companies generally create new seasonal lines in an ongoing, evolutionary manner. New lines tend to develop from previous lines, with some repetition or modification of successful styles. Styles repeated from one seasonal line to the next are called **carryovers.** The target customer, general market trends, fashion trends, color trends, fabric trends, and retailer's needs are all taken into careful consideration in the planning and development of an apparel line.

A designer typically works with a **merchandiser** to plan the overall "look" of an apparel line, the color story, the fabrics, the price, and the number of styles for each line (see Chapter 6). The designer's job includes a variety of responsibilities, such as researching the market; selecting the colors, fabrics, and garment styling for the line based on fashion direction from merchandisers; consulting with product engineers on costing factors; preparing the preliminary specification sheets; presenting technical drawings; providing suggestions for linings, interfacings, trims, buttons, and other components; and releasing the approved styles for pattern making. The merchandiser's role is to oversee that the company's needs for the line are met. This might include coordinating several lines presented by the company. The merchandiser conducts market research, develops and maintains the line estimate and price targets to meet budget objectives, reviews the designer's proposed line, and approves the line. Years of experience in design or retailing provide the perspective needed for the apparel company's merchandiser.

The creation stage of one line overlaps with the production stage of the previous line, and the selling stage of the line before that one. Thus, at any given time, designers and merchandisers are mentally handling at least three lines, each in a different stage of the product cycle. Developing a line would be much easier if one had the final sales statistics from the previous line before beginning to work on the creation stage of the new line. Unfortunately, this is not possible in the fast-paced world of fashion. Ever-increasing numbers of shopping malls, outlet malls, direct mail, and electronic shopping have provided increased opportunities for shopping. To help meet consumers' wishes, the timeline in today's apparel industry calls for creating more lines, more quickly than even five years ago. Some companies create new groups to be shipped to retail stores at frequent intervals so that fresh merchandise awaits shoppers at closely spaced intervals.

MARKET RESEARCH:
UNDERSTANDING CONSUMER MARKET TRENDS

Market research can be defined as "the systematic and objective approach to the development and provision of information for the marketing management decision-making process" (Kinnear & Taylor, 1983, p. 16). Market research is divided into two general categories: (1) basic research that deals with extending knowledge about the marketing system, and (2) applied research that help managers make better decisions (Kinnear & Taylor, p. 17). Designers and merchandisers may conduct applied market research as a part of the planning process. Trade associations, such as the American Apparel Manufacturers Association, Cotton Incorporated, and the Wool Bureau, Inc., also conduct market research, providing information that can be very beneficial to apparel manufacturers (see Chapter 3).

Consumer demand is the driving force in the apparel industry. The industry expression, "You can make it only if it sells" relates to the concept of the consumer-driven market. Thus, the success of any apparel or textile company depends on determining the needs and wants of the consumer. Applied market research includes:

- consumer research—providing information about consumer characteristics and consumer behavior,
- product research—providing information about preferred product design and characteristics, and
- market analysis—providing information about general market trends.

Each form of applied market research will provide valuable information to designers and merchandisers about the wants and needs of their target market. Some forms of market research take considerable time to conduct, analyze, and interpret. Generally, it is not possible to wait until after considerable market research has been conducted to develop an apparel line. Fashion products require a short research and development stage due to the fast-paced nature of the fashion business. Timing is crucial to the fashion item's successful selling in the marketplace.

CONSUMER RESEARCH

Consumer research provides information about consumer characteristics and consumer behavior. Conducting consumer research related to fashion items can be a challenge. Results of market research indicate that consumers often do not actually purchase what they indicate they would purchase when queried in advance. Apparel purchase decisions are based on a number of factors (such as psychological, social, and financial considerations) of which consumers are often not consciously aware.

Many companies have expanded their markets beyond U.S. consumers. The preferences of new consumer groups need to be understood. Some thriving women's activewear companies in the United States are expanding into the European market. It is important to research the French activewear consumer if the product is to succeed in this marketplace. For example, the styles of activewear apparel preferred by French women are not the same as those currently most popular in the United States. *Women's Wear Daily* reported on the French market for activewear: "Unlike American women, who have increased their participation in sports instead of doing formal aerobics, French women continue to take fitness classes. France is a country where women dress up, even when they are dressed down. Unlike the U.S., where sneakers are common week-end wear, in France women will not wear activewear when not exercising" (Weisman, 1996, p. 11).

Often color preferences in foreign markets are different from the trends seen in the United States. These preferences might be related to the country's climate, personal skin tones of the residents, or cultural heritage.

PRODUCT RESEARCH

Product research provides information about preferred product design and characteristics. When new products are developed, or existing products are modified, it is advantageous to assess how well a new or revised product will fare in the marketplace. One could survey potential consumers orally, send a questionnaire, or offer a free trial of a product in exchange for feedback. Sometimes an apparel company will conduct substantial market research before introducing a new line, especially if it is a new product type for the company. For example, Sears conducted focus group research before it ventured into a new suit market. Some large apparel manufacturers, such as JCPenney (for their private label merchandise) and VF Corporation, have been testing style preferences for years.

Is it possible to predict how apparel consumers will react to a style? Style testing techniques, refined by some of the most respected names in apparel manufacturing, show that one can predict what consumers will want to buy. Some companies use outlet stores to gather data on how consumers react to various styles and prices. JCPenney surveys mall shoppers and uses in-house video testing to guide the decisions of its buyers as well as its manufacturing operations. Focus groups guide VF Corporation's style decisions (Henricks, 1991).

Levi Strauss and Company developed a procedure to survey subjects by asking them to rate preferences after seeing a garment, a photo, or a swatch of fabric in various patterns and colors. In some cases, test stores were stocked with all the pattern, style, and color varieties. This program is called Style Pattern Apparel Testing System (SPATS). A manager of marketing research for Levi Strauss and Company provided four guidelines for a style testing program:

1. It must be fast,
2. make it easy to understand,
3. it has to be inexpensive so it won't hurt profits, and
4. style testing must be predictable (Henricks, 1991, p. 52).

MARKET ANALYSIS

Market analysis provides information about general market trends. Both long-range forecasting and short-range forecasting strategies are used for market analysis.

Long-range forecasting includes researching economic trends related to consumer spending patterns and the business climate. For example, will interest rates be increasing on money needed by an apparel manufacturer to purchase fabric? Will corporate taxes for the apparel company be increasing? Will cost-of-living expenses rise because of inflation, resulting in fewer apparel purchases by consumers? Will rising labor costs result in noticeable increases in the purchase price for apparel? All of these trends can affect the company's plans and the consumer's future purchases. Planning ahead to meet the future needs of the consumer is a critical part of continued success.

Long-range forecasting also includes sociological, psychological, political, and global trends. For example, changes in international trade policies will affect long-range forecasting. Political fluctuations among countries can affect sourcing options when planning offshore production.

Other long-range forecasting deals with changes in the apparel industry. To successfully compete in the global market, companies may need to invest in computer technology to link themselves to supply sources and retailers. Environmental concerns and quality-of-life factors are examples of long-range trends that affect apparel companies. Some companies have made the commitment to use fabrics made from recycled products, such as aluminum cans or plastic bottles. For example, the thermal underwear sold in a recent Lands' End mail order catalog was made from recycled plastic material (Recyclables, 1995) reflecting Lands' End's decision to offer products consistent with their customers' values. Jantzen, Inc., a major swimwear manufacturer, developed the "Clean Water" campaign. It focused on showing the company's commitment to social responsibility by sponsoring beach cleanups and joining forces with environmental groups to effect change. Jantzen linked forces with retailers to bring the message to customers through a donation-with-purchase program. Another type of environmental concern focuses on waste products resulting from the manufacture of textiles and apparel. Wrangler advertised its EarthWash process as an alternative to dyes and finishing processes that pollute the water supply. Advertising campaigns are structured to let the retailer and consumer know about the company's activist stance on environmental issues.

What about forecasting long-range fashion trends? Is it possible to forecast fashion trends several years in advance of a season? Long-range fore-

Figure 5.3
Jantzen's Clean Water campaign message focuses on environmental concern and responsibility.

Our new EarthWash jeans are a great buy, when you consider what you'll be saving.

EarthWash jeans are made with low-sulfide dyes, biodegradable enzymes and less water to help protect our rivers and streams. And they have all of RuggedWear's quality, value and comfort, so not only do they feel good, you can feel good about wearing them too. **Wrangler** RUGGED WEAR EARTH WASH

Figure 5.4
Wrangler's EarthWash jeans promote the importance of nonpolluting fabric processes that help protect our rivers and streams.

casting can reap benefits. For example, the *Popcorn Report* (Popcorn, 1991) predicted a trend toward "cocooning," in which people would want to stay home more in the evenings, enjoying leisure time spent in quiet rather than in restaurants, movies, or sports events surrounded by others. Evenings spent at home could signal increased consumer interest in loungewear. Thus the loungewear industry would be wise to prepare for this trend. The trend toward more casual office attire, as noted by the term "casual Fridays," has implications for the long-range planning of some apparel companies. The casual dress trend has spread to apparel markets beyond the United States. "In London's financial district, professional bankers can be spotted in turtle-necks and blazers, a move triggered in part by the expansion of U.S. branches of investment banks overseas, which have exported their casual dress policies" (Casual Fridays, 1995, p. 8).

Short-range forecasting is critical to an apparel company's success. Planning meetings are held with designers, merchandisers, planners, and sales personnel to discuss the company's short range forecasts and strategic planning. This planning includes such components as determining the desired percentage of increased sales growth for a company. For example, perhaps the company managers have determined that a five percent growth in sales should be planned. The designer for each apparel line that the company produces may be asked to increase the line with a five percent sales growth factor in mind. Using sales figures from the current selling season, the designer (and merchandiser) may select one or several styles that are selling particularly well, and add one or several similar styles to the upcoming line. Short-range forecasting also includes careful study of what the competition is doing. If competitors seem to be expanding one line, for example, the water sports category of apparel, then perhaps it would be wise to study whether this growth area would be feasible for your company.

Short-range forecasting also includes predicting changes in retailing. A retailer may be in the process of expansion, with a number of new stores ready to open in the forthcoming year. If this retailer has been a strong client of an apparel manufacturer in the past, the expansion can signal increased orders for the apparel company. As retailers file bankruptcy, merge, and divide, it is important for the apparel company to be wary of shipping goods to retailers who may be in the process of disruption.

TARGET CUSTOMER PROFILE

Each apparel line needs to have a clearly defined **target customer.** The profile, or description, of the target customer usually includes the gender, age range, lifestyle and geographic location, and price zone determined for the majority of customers. A swimwear company may produce several lines, each based on a specific target customer profile. One line may be designed for a very conservative missy customer, while other lines may range from less conservative to updated missy customers. Developing a well-defined target customer profile helps the designers and merchandisers focus the line to the specific audience, or market niche. The active outdoor sportswear company, Quiksilver, provided an excellent example of a target customer profile (Quiksilver Annual Report, 1994):

> Quiksilver, Raisins and our other labels sell to a broad age and demographic profile but our main target audience is the teen-young adult (14-25) market. Our customers are changing every year, not only due to demographics but also the continual fast-forward bombardment of media and information from the likes of CNN, MTV, magazines, movies and the Inter-Net. These kids, the so-called generation X'ers and their younger siblings, "The Gen 2000's," are spirited at an early age, threatened daily by many negative influences. These kids have new demands and tastes ever waiting to be satisfied. They listen to music groups, watch Beavis and Butthead, escape through the Inter-Net and charge through extreme sports. American youth yearns for escape and self expression and all it finds are phoney alternative cultures, attitudes and trends. Extreme sports and the outdoor world are heavy influences of fashion and most of them are individual sports that provide a quick adrenaline rush and a strong following.

Some companies develop a very detailed target customer profile. A photograph of the "typical" customer might be included with the profile statement to help merchandisers, designers, product developers, and sales representatives visualize the customer. The models used for product advertisements are also selected to portray the target customer.

GENDER. While some companies produce lines of unisex clothing (for example a T-shirt company), most lines are focused on either mens' or womens' apparel. Many companies produce both men's and women's apparel, but will have separate lines specifically designed for each gender.

AGE RANGE. For age range, junior apparel lines might profile the age of their customers as ages 15 to 25. This does not mean that a woman over the age of 25 would not wear the apparel in this line. Rather, the designer visualizes the majority of customers would be targeted toward the age 15 to 25 group and keeps this age range firmly in mind while creating the line. A company may decide to adjust the targeted age of its customer. Raising the age range of the target customer might be a logical adjustment as the average age of the population ages. Or, perhaps, the company wants to retain an established customer by broadening the age range at the older limit.

LIFESTYLE AND GEOGRAPHIC LOCATION. A study of the target customer's lifestyle might include information such as type of career, stage in career, geographic locale and population size, social or political direction, attitudes, values, and interest in fashion (for example, prefers classic looks or is a fashion trendsetter). The term "lifestyle merchandising" was coined to recognize the importance of appealing to the target customer's lifestyle choices. Lifestyle research is conducted to help define the various target groups. The proliferation of popular lifestyle magazines and mail order catalogs indicates the importance in appealing to customer's lifestyles. For example, the fitness market has a myriad of lifestyle magazines. Some apparel companies design clothing to appeal specifically to this lifestyle.

Some companies may focus a line on a specific geographic location. For example, the resort market in Florida might be a location for a targeted customer. There is a special fashion "look" to resort apparel in Florida that may not sell well in other geographic locations.

PRICE ZONE. The target customer profile also typically includes a targeted price zone, such as moderate, better, or bridge price, as discussed in Chapter 4. Each line will be planned to fall within specified prices, based on the target customer profile. Within the line, not every style of shirt will sell for the same price. There will be a range of prices, based on differences in styling and fabric variations. However, the overall prices for the line will fall within expected ranges for the determined price zone. If a company is known to produce goods in the moderate price zone, a jacket whose price is in a better price zone will look over-priced in comparison to the rest of the line. A customer would question why the price is higher than expected and would probably not purchase the jacket.

The designer always keeps the target customer profile in mind in order to create a line that will appeal to the customer. From time to time, it is important for a company to review and update its target customer profile. The target customer profile is an important component of an apparel line's marketing campaign, both to the retail "customer" and to the ultimate customer.

FASHION RESEARCH

FASHION TREND RESEARCH

Fashion **trend research** tends to be a daily activity for the designer and the merchandiser. Trend research activities include reading or scanning appropriate trade publications. Trade newspapers include *Women's Wear Daily, California Apparel News,* and *Daily News Record* (men's wear and textiles). *Women's Wear Daily* covers fabrics, fashion ready-to-wear, sportswear, furs, and financial news daily. In addition, each day of the week is targeted to specific market segments (for example, accessories, innerwear, and legwear are covered on Mondays). A few newspaper/magazine sellers offer these publications over the counter, but most are by subscription only.

Each segment of the apparel industry has specific trade newspapers and magazines directed toward fashion trends in that industry segment. Examples include *Earnshaw's Review,* focusing on children's wear industry fashion trends, *Footwear News* for the footwear industry, and *Body Fashions Intimate Apparel* for the intimate apparel industry. These trade publications require subscriptions, so they are not available for individual purchase at specialty magazine stores.

European fashion magazines, such as *French Vogue, Italian Vogue, Elegance, Collections, Vogue Homme* (men's wear) and *Vogue Bambini* (children's wear), are often helpful sources for fashion trends. Subscriptions to many of the specific fashion magazines are provided to the design team by the apparel company. For design students, these fashion magazines are available for purchase at specialty magazine stores in larger cities.

Popular fashion magazines read by the target customer are sources for fashion trend information and provide an insight into the preferences of the customer. Designers and merchandisers peruse the appropriate publications, depending on their target market. Examples of popular fashion magazines include *Vogue, Elle, Harper's Bazaar, Mirabella, W, Glamour, Allure, Mademoiselle, Self, Vanity Fair, Town & Country, Glamour, Essence, Savvy, YM, Seventeen, Details,* and *GQ.* These magazines are readily available to the public at news and magazine stands and bookstores.

Some designers and retailers subscribe to fashion trend forecasting services. Pat Tunsky in New York is an example of a company that provides fashion trend reports as one of its services. Table 5-1 lists selected color and fashion trend services. (See Chapter 3 for examples of other fashion trend forecasting companies.) These reports help designers analyze upcoming fashion trends.

Computer software programs have been developed to assist with consumer-driven fashion forecasting. One program, Consumer Outlook!, works with POS (point-of-sale) data. The software "interprets the company's POS data and uses it to spot trends that otherwise would be overlooked" (Bonner, 1996, p. 32). Consumer Outlook! shows more than total sales—it enables an

TABLE 5-1

Selected Examples of Color and Fashion Trend Forecasting Services

The Color Association of the United States, NY
The Color Committee, NY
The Doneger Design Direction, NY
Fabric & Fashion, NY
The Fashion Newsletter, Lanham, MD
International Colour Authority, Amsterdam
Margit Publications, NY
Pat Tunsky Inc., NY
Promostyl, Paris (headquarters, with subsidiary offices in NY, London, and Tokyo)
RTW Review, Milwaukee, WI
The Tobe Report, NY
Trend Union, NY and Paris
View on Color, Amsterdam

apparel company to determine specifically who is buying what, and where, taking into account factors such as weather, special events in the area, and store promotions.

Fashion trend research also involves **shopping the market.** Although this sounds like fun, it actually involves considerable concentration and constant vigilance. Merchandisers and designers look for new trends that may influence the direction of an upcoming line. Bodice design details in evening wear may inspire a similar feature in a swimwear top. One aspect of shopping the market involves visiting retail stores that carry the company's line. Talking with retailers about how the line is selling at retail provides helpful information for predicting fashion trends. Watching retail store customer reactions to the line provides helpful feedback. Studying the competitors' lines in retail stores is also important for predicting trends.

The "fantasy" aspect of trend research involves viewing the high-fashion couture and ready-to-wear collections in Paris, Milan, London, and New York. Designers and merchandisers for some apparel companies are given the assignment to view these twice-yearly collections. The high-fashion collections are often filled with avant garde styles probably not worn by the target customer. However, important fashion trends can be extracted and then modified for a moderately priced line. Specialized trade shows are held in various locations. Designers and merchandisers may attend these shows for fashion trend information as well. Some of these trade shows, such as the Men's Apparel Guild in California (MAGIC) are discussed in Chapter 8.

Some designers and merchandisers also study customers "on the street," or, if the line is an active sportswear line, then they watch potential customers on the ski slopes or at the beach. Trend research involves the collection of information from multiple sources on a continual basis. The designer does not create in a vacuum, but is influenced by everything she or he is exposed to. It is important to visit art museums, concerts, and movies and to participate in other activities that expose the designer to fashion-related trends. Fashion is a reflection of the time and the lifestyle of the society from which and for which it is created.

COLOR RESEARCH AND RESOURCES

Are there trends in colors for apparel? When color trends are reviewed over a period of time, it becomes clear that certain "staple" colors appear frequently in the fashion cycle. Black, navy, white, and beige are considered staple colors and are seen almost continuously season after season. Designers include one or more staple colors in each line. Pendleton Woolen Mills is known for maintaining a group of staple colors in its apparel lines. Pendleton's tartan navy and tartan green are examples of colors that are color matched, season after season. If a customer purchased a navy Pendleton jacket from its classic line, a pair of navy slacks purchased two years later would match the color of the jacket (unless it had faded because of improper care or excessive wear). Pendleton tracks the sales, ranked by dollar volume and color, to ensure that long-term, high-selling colors are represented in each line.

Some companies vary the specific navy color to reflect fashion influences. One season, a navy may be a violet-navy while another season the navy may be a black-navy. This lends an up-dated, fashion look to staple col-

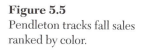

Figure 5.5
Pendleton tracks fall sales ranked by color.

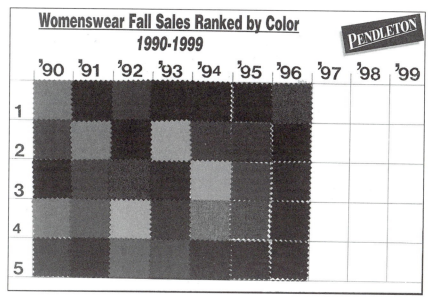

ors. If a print fabric in the line contained navy, then it would be necessary also to match the navy in the print fabric to the solid navy.

Other colors, called "fashion colors," appear less frequently over time than do the staple colors. These colors often follow cycles, reappearing in a different form from one fashion season to the next. For example, an orange-red may evolve into a blue-red which may evolve into a blue-magenta. It is interesting to follow the trend of a fashion color over a period of years. For example, a color such as aubergine (eggplant) will recur every few years. It may be slightly redder one season, while slightly bluer another season. For those who have tried to match the color of an item purchased a previous season or year, it becomes painfully obvious that the life cycle of some fashion colors is very short. Some customers have learned to purchase all color-matched pieces of a line at one time to avoid attempting later on to match the color of a pair of pants purchased a year before to a shirt one would like to purchase to wear with the pants.

Some fashion colors are more popular, and therefore tend to reappear more frequently, than others. In the United States, dark reds and wine tones tend to recur often. Orange is a color that flatters fewer people's personal coloring than some other colors, such as blue. Thus, orange does not occur as frequently in the color cycle as other colors.

Some colors tend to suit the personal coloring of Europeans or Asians or North Americans. Thus, some colors are labeled as "European" colors. For example, loden, an olive green, is more frequently seen in European apparel lines than in North American lines. Apparel designers keep in mind the ethnic coloring of their target customers as they look at color trends.

As discussed in Chapter 3, the **color forecasting services** related to textile production are also used by apparel companies. These services study color trends in textiles, apparel, home fashions, and related fields. Some color forecasting services predict color trends 18 months or 24 months in advance, while others, for a higher subscription fee, predict farther ahead. An apparel company subscribes to the color forecasting service based on the field, such as men's apparel as well as the length of advance forecast selected. Most services publish color forecasts twice a year for men's, women's and children's apparel.

Resources for color forecasting services based in the United States include The Color Association of the United States, and Pat Tunsky. A European color trend service is International Colour Authority, based in Amsterdam. Promostyl is based in Paris, with subsidiary offices in New York, London, and Tokyo. Table 5-1 lists some of the color forecasting services.

Many people wonder how color trends are determined. Does "someone" predict that ruby red will be THE color of the fall season, and that all designers will then have ruby red in their lines? Although this is not the case, color research is conducted by the color forecasting services to assist the fashion industry in the assessment of the color trends. Many U.S. forecasters rely on the color directions offered by the designer and fabric houses in

Europe and watch to see whether these colors are adopted by U.S. designers and consumer fashion innovators. Others will focus on analyzing trends in consumer color preferences through sales data.

From the wide variety of possible colors, a palette of certain hues, values, and intensities that reflect upcoming color trends will be identified by the color forecasting service. Many apparel companies subscribe to several color forecasting services. It is interesting to compare the similarities and differences of several color forecasting services for the same season.

The color palettes presented by the forecasting services are represented by a grouping of paint chips, fabric swatches, or yarn pompons, arranged attractively in a spiral bound notebook or magazine format. These charts may include up to several dozen colors. The colors selected tend to span a range of darks and lights, neutrals and fashion colors. Thus, one color service will not predict all dark colors while another service shows all light colors. Designers will be able to identify certain overall trends recurring among the various color services. After studying the color trends, designers and merchandisers will select a color palette for the upcoming season, taking into consideration the many factors important to the success of that line. A designer may note that varying shades of purple have appeared in many of the color forecasts, indicating a purple trend. Some color services provide fashion names for the color chips. The various shades of purple might be named violet, plum, dahlia, wisteria, African violet, and lavender. The specific name may be transferred to the color name used by the apparel company for that color, or a new name may be created by the apparel company to identify their company's seasonal color. The theme of a line might be linked to the color names used. For example, color names such as adobe, cactus, sage, and sandstone might be selected to correlate with a southwestern theme for a line.

FABRIC AND TRIMMINGS RESEARCH AND RESOURCES

The designer and merchandiser research the fabric and trim market in addition to studying fashion and color trends. Fashion trend research is focused on general garment silhouettes, more specific lengths (such as jacket lengths, skirt lengths), widths (such as pant leg width, lapel and necktie widths), and design detail trends (such as shawl collars, circular ruffled collars, two-button suit jackets). The color trend research is focused on guiding the selection of the color story for a specific line. The designer also undertakes fabric research, beginning with such broad fabric trends as the trend toward the use of spandex blended with wool for career apparel, or the use of microfibers for men's suits and raincoats. This research might include such trends as the use of metallic fibers incorporated into fabrics, or chenille yarns used in suitings. Resources for this type of fabric research include the same trade publications that designers use for fashion trends, as well as textile trade publications such as *International Textiles*.

Figure 5.6
Designers attend textile
trade shows for fabric
research and inspiration.

For more specific fabric trends, the fiber mills, fiber organizations, and textile manufacturers are eager to acquaint designers with the latest fibers, fabrics, and textures. Fabric manufacturers employ sales representatives who supply designers with fabric swatch cards, usually as a result of a phone call by the designer to the textile sales representative. Sample yardage can also be ordered from the sales representative. Many fabric manufacturers have showrooms—for example in New York—that display the latest fabrics. The fiber organization headquarters are excellent resources as well. For example, a designer might visit the New York office of Cotton Incorporated to research a wide range of woven and knit cotton fabrications.

A very effective way to research fabric resources is to visit one of the textile trade shows (see Chapter 3 for a discussion of these trade shows). The shows are usually held twice a year, in the fall and the spring. The American fabric manufacturers hold their textile trade shows in New York and Los Angeles. Here, many fabric manufacturers have booths displaying the latest and most enticing fabrics. Designers can place orders for **sample cuts.** Each cut is usually a three-to-five yard length, enough yardage to produce a prototype garment, to evaluate the possibilities of the fabric. The sample cuts are sent to the designer's studio after the order is placed. Sample cuts also can be ordered directly from the sales representative after the trade show.

Some designers also travel to the European textile trade shows held twice a year, to see the latest goods produced by fabric manufacturers in

Europe (see Chapter 3 for detailed information). Premier Vision, showcasing France's fabric manufacturers, occurs in Paris. Italian fabrics are shown at Ideacomo, near Milan. British fabrics are shown at Fabrex. Interstoff, held in Frankfurt, Germany, is known especially for displaying German, Austrian, and Swiss fabrics. Some designers purchase sample cuts from European fabric manufacturers. For many designers, though, these textile shows serve a similar purpose as do the couture design shows—as an inspiration and a means to sift through the multitude of ideas for trends appropriate to their target customers.

Some of the international fabric manufacturers bring their fabric lines to New York and Los Angeles to show to the American designers not able to travel to Europe. The British Woolen Show, Texitalia (Italian fabrics), International Fashion Fabric Fair, as well as Asian fabric manufacturers, are eager to attract clients who visit the textile trade shows held in New York.

Some apparel designers and product developers work with fabric manufacturers to produce custom fabrics to meet a specific need. For example, after Gore-Tex's success as a woven fabrication, active wear apparel designers longed for a knit version of the waterproof, breathable fabric. The fabric manufacturer was able to meet this need. W. L. Gore & Associates and NIKE employees work together to create special technical performance fabrics. StormFIT, (*WWD*, 1995, May 18, p. 10) is an example of "a breathable, lightweight fabric, designed to handle any combination of extreme weather, including rain, snow, sleet, ice or heat." Fabrics that have been developed by a textile producer for a specific apparel company can be restricted for use solely by the apparel company for a specified period of time. This adds exclusivity to the product, which in turn can enhance sales. Such a fabric is called "proprietary," meaning it is the property of the private owner (the apparel company).

Some types of apparel, for example outdoor activewear, are especially suited to the use of specialty trims and fasteners. A new design idea might be sparked by a novelty trim or fastener. Trims as a source of design inspiration will be discussed in Chapter 6. Research regarding new products is an important aspect for these designers and merchandisers. Product shows, trade publications, and specialty trim sales representatives are sources of information about new products.

Armed with information about market research, fashion and color trends, and fabric and trim research, the designer is ready to bring everything together in the creation of a new line.

SUMMARY

Creating an apparel line begins with research. Sales figures from the current selling season are taken into consideration as the designer and merchandiser plan the upcoming line. A fashion apparel company cannot survive long if it only repeats what has sold well in the past. Market research is often conducted to help predict what specific items or general trends will appeal to customers in the upcoming season. The designer's job responsibilities include long-range forecasting of major social, economic, retail, apparel manufacturing, and customer trends. Short-range forecasting is also tied to the economy, political climate, availability of resources, and customer needs. The target customer profile, described by age, lifestyle, and price zone, requires constant updating and careful consideration in the creation of an apparel line.

The designer conducts fashion trend research on a daily basis by reading fashion publications, attending fashion events, and developing the ability to sense the fashion mood of the times and translate it into styles for the target customer. Color forecasting services provide information for color trend research, another important component of the creation stage. The designer's apparel company may subscribe to one or more of these color services. Fabric trend research is another aspect of the designer's responsibility. This may include scrutinizing fashion publications, textile industry publications, or attending textile trade shows in New York and European or Asian fashion centers. While research is being conducted on the upcoming line, it is important to remember that the designer may also be working on fabric and style development for a subsequent line, is involved with production of the current line, and is watching the sales figures on the line selling currently in retail stores.

REFERENCES

Bonner, Staci. (1996, March). Forecasting fashion. *Apparel Industry Magazine,* pp. 32–34.

Casual Fridays: A global warming. (1995, December 13). *WWD,* pp. 8–9.

Henricks, Mark. (1991, February). Testing consumer tastes. *Apparel Industry Magazine,* pp. 50–54.

Kinnear, Thomas C., and Taylor, James R. (1983). *Marketing Research: An Applied Approach.* New York: McGraw-Hill Book Company, pp. 16–17.

Nike braves the elements. (1995, May 18). *WWD,* p. 10.

Popcorn, Faith. (1991). *The Popcorn Report.* New York: Doubleday.

Quiksilver Annual Report, p. 3. (1994).

Recyclables are a girl's best friend. (1995, January). *Outside,* p. 53.

Weisman, Katherine. (1996, February 29). France's finicky market. *WWD,* p. 11.

KEY TERMS

collection	**merchandiser**
line	**market research**
group	**long-range forecasting**
carryover	**short-range forecasting**

target customer
trend research
shopping the market

color forecasting services
sample cut

DISCUSSION QUESTIONS

1. What are some examples of trends (perhaps five years from now) that reflect long-range forecasting? How might these trends affect the apparel industry?

2. What are some examples of short-range trend forecasting (perhaps six months from now) in men's apparel, women's apparel, and children's apparel? How might these trends be reflected in an apparel line?

3. Describe what you perceive as the target customer profile of a national brand such as the Liz Claiborne sports wear line.

4. What are some current color trends in women's wear? In menswear? What color or colors do you predict will be popular next season in women's wear? in men's wear? Why do you think these colors will be popular?

5. What are some fabric trends that are on the upswing in the fashion cycle?

6. What are some examples of specific sources of research information for designers and merchandisers? How would you locate examples of these?

CAREER PROFILE

If you are particularly interested in fashion-related research or the analysis of market trends, color, or fashion trends, additional coursework in consumer behavior, market analysis, and statistics, and some related job experience may be helpful. A career in color trend forecasting is one possibility.

ASSOCIATE DIRECTOR,
International Color Trend Forecasting Organization of About 1,000 Members.

Job Description
Interpret color trends in women's, men's, and children's clothing

Typical Tasks
▌ Meet with members and prospective members

▌ Interview and write stories

What Do You Like Best About Your Job?
The fact that the subject matter or issues change constantly.

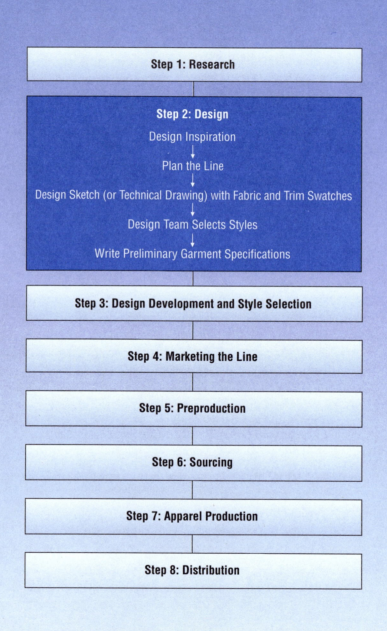

Step 1: Research

Step 2: Design

Design Inspiration
↓
Plan the Line
↓
Design Sketch (or Technical Drawing) with Fabric and Trim Swatches
↓
Design Team Selects Styles
↓
Write Preliminary Garment Specifications

Step 3: Design Development and Style Selection

Step 4: Marketing the Line

Step 5: Preproduction

Step 6: Sourcing

Step 7: Apparel Production

Step 8: Distribution

6

The Creation Stage: Design

Objectives

▌ To identify market forces that direct the company's design focus.

▌ To identify the scope of the job responsibilities of the apparel designer and merchandiser in designing a line.

▌ To explain the interrelationship between design and merchandising in developing a new season's line.

▌ To describe various sources of design inspiration.

THE MARKET NICHE

APPAREL COMPANIES USUALLY specialize in a certain type of product, such as casual clothes, swimwear, or evening wear. The apparel company's **product type** or product line is the basis for the development of the line. For example, Levi Strauss is known for its jeans, casual pants, shirts, and jackets. If you are familiar with this company, a certain type of product comes to mind when the name of the company is mentioned. Consistency in a company's product type helps the customer develop company recognition, builds product loyalty, and encourages repeat customers. Thus the designer (sometimes called the product developer) and merchandiser will develop the line for the new season with the product type as its foundation.

Figure 6.1
Consumers associate the
name of a company such
as the Gap with jeans and
casual wear.

The importance of keeping the target customer profile in mind when creating a line was discussed in the previous chapter. A strong connection exists between the type of product included in the line and the company's target customer. The blend of product type and target customer is referred to as the **market niche.** Developing and maintaining a line based on the market niche is important to the success of the apparel line. The line for the new season will include some variation of styles to appeal to the variety of customers' needs and tastes within the market niche. For example, a missy swimwear manufacturer will include some very conservative swimsuit styles, as well as some styles that have an updated look. The missy swimwear line might be divided into several groups to appeal to a variety of missy customers.

Based on the changing needs and preferences of the target customer, a company's product line may change over time. If the product line does not change at all, customers might become bored with the same look and decide that they do not need to purchase another piece so similar to pieces they

Figure 6.2
Jantzen's missy swimwear line includes styles ranging from conservative to updated looks.

already own. Perhaps a company wants to change the direction of its product from a career suit focus to a coordinated separates focus after sensing that women are no longer interested in the look of a matched suit. Or, a sportswear company may decide to add a group of golf apparel to its product line because of the growth in popularity in golf among its target customers.

Sometimes new designers and/or merchandisers are hired by a company to help revamp the product type. However, if a new look for a product is too radical, or if it is changed too quickly, it can cause problems for the retailer and the customer. Retaining the loyal customer is important, just as it is important to attract new customers for company growth. The customer who is familiar with and enjoys wearing the company's product may not "understand" the new look. Balancing the relationship among the current product look, changes that need to occur in the product to maintain interest and provide fashion change, and keeping the target customer happy is one of the responsibilities of the designers and merchandisers.

PLANNING THE LINE

The research stage of the design process—consisting of market research, as well as trend, color, and fabric and trim research—continues throughout the year for designers and merchandisers. Based on the number of lines a company produces each year, at a specified time in the year the design team must begin to develop concrete ideas for the new season's line. Each apparel company maintains a master calendar with target "due dates" for completion of the remaining stages of the flow chart shown in Figure 5-1 for the creation and production of each line. The design team looks at the due date for the finalization of a line, and works *backward* to decide when to move from the research stage to the design stage.

As discussed in Chapter 5, many larger apparel companies employ a merchandiser whose responsibility is to oversee and guide the designer or design team to determine what, when, and how much apparel to produce. Some merchandisers work with designers of several lines to oversee the coordination among the lines. In some companies, especially smaller ones, the designer also performs the job responsibilities of the merchandiser. This discussion assumes that the merchandiser and designer are separate individuals. Some companies employ both designers and product developers. A product developer takes the designer's idea and is responsible for developing the product. At other companies, the product developer performs the function of the designer.

The designer(s) and merchandiser(s) attend planning meetings during the research and design stages. At the planning meetings, the sales figures for the previous season are reviewed, sales forecasting for the new season is considered, and the overall plan for the upcoming season's line is discussed. This might include decisions about the target number of pieces to include in the line, the ratio of jackets compared to vests or the ratio of skirts compared to pants, the styles that will be repeated from the previous season, the types of silhouettes for various pieces, or a decision to try something new added to this line—perhaps a split skirt or a bodysuit.

There is an expression in the fashion business—"you're only as good as your last line"—that means a company's success is measured by how well the previous season's line sold. The designer and merchandiser have to hit the targeted sales volume with the mix of past, revised, and new styles. Due to the quantity of lines typically produced per year, the sales volume figures are not always available in time to rely solely on the number of units sold to accurately predict the strategy for the line under development. Therefore, one's intuition also becomes a part of planning the line.

Success of a line is measured by sales volume and also by **sell through** at the retail level. Sales volume relates to either the total number of units of each style sold or the total number of dollars consumers spent on the style. Manufacturers tend to measure the success of a line by the total number of units sold while retailers tend to measure the success of a line by the dollar volume. A line may sell well to the retailer, but a delay in delivery to the retailer could reduce the dollar volume at the retail store. This is one reason why another measurement tool, the line's sell through, is considered a good indicator of the line's success. Sell through denotes the percentage of items sold compared to the number of items in the line the retailer purchased from the manufacturer. A strong sell through is the goal for both the manufacturer and the retailer.

CARRYOVERS

A line of apparel typically does not consist of entirely new creations. In a new line, some styles will be **carryovers,** some styles will be modifications of good sellers, and some styles will be new designs. A carryover will repeat the same style (garment) as a successful garment from a previous season, but often in a new fabric color and texture. Thus, carryovers provide a less-expensive route to add a fresh look to a line. If the new fabric has identical textile characteristics as the previous fabric, the development cost will be minimal because the production patterns can be reused. However, if the new fabric is different—for example, it has a different shrinkage factor—a new pattern, prototype, and production pattern will need to be made.

Companies vary regarding the number of new items compared with the number of carryovers for each line. For an idea of the approximate ratio for a company that produces apparel in the moderate price zone, some companies target about one-third of the line to be carryovers, one-third as revisions of previous items, and one-third as new designs. The sales figures from the current and previous selling seasons are an important guideline in planning how many and what type of apparel to include in the new line.

LINE-FOR-LINE COPIES AND KNOCK-OFFS

A "new" style might be added to a line in another way. Sometimes while shopping the market or looking through fashion magazines, a designer or merchandiser will find a garment that seems perfect for the company's upcoming line. Thus, the designer and merchandiser may decide to create a copy of an existing garment. Copying a garment may be done in several ways. Sometimes the uniqueness of a design, for example a shirt with innovative design details, seems perfect for the upcoming line. The designer might request that a **line-for-line copy** of the shirt be made by the pattern development department and produced in a similar fabric. The new shirt would be an exact replica of the original; thus the term line-for-line copy is used.

Taking a garment that exists in a higher price zone and copying it to be sold at a less-expensive price can also be done in several ways. By selecting a less expensive fabric, a copy of the original garment could be sold at a lower price. Another way to reduce cost is to eliminate or modify some of the design detail. These two methods are used to create **knock-offs.** The new design is similar to the original, but it is not an exact replica.

Is it legal to copy an existing garment design? In the United States, there are laws to protect against copyright and trademark infringement (see

Figure 6.3
Left: The tuxedo dress as presented by Yves Saint Laurent. . .

Right. . . and the tuxedo dress as presented by Ralph Lauren.

Chapter 2). A specific "invention" in a garment (for example, a unique molding process to create a seamless panty) can be patented in the United States. However, in most countries (excluding France) the actual garment *design* is considered public domain. Therefore, it is quite common to see line-for-line copies and knock-offs in the apparel business. In 1994, French designer Yves Saint Laurent took Ralph Lauren to court in a dispute over the copying of a tuxedo dress (Tuxedo Junction, 1994).

COST, COLORS, FABRICS, AND STYLING CONSIDERATIONS

Because the cost of producing items in a line is an important factor for designers to consider throughout the design stage, many companies include cost personnel as a part of the team during the planning stage. Their role is to provide cost estimates on the new styles in the line as it develops.

During planning meetings, colors and fabrics for the new season's line are discussed. A color story will be developed based on the color research conducted before the planning meetings. Lines need a balance between some "basic" colors and some "fashion" colors (see Chapter 5). The line needs to have a cohesive look, so a great deal of time is spent deciding on the correct balance of colors. The group of colors selected may need to include a color that the planning team does not expect to sell well (for example, white used in a group of warmups) because they know that buyers expect to see this color for a balanced look in the color group.

Most garment styles will be produced in more than one color. A specific style may be available in three of four different solid colors, or in three or four color variations of the same print. The term used to designate the variety of colors available for a style is called **colorway.** Producing the same style in several colorways reduces the cost of developing the patterns and producing the garments. This variety also offers more options to retailers who might want to buy part of a line but not duplicate the same colorways as competing local retailers.

Since designers typically attend textile trade shows and are aware of the new colors and fabrics available, decisions regarding the colors and fabrics are usually made before the garment styles are determined. The new line will provide a balance among the colors, styles, and prices offered. It is important that two garments in the same line do not compete against each other for sales. Some apparel manufacturers follow a pricing strategy that specifies that the prices of two different shirt styles should not be the same—and styling differences in the two styles need to support the price difference. Other manufacturers follow an opposite pricing strategy called price averaging. In this situation, a shirt manufactured from a more expensive fabric with fewer garment details is priced to equalize a shirt manufactured from a less expensive fabric with more details. The manufacturer averages the costs of the two shirts to keep the price of both styles similar.

Thus, many factors need to be considered during the planning of the line. Among them is the overall number of items to be included in the line. Some of these items will be carryover styles from the previous line, some items will be revisions of previous styles, and some items will be new designs. Decisions are made about the balance of tops and bottoms, styling variety (such as single-breasted and double-breasted jackets), color and fabric offerings for each style, cost to produce each style, and overall pricing balance of the line.

DESIGN INSPIRATION

Throughout the planning of the line, the designer also focuses on the design inspiration for the line. This could include studying pictures of design ideas from fashion trend sources, collecting swatches of interesting fabric textures and trims, developing some innovative design details, conducting research about a historic period or another culture, or searching the market place for a "lightning bolt" idea. Designers may visit historic costume and textile collections such as the Fashion Institute of Technology's collection or the Metropolitan Museum of Art's Costume Institute, both in New York City. For designers who live in close proximity to one of the rich costume and/or textile resources, the apparel company pays an annual fee to the resource center to provide the designer with continual access to the collections. All the research information discussed in the previous chapter sifts through the designer's mind during this phase of the design process.

A THEME FOR THE NEW LINE

During the planning stage, a theme for the line might be developed based on discussions with the designers and merchandisers who are coordinating the various lines for the company. Not every group or line will have a theme, but a theme can help "sell" a group or a line to retailers and consumers. In some cases, an advertising campaign may be developed around a chosen theme. For example, a company producing an outdoor fishing group might use the theme of "chinook," the name of a breed of salmon, a popular sport fish, familiar to fishing enthusiasts.

COLOR INSPIRATION

Figure 6.4
A group within a line might be designed around a theme, such as the colorations of a species of fish.

The theme might be reflected in the colors chosen for some of the apparel. For example, the colorations seen on a chinook salmon might be an inspiration for a group of fishing apparel. Colors for fabrics used in the group might include various hues, tones, and values of the fish. A graphic design of a chinook salmon leaping up to catch a fishing fly could be created for a T-shirt in the line. A small version of the leaping chinook could be used as a motif on other pieces in the group. As another example, an Americana theme might be chosen for a group of missy pieces in a spring collection with a "country flavor" that features fabrics in ruby red, navy blue, and bisque colors in solids, small prints, and plaids.

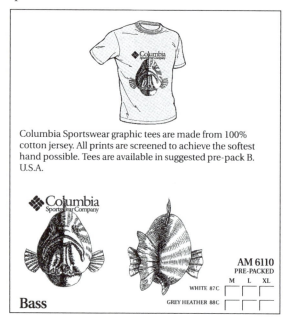

Columbia Sportswear graphic tees are made from 100% cotton jersey. All prints are screened to achieve the softest hand possible. Tees are available in suggested pre-pack B. U.S.A.

HISTORIC INSPIRATION

The high-fashion "name" designers typically develop a theme for a collection and invest heavily in marketing that theme to retailers and the public. Often the designer's theme is based on a historic or an ethnic inspiration. Fashion silhouettes or garment details popular during historic periods provide a source of design inspiration. For example, the ***Empire*** silhouette was fashionable during the early 1800s. The Empire style was named for Napoleon's empire and was worn by

Figure 6.5
The Empire style recurs periodically throughout fashion history. Shown here are examples: **a.** early nineteenth century (neoclassical), **b.** early twentieth century (Directoire), **c.** the 1960s, and **d.** the 1990s.

a.

b.

c.

d.

Empress Josephine in France. The long, tubular dress included a raised waistline located just under the bustline. Some fashion historians believe that Napoleon was inspired by the ancient Greek silhouette for this new fashion look. This style, known as neoclassical, became a fashion trend that spread throughout western Europe and the United States. The Empire silhouette reappeared in the early 1900s in the fashions of French designer Paul Poiret, seen in his "Directoire Revival" dress. Once again, other design-

a.   b.   c.

Figure 6.6
Historic fashion silhouettes often serve as a source of inspiration: **a.** the bustle
silhouette of the 1880s, as interpreted by **b.** Balenciaga in the 1940s, and **c.**
Anthony Price in the 1980s.

ers copied this style as the fashion look spread throughout Europe and the
United States. In the 1960s, the raised waistline of the Empire silhouette
appeared again, this time in an above-knee minidress version. In the early
1990s, the "Baby Doll" look of the 1960s again made fashion headlines. As
another example of historic inspiration, American designer Adrian and
French designer Balenciaga both were inspired by the bustle silhouette of
the 1880s for their designs created in the 1940s and 1950s.

A return to the fashion look of more recent decades is called **Retro**
fashion or Retro look. During the early 1990s, fashion looks reminiscent of
the decades of the 1930s, 1940s, 1950s, 1960s, and 1970s were evident in
mass fashion as well as designer collections. Retro fashions tend to not be
exact replicas of the previous fashion look, but include a "new" fashion twist.
For example, a Retro look design may be made from a currently popular fabric or include updated style details that are different from the original.

Garment details of a historic era serve as another source of inspiration
for designers. French designer Karl Lagerfeld used Renaissance fashion
details as inspiration for a Chanel design in the 1988–1989 collection. The
ruff collar popular on Renaissance clothing may inspire a group, a line, or a
collection. A sleeve detail from the Renaissance period could be an inspiration for a young girl's party dress.

Figure 6.7
Three examples of retro fashions of the 1990s *(below)* based on designs of the 1920s and 1930s *(above)* as interpreted by **a.** Lagerfeld, **b.** Gaultier, and **c.** Richard Tyler.

ETHNIC INSPIRATION

Designers may be inspired by the clothing styles of other cultures. The global environment has increased interest in products from the far reaches of the world. Designers seek inspiration from "exotic" cultures whose clothing

Figure 6.8
Karl Lagerfeld was inspired by this sixteenth-century fashion look *(left)* for an outfit in his 1988 collection *(right)*.

styles and fabrics are distinctly unique. Wearing apparel inspired from other cultures may provide a sense of adventure and vicarious enjoyment of that culture. This enjoyment can be transferred by wearing clothing inspired by another culture. Some designers travel to other locales to seek inspiration for a new line.

Asian clothing styles have been a source of inspiration historically as well as currently. *Chinoiserie* is a French term that represents a Chinese art influence. The fabrics of China were used to create Western high-fashion apparel during the 1850s. The Chinese influence on Western fashion grew during the last decades of the 1800s. In the United States, Chinese inspiration became fashionable in home fashions, china, house style details, and such clothing styles as the kimono sleeve, Mandarin collar, and frog closures. Chinese clothing and fabrics continue to inspire apparel designers today. The film *The Last Emperor* spurred a new interest in Chinese culture. After the film's release, design collections included Chinese-inspired clothing styles.

In 1995, the Costume Institute of the Metropolitan Museum of Art in New York presented "Orientalism: Visions of the East in Western Dress." This exhibition and the catalog (Martin & Koda, 1994) featured apparel inspired by Asian cultures from various decades. Included in the exhibit were several examples of Asian-inspired garments from the recent collections of American designers Ralph Lauren, Oscar de la Renta, and Todd Oldham.

Yves St. Laurent, a French couture designer, is renowned for his use of various national and ethnic groups and cultures as inspirations for his collections. He has created collections inspired by Russia, the Austrian Hapsburgs, Africa, China, Spain, and the Gypsies. American designer Mary McFadden created collections inspired by Africa and Persia, among others. In the early 1970s, British designer Zandra Rhodes traveled to the United

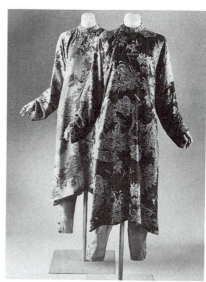

Figure 6.9
These 1994 Ralph Lauren designs *(right)* reflect an Asian inspiration *(left)*.

States to study the art and culture of American Indians. Her collection featured fabric designs filled with motifs of feathers, cactus, and other images inspired by American Indian cultures.

FABRIC, TEXTURE, AND TRIM INSPIRATION

While some designers research a specific time period or ethnic culture for inspiration, most designers of moderate price zone apparel rely primarily on studying new fabric and texture trends. The previous chapter discussed the sources of information and inspiration used for fabric research. An intrigu-

Figure 6.10
Findings such as the metal ring on this Jantzen swimsuit provide an innovative design detail.

ing fabric texture or interesting print might serve as the design foundation for a group. Several fabrics in prints, plaids, and solid colors, and in smooth as well as "textured" surfaces, might be combined to create an interesting group. During this design stage of creation, some designers work with specific fabric ideas gathered at textile shows or directly from textile manufacturers as they begin to sketch garment design ideas. Less frequently, designers might develop a design sketch, then seek the perfect fabric for it.

Special trims and findings are an important feature of some garment designs. A unique trim can transform an ordinary or classic garment into a new look. Trims inspired by Southwest American Indian cultures were a popular design addition to denim jeans, vests, and jackets for the junior market in the late 1980s. For children's apparel, special ribbons, trims, and appliqués frequently "make" the design. A unique clasp or closure on a swimsuit design can increase its appeal, or a special button on a classic jacket may create a fresh look. Designers constantly seek interesting trims and findings as a source of inspiration.

OTHER SOURCES OF INSPIRATION

The inspiration for a garment within a line or for an entire line can come from an infinite variety of sources. Sources of inspiration are often linked to the social "spirit of the times," also called the *zeitgeist*. Events and the general spirit of the popular culture might be reflected in new apparel lines, especially of high-fashion companies. Ask designers what inspired them to create a particular line. You may be surprised to learn that Japanese kites were the inspiration for a line of swimsuits or that graffiti was the inspiration for a line of sportswear.

THE DESIGN SKETCH AND SELECTION OF FABRICS AND TRIMS

HAND SKETCHES

At some point in the design stage (often influenced by the master calendar due date), the designer will begin to transform some of these inspirations into garment idea sketches. A designer might develop some garment sketches early in this stage and then have a difficult time with the remaining pieces. Is it difficult to create twenty new sweater or swimsuit designs each season? By constantly seeking inspiration from a variety of sources, most designers have plenty of new ideas.

The designer's sketches do not look like the finished artwork of a fashion illustration. In fact, some designers state that they are not good at drawing. Partially because of time constraints, some designers use a body silhouette called a *croquis*, or **lay figure**, to develop their garment design sketches. A

Figure 6.11
Designers sketch their garment design ideas on a lay figure or as front and back view technical drawings.

swimwear designer may have numerous copies of a croquis available onto which the swimsuit design idea will be drawn in pencil or marker. Other designers begin with a sheet of drawing paper and sketch both the figure and the garment idea. Some designers add color to their sketches by using colored pencils or markers. Often a back view sketch as well as the front view are shown. Some designers prefer to draw the garment design as a flat, or technical drawing of the garment, without the body silhouette.

COMPUTER-AIDED DESIGN

Computer workstations that include **computer-aided design (CAD)** software programs have become common in many apparel design studios. CAD systems used for pattern making, for pattern grading (sizing), and for marker making (developing the master cutting plan) will be discussed in other chapters. The use of CAD or graphics software programs for design sketching is an option for designers. Some of these types of computer systems are called Apparel Design Systems (ADS). Once a year (currently in the April issue), *Apparel Industry Magazine* includes a buyer's guide that lists a variety of CAD systems focusing on the features each product provides. This issue is an excellent resource for assisting in the selection of CAD software and hardware for the apparel industry.

The computer can store a croquis, or a series of croquis in various poses. The designer selects a desired pose that then appears on the computer screen. The garment sketch can be drawn onto the croquis. Existing fabrics can be scanned into the computer system. A facsimile of the fabric will appear on the computer screen. The scale of the print or plaid fabric motif can be adjusted to approximate the correct size of the motif for the scale of the drawing. This is much faster than hand drawing and coloring fabric motifs. Color printers allow output of finished drawings that accurately represent the intended fabric's color and texture.

ADVANTAGES OF CAD.   Two major advantages of using a CAD system to create designs are the time saving potential and the capability to quickly try out numerous design ideas. The designer may select a garment sketch from the previous season's line and simply modify design details for the new design for the upcoming line. This procedure greatly speeds up this phase of the design process. According to manufacturers using CAD for creating sketches,

> Throw away that pencil and paper. Forget messy charcoal and watercolor. You need a computer aided design (CAD) system to get up to speed in today's competitive marketplace. . . . Among CAD's benefits, as reported by these companies, are a savings in time and money (at the top of the list), along with more creative freedom. . . . The ability to improve and embellish merchandising and design presentations to vendors and customers also was noted, as well as enhanced precision and better quality output. (Gilbert, 1995, p. 48)

In the future, it is anticipated that advances in computer technology will allow the designer's sketch to be translated from a three-dimensional image to a two-dimensional pattern. Other predicted advances include the technology to compute the cost difference (in material usage and time to sew) between slightly different versions of a design.

Some designers may think it stifles their creativity to "sketch" on a computer. They prefer to "think" with pencil in hand. Conversely, some designers believe that using CAD increases their creative potential. As stated by Gilbert (1995),

> Even people without artistic inclinations find CAD systems very easy to use. Dave Herr of Kinney Shoe says, 'Our design system brings a new creative side to my job. I am not an artsy person; I am more of an engineer than a designer. The system and its tools have enhanced what little natural ability I have and made me creative.' (p. 49)

It has become increasingly important for designers to be proficient with CAD systems, and design students will increase their opportunities for future employment by developing the ability to "sketch" their design ideas using a computer system.

FUTURE CAD DEVELOPMENTS.   New computer technology encompasses the use of three-dimensional fabric draping. In the future, the designer might begin with a three-dimensional image of the target customer's body and "drape" fabric around the body. A Cornell University pro-

Figure 6.12
With a computer aided design (CAD) system, designers can scan a fabric image and reproduce it on the shoe design.

fessor is working on computer simulation of draping fabric over a sphere. He stated (*Human Ecology Forum*, 1995),

> When the technology is ready, it will dramatically change the way apparel designers work. Rather than designing garments with flat, two-dimensional drawings, they'll create three-dimensional images that can be rotated for viewing from different angles. As they experiment with different materials, the program will adjust the drape of the garment to reflect the characteristics of the material. (p. 15)

The concept of designing entirely on the computer may seem far off, but the reality is that in time, not only will we create the image of the garment style with replica fabric on the computer screen, but retail buyers will write their orders from the garments viewed on the screen. No prototype samples will be sewn. The cost savings compared to today's process of design development will be substantial. Other aspects of CAD systems will be discussed in Chapter 7.

TEXTILE DESIGN.   Computer aided design and graphics software programs have also entered the textile design domain. Textile designers often work for textile producers or perform free-lance design work. More frequently today than in the past, apparel designers find textile design and/or graphic design assignments a part of their responsibilities. This may include designing a graphics logo to coordinate with a print fabric used in a line, or perhaps redesigning an existing textile print. As is true with apparel design, CAD systems provide numerous advantages to textile design.

Some of the new computer textile design systems can print the newly created print design directly onto a piece of fabric. Several repeats of the printed fabric pieces can be taped together to simulate a large piece of the printed textile. Viewing a large section of the print design helps the textile designer visualize the scale, repeat, and color combination. Changes can be made immediately. This is much faster and less expensive than sending a printed paper sample to a textile mill to make a **strike off** or sample yardage of the print.

Not all textile designers agree that the advantages of using CAD systems outweigh traditional hand drawing. A textile and apparel designer who has been using CAD for more than fifteen years stated, "People today are designing solely on computers rather than experiencing the traditional textile design process. The art is going out of the process, and it shows" (Chiris, 1996, p. 16). Technology will continue to evolve, including CAD systems developed that will feel more as if the designer were actually drawing freehand.

TECHNICAL DRAWING

Some garment design sketches do not include the body silhouette. If only the garment design is drawn, without an indication of the body, the sketch is called a technical drawing, or **tech drawing.** Tech drawings are used in place of design sketches, especially in the active sportswear industry.

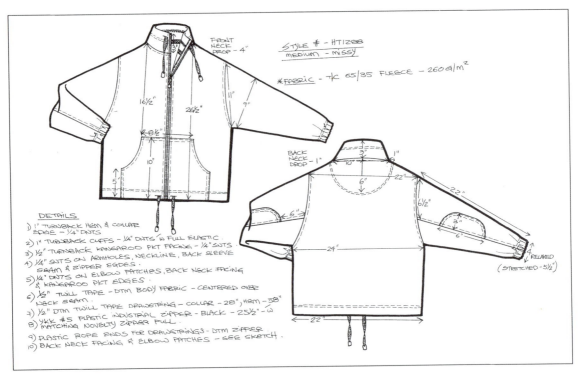

Figure 6.13
In fields such as the active sportswear industry, tech drawings are used to show design details.

Activewear garments might have more details that need to be clearly delineated compared with the "fashion" garment, where silhouette and fewer design details may be the most important aspects of the garment design. Tech drawings might include a close-up sketch of a detail such as a pocket, cuff, or collar, as well as the back view. Tech drawings are especially useful and often necessary for pattern making and production needs. Tech drawings can be drawn quickly with CAD programs. A previous season's similar CAD technical garment drawing can be used as the starting point to make modifications for the new design.

SELECTION OF FABRICS AND TRIMS

The fabrics and trims are usually selected before a design is approved for inclusion in a line. Each design idea sketch or tech drawing includes a small sample of the intended fabric, called a **swatch** that is attached to the sketch or drawing. It is essential that the fabric be chosen before a design is reviewed by the merchandiser, designer, and cost personnel for possible inclusion in the final line. Sometimes the actual fabric intended for the design is not yet available from the textile manufacturer. In these cases a facsimile fabric will be used temporarily for the design development stage. The design sketch will also include any trim swatches that will be used.

DESIGNERS WHO CREATE BY DRAPING

Some designers create a design idea three dimensionally using actual fabric as a starting point instead of beginning with a sketch of a garment. For this design process, a mannequin or dress form in the sample size is used. Fabrics vary in their **hand** and ability to drape around the body. Working with the actual fabric can be a source of design inspiration, especially for fabrics with special draping qualities, such as charmeuse or permanently pleated fabric. Fabrics that are plaid or striped or that have a large print motif are suited to creating the initial design by the **draping** process. Couture designers, and some ready-to-wear designers creating lines in the designer price zone, frequently use draping to create the initial design.

Ready-to-wear designers in the better or moderate price zones (and sometimes couture designers) might develop the design from the designer's sketch by draping in **muslin.** Muslin is an inexpensive trial fabric, similar to cotton broadcloth. It helps the designer determine silhouette, proportion, and design details, but does not have the drape of many fashion fabrics. For many fabric types and garment styles in the better or moderate price zones, muslin serves the purpose adequately. The muslin trial garment is sometimes referred to as the *toile,* a French term whose literal translation is cloth.

French designer Madeleine Vionnet created innovative bias cut garments during the 1920s and 1930s. She always draped, rather than sketched, her design ideas. She worked out the design in fabric on a small-size wooden mannequin. Her design team then draped a full-size replica in muslin. A prototype in fashion fabric was then cut using the pattern pieces developed from the muslin *toile.* Donna Karan is an example of a contemporary designer who creates designs by draping.

There are advantages to developing the design idea by draping, especially if the fashion fabric is used. Seeing the design develop, sensing the drape of the fabric, molding the fabric into a three-dimensional shape, and evolving the design during the process bring a great deal of creativity to the design process. However, draping a design may take more time than preparing a design sketch or tech drawing, and draping requires more fabric than first making a pattern and then cutting fabric from the pattern. Therefore, many designers rely on drawings for the design phase of the process.

Figure 6.14
Some designers, such as Jacques Fath, create three dimensionally by draping designs in fashion fabric on a live model.

Figure 6.15
French designer
Madeleine Vionnet
developed her design
ideas by draping on a
small-scale wooden
mannequin and perfect-
ing them later on a
full-size mannequin.

DESIGN TEAM REVIEWS LINE

Typically, many more design ideas are sketched than will appear in the final
line. At a design review session (also called a line review), the designer presents the design sketches to the review team (for example the merchandiser,
fit or production engineer, and head of sample sewing) according to the
timeline on the master calendar. Some designers present the new line as a
formal presentation with beautifully rendered drawings, fabric swatches,
and perhaps an indication of the design theme or inspiration shown on presentation boards or story boards. The designer might make an oral presentation to the design team, upper management, or private label managers to
"sell" the line. This is the first of several review processes the line must
undergo. This session might be called the first adoption meeting, with several subsequent line reviews before the final adoption. The review team discusses and evaluates the designs. The team will have determined during previous planning meetings how many items of each type of apparel item will be
possible to include in the line. Out of 60 design ideas presented for review,
perhaps only 30 or 40 sketches will be selected to continue into the design
development stage. Some of these designs will be dropped at a later stage as

Figure 6.16
At review meetings, the designer, merchandiser, and production engineer discuss the feasibility of each style in the line.

well. At other companies, the merchandisers may request that all, or most, of the designs be developed as prototypes to better visualize the product.

Guided by the total number of pieces allowed for the line, other factors enter into the decision to accept or drop designs from the line. The balance of the line is an important factor in deciding which designs should be included. For a missy career line, jacket style variations are considered so that there will be a range of styles to suit a variety of customers. For example, it is important to include a balance of the number of short versus long, boxy versus fitted, single- versus double-breasted, and collar versus collarless jackets. Solid versus plaid or print fabrics is another consideration. Skirt style variations must be balanced—short versus long, fitted versus flared, full versus pleated. The skirts need to coordinate with as many of the jacket styles as possible. The mix of classic and fashion-forward styles needs to be considered. The anticipated prices need to be similar to the previous season's prices unless a new market niche is sought. Styling needs to match price—in that a customer expects to pay more for a longer, double-breasted jacket than for a short, single-breasted style.

Other factors to consider include ease of adjusting to size variations. For example, elastic added at the sides of the skirt waistband can enhance the adaptability of a garment to fit more figure shapes, especially in the missy and larger size markets. However, for the junior market, elastic in the waistband may be considered a negative feature and could adversely affect sales.

Ease in alterations is another consideration. A wrap skirt with a curved, faced hemline is not easily shortened and cannot be lengthened. There is a constant struggle among production personnel who want the designs to be similar to previous designs and as simple as possible; merchandisers who want the line to "sell itself" in the marketplace with great prices and high quality; and designers who want highly creative, complex designs. This may explain why some companies call the conference room where design reviews are conducted the "war room."

Designs included in the final line:

▮ create a cohesive theme

▮ include an appropriate number of items and a balance of styles

▮ fit the overall merchandising orientation of the company for the season (e.g., fit the price and lifestyle of the target customer).

The merits of each design as it fits in the "big picture" of the overall line will be discussed. Sometimes design details will be modified to lower the expected cost or to coordinate better with other styles. It is important for the designer to be prolific with design ideas and to develop an impersonal attitude about the designs that are dropped from the line.

WRITING THE GARMENT SPECIFICATION SHEET

The designer often has some specific design details in mind that need to be conveyed to the pattern maker and sample sewer in order to create the sample or prototype garment at the next stage of the design process. These details, as well as other vital information, are conveyed on a **garment specification sheet,** also called a spec sheet. Examples of types of design details include the number of buttons, the size and type of buttons, any edge stitching or top stitching, the width of pleats or tucks, the spacing between pleats or tucks, the size of a patch pocket, the circumference of a skirt at the hem,

Figure 6.17
The garment specification sheet includes important information for the pattern maker and sewer as well as a drawing of the garment style and a fabric swatch.

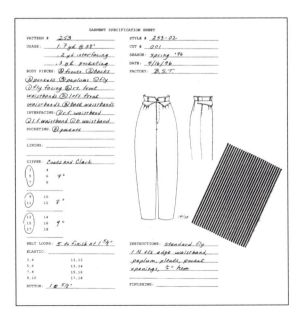

the width of the pant leg at the hem, and the finished back length of a jacket. Pocketing, lining fabric, and interfacings are also specified. Any information not specified will be decided by the pattern maker. Thus, it is the designer's responsibility to specify all garment aspects that are important to the "look" of the design. A drawing of the garment design is included on the spec sheet, along with fabric swatches. The spec sheet may also include the size specifications (see Chapter 9).

A **style number** is assigned to each new style in the line. This number (which might include a letter code as well) is coded to indicate the season/year the line will be presented to buyers, plus other information desired by the apparel company. The code may include the category, such as swimwear or sportswear. The size category of junior, missy, petite or tall might be another item included in the code. The style number is used as the style's reference throughout development, marketing, and production.

SUMMARY

In creating an apparel line, the design process follows the research process. The design team works with planning and production personnel to plan the calendar of due dates in order to provide garments to the retailer at the season's outset. The line is planned to provide the right product type for the target customer at the right time and at the right price. The sales volume and sell through at the retail level are important indicators used to plan the next line. The balance between carryover styles, revisions of popular styles from the previous season, and new styles is a critical decision to the success of the line.

The merchandiser may work with the designer to develop a theme for a new line. A theme for a line can help sell the products. An example of a color theme for a sport fishing group is one based on the colors of a sport fish. This theme can be enhanced by the use of the fish image as a graphic design on a T-shirt in the collection. Historic and ethnic clothing are sources of design inspiration, as are new fabrics, textures, trims, and fasteners.

Some designers hand sketch their garment design ideas, some use a computer aided design or graphics program, some prepare technical drawings, and some create the design idea three dimensionally in fabric by draping. The designer is responsible for creating far more design ideas than will be selected for the line. The designer is also responsible for selecting fabrics, trims, and linings for each design and specifying details such as buttons and top stitching. The garment specification sheet includes all the pertinent information required to complete a pattern and prototype of the design.

REFERENCES

Chiris, Stuart. (1996, February 27). CAD: Help or hindrance in the creative process? *WWD*, p. 16.

Gilbert, Laurel. (1995, July). CAD comes of age. *Bobbin*, pp. 48–52.

Human Ecology Forum, (1995, Spring). Cornell University College of Human Ecology, 23(2), 13–15.

Mackrell, Alice. (1990). *Paul Poiret,* New York: Holmes & Meier.

Martin, Richard, and Koda, Harold. (1989). *The Historical Mode.* New York: Rizzoli International Publications.

Martin, Richard, and Koda, Harold. (1994). *Orientalism: Visions of the East in Western Dress,* New York: Metropolitan Museum of Art. Distributed by Harry N. Abrams, Inc.

Saint Laurent, Yves, Vreeland, Diana et al. (1983). *Yves Saint Laurent.* New York: Metropolitan Museum of Art.

Tuxedo Junction: YSL, Ralph square off. (1994, April 28). *WWD,* pp. 1, 15.

KEY TERMS

product type	**lay figure**
market niche	**computer aided design (CAD)**
sell through	**strike off**
carryover	**tech drawing**
line-for-line copy	**swatch**
knock-off	**hand**
colorway	**draping**
Empire	**muslin**
Retro	*toile*
zeitgeist	**garment specification sheet**
croquis	**style number**

DISCUSSION QUESTIONS

1. What are some possible themes for a high-fashion eveningwear collection?
2. What are some possible themes for a junior sportswear line?
3. What are some current societal trends (*zeitgeist*) that might provide an inspiration for a group or line of apparel?
4. What might be an example of an "unconventional" source of design inspiration?
5. What are some of the job responsibilities of a merchandiser and a designer in the design stage of the design process? What are some activities that might be helpful for you to accomplish as students to help prepare you for these job responsibilities?

CAREER PROFILES

If you are considering a career as a designer or merchandiser for an apparel company, what would your job description entail and what are some typical tasks that you would perform?

ASSISTANT DESIGNER, *Privately Owned Sportswear Company*

Job Description
Assist the design director and manager.

Typical Tasks
- Create catalog of the seasons prototype garments—computer illustrations and colorways of all garments
- Create and weave up yarn dyes on the computer and scan in prints
- Prepare all of the information necessary for the textile mills to do strike offs and handlooms
- Update and change CAD/CAM data when changes in colors are made
- Design garments from initial sketches through fit sessions
- Special computer projects for sales reps (requiring drawing garments, coloring up, and making minicatalogs)
- Work with all fit models
- Work with all overseas correspondence in the absence of the designer

What Do You Like Best About Your Job?
The variety of work, working on the computer with many fun programs, designing, and the people.

DESIGNER, *Publicly Owned Sportswear and Athletic Shoe Company*

Job Description
Work with one marketer to design the running and cycling lines and another marketer to design the All Conditions Gear line. Work with graphic designer and textile designer as an integral part of the line.

Typical Tasks
- Ideation, direction, image, and concept for the season's lines
- Research fabric vendor resources
- Select fabrics
- Work with three pattern makers
- Provide follow-through to production of all garments in lines
- Give presentation on the line to up to six groups of people for feedback

What Do You Like Best About Your Job?
Apply my vision to a product, to determine a way to do something differently.

Attributes of a Designer
Creative flair, good technical knowledge, confidence (not to be confused with arrogance or close mindedness), inspired individual everyday, all the time.

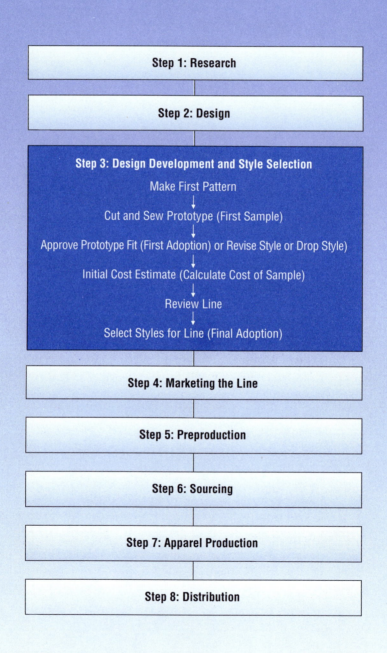

Step 1: Research

Step 2: Design

Step 3: Design Development and Style Selection

Make First Pattern
↓
Cut and Sew Prototype (First Sample)
↓
Approve Prototype Fit (First Adoption) or Revise Style or Drop Style)
↓
Initial Cost Estimate (Calculate Cost of Sample)
↓
Review Line
↓
Select Styles for Line (Final Adoption)

Step 4: Marketing the Line

Step 5: Preproduction

Step 6: Sourcing

Step 7: Apparel Production

Step 8: Distribution

7

Design Development and
Style Selection

Objectives

▌ To describe the steps required to develop a sketch into a prototype
garment and to prepare the garment for design team review.

▌ To identify the advantages and disadvantages of using a computer
Pattern Design System for pattern making.

▌ To explain the reasons why a style might be eliminated from the line
during the review process.

▌ To describe some of the style factors that influence the estimated cost
of a new garment style.

▌ To compare the traditional development process used to take a
garment sketch into a retail garment with alternative methods, such
as private label manufacturing, specification buying, and mass
customization.

AT THIS POINT in the design process, the "line" for the new season consists
of a group of sketches with fabric swatches that have made it through the
design team's preliminary selection process. This chapter discusses how the
first pattern is developed from the designer's sketch, swatch, and garment

specification sheet, and how the prototype garment is cut and sewn from the first pattern. The prototype is then tried on a fit model whose body measurements match the company's size standard. The designer, merchandiser, pattern maker, and production engineer analyze the fit and design, and discuss cost factors. A preliminary cost estimate is calculated. This is an important factor in deciding the feasibility of producing the style. Changes may be made to the prototype, or perhaps a modified prototype will be cut and sewn. This process continues with all the styles for the line. The styles in the line are reviewed, and final decisions are made to determine which styles will be included in the final line. Viewing the development of a new style from its sketch (or the first drape) to a finished prototype is an exciting part of the design process. On the other hand, it can be a difficult decision to cut some styles from the line after seeing the prototypes and liking all of them.

This chapter focuses on the development process typically used by apparel companies who manufacture **brand merchandise.** This is apparel whose brand labels are well recognized by the public, including Levi Strauss, Liz Claiborne, and Jantzen. Later in the chapter, alternative development processes are discussed. These include **private label manufacturing** and **specification buying,** in which retailers are a part of the design team and/or are in charge of the manufacturing process. Increased vertical integration and changes in the design-retail relationship during the 1980s led to the growth and expansion of these alternative development processes. Changing roles and relationships between design and retail will continue in our complex economic market.

DESIGN DEVELOPMENT

The fashion development or design department (also called the design development or product development department at some companies) usually consists of designers (and product developers), and assistant designers. At some companies, the pattern makers and production engineers (also called cost engineers or product technicians) are a part of the design development team. If the apparel company also has production pattern makers, they may be a part of the design department.

As discussed in Chapter 6, some designers sketch an idea for a new style as the preliminary design step. After the design team has approved the style for development, the designer's sketch, fabric swatch, and garment specification sheet are delivered to the fashion or **design development department** to begin the pattern making process. For apparel manufacturers who use contractors, the first pattern may be developed by the contractor, or the pattern may be developed by the apparel manufacturer. The responsibility for developing the first pattern is fairly common for contractors located in Asia.

Other designers prefer to drape the preliminary design idea using either muslin or a fashion fabric on a mannequin or dress form. After careful markings have been made, the fabric pieces of the draped design are removed from the mannequin. The "drape" is then ready for pattern making.

MAKING THE FIRST PATTERN

The pattern maker may work with paper patterns, or the pattern might be created using a computer aided design system. There are similarities between both methods in the pattern making process, but also some differences. Both pattern making methods will be discussed.

In some companies, the designer is also the first pattern maker. This tends to occur in very small companies or in some specialty areas, such as children's wear. Some designers enjoy being involved in the development of their design ideas from sketches into patterns and then prototypes. Some designers find that their design ideas evolve during development and that they modify the design during the process of making the pattern and/or sewing the prototype.

TRADITIONAL PATTERN MAKING. From the designer's sketch, the assistant designer or pattern maker begins the pattern-making process, called **flat pattern** design. The pattern maker's role is critical to the accurate translation of the designer's idea. An existing pattern is used to begin the new design. This pattern could be a basic pattern (also called a **block** or a **sloper**) in the company's sample size. For example, a basic shirt block might be used as the basic pattern for a new shirt style. The pattern maker creates the new pattern by adding pattern design details such as a collar, pocket, button band, back yoke, and sleeve pleats to the basic pattern as indicated in the designer's sketch.

Figure 7.1
Tagboard patterns from previous seasons are used as reference for new pattern styles.

Another route frequently used by the pattern maker is to select a similar style from a previous season. For example, a shirt style for a new season might be similar to a pattern that has already been made. Modifying an existing pattern can be a much faster way to create the pattern for the new style. Selecting the most appropriate previous style for the starting point of a new style may require some discussion between the assistant designer or pattern maker and the designer. Or, the designer might make a note on the sketch suggesting a previous style from which to begin. It is important that the pattern maker accurately assess from the sketch the overall silhouette desired, the amount of ease (from very snug to very oversized), and the designer's desired proportions for the design details.

The existing basic pattern as well as stylized patterns are often made of a heavy weight paper called **tagboard,** oaktag, or "hard" paper. (It is similar in weight to the paper used for file folders.) This heavy paper is sturdy and the edges can be traced rapidly to copy a pattern as the beginning point for the new pattern. Traditional pattern making procedures require that the pattern maker trace the base pattern onto either pattern paper, called "soft" paper, or that new patterns are made directly onto new hard paper. Style details are developed, collars can be created, new sleeves designed, and pleats or gathers added in order to create the pattern pieces for the new style.

The intended fabric is an important consideration during pattern making. For example, the amount of gathers to incorporate into a sleeve depends on the hand or tactile qualities of the fabric specified by the designer. The pattern maker may experiment by gathering a section of the intended fabric or a facsimile fabric to better determine the ideal quantity of gathers. To develop patterns for garments made from stretch fabrics, it is necessary to know the exact amount of stretch in all directions of the fabric. The pattern maker selects the base block or previous style pattern to correspond to the specific stretch factor of the intended fabric for the new style. Fabric shrinkage is another pattern making consideration. The fabric sample has been wash tested to accurately determine its shrinkage in all directions. The pattern is made sufficiently larger to account for the shrinkage factor. The pattern maker not only needs pattern making expertise to interpret a garment illustration into a pattern, but also must be knowledgeable about production aspects so the pattern can be made feasibly and cost effectively in the factories.

PATTERN MAKING USING COMPUTERS. Computer pattern making has been used in some apparel companies since the early 1980s. Many apparel companies use **pattern design systems (PDS)** for some or all of the pattern making functions. The pattern making process is similar to the flat pattern process previously discussed. The basic patterns or blocks and all previous style patterns are stored in the computer's memory. To begin a new style, either a block, such as a basic shirt block, or a similar style from a previous season is pulled from the computer's memory and appears on the screen. The pattern maker uses a mouse, cursor, or stylus (which looks similar to a pen) to select specific areas to change on the pattern. Pattern making commands are either selected from a menu shown on the screen or typed onto a keyboard. Once the pattern pieces are completed, the pattern can be plotted (drawn) in full size.

New computer technology continues to bring remarkable advances in the ease of use, adaptability, and cost effectiveness ("CAD users report payback within one year," 1993). Some of the advantages of PDS include:

Advantages

Speed: All basic patterns, or base blocks, and previous styles are stored in the computer's memory. A pattern maker begins by calling up the selected previous pattern. No tracing of an existing pattern is required. Tedious pattern making tasks, such as tracing a pattern piece to make a facing, are accomplished with a fast copy command. The pattern making programs add selected seam allowances and hem allowances to selected edges very quickly. The lengths of two seam lines can be compared for accuracy with a computer command. Markings and labels such as grainlines and notches are stored in a special "library" and quickly added to the pattern pieces. Gathers can be added by indicating on the block shown on the monitor where and how much the pattern maker wants the pattern to be enlarged. The pattern piece is spread instantly, compared to slashing a paper pattern in several places, then spreading the pattern and inserting pattern paper. If the design is modified later in the design process, changes in the pattern can be made more quickly by PDS than is usually required to modify a paper pattern.

Accuracy: Using CAD eliminates the incremental growth that can occur when hand tracing a pattern because of the thickness of the pencil lead. Seam lengths and seam allowance widths are more exact than is possible by hand.

Ergonomic Concerns: Sitting or standing at a computer workstation can be easier on the body ergonomics compared to bending over a pattern table. It is usually not necessary for the pattern maker to cut out soft or hard paper patterns when making a pattern by computer, saving wear and tear on the hands.

Integration with Production: Later in the process, production is faster if the pattern pieces have been stored already in the computer (versus the time required to input the pattern pieces for computerized grading and marker making). This process will be discussed in Chapter 9.

Although the advantages of PDS are many, some pattern makers and company executives note that there are disadvantages.

Disadvantages

Cost: The initial cost of a PDS workstation is high, although some of the new technology systems cost less than earlier versions. Some apparel manufacturers, especially smaller companies, may not see a substantial return on their investment for a number of years. A workstation must be used a specific number of hours per day, every day, to be cost effective. If a company produces only a limited number of new styles per season, the PDS system will not be utilized to its maximum. Leasing time and/or space on an owner's CAD system is being done by some small manufacturers (Christmas, 1994). Several small apparel companies might join a cooperative to "buy" time on a PDS workstation ("Computer center opens," 1995). Another aspect of cost deals with training costs for pattern makers. Typically, pattern makers are sent to the computer company's headquarters for a week or two of intensive training on the system. In addition, there is the "lost time" while training occurs and the slower speed to make patterns while the new system is being learned. During the transition time, some pattern styles may still be made faster on the table from existing patterns, while some new styles will be made on PDS and stored in the computer. Thus, both PDS and paper patterns will be used for a while, which can create complications.

Visualization of the Full Size: For pattern makers who are experienced at pattern making in full size, the use of PDS requires a visual adjustment to the scale of pattern parts as seen on the computer screen. When working by hand, the pattern maker slashes the pattern for gathers and spreads the pattern the desired amount. These decisions are based on what looks correct visually. When pattern makers use PDS, they select the quantity of gathers to add. The pattern, with the predetermined quantity of gathers, then appears on the screen. If the quantity of gathers seems too great or too small, it takes very little time with PDS to undo the maneuver and request a different quantity of gathers. With experience it becomes easier for pattern makers to visualize scale on a CAD system.

User Friendliness: One of the hurdles with learning a computer system is memorizing the commands and the various steps needed to complete a process. Some of the early PDS systems were not "user friendly." Recently,

Figure 7.2
Pattern Design Systems such as Gerber's AccuMark provide speed and accuracy in making patterns for new styles.

great strides have been made in the language used for commands, and in the use of "real size" pattern tables instead of smaller sensitized screen areas for pattern making. For example, the Silhouette™ system developed by Microdynamics in the early 1990s allows pattern makers to work from full-size patterns on a special sensitized "pattern" table. This system can reduce the time it may take pattern makers to feel comfortable with a PDS system.

"Down" Time: For apparel companies located in very large cities, expert service representatives may be a quick phone call away when a computer system malfunctions or "goes down." However, for some companies, a malfunctioning workstation can cause great problems and affect the subsequent production steps. Any delays can be extremely costly to the manufacturer and retailer.

Figure 7.3
After a pattern is completed on the pattern design system, the pattern pieces are drawn full size on a plotter.

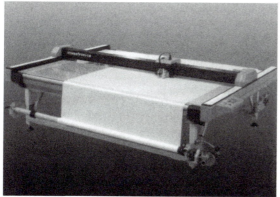

Ergonomic Concerns: There are ergonomic concerns for computer users. For example, repetitive motion syndrome is a wrist injury resulting from frequent use of a keyboard. Newer CAD software systems use a mouse to select options more frequently than using a keyboard. This greatly reduces the potential for wrist injury. Other concerns include correct table height for the individual and an ergonomically designed chair.

The future will bring an increased number of apparel companies using PDS. Cost of PDS workstations may be reduced as more price competition among CAD companies develops or technology costs decrease (Belleau & Didier, 1989). Or, as larger companies upgrade their systems, they may sell used PDS workstations at a price that is acceptable to smaller companies. Some larger apparel manufacturers already rely completely on computer-generated pattern making.

There are computer software programs that provide an interface between the pattern making process and the garment specification sheet. One system is designed to allow the pattern maker to write the spec sheet as the pattern is being made on PDS. A file of potential sewing steps is retrieved and edited on one screen while the pattern is being made and viewed on another screen. The possibility of an error in the spec sheet is reduced when the pattern maker writes the spec sheet simultaneously with the pattern making process.

PATTERN MAKING FROM A DRAPED DESIGN. As discussed in Chapter 6, some designers, especially in the couture, designer, and bridge price zones, create the initial garment by draping the design on a mannequin. The fabric, either expensive fashion fabric or muslin, is "draped" onto the sample size mannequin. The design is developed by cutting into the fabric, molding the fabric to the desired shape, and then pinning the fabric

Figure 7.4
A new style may be developed in muslin before a prototype is made in fashion fabric.

in place. After finalizing all aspects of the design, the style lines and construction details of the drape are very carefully marked in preparation for removal from the mannequin. The fabric pieces are removed and laid flat over pattern paper. The shapes of the pattern pieces are traced onto paper, then the pattern is perfected and finalized with markings such as grainlines, notches, buttonholes, correct seam and hem allowances, and facings.

Regardless of the procedure by which the pattern is made—from a draped design, by using traditional flat pattern design, or by using PDS—the full-size final pattern is now ready to cut and sew.

MAKING THE PROTOTYPE OR SAMPLE GARMENT

As noted earlier, some apparel manufacturers develop the line, create the design sketches with fabric swatches, and write the garment specification sheet. They then use contractors, either domestic or off-shore, to actually manufacture the garments. The steps in-between, those involving the making of the pattern and cutting and sewing the **prototype** or sample, may be performed by either the apparel company or the contractor.

For those apparel companies that use contractors, it could be advantageous for the apparel company to have the capability to develop the pattern and prototype in-house. There are inherent time delays, as well as potential communication and visual interpretation problems when using contractors to develop the pattern and prototype. In addition, not all contractors use an identical base pattern for pattern making; this can cause differences in the fit of the finished stylized garment. A number of factors must be considered by each apparel manufacturer regarding the pattern making, grading, and marker making responsibility.

Figure 7.5
The sample fabric
is cut by hand for the
prototype.

SAMPLE SEWING. Apparel companies who sew the prototype in-house have a **sample sewing department.** The completed pattern is delivered to the sample sewing department, with a swatch of the intended fabric (the fabric to be used for the actual garment) and the garment specification sheet. If the intended fabric is available (sometimes as a sample cut ordered from the textile mill), it will be used to make the prototype garment. Sometimes the intended fabric is not yet available, so a substitute or facsimile fabric, as similar as possible to the intended fabric, will be used.

The garment spec sheet will indicate any special cutting instructions. For example, a shirt with back yoke may require that the shirt's striped fabric be cut on lengthwise grain for the body, sleeves, and collar, and crosswise grain for the yoke. Stretch fabrics for swimwear and bodywear may require some pattern pieces be cut with greatest stretch in the horizontal direction while other pattern pieces will be cut with greatest stretch in the vertical direction. The cutter will match plaids where specified and make other decisions about layout. The cutter will cut all pieces needed for the prototype, including pocketing, interfacings, and linings. The pattern is removed from the fabric after cutting, then the pattern is usually returned to the design department rather than accompanying the fabric pieces of the prototype.

The **sample sewer** who sews the prototype is highly skilled in the use of a variety of sewing machines as well as in the production processes used in the factories. Without an instruction sheet and rarely consulting the pattern pieces, the sample sewer sews the entire prototype garment. The sample sewer moves from one piece of equipment to the next, until the garment is finished. This differs from production sewers who generally perform only a few steps in the sewing sequence on each garment and remain at one piece of sewing equipment. The sample sewer may need to send a section of a pro-

Figure 7.6
The pattern maker and the sample sewer discuss possible alternatives for a pocket detail.

totype to another area for work. For example, a logo may need to be embroidered onto a shirt front after it is cut out and before the shirt is sewn. Keeping the work flowing smoothly is also part of the process. Generally, for companies who produce prototypes in-house, the prototype is completed within a few days after cutting.

If the design department is near the sample sewing room, the sample sewer might consult with the pattern maker regarding a specific sewing process or technique, or they may discuss possible alternatives to a pattern solution. A team approach among pattern maker, cutter, and sample sewer is an advantage. After the sample sewer finishes making the prototype, it is sent back to the design department for evaluation. Often the pattern maker reviews the prototype first to assess whether any changes need to be made before the style is reviewed by the designer and merchandiser.

APPROVING THE PROTOTYPE. The fit of the company's products is a way to achieve product differentiation. Therefore, an assessment of how each style fits can be very important to a company. A **fit model** is used to assess the fit, styling, and overall look of the new prototype. The fit model is a person selected to represent the body proportions that the apparel company feels are ideal for its target customer and that correspond to the basic pattern size used to make the prototype. Some fit models, called in-house models, may work for the company in another capacity and are asked to try on prototypes as needed as a part of their job duties. Other companies hire a professional fit model who may work for a number of apparel companies. With professional fit models, specific appointments will be made for fit sessions, requiring both lead time to book the appointment and on-time delivery of prototypes for the fit session. Fit models can provide valuable information about the comfort and ease of the garment.

Men's wear fit models tend to have well-proportioned bodies and usually are about 5'10" to 6 feet in height. In missy apparel, fit models differ from runway models and photographic models. A missy fit model has body proportions that are "average," with a height of 5'5" to 5'8" as compared to the tall and svelte runway models. Large size and petite fit models are used for their respective size categories. In children's wear, the fit model outgrows the sample size very quickly, leaving the apparel company searching for a new fit model every few months.

In junior and missy apparel, there is wide variation of body dimensions within one size among apparel companies (Workman, 1991). For a pant created to fit an individual with a 25-inch waist, one company may use a 36-inch hip measurement for its size standard and another company may use a 37-inch hip measurement. The pattern's crotch depth may also differ at various companies. Finding the "perfect" fit model for an apparel company can be a challenge, especially for swimwear and innerwear companies whose garments fit close to the body. The model's cup size and bust contour are factors in selecting the fit model. Some fit models are in very high demand, especially in the more populated market centers.

When several prototypes are ready for assessment, a fit session is scheduled with the fit model. While the garment "fit" is a part of the assessment, much of the discussion between designer and assistant designer/pattern maker may focus on the prototype's overall style and garment details. Sometimes production engineers are asked to provide feedback about potential difficulties in factory production of the style. If any of these aspects need revision, either the existing prototype will be redone, or the pattern will be revised and a new prototype will be cut and sewn. The final design will be approved by the designer and/or the merchandiser. The prototype might be eliminated at this point if reworking the design does not seem feasible.

New fabrics are tested for such properties as color fastness, crocking, pilling, and abrasion early in the design process. After the prototype has been completed, a wash test might be performed on the finished garment. A typical washer and dryer used for home laundering would be used. For the wash test performed on garments to be sold in other countries, the type of laundering equipment used by the customer might be used to simulate the conditions under which the garment will be laundered. Occasionally, problems arise after laundering a garment that were not evident when the individual fabrics or trims were tested.

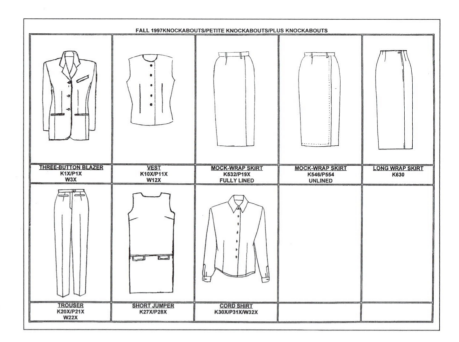

Figure 7.7
The preliminary line sheet is used by the design team during the development process of the line.

PRELIMINARY LINE SHEET. A tech drawing of each new style in the group or line will be added to a **preliminary line sheet.** Fabric swatches and other pertinent details might also be listed. The line sheet is used within the department to help all the team members keep track of the styles in the group. The preliminary line sheet will be developed into the line brochure, or line catalog, used later to market the line.

DETERMINING THE COST ESTIMATE

The cost to mass produce the style is an important consideration in the selection of styles for the final line. Thus, preliminary costing needs to occur prior to the decision to adopt or reject a style. An **initial cost estimate** (also called precosting) for the style is based on several important components. The cost of the materials is estimated based on the number of yards of fabrics required to make the prototype. The quantity of all materials used must be included, such as interfacing, pocketing, and lining, and findings, such as elastic, zipper, buttons, and trims. A **marker** is the term used for the layout plan of the pattern pieces. The **costing marker** refers to the layout plan for the pattern pieces used to determine the yardage for the new style. If the pattern was made using PDS, the yardage (called **usage**) can be determined by making a costing marker on the computer. The pattern pieces for this style have been stored in the computer and can be brought up on the com-

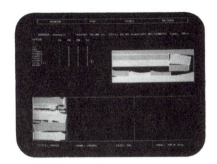

Figure 7.8
A costing marker created from the pattern pieces stored in the Pattern Design System is used to determine the quantity of material required for one garment.

puter screen. The pattern pieces can be arranged using the cursor or stylus and viewed on the computer screen within a rectangular space representing the width and length of the intended fabric. Various layouts can be analyzed to determine the best arrangement of pattern pieces for the least quantity of fabric. This process is repeated for the lining and other materials required.

In theory, the quantity of each fabric needed to produce one medium-sized garment multiplied by the cost of the fabric to the apparel company is added together to arrive at a total materials cost. If the company produces the same number of small sizes and large sizes, then using the size medium to "average" the quantity of fabrics needed should provide a good estimate of the yardage. However, if the company in fact, sells many more size small than size large, the "average" cost of materials would be higher than the actual cost. Conversely, if many more size large items were sold than size small items, then the "average" cost of materials would be too low. Therefore, some companies may use another size to calculate their "average" usage. The quantity multiplied by the cost to the apparel company is calculated for sundries (also called notions or findings) and trims. The total is the "materials" cost.

The other major component of the initial cost estimate is the cost of labor to sew the style. The labor cost is determined by estimating the number of minutes it will require to cut and sew the garment multiplied by the cost per minute of labor for a specific sewing factory. For an accurate cost estimate, it is necessary to select a possible site for production since labor costs vary considerably around the world. In some countries, the labor cost varies month by month. One approach to estimating the labor cost for a new style is to use the known cost of labor to sew a similar garment from the previous season. Due to economic and political conditions, it may not be feasible to use the same factory that produced a similar style for the previous season. At this point in the development process, the estimate *is* just an estimate. An exact cost will be calculated later. As production time nears, costs might be researched in several countries to select the source country for the best cost of production. Shipping and other related costs, discussed later, need to be estimated and added to the initial cost estimate as well.

Designing a product based on **target costing** works a little differently from the sequence discussed previously. Jantzen uses target costing to develop its missy and junior swimwear lines. The designer's sketch is reviewed by the cost engineer, called a product technician. The cost is carefully estimated from the designer's sketch. The design team works out garment details and construction factors to bring the design within the required cost for the styles in the line. The design sketch is reworked and approved, then a prototype garment is cut, sewn, and approved. Each style that is approved is added to the line composed of five groups with three to four styles in each group.

The material, sundries, and trims cost plus the labor cost are totaled to determine the initial cost estimate. Cost is used as a determining factor in the next stage in the style development process.

STYLE SELECTION

Each style in the new line goes through a similar process of development and costing. When all the styles have received the designer's and merchandiser's approval, the line is ready for design review. Because of the lag time in receiving some fabrics, the review garments may have simulated textile elements in order to visualize the style in the intended fabric. Sometimes a print or stripe is painted onto a fabric to simulate the final textile. On occasion, these simulated prototypes are even used for promotional photos as the difference between the mockup and the actual garment will not be apparent in the photograph.

PRESENTING AND REVIEWING THE LINE

On the scheduled calendar date, the new line is presented for review. The merchandiser, designer, assistant designer, production engineer, and any other team members (such as a selected sales representative) assemble for the line review. Upper management may be included in the review session. The individual garment styles may be displayed on walls in the conference room or "war room." Or, fit models may try on the garments to present the styles to the review team.

Figure 7.9
The design team carefully reviews each style in the line. The line that will be shown at market is determined at the final adoption meeting.

Sometimes the designer or merchandiser begins the review session with a presentation. Design presentation boards or concept boards may be included as a part of the presentation, showing fabrics, various colorways, inspirational pictures, and garment sketches. The presentation might include information about the concept or inspiration for the line, about how the styles coordinate or work together, and about the intended customer profiles for various styles within the line. It may be to the designer's advantage to "sell" the styles in the line to the company review team.

Each style in the line is reviewed by the team to determine how well the style works in areas such as:

Cost: Is the estimated cost within the range of the target customer's expectation? Is its cost proportionate to that of other similar styles? Are there changes in design that might reduce the cost? Could less expensive buttons be substituted? For companies that do cost averaging among several similar items (see Chapter 6), is this approach feasible?

Production: Are there any potential difficulties in production? Could anything be changed to make production easier or less expensive? Could a seam be eliminated?

Styling: Does the style fit the "look" of the target market? Or, does the styling look too fashion forward or too conservative when compared with the rest of the line? Could pockets be added if this is important to the customer? Does the style look sufficiently different from competitor's styles?

Fits in Line: Does the style work well with other styles in the line? Is there another style so similar that they will compete against each other? Or, is the style so different from others so that it looks out of place in the line?

Fabric/Trims: Are there potential problems with the fabric? If the fabric is new to the line, will it snag, pill, or wrinkle? Has the fabric been adequately tested? Are there potential problems with lengthy lead time required for a fabric, or high minimum yardage requirements by the textile mill?

Each of these points, as well as others, is discussed by the review team for each of the styles in the line.

SELECTING THE STYLES FOR THE LINE (OR FINAL ADOPTION MEETING)

At the conclusion of the line review, some of the styles will be eliminated and some changes may be required in a few styles. The line is honed to develop a tight group of styles with the hope that all styles will sell well at market.

Occasionally, one or more styles is included in a line that the review team speculates may not sell well to the retail buyers. This may be done for several reasons. With some lines, a "color balance" is needed when showing the line to retail buyers. For example, although windbreakers that are predominately white probably will not sell as well as those that are colored, a line without any white may not look appealing to buyers. So one or several windbreaker styles with white are included to provide a visual balance to the line. Or, a company may want to experiment with a slightly more fashion forward look. The line may include one or two jackets with more updated styling than has been shown in the past to see how the retail buyers react to these styles.

DETERMINING THE FINAL COST

The final cost for each style to be shown in the new line must be determined before showing the line at market. Calculating the cost requires knowledge about production techniques and facilities. Production (or cost) engineers use known costs as well as estimated costs for unknown factors to arrive at the final cost. There is always the possibility that a style will actually cost more than was calculated, or perhaps, less than calculated.

Contractors can be asked to: (1) examine a prototype garment, (2) sew a sample garment, and thus provide a labor cost estimate, or (3) review a complete and detailed spec sheet and provide a firm cost. Establishing as accurate a cost as possible is important to the successful financial outcome of the line. A design that sells well but is underpriced can be a disaster to the apparel company. The amount that is calculated at this time is called the **cost.** This is the manufacturer's cost to produce the goods. The **wholesale price** will be the price shown to the buyers at market and will be the amount that the retail store will pay the apparel company for the goods. The wholesale price includes the manufacturer's profit as well as the funds needed to

Figure 7.10
The production engineer and designer confer regarding the final cost to produce the new style.

TABLE 7-1

Cost to Manufacture a Pair of Cotton Pants

STYLE # 8074

Quantity	Price	Amount	Sub-total
1. Material			
fabric @ 58" 1.7 yd	$ 2.90	$ 4.93	
interfacing .2 yd	$ .55	$ .11	
Total Material Cost			$ 5.04
2. Trim/Sundries			
buttons 1	$ 2.00/gross	$ .02	
zipper 7" 1	$ .13	$ .13	
Total Trim/Sundries Cost			$ .15
3. Labor			
cutting ($75 for 200 units)	$ .38		
sewing labor .5 hour @ $8.00/hr.	$ 4.00		
marking ($45)	$ .23		
grading ($70)	$ .35		
Total Labor Cost			$ 4.96
4. Other			
packaging/hangar, hangtag, labels	$ .15		
freight	$ .35		
duty			
shipping agent, consolidator fees			
Total Other Cost			$ .50
5. Cost to Manufacture		**Total**	**$10.65**

run the business. Some apparel companies double the cost to manufacture to arrive at the wholesale price. Table 7-1 shows an example of the cost to manufacture a pair of cotton pants.

MARKETING

Now that the new line is ready to be shown to retail buyers, additional samples need to be made so that sales representatives throughout the country or world can sell the line by showing samples to retail store buyers. The marketing process involved in selling the line will be discussed in detail in Chapter 8.

Figure 7.11
The line might be shown in a presentation to the company's sales representatives before the line is marketed to retailers.

ORDERING AND MAKING SALES SAMPLES

Each sales representative and/or each market center showroom will require a representative group of styles from the new line to show to the retail store buyers. Because of cost limitations, not every style in every colorway will be made for sales representatives' samples. As soon as the line has been finalized, the styles that will be made as samples to sell the line at market are selected. The quantity of fabric as well as linings, buttons, zippers, and other supplies required for the samples is calculated and ordered. If the textile producer is late in delivering the ordered fabrics, complications in producing the samples, also call **duplicates,** on time may occur. Late arrival of fabric could result in the samples not arriving in time for the sales representatives to show at market.

Contractors or the apparel company's sewing factories cut and sew the sample garments. If any production difficulties arise during this small production run, there is an opportunity to make an adjustment to ensure a smooth run during production of the retailer's goods. Late delivery of samples from the sewing facility could also cause complications at market.

The apparel company may also produce a fashion show and visual presentation of all the company's lines at a special event for the company's sales representatives. The purpose of this showing is to create enthusiasm for the new season's goods and to help the sales force sell the line. The line's designer (and merchandiser) may be responsible for producing the line showing. There might be social events, such as golf or tennis tournaments, with friendly competition along the sales force to support the "company spirit."

LINE BROCHURE OR CATALOG

As soon as the new line has been finalized, a **line brochure** (also called a line sheet) is prepared. This is a catalog, usually with color illustrations, of all the styles available in the line in all or some of the various colorways available for each style. Color photographs of featured styles may also be included. Charts show the sizes and colors available for each style and can serve as order sheets as well. The line brochure is used by sales representatives and buyers to augment the sample garments shown during selling and to use later for reorders from the retailer's store.

Most companies use specialized CAD or graphics software to produce the color illustrations of the garments for the line brochure. The technical capabilities of these computer systems allow the actual fabric prints to be scanned. The print scale can be reduced to coincide with the size of the garment illustration for the line brochure. In addition, a plaid motif on a collar can be adapted so that the plaid contours around the neck shape.

It is important to maintain accurate color rendition between the actual fabric and the printed colors in the line brochure. Retail buyers expect the finished goods to match the colors depicted in the line brochure. In the early years of computer technology, color printers often made accurate color rendition difficult to achieve. New color print technology has improved both in the time needed to prepare accurate color rendition and in the trueness of the color reproduction. Some apparel companies show actual fabric swatches in their line brochures, or send a set of fabric swatches with the brochures. Seeing the actual fabric texture, plaid repeat, or variety of colorways helps sell the line to the retail buyers.

PLACING ORDERS AT MARKET AND CANCELED ORDERS

It is important to keep in mind that not every style that makes it through the review process and is presented in the line to buyers will be produced by the factories. Usually only those styles that have a sufficient number of orders from retail buyers will be produced. At the time the buyer places the order for a specific style, in specified colors and sizes, the order is tentative. Whether or not a specific style in a specific color will be produced is based on the cumulative orders from other retail buyers. The style will be produced only if the minimum number of orders for the style and color is achieved. The minimum number of items required to put a style into production varies according to many factors. Sometimes a minimum order is based on the fabric manufacturer's minimum yardage requirement. Or, the minimum order might be determined by the contractor who will sew the style. In some cases, a minimum of 300 units might be required, while with another company, the minimum order might be 3,000 units.

Thus, retail buyers place orders not knowing for certain if every style they order in the preferred color will be produced. In addition to insufficient orders, another common reason why buyers' orders are canceled is lack of availability of the fabric from the textile manufacturer. The textile company will produce the fabric only if a sufficient number of yards has been ordered by apparel companies. As you can imagine, there is a snowball effect in these related industries. Other reasons for canceled orders can include a variety of production problems, both with the textile manufacturer and with the apparel production facilities. With off-shore production, natural disasters and political crises can be involved in an inability to meet retailers' orders.

When a retailer's order for a style cannot be filled by the apparel company, the retailer may be willing to accept a substitute style or color. Or, the retailer may cancel the order, filling in any gaps in apparel style choices on the retail floor with merchandise from other companies.

TERMS OF AGREEMENT FOR ORDERS

As orders are placed by the retailer for styles in the new line, delivery dates and payment terms are arranged between the apparel company and the retailer. If the apparel company does not meet the delivery date, the apparel company may be required to take a reduced payment for the shipment or the retailer may be allowed to cancel the order. Late delivery may be the result of fabric arriving late from the textile manufacturer, production delays with the contractor, or delays in transportation. With off-shore production and the resultant time needed for communication and transportation, delays can be a problem. An apparel company may have to yield to the much greater cost of air shipment in place of sea transportation to avoid a late penalty and risk losing the business of the retailer.

The apparel company needs to be aware of financial problems facing the retailer, especially in today's marketplace of mergers, takeovers, and bankruptcies. For example, on the eve of a predicted announcement of bankruptcy by a major retailer, the management of a large apparel company faced the decision of whether or not to ship a large order to the retailer. If the retailer remained in business, the late shipment penalty would cost the apparel company substantially. However, if bankruptcy did occur, the apparel company might have lost far more money by shipping the goods. These are difficult management decisions.

COMPUTER APPLICATIONS LINKING DESIGN, STYLE SELECTION, AND MARKETING

The apparel company invests a substantial amount of money in the development of each new style—including making the first pattern, cutting and sewing the prototype, and approving the fit of the prototype before estimating its cost. If an insufficient number of orders for a style is placed at market,

Figure 7.12
A computer aided design system can be used to show buyers styles in a line with simulated images of the fabrics.

the style will not be produced and the money spent on development of the style will have been wasted.

The development of three-dimensional computer technology has provided a fast and cost-effective alternative to the traditional method of product development from pattern to prototype. Using a CAD system, it is possible to "show" a line of apparel in which each style is viewed on a computer screen. The intended fabric color and print of the style will be shown, including fabric folds and shadows, so that it looks like a photograph of an actual prototype. "The fabric is draped over the form, automatically simulating an image so real that it can be used for storyboards, advertisements and catalogs. Most importantly, designers and manufacturers dramatically reduce sample making costs" (Freedman, 1990, p. 12). Although these computer draping systems are expensive, the savings afforded by eliminating the cost to produce prototypes is easily justified (Freedman, 1990).

Retail buyers and sales representatives can view the line and place orders without the manufacturer producing actual prototypes. Pieces of the line can be combined in a video presentation to show a variety of coordinating combinations. Video presentations can be customized for a specific customer. A photograph of the customer's site can be "dubbed" in the background. For example, "One uniform manufacturer uses its CAD system to

Figure 7.13
A catalog page from a video line brochure provides another alternative for the retailer to order styles.

create presentations for buyers that visualize what the uniforms actually will look like in a particular environment" (Gilbert, 1995, p. 49).

Another advantage of computer-generated buying is that key buyers can "forecast" the hot-selling styles.

> A CAD system allows you to illustrate a concept or line without ever making a sample. Let's face it, the name of the game in today's marketplace is Quick Response. By eliminating the sample making process, you can get early numbers from key accounts for use in forecasts, which will greatly reduce lead times and overruns. (Gilbert, 1995, p. 48)

Use of CAD-created presentations for ordering new styles and entire new lines will undoubtedly increase in the future. As more aspects of design, development, and production are computerized and software programs fully integrated, the time savings increases exponentially. The new style can be created by the designer on a three-dimensional CAD system, revised by the design team, shown to buyers (even in remote locations by means of a modem link), and orders placed without the cost of developing a prototype. The newest CAD technology is demonstrated at the Bobbin Show held each September in Atlanta. A viewer wrote about the ModaCAD system shown at the Bobbin Show, "A designer could pull up a style on a system in Los Angeles, and show it to a buyer in New York" (Greco, 1995, p. 68).

Integrated computer systems among computer-generated garment design, pattern, and material utilization have been developed to enhance the entire process of creating a new line. Linking the computer aided design system to the computer integrated manufacturing system provides the maximum cost efficiency, speed, accuracy, and quality. For example, it is possible to predict the efficiency of the fabric usage for a style, and to revise the garment design for a more efficient utilization without going through the pattern-making process. Computer Design Inc. has developed DesignConcept 3D, software designed for the form-fitted apparel market, that allows users to see how changes in two-dimensional and three-dimensional patterns affect material utilization, cutting costs in fabric waste (Greco, 1995). Chapters 9 and 11 discuss computer applications in the pattern development and production processes.

MASS CUSTOMIZATION

The more traditional approaches to developing a design for a target market have been discussed. The pattern is developed based on a company's target customer "standard body." The "standard" size apparel fits some bodies better than others. With the advent of new computer-linked technology, a different type of custom apparel is possible than the custom-made apparel pro-

Figure 7.14
Mass customization is made possible by computer technology.

A sales clerk measures the customer using instructions from a computer as an aid.

The clerk enters the measurements, and adjusts the data based on the customer's reaction to samples.

The final measurements are relayed to a computerized fabric-cutting machine at the factory.

Bar codes are attached to the clothing to track it as it is assembled, washed and prepared for shipment.

duced by personal tailors or dressmakers of the past. The new computer technology, which links the customer at the retail store to the apparel factory, has resulted in **mass customization.** Three-dimensional computerized body imaging is used to "scan" the body dimensions of the customer, or body measurements can be taken with a tape measure.

A modem connects the retailer's computer to the apparel factory's computer. The body dimensions can be translated into specific differences between the "standard" pattern and the customer's needed adjustments. The pattern changes are made by computer calculations, and a customized pattern is plotted. From this pattern, the customized garment is cut and sewn, then shipped to the retailer. The customer may return to the retail store for a final "fitting" for pant hemming and other minor adjustments handled by the retailer before receiving the finished goods.

Another type of customization includes the option of viewing a digitized image of your body in various outfits you have selected in place of trying on clothing in a retailer's fitting room. Once the shopper has selected an outfit from those choices seen on the video screen, the order would be custom cut for the purchaser. While this process is years away, it is a likely prospect in the future. An article in the *Wall Street Journal* (Lee, 1994) described the process:

> Modern clothes are designed to fit mannequins, not imperfectly proportioned humans. Now a research consortium has come up with a device called a body scanner that will allow people to buy clothes that precisely fit.
>
> With this device, a shopper would enter a store, slip into a bodysuit and be measured three-dimensionally from head to toe. Then the customer could select a shirt, pants or a dress from the racks or from digitized images of clothing on a kiosk or television screen. Using the body scan as an electronic paper doll, shoppers could superimpose garments onto their bodies to see how they look. If the customer wants an item, he or she could electronically zap the scan and the order to the manufacturer, which would create a custom-cut garment. The scan could be stored and reused for future purchases. (p. B1)

The Textile/Clothing Technology Corporation, $(TC)^2$, consists of a research team and facility located in Cary, North Carolina (see Chapter 1). It is funded by contributions from the apparel industry and the U.S. government. One of the projects that $(TC)^2$ has been developing since the early 1990s is optical, noncontact measuring technology (Abend, 1992).

The future will include additional adaptations. Perhaps the pattern will be customized and the garment cut and sewn while the customer shops at one of the megamalls, returning a few hours later to collect the finished product. Customization for mass manufacturing may become an apparel production/retail trend.

PRIVATE LABEL AND SPECIFICATION BUYING

We have traced the progress of a style from its creation through its development stages using a model based on the marketing channel traditionally used for brand merchandise in the apparel industry. The apparel company conceives the design, controls manufacturing, and then markets the product to the retailer. The retailer awaits the product, then decides whether or not to purchase the style in anticipation of the retailer's customer desiring the product. A profit is expected at each step of the marketing channel. Traditional manufacturing involves several profit-making steps, including the sewing contractor and the sales representative. The final cost of the product usually reflects the number of profit-making steps.

As the cost of apparel has escalated in recent years, retailers and apparel companies have sought ways to reduce costs and increase their share of the profit. Using off-shore production in countries with lower labor costs is one solution. Another approach is to reduce the number of steps involved in the marketing channel. By reducing the number of profit-making steps, either the cost of the product can be reduced or the profit to the remaining companies can be increased (or both). If a retailer works directly with an apparel company to cocreate a product or a line, the sales representative's position is no longer needed. If a retailer decides to create a product to sell in its retail stores and goes directly to a sewing contractor, the apparel company's services are not needed. These are examples of private label (first example) and specification buying (second example). In today's marketplace, there are various ways in which the creation and development of an apparel line occurs. Table 7-2 shows several examples of possible design-retail relationships of the marketing channel.

PRIVATE LABEL

The British retailer, Marks and Spencer, has been a leader in private label apparel since its merchandise development department was established in the 1930s (Ewing, 1992). Each decade since, more retailers have decided to enter the private label business. "The shift to private label is a matter of money: Stores get a higher profit margin on in-house brands—as much as a third more than on national brands" (Agins, 1994, p. B1). There are other reasons retailers decide to offer private label merchandise. "With factory-outlet malls and off-price stores now flooded with designer clothes and other national brands, department stores are using house brands to present exclusive merchandise and to address the lifestyles and demographics of their customers" (Agins, p. B1). Presenting exclusive merchandise to the customer who wants to associate with the retailer's image is an increasingly important retail trend.

Private label merchandise includes (Bohlinger, 1990):

1. putting the store's label on a slightly changed manufacturer-developed product line,

2. purchasing private label product line from manufacturers who develop and manufacture exclusively for retailers that have private label goods,

TABLE 7-2

Marketing Channels

SCENE ONE: TRADITIONAL MARKETING
Garment carries label of apparel company, e.g., Pendleton

Channel:

Apparel Company	(makes profit)
Pendleton Designer creates line	
Sewing Contractor	(makes profit)
Pendleton writes garment specifications	
Apparel Company's Sales Representative	(makes profit)
Retailer	(makes profit)
Customer	

SCENE TWO: PRIVATE LABEL MARKETING
Garment does not carry label of apparel company, may have label of mass retailer, e.g., Jantzen makes swimsuits for JCPenney with Penney's label

Channel:

Apparel Company	(makes profit)
Jantzen Designer meets with Penney's buyers to plan Penney's line with styling for Penney's customer (fabric usually not same as Jantzen's either)	
Jantzen/Penney's write garment specifications	
Sewing Contractor	(makes profit)
Retailer = JCPenney	(makes profit)
Customer	

e.g., Nike creates apparel lines specifically for Foot Locker, Lady Foot Locker, and Mervyn's that do not carry the Nike label. Cole of California creates swimwear for Lands' End.

(continued)

3. selecting private label goods developed by a resident buying office for their noncompeting member retailers, and

4. developing and manufacturing merchandise under the store's own private label (actually specification buying).

   Some specialty retailers sell 100 percent private label merchandise (e.g., The Gap, The Limited). These are known as retail store brands (see Chapter 4). Most department stores strive toward a balance between national brands and their private label merchandise. For example, Macy's offers a variety of private label lines, such as Charter Club, Morgan Taylor, Christopher Hayes,

Marketing Channels

SCENE THREE: SPECIFICATION BUYING
Garment carries label of retailer, e.g., Macy's apparel has label of Charter Club

Channel:

Sewing Contractor   (makes profit)
   Macy's buyers meet with contractor
   or an agent for contractor,
   e.g., in southeast Asia, to write garment
   specifications for:
   (1) a garment such as a polo shirt in a
   number of specific colors
   (2) a group such as washed silk jacket,
   vest, pants, shorts in specific colors

Retailer = Macy's   (makes profit)

Customer

SCENE FOUR: SPECIFICATION BUYING
Garment carries label of retailer

Channel:

Target
   Staff Designer creates line,
   writes garment specifications

Sewing Contractor   (makes profit)

Retailer = Target   (makes profit)

Customer

and Austin Grey, in addition to the national brands, such as Levi Strauss, Liz Claiborne, Koret, and Pendleton (see Table 7-3). Some retailers link their private label lines to celebrities to enhance the stature of the label and the retail store. Kmart offers a Jaclyn Smith label and Wal-Mart sells a Kathie Lee apparel line. Quality private label products offered at a good price can build and maintain store loyalty and private brand loyalty among customers. According to a retail analyst for Paine Webber, "The current picture shows that the consumer isn't nearly as interested in the label as the price/quality relationship" (Abend, 1995, p. 68). Indeed, "strategic priority for private brands is to drive sales and margins higher; and secondary to provide exclusivity" (Lewis,

TABLE 7-3

Selected Private Labels

STORES	PRIVATE LABELS
Abraham & Straus, The Bon Marché, Sterns, other Federated divisions	Adirondack, Allen Solly, Saville Row
Dayton's, Hudson's, Marshall Field's (division of Dayton Hudson)	Country Shop, Field Gear
JCPenney	Hunt Club, Stafford, The Original Arizona Jean Company, Towncraft, Worthington
Kmart	Jaclyn Smith, Knightsbridge, Saugatuck Dry Goods
Macy's	Aeropostale, Austin Grey, Charter Club, Christopher Hayes, Jennifer Moore, Morgan Taylor, I.N.C.
Mervyn's	Cambridge Classics, Cheetah, Partners, Sprockets
Nordstrom	Hickey Freeman shirts and ties, Norsport, Evergreen, Classiques Entier, Baby N
Saks Fifth Avenue	Real Clothes, The Works
Sears	Carriage Court, Fieldmaster, Freeze Frame, Inner Most Intimates, Mainframe, Max Active, Middlebrook Park
Target	Greatland

1995, p. 16). The private label share of major apparel product categories has grown slightly or remained constant in recent years (see Table 7-4).

According to industry analysts (Lewis, 1995, p. 16), the most appropriate products for private labels are:

■ moderate and entry price-point categories,

■ basic apparel,

■ easy-fit apparel,

■ categories with weak or no competing major brands,

■ products that have a lower presence by manufacturers of brands, and

■ jeans for low risk/ease of entry and a price-point alternative to major brands.

JCPenney launched its Arizona jeans brand in late 1989. Its growth has far surpassed industry executives' forecasts. In the first five years after the

Figure 7.15
The Jaclyn Smith line of apparel offered by Kmart enhances the status of the label and the retailer.

brand's introduction, sales grew to over $500 million. "It ranks among the top 10 best-selling jeans brands across all distribution channels nationwide" ("Private Label," 1996).

The competition between national brands and private label apparel is related to the garment's styling and price. Analysts contend (Lewis, 1995, p.16) that "traditional manufacturer's brands perform better against productivity and marketing measures, while private brands rate better against financial measures." Manufacturer and private brands rate the same on factors such as logistics support, available range of sizes/styles/colors, and on average inventory investment. The styling of basic garment styles, such as polo shirts, shorts, casual pants, and jeans, makes differentiation between a national brand and a private label item difficult to discern. These garments are well suited for private label manufacturing. Another criterion for selecting the type of apparel goods for private label development depends on the fashion cycle. Trying to develop private label merchandise for trendy or high fashion apparel puts the burden of risk of unsold goods at the wane of the fashion cycle on the retailer's shoulders. Less risk to the retailer is involved when goods with "classic" styling and long-term sales potential are produced.

A retail product development model was developed by Gaskill (1992) to identify the processes and the intervening factors that impact the development of private label goods. The development process depicted in the model

TABLE 7-4

Private Label Share of Major Apparel Product Categories

APPAREL CATEGORY	PRIVATE LABEL SHARE
Men's Tops	32%
Men's Bottoms	25%
Boys' Tops	35%
Boys' Bottoms	32%
Women's Tops	36%
Women's Bottoms	36%
Girls' Tops	33%
Girls' Bottoms	36%

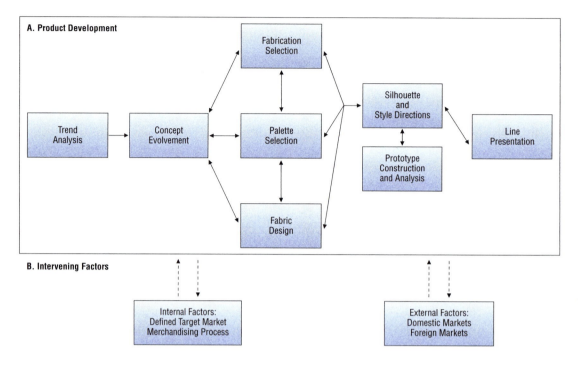

A. Solid arrows indicate the direction and evolvement of product from concept to the final phase of line presentation.
B. Broken arrows indicate the intervening forces which impact upon the development process: merchandising, target markets, and trends (domestic and foreign).

Figure 7.16
The retail product development model identifies the processes and intervening factors that influence the development of private label goods.

is similar to the steps in the design/manufacture/retail process used by most apparel manufacturers. Arrows indicate the direction and evolution of a product during its development. For example, it may move back and forth between style development and fabric selection. The model identifies intervening factors as internal (defined target market and merchandising process) and external (domestic markets and foreign markets). These factors also serve as important variables in the development of nonprivate label apparel products as well.

SPECIFICATION BUYING

The other significant change from the traditional apparel marketing channel focuses on retailer-initiated design-manufacture of apparel goods. Rather than using the apparel company's design and development staff as is done with private label goods, the retailer works directly with sewing contractors (or their agents) to reduce the number of marketing channels, thereby reducing cost and/or increasing profit to the retailer. Thus, the retailer assumes the responsibility of designing the product as well as overseeing its production. The garment specifications are written by the retailer's staff; thus the term "specification buying" was coined. Retail buyers or product developers on the retailer's staff might be responsible for sourcing the production of the goods. Tomorrow's retail buyer may need to be a production expert. "As retailers become more private label-oriented and therefore more production-oriented, they are more frequently staffing offices with product development experts and production managers" ("Tomorrow's buyer," 1988, p. 20). Individuals with expertise in both merchandising management and design may enhance the career options for future professionals in the field.

With the development of the product in the hands of the retailer, the creative possibilities are expanded when compared with traditional private label goods in which knockoffs or classic styles are often produced, according to Bernard Wolford of Kurt Salmon Associates ("Tomorrow's buyer," 1988). Retailers such as Target have a product development staff, including designers, in charge of specification buying.

There are advantages to the retailer in dealing directly with the contractor for production. From the contractor's viewpoint, working directly with the retailer has certain risks. Some of the risks were discussed by the president of Louie Bernard. "These scenarios put a lot of risk on the contractor, which serves as the bank" (Moore, 1995, p. 56). With specification buying, the contractor usually carries the financing for the materials during the production process. After delivery of the goods to the retailer, the contractor is paid for both labor and materials. This is different from the traditional market channel discussed earlier, in which the apparel company often carries the financing of the materials. As these new marketing channels expand and are modified, the advantages, disadvantages, and risks to contractor and retailer may vary as well. One future trend is that some retailers will own their production facilities.

SUMMARY

The design development stage in the progress of a new line begins with the delivery of the designer's sketch. Development of the new style includes making the first pattern using either traditional paper pattern making techniques or computerized PDS. An alternative to relying on a designer's sketch is a draped design, in which the designer creates the new style using fabric pinned directly to a mannequin. This drape is then transferred into a paper pattern.

From the pattern, a prototype is cut and sewn by a sample sewer, using the intended fabric (or a substitute facsimile if the actual fabric is not yet available). The new prototype is tried on a fit model for review of the design and fit by a design team, and revised if necessary. Sometimes several prototypes are sewn in order to perfect the design. The cost for the final design is estimated. The line is reviewed again, at which time each style is scrutinized carefully by the design team. The final line consists of styles that have been approved. Additional samples of styles in the line are sewn for sales representatives, and a line brochure and other types of materials are prepared for marketing purposes.

Computer applications in design development continue to expand. Each year, more apparel companies realize the need to utilize this technology in order to survive in today's marketplace. The computer integration of design, pattern making, and production is another critical step for future survival.

The changing structure of apparel marketing channels will continue to bring changes in the relationship among apparel company, contractor, sales representative, and retailer. Trends in the apparel industry include mass customization, private label, and specification buying.

REFERENCES

Abend, Jules. (1995, June). Private labels, brands square off. *Bobbin*, pp. 66–75.

Abend, Jules. (1992, May). Time is of the essence at $(TC)^2$. *Bobbin*, pp. 24–25.

Agins, Teri. (1994, September 26). Big stores put own labels on best clothes. *Wall Street Journal*, pp. B1–B2.

Belleau, Bonnie, and Didier, Jacqueline. (1989). Computer technology use by Louisiana apparel manufacturers. *Clothing and Textiles Research Journal*, 7 (1), 47–55.

Bohlinger, Maryanne Smith. (1990). *Merchandise Buying* (3rd ed.). Boston: Allyn and Bacon.

Cad users report payback within one year. (1993, September). *Apparel Industry Magazine*, pp. 76–80.

Christmas, Bobbie. (1994, June). Atypical contractor. *Apparel Industry Magazine*, pp. 30–31.

Computer center opens. (1995, May 24). *WWD*, pp. 22–23.

Ewing, Elizabeth. (1992). *History of Twentieth Century Fashion* (3rd ed.). Lanham, MD: Barnes & Noble Books, pp. 137–138.

Freedman, Linda. (1990, April). New developments in computer-aided draping. *Apparel Manufacturer*, pp. 12–14.

Gaskill, LuAnn Ricketts. (1992). Toward a model of retail product development: A case study analysis. *Clothing and Textiles Research Journal*, 10 (4), 17–24.

Gilbert, Laurel. (1995, July). CAD comes of age. *Bobbin*, pp. 48–52.

Greco, Monica (1995, August). CAD intros accommodate multi-systems' integration. *Apparel Industry Magazine*, pp. 64–74.

Kurt Salmon Associates. (1996, January). Soft goods outlook for 1996. *Apparel Industry Magazine*, pp. 46–59.

Lee, Louise. (1994, September 20). Garment scanner could be a perfect fit. *Wall Street Journal*, pp. B1, B6.

Lewis, Robin. (1995, November). What's in a name? Supplement to *Daily News Record*.

Moore, Lila. (1995, April). The two-edged sword. *Apparel Industry Magazine*, pp. 54–60.

Private label jeans mount aggressive attack on market. (1996, February). *Stores*, pp. 68–69.

Tomorrow's buyer: A production expert? (1988, June). *Stores,* p. 20.

Workman, Jane. (1991). Body measurement specifications for fit models as a factor in clothing size variation. *Clothing and Textiles Research Journal, 10* (1), 31–36.

KEY TERMS

brand merchandise	**fit model**
private label	**preliminary line sheet**
manufacturing	**initial cost estimate**
specification buying	**marker**
design development department	**costing marker**
flat pattern	**usage**
block	**target costing**
sloper	**cost**
tagboard	**wholesale price**
Pattern Design Systems (PDS)	**duplicate**
prototype	**line brochure**
sample sewing department	**mass customization**
sample sewer	

DISCUSSION QUESTIONS

1. Discuss how an apparel company interested in converting from paper pattern making to a Pattern Design System might decide what system to purchase.

2. As a merchandiser for an apparel company, what are reasons why you might recommend a style be dropped from the line during a line review session?

3. As a retail buyer, what are advantages to viewing an apparel line on a computer screen as compared with a market showroom?

4. As a retailer, what are some advantages in producing private label merchandise?

5. As an apparel company, what are some advantages in producing a special private label apparel line for a retailer?

6. As a retailer, what are some potential problems in producing apparel by specification buying?

CAREER PROFILES

If you are considering a career in the development area as an assistant designer/pattern maker, cutter or sample sewer or supervisor, or specification technician, what would your job description entail and what are some typical tasks that you would perform?

PATTERN MAKER: SENIOR APPAREL PATTERN MAKER,
Publicly Owned Athletic Shoe and Sportswear Manufacturer

Job Description
Create fit approved and manufacturable pattern from design sketches in a timely manner ensuring design concepts are correctly interpreted and production capabilities are considered. Manage approximately 90 to 150 styles annually from inception through distribution. Provide construction, specification, and fabric utilization expertise for the design and development of apparel.

Typical Tasks
- Draft prototype patterns on CAD/CAM
- Develop preliminary specifications and construction details for sewers and engineers
- Collaborate with design, development, and engineering departments to interpret sketches into cost effective production styles
- Monitor fit sessions, review garments for accuracy of measurements and construction details, revise patterns
- Calculate and provide fabric utilization information throughout the development process
- Oversee the sample making process on assigned styles
- Prepare traced patterns, specifications, construction details, usage and special grading requirements for contractors' samples

What Do You Like Best About Your Job?
The challenge that each season brings of taking new design ideas and creating the new construction methods necessary to reach the end goal of a garment that can be mass produced.

PATTERN MAKER/GRADER, *Publicly Owned Sportswear Company*

Job Description
Interpret designer's sketches into mechanically accurate and manufacturable patterns that fit according to company standards. Translate body measurement standards into growth values and apply to base size patterns for generation of a production size range.

Typical Tasks
- Make swimwear and cover-up patterns on the PDS system, including grading, creating production file, print style report
- Write construction specification sheets
- Process carryover styles and perform necessary research to make sure the best retro pattern is used and the fabric, etc., is compatible with the new style
- Attend team meetings to communicate with other workers

What Do You Like About Your Job?
The challenge of trying to develop some of the more difficult patterns, the people, and the communication.

SPECIFICATION BUYER, *Large Mail Order and Shoe and Sportswear Manufacturer and Retailer*

Job Description

This position is responsible for assisting the product engineer in the documentation of all sample reviews and the follow-up communication to vendors relating to specification development, product evaluation, and control of specification files.

Typical Tasks

- Responsible for fit reviews
- Create specification packages (bill of materials, construction, size specs)
- Sketch front and back details of garments
- Read electronic mail from product engineer and domestic and overseas vendors
- Tag, log, and track all incoming samples
- Perform engineer's tasks when needed
- Complete counter sample reviews and preproduction reviews

What Do You Like Best About Your Job?

I enjoy communicating with so many people, such as team-product engineers, product managers, product developers, and domestic and overseas vendors.

SAMPLEROOM SUPERVISOR, *Publicly Owned Sportswear and Athletic Shoe Company*

Job Description

Ensure sample sewing room functions smoothly, sewing is completed, garments constructed and embroidery finished in a timely manner, correctly, and to quality standards. Supervise staff of 12 to 20.

Typical Tasks

- Select, train, and develop the sample room staff
- Manage workflow of more than 400 styles per season, requiring three to seven prototypes per style
- Oversee production of garments
- Organize and deliver line list orders
- Solve problems related to pattern requirements, construction, and fabric
- Coordinate work of contractors, screenprinter, and embroiderers
- Act as liaison between sewers and pattern makers. Communicate with engineers, developers, and pattern makers to solve construction and quality problems and to improve sample making process

What Do You Like Best About Your Job?

Working in research, design, and development. I work in a very creative atmosphere with very talented people.

Step 1: Research

Step 2: Design

Step 3: Design Development and Style Selection

Step 4: Marketing the Line

Order Fabrics for Sales Samples (Duplicates)

Order Duplicates for Sales Samples

Final Costing

Sales Representatives Show Line at Market

Retail Buyers Place Orders

Step 5: Preproduction

Step 6: Sourcing

Step 7: Apparel Production

Step 8: Distribution

8

Marketing an Apparel Line

Objectives

▮ To summarize the marketing process within apparel companies.

▮ To describe the history, function, and activities of U.S. apparel market centers, marts, market weeks, and trade shows.

▮ To examine the selling function of apparel companies, specifically the role of sales representatives and showrooms.

▮ To outline the distribution and sales promotion strategies used by apparel companies.

THE ROLE OF MARKETING

AS DISCUSSED IN Chapters 4 and 5, the term **marketing** is used to describe the process of:

1. Identifying the target market, and
2. Developing the marketing mix. This includes developing

   ▮ the product or service,

   ▮ the company's pricing strategy,

   ▮ the company's promotional strategy, and

   ▮ the company's place strategy (where the products are to be sold).

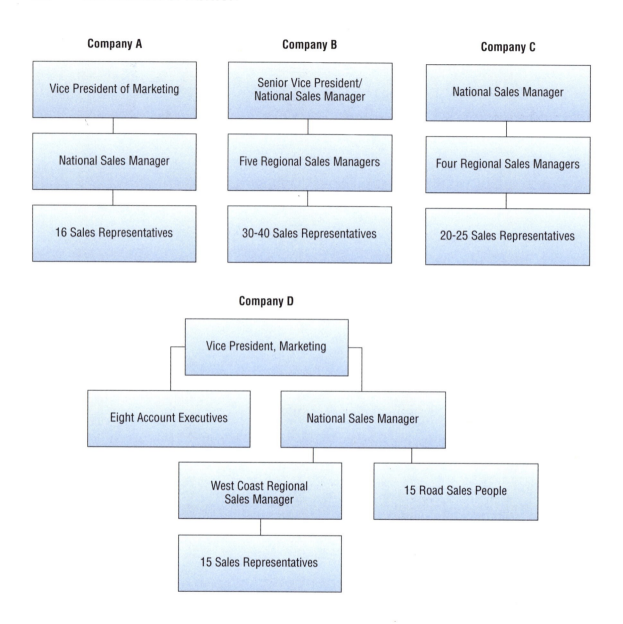

Figure 8.1
Examples of Marketing Division organizational structures.

Because most apparel companies approach their business from this marketing orientation, the marketing process has been a part of all stages of line development, from research through production. Using this marketing approach, successful apparel companies have accurately identified and assessed the wants and needs of their target market and produced goods that meet the needs of these consumers. Now the manufacturer must make sure the product gets to the target customer.

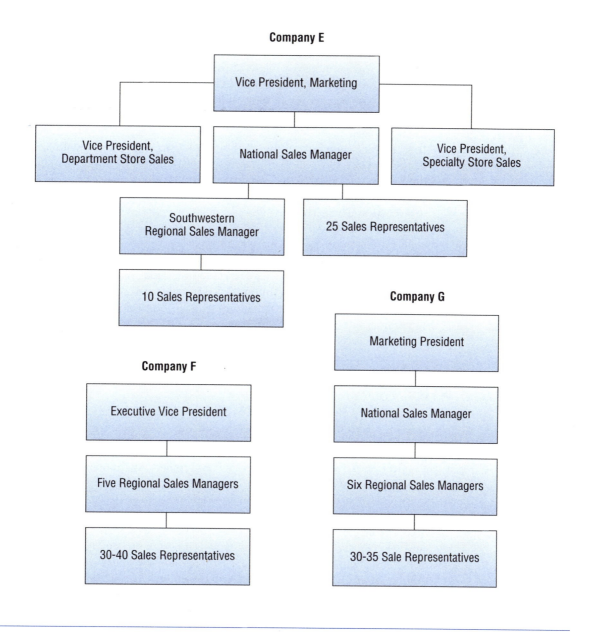

Within the organizational structure of an apparel company, the area called "marketing" typically focuses on developing sales, promotion, and distribution strategies (see Chapter 4). Marketing divisions or departments in apparel companies are organized in a number of ways depending on the size and goals of the company. Figure 8-1 shows a variety of organizational structures for marketing divisions of apparel companies. Although the marketing area of an apparel company is most often associated with promotion and sales of the products, it should be noted that without an accurate under-standing of the target market and without designing and producing goods and services that meet the needs of the target market, even the best of pro-motional strategies will undoubtedly fail. Thus the marketing of apparel products connects the research conducted previously with the appropriate strategies for getting the product to the consumers at the right price and in the right place.

The term **market** can be used in several ways. One may say that a par-ticular product has a market, meaning that there is consumer demand for the product. Chapter 5 discussed research used in assessing the consumer demand or market for a product. The term market can also be used to refer to a location where the buying and selling of merchandise takes place. For example, retail buyers often talk about going to market to purchase mer-chandise for their stores. One can also market a product, meaning that the product will be promoted through the media and public relations efforts. This chapter examines apparel markets as locations where apparel compa-nies sell their merchandise to retailers. It also explores the distribution and promotional strategies that apparel companies use in marketing their goods to retailers and consumers.

MARKET CENTERS, MARTS, MARKET WEEKS, AND TRADE SHOWS

GROWTH OF MARKET CENTERS AND MARTS

Historically, New York was the first market center in the United States. Buy-ers from large, up-scale stores would travel to New York once or twice a year to view the new apparel lines and purchase merchandise for their stores. In addition, manufacturers' salespeople would travel from town to town within a specific region inviting buyers from local stores to see the lines in a hotel room or in the retailers' stores. With the growth of apparel manufacturing and retailing in the 1950s, regional market centers were beginning to be estab-lished. In the early 1960s, the first regional apparel marts were built. Cur-rently, any city where apparel marts and showrooms are located can be viewed as a market for apparel lines. The term **market center** is sometimes used to refer to those cities that not only house marts and showrooms, but also have important manufacturing and retailing industries. In the United States, these cities include New York, Los Angeles, Dallas, Atlanta, and Chicago.

MARTS. A **mart** is a building or group of buildings that house showrooms in which sales representatives show apparel lines to retail buyers. Most major cities have marts (except for New York); some are devoted entirely to apparel, accessories, and related goods (e.g., Los Angeles' CaliforniaMart); some also house showrooms for a variety of types of products (e.g., Portland, Oregon's Montgomery Park). Figure 8-2 shows the location and names of the major

1. **Atlanta**
   Atlanta Apparel Mart
   at the Atlanta Market Center
   250 Spring Street, NW
   Atlanta, GA 30303
   (404) 220-3000

2. **Birmingham**
   Birmingham Apparel Mart
   at the Birmingham Jefferson Civic Center
   One Civic Center Plaza
   Birmingham, AL 35203
   (203) 871-3305

3. **Boston**
   Bayside Merchandise Mart
   at the Bayside Expo Center
   150-160 Mt. Vernon Street
   Boston, MA 02125
   (617) 825-4040

4. **Charlotte**
   Charlotte International Trade Center
   200 North College Street
   Charlotte, NC 28202
   (704) 335-9100

5. **Chicago**
   Chicago Apparel Center
   350 North Orleans Street
   Chicago, IL 60654
   (312) 527-7777

6. **Dallas**
   International Apparel Mart
   International Menswear Mart
   2300 Stemmons Freeway
   Dallas, TX 75258
   (214) 879-8300
   http://the-center.synapse-group.com/
   dmc@the-center.synapse-group.com

7. **Denver**
   Denver Merchandise Mart
   451 East 58th Avenue
   Denver, CO 80216
   (303) 292-6278

8. **Kansas City**
   Kansas City Market Center
   1775 Universal Avenue
   Kansas City, MO 64120
   (816) 241-6200

9. **Los Angeles**
   California Mart
   110 East Ninth Street
   Los Angeles, CA 90079
   (213) 620-0260

10. **Miami**
    Miami International Merchandise Mart
    777 NW 72nd Avenue
    Miami, FL 33126
    (305) 261-2900

11. **Minneapolis**
    Minneapolis Apparel Market
    Hyatt Merchandise Mart
    1300 Nicolette Mall
    Suite 4052
    Minneapolis, MN 55403
    (612) 333-5219

12. **New York**
    Fashion Center Headquarters
    249 West 39th Street
    New York, NY 10018
    (212) 764-9600

13. **Pittsburgh**
    Pittsburgh Expo Mart
    105 Mall Boulevard
    Monroeville, PA 15146
    (412) 856-8100

14. **Portland**
    Portland Apparel Mart
    Montgomery Park
    2701 NW Vaughn Street
    Portland, OR 97210
    (503) 228-7275

15. **Seattle**
    Seattle International Trade Center
    2601 Elliot Avenue
    Seattle, WA 98121
    (206) 223-6819

16. **San Francisco**
    The Fashion Center
    699 Eighth Street
    San Francisco, CA 94103
    (415) 864-1561

Figure 8.2
U.S. apparel markets and marts.

market centers and regional marts in the United States. All marts also include exhibition halls that are used during **market weeks** (primary times during the year in which lines are shown to retail buyers) for temporary showrooms for apparel companies or sales representatives who do not have permanent showrooms at that mart. To facilitate the buyers' trips to market, apparel marts publish directories for market weeks that list the apparel lines being offered, sales representatives, and services available at the mart.

RETAIL RELATIONS PROGRAMS. After experiencing growth throughout the 1980s, most apparel marts have seen business stabilize. Some have even seen it decline in the 1990s. As a result, greater competition has led marts to increase efforts to attract buyers through various services designed to make the buyer's job easier. For example, in response to shorter turn around times and faster delivery of apparel and because buyers are purchasing less merchandise more often, the larger marts are open year round; typically five days a week, 52 weeks a year. This allows buyers to come at any time during the year, not just during market weeks.

Most marts currently have on-going retail relations programs, including a number of services designed to assist retail buyers. These services include educational seminars (e.g., visual merchandising, new merchandising strategies), fashion shows, trunk shows, credit and financing assistance, discounts on travel expenses, and entertainment (e.g., concerts, food fairs). In recent years, a number of marts have offered seminars focusing on international markets. Topics include how to do business in Mexico, labeling requirements for exporting goods, and other issues surrounding exporting.

Although the growth of apparel marts outside of New York was primarily due to the need for regional market centers, the larger apparel marts (e.g., CaliforniaMart in Los Angeles, International Apparel Mart in Dallas) have become more than regional centers that cater to store buyers in the local area and from surrounding states. Because of their expanded services, they are now considered national and international resources; many marts are working to attract international buyers from Mexico, Canada, Central and South America, Asia, and Europe. In fact, CaliforniaMart now offers onsite Spanish-English interpretation services free to its tenants.

Marts are sometimes viewed as self-contained in that they generally house consultants' offices, restaurants, banks, hotels, auditoria, health clubs, and other services for retail buyers. Marts may also be involved in many aspects of the apparel industry. For example, the CaliforniaMart includes offices of major trade publications, consumer publications, buying offices, trade associations, and textile manufacturers. Thus, when a buyer comes to market, the mart serves as a one-stop location for all of their needs.

MARKET WEEKS AND TRADE SHOWS

MARKET WEEKS. Market weeks are the times of the year in which retail buyers come to showrooms or exhibit halls to see the seasonal fashion lines.

During market weeks, retail buyers review many manufacturers' lines and purchase merchandise for their stores. They typically come to market weeks with a specific amount they can spend (referred to as "open-to-buy") for specific categories of merchandise. Marts generally sponsor a variety of market weeks throughout the year, each focusing on a particular product category (e.g., women's, juniors, men's, children's, bridal, swimwear, etc.) and fashion season (e.g., spring, summer, resort, fall, holiday). Market weeks may also be sponsored in conjunction with an industry trade association. For example, recently the CaliforniaMart juniors and contemporary spring market week was held in conjunction with the International Swimwear/Activewear Market's (ISAM) swimwear show and the Big Blu Jeanswear show. Through these joint efforts, buyers are exposed to a greater variety of apparel manufacturers at a single location. Table 8-1 outlines the typical months in which U.S. women's and children's ready-to-wear market weeks are held for each fashion season.

Market weeks provide advantages for both the apparel manufacturer and the retailer. For the apparel manufacturer, sales representatives can show the new lines to a large number of retail buyers in a very short period of time. They can talk with the buyers and acquire information regarding retail trends. Based on buyer interest, they also can determine which pieces in the line will eventually be put into production. In addition, through such market week activities as fashion shows, apparel companies can receive publicity for their lines. For retailer buyers, market weeks allow them to review a large number of apparel lines in a very short period of time. By attending seminars held during market weeks, they are also able to acquire information about fashion trends, advertising, visual merchandising, and a number of other topics. In addition, buyers can also become aware of new lines that they may want to purchase for their stores. Thus market weeks are important times for the apparel companies in determining the success of their lines.

TRADE SHOWS. Some trade associations or trade show producers sponsor their own shows for the purpose of promoting lines of apparel or accessories. These **trade shows,** lasting anywhere from three to eight days, are

TABLE 8-1

Market Week Dates

FASHION SEASON	MARKET WEEKS
Summer	January
Fall I	NY: February to March, All others: March to April
Fall II	NY: April to May, All others: June
Resort	August
Spring	October to November

Figure 8.3
Through the use of temporary showrooms, trade shows provide opportunities for companies to show their lines to retail buyers.

typically located at large hotels or convention centers. For example, the Accessories Circuit, Fashion Footwear Association of New York, and Fashion Coterie trade shows are often held at New York's Plaza Hotel; the Ladies Apparel Show Vegas (LAS Vegas) and the Children's Trade Expo Vegas (CTE Vegas) are both held at the Sands Hotel Expo and Convention Center in Las Vegas. New York's Jacob K. Javits Convention Center is the home of trade shows such as the New York Premier Collections, International Fashion Boutique Show, International Fashion Fabric Exhibition, and the International Fashion Kids Show. The Las Vegas Convention Center has been a growing hub for a number of trade shows, including the Men's Apparel Guild in California (MAGIC) Show which moved from Los Angeles for larger quarters and the women's counterpart, WWD/MAGIC. Some companies rely heavily on trade shows for showing their lines; others show their lines primarily during market weeks in New York and/or apparel marts and may attend only one or two trade shows. Table 8-2 lists typical market weeks and trade show dates.

U.S. MARKET CENTERS

NEW YORK CITY

New York City (NYC) is considered the preeminent U.S. market center for apparel and accessories. As noted in Chapter 1, NYC has a long history and tradition of being the heart of apparel manufacturing and marketing in the

Figure 8.4
The Men's Apparel Guild in California (MAGIC) is a cosponsor of Women's MAGIC, a trade show of women's apparel and accessories.

United States. Interestingly enough, NYC is the only U.S. market center that does not have an apparel mart. Instead, showrooms are located throughout a portion of Manhattan known as the "garment district," the "garment center," or what NYC refers to as the "fashion center." NYC's fashion center is an area in mid-town Manhattan located between Fifth Avenue and Ninth Avenue and between 35th Street and 41st Street. The central point is Seventh Avenue (designated as "Fashion Avenue" in 1972) and Broadway. The fashion center started as a manufacturing center, but the cost of space in the city has turned it into a designing, marketing, and sales center. Much of the manufacturing now occurs in nearby locations outside of Manhattan where costs are lower. However, even today New York State remains one of the largest apparel manufacturing centers in the United States.

Currently the fashion center includes approximately 450 buildings with fashion industry tenants and more than 4,500 showrooms and factories. It is estimated that 22,000 out-of-town buyers visit the fashion center every year. For companies who also have their design headquarters in NYC, showrooms are often in the same building—if not on the same floor—as the design area. Although NYC is the home of marketing efforts for a wide variety of companies, the NYC market is best known for women's apparel and for designer

TABLE 8-2

Market Week and Trade Show Calendar
(Note: months may vary slightly from year to year)

JANUARY

U.S.

New York RTW market (summer)	NYC
RTW markets (summer)	LA, Dallas, Chicago, Atlanta, etc.
NY Accessory Market Week	NYC
NY Intimate Apparel Market weeks	NYC
NAMSB Show	NYC
International Fashion Boutique Show (RTW)	NYC
International Kids Fashion Show	NYC
Fashion Accessories Exposition (or February)	NYC
Accessorie Circuit trade show (accessories)	NYC
Los Angeles International Textile Show	LA

International

Haute Couture Collections (spring)	Paris
Designer Men's Collections	Paris
Alta Moda Roma (couture) Collections (spring)	Rome
Hong Kong Fashion Week	Hong Kong
Tokyo Fashion Week	Tokyo

FEBRUARY

U.S.

New York RTW market (fall I) into March	NYC
New York Premier Collections (fall I) trade show	NYC
International Swimwear/Activewear Market (ISAM)	LA
Super Show (sportswear)	Atlanta
Action Sports Retailer Show	San Diego
MAGIC International trade show	Las Vegas
WWD/MAGIC	Las Vegas
Fashion Footwear Association of New York (FFANY)	NYC
Fashion Coterie trade show	NYC
Take Off (Interstoff)	Frankfurt

MARCH

U.S.

New York RTW market (fall II) into April	NYC
RTW markets (fall I) into April	LA, Dallas, Chicago, Atlanta, etc.

NY Accessory Market Week	NYC
NY Intimate Apparel Market Week	NYC
NAMSB show	NYC
International Fashion Boutique Show	NYC
International Kids Fashion Show	NYC
International Fashion Fabrics Exhibition (spring/summer)	NYC

International

Premiere Vision (fabrics, spring/summer)	Paris
Ideacomo (fabrics, spring/summer) or April	Lake Como
Interstoff World (fabrics)	Frankfurt

APRIL

U.S.

Bridal Market Weeks	NYC, Chicago, Atlanta
Texitalia (fabrics, spring/summer)	NYC
Los Angeles Textile Show (fabrics, spring/summer)	LA

International

Interstoff Season (fabrics, spring/summer)	Frankfurt
Interstoff Asia (fabrics)	Hong Kong
Igedo (RTW)	Dusseldorf

MAY

U.S.

NY Accessory Market Week	NYC
NY Intimate Apparel Market Week	NYC
Fashion Accessories Expo	NYC
Accessorie Circuit (accessories) trade show	NYC

JUNE

U.S.

RTW markets (fall II)	LA, Dallas, Chicago, Atlanta, etc.
International Fashion Boutique Show	NYC
NAMSB Show	NYC

JULY

U.S.

International Swimwear/Activewear Market (ISAM)	LA

(continued)

TABLE 8-2 (continued)

International

Haute Couture collections (fall/winter)	Paris
Mens' Designer collections	Paris
Alta Moda Roma (couture) collections (fall/winter)	Rome
Hong Kong Fashion Week	Hong Kong
Tokyo Fashion Week	Tokyo

AUGUST

U.S.

NY RTW market (resort)	NYC
RTW markets (resort)	LA, Dallas, Chicago, Atlanta, etc.
NY Accessory Market Week	NYC
NY Intimate Apparel Market Week	NYC
Accessorie Circuit (accessories) trade show	NYC
FFANY (shoes)	NYC
Fashion Accessories Expo	NYC
International Kids Fashion Show	NYC
International Fashion Boutique Show	NYC
WWD/MAGIC (or September)	Las Vegas
Action Sport Retailer Show	San Diego

International

Igedo (RTW)	Dusseldorf

SEPTEMBER

U.S.

Ladies Apparel Show Vegas	Las Vegas
MAGIC International	Las Vegas
NY Premier Collections	NYC

and bridge price zones. Virtually all name designers (e.g., Calvin Klein, Donna Karan, Ralph Lauren, Isaac Mizrahi, etc.) have offices in New York and sponsor extravagant runway shows during NYC market weeks. In recent years many designers have held their runway shows in tents in Bryant Park as part of "7th on Sixth," a show organized by the Council of Fashion Designers of America.

In an effort to facilitate buyers' trips to NYC, certain buildings have tried to specialize in specific apparel categories. For example, 1411 Broadway houses many swimwear manufacturers. However, despite some attempts to specialize buildings, NYC, in general, is not very convenient for retail buyers who must go from building to building to visit showrooms dur-

Fashion Coterie trade show	NYC
The Bobbin Show (sewn products industry)	Atlanta

International

Interstoff World (fabrics, fall/winter)	Frankfurt

OCTOBER

U.S.

NY RTW market (spring) into November	NYC
RTW markets (spring) into November	LA, Dallas, Chicago, Atlanta, etc.
NY Intimate Apparel Market Week	NYC
NY Accessory Market Week	NYC
International Swimwear/Activewear Market (ISAM)	LA
International Fashion Boutique Show	NYC
International Kids Fashion Show	NYC
International Fashion Fabric Exhibition (fall/winter)	NYC
Los Angeles International Textile Show (fall/winter)	LA

International

Premiere Vision (fabrics, fall/winter)	Paris
Interstoff (fabrics, fall/winter)	Frankfurt
Ideacomo (fabrics, fall/winter)	Lake Como

NOVEMBER

U.S.

Texitalia (fabrics, fall/winter)	NYC

DECEMBER

No major market weeks or trade shows

ing their buying trips. Resources for accessories, for example, are spread throughout the garment district, adding to the inconvenience. Thus in comparing the NYC market with the "regional" apparel marts, NYC is often viewed as less personal and more overwhelming. To add greater convenience for retail buyers, the Fashion Center Business Improvement District (FCBID), funded by property owners devoted to the garment industry, was created to provide additional services and capital improvements to enhance the fashion center. FCBID has developed maps with buildings color-coded according to primary industry use and has hired sanitation and security crews to help clean up the area and provide for a safer environment.

Figure 8.5
New York City's Fashion Center, located in mid-town Manhattan, is the home of thousands of showrooms and factories.

Given the fact that the city is expensive, crowded, and inconvenient, why does NYC continue to serve as an important market center? In addition to its historic foundation as a fashion center, NYC offers companies access to fabric suppliers, consultants, advertising agencies, offices of major trade associations, and publishing companies located in the city. As a cultural center, designers can draw inspiration from the continuous influx of art, theater, dance, opera, and other cultural events. They can also view historic costume and textile collections at the Metropolitan Museum of Art and the Fashion Institute of Technology. In addition, because so many companies have showrooms in NYC, the NYC market remains a "must attend" for many buyers regardless of whether they attend market weeks elsewhere.

LOS ANGELES

Whereas NYC is considered the primary market center on the east coast, Los Angeles (LA) is considered the primary market center on the west coast. LA is home to the CaliforniaMart, which opened in 1964 with 700 permanent showrooms. Its 13 floors currently house more than 1,500 showrooms

Figure 8.6
Los Angeles is the site of the CaliforniaMart, the largest apparel mart on the west coast.

representing 10,000 lines. The New Mart, across the street from the CaliforniaMart, provides additional space and has showrooms for many designer and contemporary resources. The menswear building is home to the California International Menswear Market (CIMM). As a result of a recent $14 million remodeling, the CaliforniaMart has become one of the most technologically advanced of the market centers. It includes a videoconference center, satellite broadcasting studio, and automated faxback system by which buyers and retailers can receive the most current CaliforniaMart information automatically on their own fax machines. The CaliforniaMart caters to retail buyers primarily in the western and southwestern states (e.g., Arizona, New Mexico, Nevada, Utah, Oregon, Washington, and Idaho), but is attracting a greater number of international buyers.

LA also has a large apparel manufacturing industry. This is primarily because of the availability of skilled workers, typically immigrants from Mexico. When we think of California, casual apparel and sportswear come to mind; LA is best known for sportswear and swimwear manufacturing. Companies with headquarters in the LA area include Authentic Fitness, Catalina, Ocean Pacific, Guess?, Inc., Carole Little, Quiksilver, LA Gear, and Z-Wear, to name a few.

CHICAGO

The Chicago Apparel Center caters primarily to the northern and mid-western region of the United States (e.g., Illinois, North Dakota, South Dakota, Minnesota, Michigan, Indiana, Wisconsin, and Iowa). Built in 1977, the Apparel Center is located next to the Chicago Merchandise Mart. During market weeks, the Apparel Center's 140,000 square foot Expo Center can accommodate 500 booths from temporary vendors. Some consider the

Figure 8.7
The Chicago Apparel Center is the largest apparel mart in the northern and mid-western region of the United States.

Apparel Center's bridal market, which now includes an entire floor consisting of more than 60 manufacturers, to be second only to New York's. Chicago is also home to historically significant manufacturers and retailers. The headquarters for Sara Lee Corporation (owner of L'eggs and Hanes), and Hartmarx, a prominent manufacturer of men's wear as well as women's apparel, are in Chicago. Retail institutions such as Sears Roebuck & Co. and Montgomery Ward, are also headquartered in Chicago.

DALLAS

In the south, Dallas has become the key apparel market center. The International Apparel Mart and International Menswear Mart (formerly the Dallas Apparel Mart/Menswear Mart) is part of the Dallas Market Center Complex, which includes other merchandise marts (i.e., The World Trade Center, Trade Mart). The Dallas Apparel Mart opened in 1964 and the Menswear Mart opened in 1982. Currently, the International Apparel Mart and International Menswear Mart houses approximately 1,100 permanent showrooms (1.8 million sq. ft in the apparel mart and 400,000 sq. ft. in the adjacent men's apparel mart). Both permanent and temporary showrooms offer retail buyers more than 14,000 manufacturers' lines. The International Apparel Mart and International Menswear Mart cater not only to retail buyers from Texas, Arkansas, Oklahoma, and Louisiana, but also attract buyers from Mexico and Central America. Dallas is sometimes viewed as a fashion barometer in that what sells at the International Apparel Mart and International Menswear Mart is typically what is going to sell across the country. In fact, some New York companies use Dallas as a test market for new lines.

Figure 8.8
The Atlanta Apparel
Mart's fashion theater
is used for promotional
events.

ATLANTA

The Atlanta Apparel Mart is part of the Atlanta Market Center, which also includes the Merchandise Mart (opened in 1961) and the Gift Mart (opened in 1992). The Apparel Mart opened in 1979 with seven floors. In 1989, the Apparel Mart expanded to 15 floors including a large fashion theater. It has the capacity to house 2,000 showrooms and 11,000 apparel and accessory lines, including more than 800 children's wear lines. Because NYC does not have a mart, the Atlanta Apparel Mart is the largest mart on the east coast, catering primarily to states in the east and southeast (e.g., Georgia, South Carolina, North Carolina, Florida, Alabama, Mississippi, Tennessee, Kentucky, and Virginia). In the early 1990s the mart, hard-hit by the recession, consolidated and reorganized the women's wear showrooms and transformed the lower floors to the International Sports Plaza which was linked to the 1996 Olympic Games held in Atlanta. With the passage of the North American Free Trade Agreement (NAFTA), the Atlanta Mart has also seen a growth in the number of international buyers attending the mart.

OTHER REGIONAL MARKETS

In addition to these market centers, smaller regional marts also exist in many U.S. cities. Although these marts cater to a more localized clientele, with the increase in turn-around and the fact that retail buyers are buying less merchandise more often, they have grown in importance. The most prominent of these regional marts are in Miami, San Francisco, and Seattle.

MIAMI. The Miami International Merchandise Mart contains more than 500 showrooms. Known for sportswear and children's wear, growth in Miami's apparel industry was a result of Cuban immigration in the 1960s. During the 1980s, Miami saw change and increased growth in its apparel industry because of the arrival of off-shore production, particularly production in Caribbean Basin countries. As will be discussed in Chapter 10, in "807" and "807A" production, goods cut in the United States can be sewn in other countries (to take advantage of lower wages) and tariffs are applied only to the value added to the goods. Because of Miami's proximity to many low-wage production centers in Central and South America as well as the Caribbean, Miami has attracted a number of apparel manufacturers who produce off shore.

SAN FRANCISCO. In 1981 the San Francisco Apparel Mart was built to cater to northern Californian retailers. Although San Francisco had a thriving fashion industry, the San Francisco Apparel Mart failed because of a lack of marketing support for its tenants. Then in 1990, the Fashion Center in San Francisco was built and catered to northern California and the Pacific Northwest, as well as to Nevada and Utah. The Fashion Center was sold in 1996. San Francisco is the third largest apparel manufacturing center in the United States, after New York and Los Angeles. Many large companies have headquarters in San Francisco, including Levi Strauss, Esprit de Corp, Jessica McClintock, and Koret of California.

SEATTLE. The Seattle International Trade Center, which opened in 1977, is an important regional mart for buyers in Washington, Oregon, Idaho, Montana, Alaska, and British Columbia. Seattle is famous for its men's and young men's sportswear and outerwear manufacturers. In the late 1970s, Seattle was the home to Brittania Sportswear, then the largest privately owned sportswear manufacturer in the United States, with annual sales of $300 million. In Brittania's wake came a second generation of sportswear companies that achieved success in the 1980s, including Seattle Pacific Industries (Union Bay, Re-union), Generra, Code Bleu, Heet, Only Stuff, Bench, M'otto, b.u.m. equipment, Shah Safari, and Sahara Club. Proximity to Asian contractors is an advantage for Seattle companies that import. With the inclusion of established outdoor wear companies, such as Eddie Bauer and Recreational Equipment Incorporated (R.E.I.), and successful retailers, such as Nordstrom, Seattle has gained prominence in the fashion industry.

Seattle is also known for its preline showings held prior to the Men's Apparel Guild in California (MAGIC) Show. This marketing activity began when Brittania starting showing lines to a few buyers prior to market weeks. Since then, the preline tradition has grown and now includes organized showings by most Seattle manufacturers.

OTHER MARTS. Marts can be found in a number of other cities, including Birmingham, Boston, Charlotte, Denver, Kansas City, Minneapolis, Pittsburgh, and Portland, Oregon. These general merchandise marts typically house permanent showrooms for a variety of merchandise, only some of which may be devoted to apparel and accessories. These marts sponsor apparel market weeks relying on traveling sales representatives who set up temporary showroom booths. These markets cater to buyers within a fairly small region (primarily within a 250 mile radius of the mart). However, for these buyers, attending a regional market is much less costly and time consuming than traveling to a larger apparel mart or to NYC. In addition, even for buyers who attend other markets, they may attend these regional markets to supplement their stock between major market weeks.

THE SELLING FUNCTION

The selling function of apparel companies is handled in one of two ways: through the use of **corporate selling** or through the use of **sales representatives** and **showrooms.** With private label merchandise (i.e., private label brands and store brands) this "selling" stage is by-passed entirely. This is because merchandise is designed and produced for a particular retailer.

CORPORATE SELLING

Most apparel companies rely on sales representatives to perform the selling function, but a few rely on corporate selling. Corporate selling is typically used by some companies that manufacture designer price zone merchandise and sell to a limited number of retailers. For example, designer Zoran sells to a only a few retailers in New York City. Corporate selling is also used by very large companies that sell moderately priced merchandise to large corporate retailers. In these cases, selling is often done through their corporate headquarters without the use of sales representatives or showrooms.

SALES REPRESENTATIVES AND SHOWROOMS

The sales representative or "sales rep" is the individual who serves as the intermediary between the apparel manufacturer and the retailer, selling the apparel line to retail buyers. Other names for sales representatives are vendor representative, account executive, and manufacturer's representative.

Showrooms are the room(s) used by sales representatives to show samples of an apparel line to retail buyers. Depending on the size of the company, showrooms can be elaborately decorated or very simple in design. They always include display racks for the apparel samples and tables and chairs for the retail buyers.

Showrooms can be either permanent or temporary. Permanent showrooms are located in buildings in NYC's fashion center, in apparel marts, in buildings adjacent to marts, or as part of a company's headquarters or production facilities. During market weeks, temporary showrooms or booths are set up by companies or sales representatives who do not work out of a permanent showroom. Some sales reps always use temporary showroom/booth space during market weeks. Some companies will use temporary showroom/booth space to "test the water" in a new region during a market week without having to commit to a sales rep or the mart on a permanent basis. Although using temporary space can provide companies with a feel for the mart and the sales opportunities, there are also disadvantages. Because buyers are looking for a customer service orientation from sales reps, they may need greater assurance of continued service from reps who do not have a permanent showroom.

TYPES OF SALES REPRESENTATIVES AND SHOWROOMS. One of the most important decisions made by apparel marketers is whether to open an exclusive corporate showroom with company sales representatives or to use established independent **multiline sales representatives.** The primary difference between the two is that company sales reps work for a particular company and are housed in corporate showrooms owned by the company; independent multiline sales reps work for themselves and typically represent lines from several different, noncompeting but related, companies. For example, a multiline sales rep may offer a variety of noncompeting children's wear lines from several companies. In addition, this sales rep may also represent lines of children's toys and nursery accessories. Both company and multiline sales reps are assigned and work in a geographic territory **(regional sales territory)** which may be quite large (e.g., the West) or quite small (e.g., northern California) depending on the company and product line.

Figure 8.9
Sales representatives are typically assigned to a regional territory. Russell Athletic has four regions plus Canada.

To Contact the Athletic Sales Representatives in Your Region, Call				
RUSSELL ATHLETIC SOUTH 770-979-3750	**RUSSELL ATHLETIC NORTHEAST** 410-859-4944	**RUSSELL ATHLETIC MIDWEST** 614-890-1622	**RUSSELL ATHLETIC WEST** 702-359-1800	**CANADA** 519-448-1381
3250 Highway 124 P.O. Box 989 Snellville, GA 30278	Baltimore Commons Business Park 7464 New Ridge Road Suite 4 - Box 348 Hanover, MD 21076-3101	623C Park Meadow Westerville, OH 43081-2876	545 Coney Island Drive Sparks, NV 89431-6158 P.O. Box 1650 89432-1650	HD Brown Enterprises 23 Beverly Street, E. St. George, Ontario Canada NOEINO

The main criteria used in deciding whether to use a corporate show-room or multiline sales rep are the type of product line and the amount of business the company is expecting to do. The **corporate showroom** is appropriate for companies with large sales volume in a particular region of the country. For some marts, it is recommended that the company should be capable of producing at least $1 million in sales at the mart in order to support a corporate showroom. Corporate showrooms are managed by company sales representatives who represent the lines of only that company. (It should be noted that because company sales reps generally represent large companies, most are based in a showroom). Company sales reps may work on salary plus commission or on a straight commission basis, depending on the sales philosophy of the company. If the company pays the sales rep's expenses, which is often the case for company sales reps, then commission is lower than if expenses are not paid. In addition to managing the showroom, company sales reps may travel to other mart's market weeks and trade shows and may also visit retail accounts. Road travel is most typical for lines in the moderate price zone. For this type of merchandise, apparel manufacturers can often get sample lines to the sales rep prior to market weeks, allowing the sales rep to travel to accounts and sell outside of market weeks. Because of the costs associated with producing samples of designer and bridge lines, companies that produce these lines may only have one or two sample lines per season. Thus the sample line may travel from one city to another for their market weeks.

Corporate showrooms have advantages and disadvantages. With a corporate showroom, the staff can devote 100 percent of its time to the company's line(s) and the company's customers. In addition, the showroom can better portray the company's image and style of merchandise to retail buyers. However, a corporate showroom is an expensive investment. Space is leased from the mart and leases should be evaluated in terms of services offered (e.g., janitorial services, utilities, mart-sponsored promotional activities, directory listings), as they can vary from mart to mart.

Rather than opening a corporate showroom, many companies choose to go with an independent multiline sales representative. Multiline sales representatives typically work for small manufacturers who cannot afford or do not want to hire their own sales representatives. The multiline sales rep works on straight commission, typically 5 to 10 percent of the wholesale price of goods that are shipped by the company. This means that if the company ships $100,000 (wholesale) in goods sold by the sales rep, the sales rep would receive 5 to 10 percent of this amount ($5,000 to $10,000) as payment. Independent multiline sales reps must pay all of their own expenses, including the cost of leasing and furnishing showrooms (if they have one), travel expenses to market weeks or to visit retailers, and in some cases, to purchase the samples of the lines from the manufacturer.

For smaller companies, using an independent multiline sales representative can have several advantages. The main advantage is that no initial capital investment in the showroom is needed. In addition, established sales

TABLE 8-3

Comparisons Between Corporate Showrooms and Multiline Sales Representatives

	ADVANTAGES FOR THE MANUFACTURER	DISADVANTAGES FOR THE MANUFACTURER
Corporate Showroom	▌ control over image of showroom possible ▌ staff can devote 100% of time to line	▌ capital investment necessary ▌ lease agreements might vary from mart to mart
Multiline Sales Representative	▌ no initial capital investments needed ▌ established reps know local accounts ▌ buyers are exposed to related, but noncompeting, lines in the same showroom	▌ in addition to commission, there may be other promotional expenses ▌ determining right fit between sales rep and line might be difficult ▌ rep might not devote adequate time to the line ▌ lack of control over image of the showroom

reps are typically familiar with local accounts and can promote the line with buyers. Although the initial costs of going with an independent rep are less than with opening a corporate showroom, additional expenses to be expected include fees for market week activities, cooperative advertising expenses, costs for hospitality service, and fashion shows. Some companies will begin with an independent rep and then, as they grow, move into their own corporate showroom.

Finding the right fit between the product line and the sales representative is important to both the apparel company and the sales rep. Companies want to find a rep who has access to the types of retailers appropriate for the product line. Independent multiline sales reps should not represent competing lines. The company must be assured that the sales rep will spend the appropriate amount of time in promoting their line(s). Another consideration is whether the sales rep is needed to travel to different retail accounts prior to market weeks. Table 8-3 compares the advantages and disadvantages of corporate showrooms and multiline sales representatives.

JOB FUNCTIONS OF THE SALES REPRESENTATIVE. The sales representative (whether a company sales rep or an independent multiline sales rep) performs a number of job functions, including selling activities, selling support activities, and nonselling activities (Howerton & Summers, 1988). The most obvious of the functions that sales representatives perform are the *selling functions*. These include:

Figure 8.10

Top: In addition to selling merchandise to retail buyers, sales representatives also manage showrooms or trade booths.

Bottom: Temporary showrooms or booths are often set up during market weeks to show lines to retail buyers.

- showing lines to retail buyers and demonstrating product features,
- negotiating terms of sale, and
- writing orders for merchandise.

In negotiating the terms of sale, the sales representative and retail buyer will focus on several areas including:

- delivery time—how fast can the goods be delivered.
- guarantees related to whether styles ordered will, in fact, be produced.
- reorder capabilities and timing of the reorders. This is especially important for basic merchandise such as jeans or hosiery where continuous inventory is essential for optimum sales.

- cooperative advertising allowances—will the manufacturer or retailer help pay for advertising?
- discounts if bills are paid within a certain period of time.
- discounts if a certain quantity is purchased.
- markdown allowances—is any credit given on goods that had to be marked down?
- availability of promotional tools such as gift-with-purchase promotions or displays.

Sales representatives also perform a number of activities that *support and expand the selling function.* These include:

- advising retail buyers regarding trends in consumer behavior,
- providing retailers with product and merchandising information,
- training buyers and/or salespeople to promote and advertise the merchandise,
- ordering and reordering merchandise for retailers to guarantee sufficient inventory,
- dealing with complaints from retail customers regarding merchandise orders, and
- promoting customer relations.

In addition, sales representatives perform many *nonselling activities* including:

- making travel arrangements,
- writing reports for the company and keeping books of account,
- attending sales meetings,
- participating in market week activities, such as fashion shows, and
- attending to showroom or trade booth management and maintenance.

Although the career paths of sales representatives vary greatly, many sales representatives have retail buying experience before becoming a sales representative. With this background, they understand the retail buying process and can address the needs of retail buyers.

MARKETING STRATEGIES

DISTRIBUTION POLICIES

The primary goal of a company's distribution policies is to make sure the merchandise is sold to stores that cater to the target market audience for whom the merchandise was designed and manufactured. Thus it is important for apparel marketers to identify store characteristics and geographic areas that will optimize the availability of the merchandise to the target customers. For example, a manufacturer of designer-priced men's suits may identify specialty stores in areas whose residents have above average incomes as its primary retail customer. A manufacturer of moderate-priced women's sportswear, on the other hand, may identify department stores as its primary retail customer. Once these basic criteria are established, apparel marketers must next decide on the company's policy regarding merchandise distribution. In general, there are two basic distribution policies:

- **open distribution policy** in which the apparel company will sell to any retailer who meets the basic characteristics and
- **selected distribution policy** in which apparel companies establish more detailed criteria that stores must meet in order for them to carry the apparel company's merchandise. Typically the criteria focus on expected sales volume, geographic area, and store image. For example, some apparel companies will only sell their merchandise to one or two retailers within a certain geographic region; others will only sell to retailers that portray an image that is consistent with the merchandise; others will only sell to retail accounts that can purchase a certain amount of merchandise.

Based on these decisions, apparel marketers focus on retail accounts that are consistent with their distribution policy. Distribution strategies will be further discussed in Chapter 12.

INTERNATIONAL MARKETING

As U.S. companies expand their businesses to include foreign markets, it is important to review the ways in which apparel is marketed internationally. There are four basic ways of marketing internationally (Ellis, 1995, p. 10):

1. Direct sales—selling directly to foreign retailers through independent or company sales representatives.
2. Selling through agents—in some cases U.S. apparel companies prefer to use international agents to handle the selling function in other countries. These agents have expertise in market demand, import/export issues, and international currency issues. Therefore, they can facilitate the establishment and processing of international accounts.
3. Selling through exclusive distribution agreements—in some cases U.S. apparel companies have established agreements with specific international retailers for the exclusive distribution of the apparel line.
4. Marketing through foreign licensees in a specific country or region—in these cases, licensing arrangements with foreign companies facilitates the marketing of the goods internationally.

SALES/PROMOTION STRATEGIES

Apparel companies essentially have two groups of customers who need to know about their lines: retailers and consumers. Thus sales promotion strate-

LITTLE WHITE SUIT

LIZ CLAIBORNE COLLECTION

The ultimate simplicity. Fitted short jacket, $168.
Shell at here skirt, $88. In linen/rayon, 4–14. Selected stores.

ROBINSONS-MAY AND LIZ CLAIBORNE INVITE YOU TO PARTICIPATE
IN THE 3RD ANNUAL REVLON RUN/WALK FOR WOMEN

Join the Liz apparel brands and receive a center by participating in the
RUN/WALK for Women on Saturday, May 11 at the Greystone Hills
Recreation Center across the street from Fox Studios in West Los
Angeles. Registration forms available at all Los Angeles County
Robinsons-May stores in the Liz Claiborne department.

REVLON
RUN/WALK
FOR WOMEN

ORDER ANY TIME TOLL FREE 1-800-633-1224

ROBINSONS·MAY

Figure 8.11
Coop advertisements
are often used to connect
a brand name with a
retailer in consumers'
minds.

gies developed by apparel companies will focus on both of these customers. Apparel companies use a number of promotional strategies to let retailers and consumers know about their merchandise. Decisions regarding promotional strategies are based on the company's advertising budget, characteristics of its target market, characteristics of the product line, and area of distribution. Promotional strategies include publicity, advertising, and other promotional tools made available to retailers.

ADVERTISING. Through paid **advertising**, apparel companies buy space or time in the print or broadcast media to promote their lines to retailers and consumers. Although some large companies may have "in-house" advertising departments, most companies hire advertising firms to develop campaigns for them. Large companies that manufacture name brand or designer merchandise (e.g., NIKE, Ralph Lauren, Calvin Klein) can spend millions of dollars per year on advertising. Companies can also share the cost of the advertisement with a retailer, trade association, or another manufacturer through **cooperative or "coop" advertising.** For example, an apparel company and retailers may share the cost of an advertisement that features both the merchandise and the retailer. The specific print and broadcast media used in advertising campaigns depends upon the advertising budget, target audience, product line, and company image. For example, a company may rely on advertisements in trade publications, such as *Women's Wear Daily* or *Daily News Record,* when targeting retailers. When targeting consumers, a designer such as Donna Karan or Calvin Klein may focus on slick print advertisements in fashion magazines; a company that manufactures national brand name merchandise such as Russell, Levi's, or NIKE may use television ads to reach a wide audience.

PUBLICITY. Although the effect of **publicity** is the same as advertising (to promote lines to retailers and to consumers), unlike advertising, publicity is not controlled by the marketer. With publicity, the company or the company's line is viewed as "newsworthy" and thus receives coverage in the print media or on television or radio. For example, press coverage of designers' runway shows often results in news stories and photographs or videos of the designers' collections in trade (e.g., WWD) or consumer newspapers, magazines, or on television. Sometimes the company will create news by sending out news releases about its company or lines. The primary advantage of publicity to the apparel company is that the company does not have to pay the

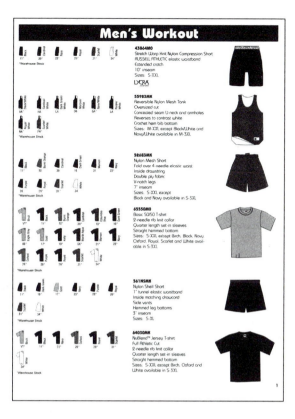

Figure 8.12
The line brochure or catalog shows all of the styles, sizes, and colors available for a line. Sales representatives and retail buyers use the line brochure to place orders.

media source for including information about the company. The primary disadvantage of publicity is that the company has little control over how the company or its merchandise will be portrayed.

OTHER PROMOTIONAL TOOLS. A number of other tools are provided by apparel companies to promote their lines to retailers and to consumers. These include:

▪ *Catalogs and line brochures or line sheets.* Catalogs and line brochures or line sheets provide important information about the line to retail buyers. They include photographs or drawings of the items in the line along with style numbers, sizing information, colors (some may even include fabric swatches), and information regarding ordering procedures and guidelines.

▪ *Direct mail inserts.* As a form of cooperative advertising, manufacturers may provide promotional inserts to be included with retail store mailings (e.g., credit card bills).

▪ *Visual merchandising tools.* A variety of visual merchandising tools may be provided by apparel companies. These can range from posters and signs to

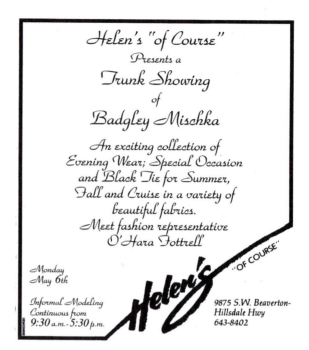

Figure 8.13
Trunk shows are used to promote apparel lines to prospective customers.

setting up actual in-store shops and providing all the necessary fixtures (e.g., Ralph Lauren in-store shops).

▌ *Trunk shows.* Typically, a retail buyer will not purchase a company's entire line for their store. Through the use of **trunk shows,** a representative from the company (or the designer him/herself) will bring the entire line to a store. Customers invited to attend the showing can purchase or order any piece of the line whether or not it will be carried by the store. Designers often make appearances at their trunk shows to promote their collections. Trunk shows can benefit retailers, consumers, and the manufacturers. For retailers, trunk shows provide an opportunity to offer an exclusive service to their customers. They also provide feedback from their customers about their tastes and preferences. Customers benefit because they have access to the full line of merchandise. Manufacturers use trunk shows to promote not only their lines, but also to get reactions of consumers to their merchandise.

▌ *Videos.* Manufacturers may provide videos for use by retailers in training their sales associates about the line or in promoting the line to consumers. For example, videos may be used to demonstrate visual displays, to demonstrate product usage, or to give fashion or styling information.

▌ *Merchandise representatives.* A growing trend is the use of "specialists," "merchandisers," or "sales executives," who are either paid partly by the apparel company and partly by the retailer or entirely by the apparel company, but work in the retail store(s). These individuals are located in one store or may travel to various stores within a region. Their role is to educate the retail sales staff and consumers about the merchandise, to demonstrate display procedures, and to get feedback from the retailers and consumers for the apparel company.

- *Press kits.* Photographs, press releases, television or radio spots, and other information are sometimes provided by manufacturers for publicity purposes or for retailers to use in advertisements.

SUMMARY

The marketing of apparel products connects market research with the appropriate strategies for getting the right product to the target consumers at the right time, at the right price, and in the right place. Markets for apparel lines can be any city where apparel marts and showrooms are located. Market centers (New York City, Los Angeles, Dallas, Chicago, and Atlanta) are large markets with important manufacturing and retailing industries. All U.S. market centers, except New York City, have an apparel mart that houses showrooms and exhibition halls used during market weeks. Marts can also be found in a number of other cities throughout the United States. In New York City, showrooms are located in buildings throughout the fashion center in midtown Manhattan. During specific times of the year, known as market weeks, buyers come to apparel markets to purchase merchandise for their stores. They may also attend trade shows sponsored by apparel marts or trade associations.

The selling function of apparel companies is handled either through corporate selling or through sales representatives who work out of permanent or temporary showrooms. Sales representatives serve as the liaison between the manufacturer and retailer. Some sales representatives work from a corporate showroom and focus on the line(s) of one company; others are multiline sales reps, representing lines from a number of related but noncompeting lines. The job of sales representatives includes both selling as well as nonselling functions.

Apparel marketers will develop distribution and promotional strategies for their company. In general, there are two basic distribution policies: open distribution and selected distribution. These policies help determine which retail customers will be the focus of selling efforts. Sales promotion strategies of apparel companies are directed to both retail customers and consumers. Strategies may include advertising, publicity, and other promotional tools.

REFERENCES

Cedrone, Lisa. (1991, December). Moving in on the marts. *Bobbin*, pp. 75–80.

Corwin, J. Blade (1989, March). What it takes (& pays) to sell. *Bobbin*, pp. 76–82.

Ellis, Kristi. (1995, October). U.S. firms look overseas. *WWD*, p. 10.

Foxenberger, Barbara. (1994, April). West coast harbors apparel niches. *Apparel Industry Magazine,* pp. 18–26.

Friedman, Arthur (1994, August 3). FCBID building a better SA. *WWD,* pp. 20–21.

Howerton, Renee, and Summers, Teresa A. (1988, Spring). Apparel sales representatives: Perceptions of their roles and functions. *FIT Review, 4* (2), 10–18.

Lytle, Lisa. (1990, October). The west side story. *Earnshaw's Review,* pp. 99–106.

Mart to mart. (1993, March 8). *California Apparel News,* pp. 28–34.

Smarr, Susan L. (1988, April). Seattle: Supersonic sportswear star. *Bobbin,* pp. 75–78.

KEY TERMS

marketing	**multiline sales representative**
market	**regional sales territory**
market center	**corporate showroom**
mart	**open distribution policy**
market week	**selected distribution policy**
trade show	**advertising**
corporate selling	**cooperative (or coop) advertising**
sales representative	**publicity**
showroom	**trunk show**

DISCUSSION QUESTIONS

1. Interview a retail buyer in your community. Document the type of retailer (e.g., specialty store, department store) and the type of merchandise offered (e.g., children's wear, men's wear). Ask the buyer which markets or trade shows he/she attends and why? Bring the results from your interview to class and compare your findings with those of your classmates. Are there any patterns in market attendance related to geographic area, type of retailer, or type of merchandise?

2. Find two examples of "coop" print advertisements in either a trade publication or a consumer publication (e.g., fashion magazine). For each advertisement, analyze what companies/associations joined forces in the advertisement. What are the advantages and disadvantages for the companies in using coop ads as part of their promotional strategy?

CAREER PROFILE

The marketing of apparel has career opportunities for individuals who manage apparel marts, organizers of market weeks and apparel trade shows, sales representatives, and those involved with such promotional activities as advertising and public relations. For these careers, an understanding of the marketing process, product knowledge, creativity, organizational skills, analytic skills, and negotiation skills are important.

FIELD SALES REPRESENTATIVE, *Designer Hosiery Company*

Job Description
Sell basic stock and seasonal merchandise to the hosiery buyers for major department stores and specialty stores within a specific region; service the accounts that carry the merchandise within the sales territory.

Typical Tasks
- Do six-month merchandise plans in retail and cost dollars
- Write orders
- Obtain buyers' approvals for orders
- Visit store accounts
- Talk to sales associates about the merchandise
- Entertain buyers and divisional merchandise managers
- Make sure goods are shipped as planned
- Keep in close contact with buyers and report on status of orders
- Plan and help with store promotions
- Analyze sales (do spreadsheets of sell-throughs and stock-to-sales ratios and stock-turns for each stock-keeping unit by store)
- Plan model stocks (13 week supply) based on sales analysis (basic stock fill-in orders or automatic reorders are based on the model stock plans)
- Hire and supervise merchandisers who also visit store accounts and conduct inventories

What Do You Like Best About Your Job?
It is like running your own business. I can work out of my home. Although there is travel involved, the advantage is that I am not tied to a desk; I can visit stores and see the region. The hours and money are better than in some positions in retail.

Other
Sales representatives typically have experience in retail (especially experience in retail buying) before moving into sales. College degrees are also important.

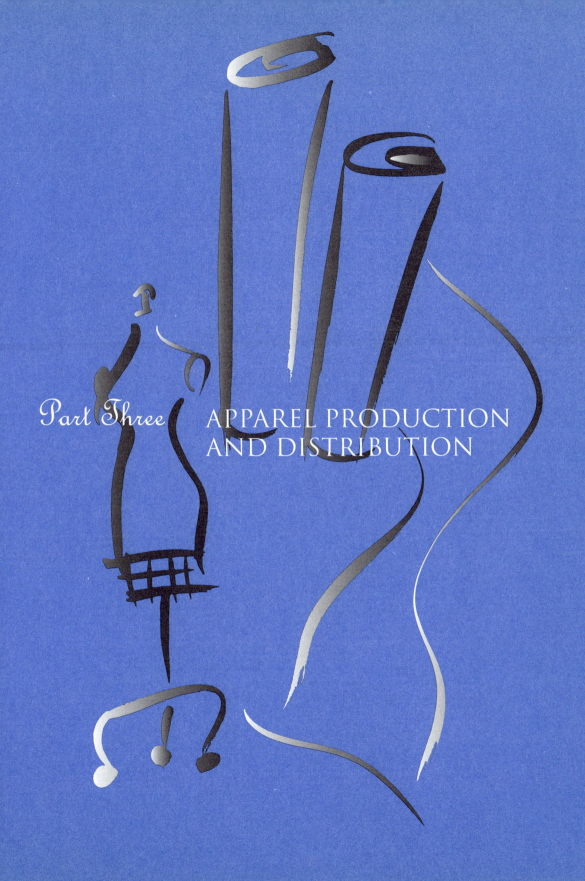

Part Three APPAREL PRODUCTION AND DISTRIBUTION

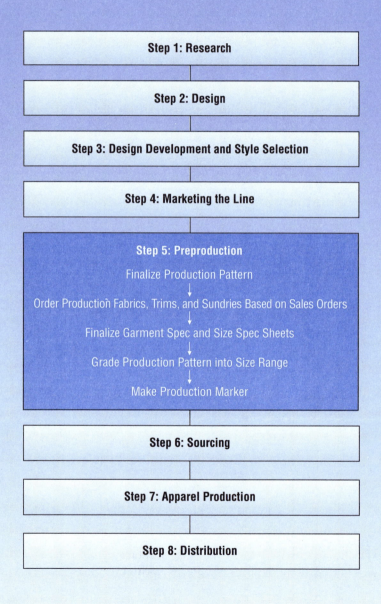

Step 1: Research

Step 2: Design

Step 3: Design Development and Style Selection

Step 4: Marketing the Line

Step 5: Preproduction

Finalize Production Pattern

Order Production Fabrics, Trims, and Sundries Based on Sales Orders

Finalize Garment Spec and Size Spec Sheets

Grade Production Pattern into Size Range

Make Production Marker

Step 6: Sourcing

Step 7: Apparel Production

Step 8: Distribution

9

Preproduction Processes

Objectives

▌ To describe the process and timing used by apparel companies to order production fabrics and trims.

▌ To discuss the importance of color control in ordering production fabrics and trims.

▌ To describe the stages used to finalize a production pattern, grade the pattern, and create a production marker.

▌ To describe some of the factors influencing pattern grading, including grade rules, the size range and styling cost considerations, and grading processes.

▌ To discuss advantages to the apparel company of computer grading and marker making compared with other grading methods.

PRODUCTION ORDERS

THE SALES FORCE has shown the new line to retailers during market weeks and the retail buyers have placed their orders with the apparel company. As discussed in Chapter 7, it is only those styles in specific colors and sizes that meet the company's required minimum that will continue in the develop-

245

ment process. Usually, styles that do not attain the minimum number of orders will be dropped from the line. Sometimes after a week or two of selling the line, a manufacturer will decide to drop a style that is not selling well. For the style we are following through the development process, let us imagine that a sufficient number of orders has been placed for the style in specified colors and sizes to warrant a production run of the style.

FACTORING

Apparel manufacturers, contractors, and retailers need to have the financial means established for a credit line or cash advance to "buy" in advance of the season in which payment is received. While traditional bank loans may be a possibility, the nature of the apparel business deters some banks from loaning money. Another financing system is used in the apparel industry. The term for the financial arrangements used in the apparel business is called **factoring.** Factoring is "the business of purchasing and collecting accounts receivable or of advancing cash on the basis of accounts receivable" (Young, 1996, p. 1).

Factoring firms are the companies that manage the accounts receivable in the apparel industry. The apparel business has a distinct financial risk factor. Mergers and bankruptcies in the entire fiber-textile-apparel-retail complex in the 1980s caused the consolidation of factoring firms. Though only a few firms remain, the competition for business is intense, resulting in lower rates than in the 1980s. However, the interest rates tend to be higher than a regular bank loan or line of credit.

Before production can begin, the financial arrangements must be approved by the company's factoring firm. The textile producer checks the apparel manufacturer's credit, and the apparel manufacturer checks the retailer's credit. After approval of credit, production can proceed. Some manufacturers will decide to take an account on their own, without the factor's approval. In this situation, the manufacturer carries the financial risk.

CUT ORDERS

When either (a) a targeted number of orders for a style has been placed by retailers and received by the manufacturer, or (b) the apparel manufacturer decides to produce a style prior to receiving orders, a production cut order is issued. The cut order specifies the number of items in each color and each size that will be included in the production run. The cut order will include the date when the goods must be delivered to each retailer. Thus, the production schedule is calculated from end to beginning, that is, from the retailer's delivery date backwards to the date when production of the goods must be finished to the date production must begin to the date when the fabrics, trims, and sundries must be ordered.

ORDERING PRODUCTION FABRICS, TRIMS, AND SUNDRIES

In the ideal situation, the apparel company would wait until the majority of retail buyers had placed their orders before ordering the large quantity of fabrics from the textile producers (for example, a production run might require 6,000 yards of fabric), as well as the trims and sundries (findings or notions) for all the styles in the new line. In such a situation, there would be no financial risk of ordering fabric that would not be needed. Similarly, other apparel companies would also wait to order fabrics until they knew exactly how much of each fabric in their lines would be needed. The textile producer, not wanting to risk manufacturing excess fabric, would also wait until the apparel companies had ordered fabric before beginning to produce production yardage. Thus, in this situation, the apparel company would have to wait weeks, or even months, for the production yardage to arrive at the sewing facility. Producing the apparel goods would probably take several more weeks. As you can imagine, these cumulative delays would be so lengthy that the retailers would not receive the goods at the peak selling time.

In reality, few apparel companies can afford to wait until all or nearly all of the buyers' orders are placed before ordering fabric for the line. Therefore, apparel companies use a variety of means to determine how much yardage to order and when to order the yardage from the textile producers. These methods include:

- early production of proven sellers in basic colors,
- the use of pre-line selling,
- the use of early-season lines to predict sales,
- the use of test markets, and
- the use of past sales figures.

Some companies will project production estimates of some of the more "staple" styles and colors, especially if these are carryovers from a previous season. Some colors are known to sell especially well. For example, a skiwear manufacturer knows that black or navy blue ski pants will sell well every year. Therefore, they may decide to begin production early on several styles of "proven sellers" in these basic colors. Early production also allows the company to maintain a constant production flow in order to avoid times when the factories are overcommitted.

Pre-line selling occurs after the prototype styles are completed but before any sales samples have been produced. Key retail accounts may be invited by the apparel manufacturer to preview the line of prototypes and place orders. The retailers involved in preselling account for a sizeable portion of the total sales for the line and may represent a large geographic area. Therefore their opinions are valued. Advantages to the manufacturer include (a) knowing which styles will sell well, so that fabrics may be ordered early, (b) maintaining a strong working relationship with key retail accounts, and (c) receiving feedback from retailers about styles that might sell better if changes were made. A disadvantage, though, is that the style has not been produced in the factory and therefore unknown factors may require a later change in the style. Pre-line selling helps companies forecast demand for products and thus maintain a "competitive edge." The company can be ready with an adequate quantity of anticipated successful products and avoid producing poor-selling styles.

Swimwear companies might use an early-season line to help predict which styles will sell well. An early January line of swimsuits sold in resorts in Florida could be used to help forecast production of the spring line to be introduced to northern climates in April. Some of the hot-selling styles from Florida retail sales could be put into production for the main selling season before the line is sold at market to retailers in the other areas. Sometimes a specific region is targeted as a "test market" for a new line, in which a small production run of the new line will be placed in key stores. Occasionally, an apparel company has its own store, in which sales help forecast production quantities.

Past sales figures and the opinions of leading sales representatives and leading retail buyers might be used to determine which styles and colors might go into early production. Using as much information as possible as early as possible, production yardage, trims, and sundries are ordered from the various **vendors** (also called **sources** or **suppliers**) of textiles, textile converters, trims, and sundries. Many variables influence the selection of vendors. Lead time needed to secure the goods is one consideration. Other factors include past history of on-time delivery, the quality of goods, whether the vendor participates in Quick Response, the minimum yardage or quantity of an order, and the financial stability of a vendor. Some manufacturers will review bids from various vendors as part of the decision process. A review of the Bobbin Show in Atlanta described a computer software program: "with built-in cost analysis and international sourcing and dual language capabilities, KARAT™'s software allows a user to easily develop cost comparisons for intelligent design and sourcing decisions" ("Bobbin show," 1995, p. 60). Clearly, many factors are important considerations in the selection of vendors.

Not all printed fabrics are printed by the textile mills that produce the fabrics. Sometimes the fabric is printed by a textile converter to the specific textile design requested by the apparel manufacturer (see Chapters 3 and 6). The apparel company works with textile converters as well as textile mills. The fabric might be purchased from the textile mill, then sent to a textile converter to print the fabric before arriving at the cutting facility. This situation requires careful scheduling to ensure that the printed fabric is ready on time.

As discussed in Chapter 6, most fashion fabrics are selected during the design phase of the process. The design team has viewed samples at textile trade shows and textile showrooms. Original artwork for a textile design might have been purchased to be used to create a print fabric to the specifications of the apparel company. These fabrics require substantial lead time for orders and therefore occur early in the design/production process. Other

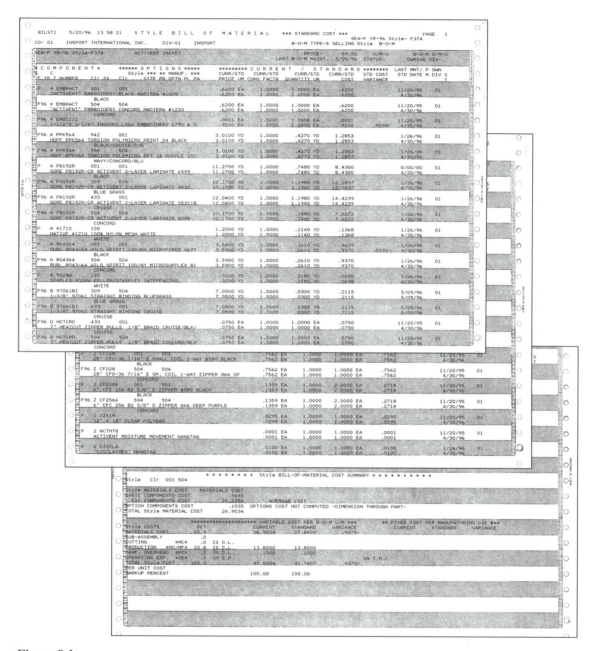

Figure 9.1
The bill of material is used to order and track all components. Some garment styles require an extensive number of fabrics and trims.

staple fabrics, such as linings and interfacings, as well as some fashion goods, such as cotton poplin and broadcloth and wool crepe and jersey in staple colors or piece-dyed textiles, can be purchased closer to production. Fabric sourcing for these types of staple goods might be very suitable for computer on-line sourcing. Textile producers are incorporating on-line technology that uses several automated sourcing services. The apparel manufacturer can view and order textiles using custom searches (Greco, 1996). For goods already produced and awaiting shipment at the textile producer, on-line sourcing is a viable option because it allows late-cycle ordering, which has advantages to the apparel manufacturer.

COLOR CONTROL

Chapter 7 discussed the requirement that the prototype accurately match the color as it will be shown in the line brochure. It is also important that the color of the production garments match the prototype as shown to retail buyers. **Color control** is a term used to describe the color matching requirement. Staff in the design development department might be responsible for working with the textile, trims, and sundries producers to maintain exact color matching of all components in each style and to ensure that all products in the entire production run maintain the specified color match. Color matching may begin at the prototype stage, if a textile is to be dyed to match a color chip or swatch provided by the apparel company. If available, the specially dyed sample goods are used to make the prototype. Trim, sundries, and production yardage will be ordered to match the prototype color.

It is important to the consumer, and thus to the retailer and the apparel producer, that colors remain consistent throughout all the components that are used to make a style. First, the color of the body of the style needs to match the color intended by the design team. This could require that the textile producer submit multiple test samples until the "perfect" color is achieved. The trims and sundries such as buttons, zippers, and thread must match the body color. If the color of the rib knit used for the sleeve band of a rugby shirt is not the same shade as the body of the shirt, the consumer may quite likely decide not to purchase the item. Thus, when contractors supply the trims and sundries for the products they make, it is important that they receive approval of the color match from the apparel company. For contractor-provided matched goods, the term **commercial match** might be used to describe an acceptable color match.

All pieces of an outfit, and those styles that are to coordinate in a line, need to match exactly. Mismatching can occur if strict color control is not maintained. Even with adherence to color control, various dye lots of a specific fabric may not match exactly. Therefore, it is important to code all fabric bolts with the dye lot number, and to maintain accuracy in matching dye lots throughout the production and distribution process. Often an apparel company uses one sewing contractor for the suit pants production and another for the suit jacket. Each contractor receives a shipment of "matching" fabric from the textile producer. If dye lots are not matched, the suit pants might be a slightly difference shade from the suit jacket. This discrepancy may not be noticed until the goods arrive at the apparel company's distribution center, the retailer's distribution center, or the retail selling floor, where the sale may be lost.

LAB DIP

To ensure that color matching will be as perfect as possible, the source (textile vendor or supplier) will supply a sample of the product in the color requested. The sample is called a **lab dip,** because it usually means that the fabric swatch (or button) has been dipped in a specifically prepared dye bath in the "lab." Each fabric, trim, and sundry that is to match the season's color choice will require approval on a form supplied by the apparel company. Sources (textile vendors or suppliers) submit lab dips for all the individual items required in a line. Since various blends of fabrics and other materials absorb dyestuffs differently, accurate color matching of all components may require multiple attempts by suppliers. The manufacturer may require that the source submit color fastness and light fastness textile test results for each sample. The tests are performed by approved textile testing laboratories. These testing procedures are especially important for certain fabrics, such as nylon fabrics in neon bright colors. The approval process requires time and accurate recordkeeping.

PATTERN FINALIZATION AND WRITTEN DOCUMENTS

The pattern for the style that has been approved for production needs final preparation. Every detail needs to be perfect for production to run smoothly. Sometimes, minor pattern adjustments need to be made to improve ease of production. The production pattern, which has been made in the company's sample size, is then ready for **grading,** that is, each individual piece of the pattern is remade in each if the sizes specified. Next, all the pattern pieces in all the sizes are arranged into a master cutting plan, called a **production marker.** The style is ready to move to the next stage, production cutting and sewing operations.

FINALIZING THE PRODUCTION PATTERN

A specialist called a pattern engineer or **production engineer** may be part of the team that is responsible for preparing the pattern for production. Production engineers are familiar with factory mass-production processes and types of equipment. The pattern may need some minor changes to facilitate production. The production engineer would be responsible for suggesting such changes in the pattern and might also be responsible for suggesting the specific factory where production would best be accomplished.

All markings for factory production must be perfect, including notches to ensure accurate matching of one piece to its mate, buttonholes, and pocket placement. One forgotten notch marking can cause production problems, especially since this marking would be missing on the pattern piece for the entire size range after grading the pattern. If the first pattern had been

a.

SPORTCO SPEC SHEET   DATE: 3-28-96   REV DATE: 4-4-96   **F374**
STYLE: F 374   DESCRIPTION: OUTERWEAR JACKET   SIZE: S-M-L
FINAL NAME: ACTIVENT JACKET
SEASON: F'96   OFF SHORE: ___   DOMESTIC: X   BLOCK: NEW

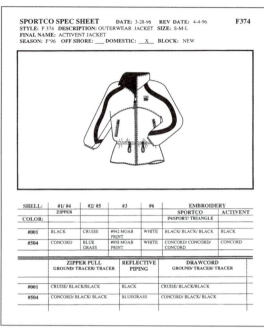

SHELL:	#1/ #4	#2/ #5	#3	#6	EMBROIDERY	
	ZIPPER				SPORTCO	ACTIVENT
COLOR:					IN/SPORT/ TRIANGLE	
#001	BLACK	CRUISE	#942 MOAB PRINT	WHITE	BLACK/ BLACK/ BLACK	BLACK
#504	CONCORD	BLUE GRASS	#958 MOAB PRINT	WHITE	CONCORD/ CONCORD/ CONCORD	CONCORD

	ZIPPER PULL	REFLECTIVE	DRAWCORD
	GROUND/ TRACER/ TRACER	PIPING	GROUND TRACER/ TRACER
#001	CRUISE/ BLACK/BLACK	BLACK	CRUISE/ BLACK/BLACK
#504	CONCORD/ BLACK/ BLACK	BLUEGRASS	CONCORD/ BLACK/ BLACK

b.

SPORTCO SPEC SHEET   DATE: 3-28-96   REV DATE: 4-4-96   **F374**
STYLE: F 374   DESCRIPTION: OUTERWEAR JACKET   SIZE: S-M-L
FINAL NAME: ACTIVENT JACKET
SEASON: F'96   OFF SHORE: ___   DOMESTIC: X   BLOCK: NEW

SHELL #1	SHELL #2	SHELL #3	SHELL #4
VENDOR: W.L. GORE	VENDOR: W.L. GORE	VENDOR: WELLER CALIF. PRINTS	VENDOR: DURLINGTON
FAB #: ACTIVENT #P3462R-CR	FAB #: ACTIVENT #P3462R-CR	FAB #: MOAB POLYMICRO PRINT	FAB #: 804364
WIDTH: 56"	WIDTH: 56"	WIDTH: 44/45"	WIDTH: 57/59"
CONTENT: 100% POLYESTER	CONTENT: 100% POLYESTER	CONTENT: 100% POLYESTER	CONTENT: 100% NYLON MICROSUPPLEX
PIECES:	PIECES:	PIECES:	PIECES:
2 LW. FR. - 01	2 UP. FR. - 06RT - 06LF	2 FR. SP. - 10	1 CS. - 12
	2 SL. - 08	2 BK SP. - 11	2TP. PK. - 13
2 WELT - 05	2 FR. SP. - 10	2 IN. CL. - 09	2 UN. PK. - 14
1 MD. BK. - 03	2 BK. YK. - 07		
	2 BK SP. - 11		
1 ST. FLY - 16	1 CL. - 09		

	SHELL #5	SHELL #6	SHELL #7
1 LW. BK. - 02	VENDOR: EASTRIVER	VENDOR: NATIVE TEXTILES	VENDOR: APPAREL MFG. SUPPLY
1 VT. HEM - 04	FAB #: 95661	FAB #: 45670 WHITE NYLON MESH	FAB #: 9024 PELLON
			WIDTH: 48"
	WIDTH: 60/62"	WIDTH: 63/64"	CONTENT: POLY/RAYON BLEND
	CONTENT: 82% NYLON/ 18% LYCRA	CONTENT: 100% NYLON	PIECES:
	PIECES:	PIECES:	2 WELT - 05
	BINDING	1 BK. MESH - 15	1 CL. - 09
			1 ST FLY INTER -17

TRIMS:

VENDOR	ITEM	ITEM #	PLACEMENT	YIELD/QTY
KLR INC	28" ZIPPER	CFO 36 7/16" E	CENTER FRONT	1 EA.
KLR INC.	6" ZIPPER	CFC 256 5/8" B2E	FRONT POCKETS	2 EA.
WEARLITES	FASHION CORDING	7" HEAT CUT ZIPPER PULL	FRONT ZIPPER SLIDER	1 EA.
SPORTCO	EMBROIDERY "ACTIVENT"		CENTER BACK COLLAR	1 EA.
	EMBROIDERY	1793 STITCH COUNT- 1 1/2"X 1 1/2"	LEFT FRONT CHEST	1 EA.
WEARLITES	REFLECTIVE PIPING	NO FILL #TPW53	BACK VENT	.7
WEARLITES	1/8" CORDING ON SPOOLS		WAIST	1.45
BRITEX	ELLIPSE CORDLOC - BLACK	350-0000-5614	ON SHOCKCORD AT WAIST	2 EA.
FASTENER SUPPLY CO.	WASHER NICKEL	#C82	FRONT WAIST	4 EA.
FASTENER SUPPLY CO.	EYELET BRASS - GROMMETS	#A289	FRONT WAIST	4 EA.
MVL	END FOLD BRAND LABEL W/ SIZE - FOR WOMEN	771249 B 8/30	CENTER BACK NECK ON MESH	1 EA.
SPORTCO	WASH LABEL	46	UNDER BRAND LABEL	1 EA.
SPORTCO	DISCLAIMER SOABAR		UNDER WASH LABEL	1 EA.
FACTORY REPS CO.	12 X 18 POLYBAG - SEALED W/ TAPE			1 EA.
MVL	I.D. TAG: WOMEN'S	W01	SWIFT-TACHED DIRECTLY INTO LEFT LOWER SLEEVE	1 EA.
WL. GORE	HANGTAG: ACTIVENT		SWIFT-TACHED DIRECTLY INTO LEFT LOWER SLEEVE	1 EA.
MVL	HANGTAG: DISCLAIMER		SWIFT-TACHED DIRECTLY INTO LEFT LOWER SLEEVE	1 EA.

c.

CONSTRUCTION PAGE

STYLE: F374   DATE: 3-28-96
SEASON: F'96   REVISED: 4-4-96

CUTTING:

SEAM ALLOWANCE: 3/8" ON ALL SEAMS.

TOPSTITCHING: 1/4" TOPSTITCH ON FRONT ZIPPER, COLLAR, AND SPLICE SEAMS. EDGESTITCH WAIST CASING. STITCH VENT TO BODY AT CENTER BACK AND 5" IN FROM EACH SIDE SEAM (TOTAL OF THREE TACKS).

HEM ALLOWANCE: LYCRA BINDING ON CUFFS. BOTTOM HEM: 3/8" DOUBLE ROLL.

THREAD: LOOPER OF OVERLOCK SHOULD BE WHITE, NEEDLE TO MATCH SHELL #1.

ELASTIC:
RUBBER:

BUTTONS OR SNAPS: FOUR REINFORCED GROMMETS AT WAIST FOR DRAWCORD.

ZIPPERS: ONE 28" SMALL COIL ZIPPER FOR FRONT CLOSURE. TWO 6" POCKET ZIPPERS. PULLS: ONE 7" HEAT CUT PULL FOR FRONT ZIPPER, KNOT AT ENDS.

BAR TACKS: ONE AT EACH SLEEVE BINDING (2).

WELTS: TWO SINGLE WELT ZIPPER POCKETS, FINISHING 1/2" X 6 1/2" WITH WELT OPENING DOWNWARDS, ZIPPER SLIDER AT TOP WHEN CLOSED.

MISCELLANEOUS: REFLECTIVE PIPING IN BACK VENT. STORM FLY TO BE SET AT TOP EDGE OF COLLAR.

DRAWCORD: DRAWCORD IN WAIST CASING, WITH TWO LOCKS, KNOTTED AT ENDS.

LABEL: END FOLD BRAND, WITH CARE CONTENT AND DISCLAIMER, CENTER BACK NECK ON-MESH.

LOGO: EMBROIDERY 1) SPORTCO - LEFT FRONT CHEST: SEE MEASUREMENT PAGE FOR PLACEMENT. 2) ACTIVENT: CENTER BACK COLLAR - SEE TEMPLATE FOR PLACEMENT.

PACKAGING: I.D. TAG WITH STYLE NUMBER MUST BE VISIBLE THROUGH POLYBAG.

Figure 9.2
a. The garment specification (spec) sheet includes important information for producing the style as requested. **b.** Fabric, trim, and sundries are specified on this page of the garment spec sheet. **c.** This page of the garment spec sheet details construction-related instructions.

made on a pattern design system (PDS), any changes at this stage might be accomplished very quickly because the pattern is already in the computer system (see Chapter 7).

FINALIZING THE GARMENT SPECIFICATION SHEET

At the time the designer's sketch or drape of the style is delivered to design development, a garment specification sheet accompanies the design (see Chapter 7). The spec sheet lists all fabrics, sundries, and important construction details, including placement of a logo, label type and label placement, and color for top-stitching thread. Any changes that may have occurred during the development of the style must be transferred to the garment spec sheet. Any requested change not transferred to the spec sheet can cause difficulties in production. If a computer is used to create and maintain the spec sheet, all changes can be made very easily as soon as they have been approved. Some of the computer systems are integrated so that a change made on the spec sheet will automatically be changed on any other necessary documents. Technology shown at the Bobbin Show ("Bobbin show," 1995, p. 58) was described as follows: "Integrated systems and product development systems featured real-time information capabilities, including the graphic integration of style and product descriptions and the immediate feedback of information on such sectors as costing, bill of materials and inventories." Some computer systems include bilingual and multilingual flexibility, especially helpful when working with off-shore sources.

FINALIZING THE PRODUCTION SEQUENCE

Included with the written documentation that accompanies the style will be additional production instructions related to the production sequence. The production engineer or product technician often determines the sequence of steps (what will be sewn first, second, third, and so forth) required for factory production of the style. If the style were to be made in a factory owned by the apparel company, the production engineer would be an employee of the apparel company. If a contractor were to be used for production, a contractor's production engineer would determine the production sequence. The sequence of production is related to the cost of manufacturing the goods. Therefore, the production sequence may have been determined at the time the final cost was calculated, as discussed in Chapter 7.

Experienced production engineers can examine a finished sample garment and quickly provide a reliable estimate of the number of minutes (and thus the actual labor cost) required to sew a specific style. One of the reasons why production engineers are often included in the development design team (see Chapter 7) is that their engineering and costing experience is highly valu-

Figure 9.3

Union Special, an industrial sewing machine producer, illustrates a typical production sequence for manufacturing jeans.

able as a factor in styling decisions. Computer software programs can be used to help analyze cost in comparing various production sequence options.

SIZE SPECIFICATIONS

The actual measurements at specific locations of the finished goods for each of the sizes specified for the style will be listed on a **size specification** or measurement chart. Or, the size specifications might be listed on the same document with the garment specification sheet. For each size to be produced, size specifications for a jacket style might include the chest circumference, jacket hem circumference, back length from neck to hem, neck circumference, sleeve length, and waist circumference listed in chart form. This dimensional information is important to maintain accurate sizes, especially if several factories will be used to produce a large order. Two jackets in the same style and size may fit differently if one factory is less accurate in sewing than another. Some computer pattern design systems include a feature that allows the pattern maker to request the dimensions at specific points on the pattern. The pattern maker completes the size specifications on a separate computer screen during the pattern making process. This saves considerable time compared with hand-measuring each of the specified locations on the pattern pieces. The software can provide the size specs in metric measurements as well as Imperial for contractors who use the metric system.

MEASUREMENT PAGE

STYLE: F 374   DATE: 3-28-96

SEASON: F'96   REV. DATE: 4-4-96

SIZE:	TOT. + OR -	S	M	L
CENTER BACK LENGTH	1/2"	28"	28"	28"
ON THE HALF CHEST: AT UNDERARM	1/2"	22 1/2"	24"	25 1/2"
ON THE HALF HEM: AT BOTTOM OF SIDE SEAM	1/4"	21 1/4"	22 3/4"	24 1/4"
SLEEVE LENGTH: FROM NECKLINE	3/8"	29 1/4"	30"	30 3/4"
ON THE HALF SLEEVE OPENING: RELAXED	1/4"	3 1/2"	3 1/2"	3 3/4"
ON THE HALF NECK OPENING:TOP OF COLLAR	1/4"	9 3/8"	9 3/4"	10 1/8"
DRAWCORD AT WAIST	TOTAL MEASURE	47"	50"	53"

LOGO PLACEMENT - TO CENTER OF LOGO

SIZE	DOWN FROM RAW EDGE- CENTER FRONT NECK	OVER FROM CENTER FRONT
S	1 1/4"	4 3/4"
M	1 1/4"	5"
L	1 1/4"	5 1/4"

Figure 9.4
Small, medium, and large size specifications are listed on the garment spec sheet, along with the tolerances allowed at each specified garment location.

The size specifications also include a **tolerance,** listed usually as a +/− in inches that provides for a narrow range of acceptable dimensional measurements. The tolerance amount might be 1/2 inch for larger circumferences (such as the chest) or lengths, and 1/4 inch for smaller circumferences (such as the neck) or lengths. The stated dimensions, with allowable tolerance, serve as a contract between the apparel company and the sewing facility. If dimensional accuracy is not maintained within the tolerance range, the goods can be rejected by the apparel company.

The apparel company's quality assurance department is usually responsible for checking the finished dimensions of the delivered goods. Since it would be too time consuming to measure the specified dimensions of every garment in an order, a sampling technique is used to measure a specified number of garments in specific sizes. If goods sewn by a contractor must be rejected due to size inaccuracy, the apparel company may miss the deadline for delivery of goods to the retailer. Therefore, it is important for apparel companies to select carefully the contractors with which they do business.

GRADING THE PRODUCTION PATTERN

Pattern grading involves taking the production pattern pieces which have been made in the sample size and creating a set of pattern pieces for each of the sizes listed on the garment spec sheet. The written documents and production pattern are delivered to the pattern grading and marker making department, if the apparel company is responsible for the grading and marker making operation. As mentioned in Chapter 7, when contractors are used for production, they will be responsible for one of the following:

▌ making the first pattern and production pattern, grading and making the marker, cutting and sewing, or

▌ making the production pattern, grading and making the marker, cutting and sewing, or

▌ grading and making the marker, cutting and sewing, or

▌ cutting and sewing (termed "CMT" for cut, make, and trim) only.

Some apparel companies that use contractors prefer to take responsiblity for grading and marker making. This minimizes the risk to the apparel company and ensures that the contractor is not responsible for any errors in pattern grading or marker making. However, if anything is not correct on the pattern or marker, the contractor can blame the manufacturer for a late delivery or other problem. For the manufacturer who provides the marker, maintaining an even work flow in grading and marker making is difficult, especially when the time frame for producing a season's line—determining that a style will be produced and having the marker ready for cutting—is very tight.

GRADE RULES

Grading requires different amounts of growth (for a larger size) or reduction (for a smaller size) at various points on the pattern piece. Thus, it is not possible to place a pattern piece into a photocopy machine and enlarge or reduce the pattern piece uniformly. The amounts and locations of growth/reduction are called the **grade rules.** There is no industry standard for these grade rules and some companies guard carefully their grade rule standards.

Pattern grading is more complex than it may appear. There are different grade rules for jackets with set-in sleeves, raglan sleeves, kimono sleeves, and shirt sleeves. Style variations magnify the complexity of the different grade rules. For example, a raglan sleeve style shirt could also include a front panel, so the grade rules would need to be modified for the extra style line added to the shirt front.

SIZE RANGE AND STYLING COST CONSIDERATIONS

Depending on the style and the apparel company's policy, the size range might include a large number of sizes, for example, from size 4 to size 18 for a missy dress. Another apparel company might produce garments in a size range of small, medium, large, and extra large (designated S-M-L-XL). The cost to grade a pattern with many pattern pieces into a wide range of sizes may cost considerably more than the cost to grade a pattern with only a few pattern pieces in just four sizes. These cost differences are considered from the design stage onward. Another cost variation related to styling concerns designs that are asymmetrical—that is, different pattern pieces are required for the left and right halves of the body. An asymmetrical design might also require different left and right facings, as well as interfacing patterns. Each separate pattern piece needs to be graded, multiplied by the number of sizes in the size range. Thus, asymmetrical designs can be more costly to grade if using traditional grading technology.

The fabric selected may influence the size range in which the style will be produced. Some fabrics will look best in a narrow size range. Based on the scale of a plaid size and repeat, a plaid pleated skirt in missy sizes may look attractive only in certain mid-sizes, for example in sizes 8 through 16. It would be ideal to select a fabric that looks good in a wide size range, but this is not always possible. Some styles look best in certain sizes. Thus, the style may not be offered in the smallest or largest sizes.

GRADING PROCESSES

The pattern grading process can be accomplished by a variety of methods, and there are several approaches to these methods. Computer grading, combined with computer marker making, has gained widespread acceptance. It is the method of choice for apparel companies and contractors that can invest in a computer grading and marker making system. Other processes include hand grading and machine grading.

HAND GRADING. The fundamental process is called hand grading. This process requires a ruler, pencil, and paper as the minimum tools. Using the production pattern pieces, the pattern grader (person grading the pattern) traces a copy of the pattern piece, moving the pattern piece the distance designated by the grade rules at specific points throughout the tracing process. Some hand graders use special grading rulers or graph paper as aids to grading.

MACHINE GRADING. Pattern grading machines are used by some companies to speed the grading process. The grading machine is equipped with two dials—one for width increase/decrease and the other for length increase/decrease. The pattern piece is clamped into or taped to the grading machine, and paper is laid beneath. The pattern is traced in sequence by moving the dials on the grading machine to correspond to the grade rules at designated points on the pattern piece.

COMPUTER GRADING. Although machine grading is faster than hand grading, computer grading is much faster than either of these methods. Computer programs for pattern grading and marker making have been in use since the 1970s. For companies that utilize computer systems to grade

Figure 9.5
Some pattern graders use a grading machine to speed the process of grading patterns into the entire size range.

and make markers, this department may be called **Computer Grading and Marker Making (CGMM)**. Many apparel companies began their shift to computerization with a CGMM department. Computers for use in pattern making and design areas are much more recent. Although the investment in hardware, software, and employee training is substantial, the cost savings is quickly evident for companies that have a substantial quantity of work. For example, Jantzen helped pay for its investment in computer equipment by running two shifts per day and serving as a CGMM facility for other apparel companies in the area who paid for grading and marker making services.

For companies that use a computer pattern design system (PDS) for the production pattern, the pattern is ready for computer grading. Some companies, however, converted to computer grading before they began to use computers to make the patterns. For these companies, it is necessary to input the tagboard production pattern into the computer before grading can be done. The process of inputting a pattern piece into the computer can be done by "tracing" the pattern piece or by scanning the piece. To "trace" a pattern piece, a table called a **digitizer** is used. The digitizer is sensitized at very small increments in both vertical and horizontal directions. These correspond to the x and y coordinates displayed on the computer monitor. The pattern piece is laid in place on the digitizer (also called the digitizing table) and "traced" using a hand-held cursor. The traced pattern piece appears on the computer monitor. During the tracing process, the pattern grader uses a keypad on the cursor to input the specific grade rules at the desired locations. The pattern grader must plan the grade rules to be used, which may require a great deal of thought and pattern grading experience for some complicated styles.

Scanning equipment can input the pattern piece information, including piece perimeters, grade points, and notches. Stripe lines used to match pattern motifs on the fabric and grainlines can be read from the pattern. The scanner will reorient a pattern piece as it is scanned, if the pattern piece enters the scanner askew. Patterns can be scanned from a traced drawing, from a tagboard pattern, or a plastic pattern piece (GGT AccuMark Scan 100 brochure).

The computer system not only calculates the graded dimensions for the entire size range, but also develops smooth necklines, armholes, waistlines, and other curves. Each pattern piece can be viewed on the monitor as a "nest," with all of its sizes nested together. This helps the grader decide if a grade rule is incorrect or a curve is not adequately smoothed. By using the horizontal and vertical coordinates for a specific point, corrections can be made without starting over. The pattern pieces for a style can be graded more quickly by computer than by machine or by hand. To check the grade, a full size or a miniature version of the graded nest can be printed or plotted.

Newer PDS programs include the option to select a grading function as the pattern is being made. These PDS systems are integrated so that the pattern blocks used to begin making the style have specific grade rules "embedded" in the pattern blocks. Once the pattern has been completed, the grading is completed automatically. Lectra systems (a major developer of PDS) has introduced a grading package ("Lectra demonstrates," 1995) that:

> enables the operator to distribute the new measurements to all affected pieces automatically, without having to manually choose each pattern piece to be graded.

Figure 9.6
A scanner is used to input pattern pieces directly into a CAD system if the pattern was not made using a computer system.

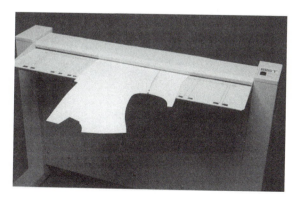

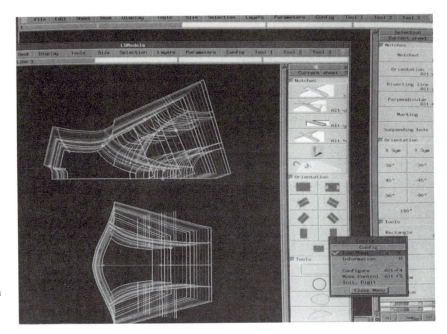

Figure 9.7
Computer screen shows a nested grade of front and sleeve pattern pieces.

> For example, when a measurement change is made on the front shirt piece, the program automatically modifies the measurements of the opposite front, side and back pieces, which will save pattern makers substantial time and effort. (p. 62)

Other improvements to increase speed and ease of use while reducing the possibility of grading errors are in the future.

MAKING THE PRODUCTION MARKER

A costing marker, used to calculate the yardage required for one garment, was discussed in Chapter 7. At this stage in the process, another type of marker is required. The production marker is the full-size cutting layout of all the pattern pieces for all the sizes specified for the style. The marker is drawn on paper, showing the outline of all the pattern pieces. A tightly arranged layout is the goal for the marker, so that very little fabric is wasted. The waste, called **fallout,** represents fabric that cannot be used, and thus money lost to the apparel company. The efficiency of a marker's layout plan (marker efficiency) is measured in the percentage of fabric utilized. Thus, a high utilization percentage represents a cost-effective marker. Highly efficient markers attain utilization in the high 80 or into the 90 percentile figures.

If a pattern for a style requires 10 pattern pieces, and 7 sizes are produced, the marker will include 70 pattern pieces. Sometimes, a marker is planned to

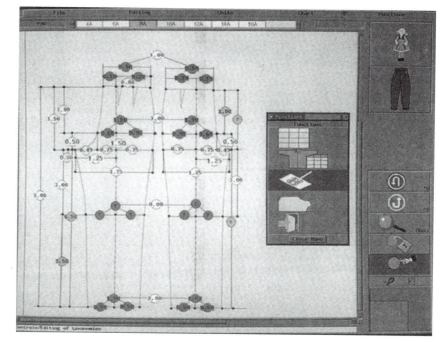

Figure 9.8
Some computer programs provide tools to allow faster grading processes, measurements of pattern dimensions, and electronic sharing of graded patterns with production facilities.

have two sets of pattern pieces in the most frequently purchased sizes, those in the mid-size range. Therefore, the marker for a missy style could have two sets of sizes 10 and 12, for a total of 90 pattern pieces for the marker. Arranging all the pattern pieces into an efficient layout can be a challenge.

MARKER MAKING BY HAND

Marker making by hand begins by planning the layout on a long sheet of paper (perhaps 21 feet long), the width of the fabric to be cut. The tagboard pattern pieces are shifted into the tightest arrangement. The outlines of all the pattern pieces are traced onto the paper beneath. The pattern pieces are removed, and the marker is laid onto the stacked layers of fabric. The cutter follows the drawn outlines of the pattern piece on the marker. Typically, the marker paper is of double thickness. It can be carbonless or have carbon between the layers, so that a copy of the original marker is made at the same time. Thus, after the original marker has been cut up, a reference copy remains. This copy can be traced again, if another production order for the same style is received. If a similar style is produced later, the marker maker can refer to the file of markers to help guide the layout plan for the new style.

OTHER MARKER MAKING METHODS

Some apparel companies and contractors continue to make markers by hand. Other methods, developed to increase the speed and efficiency of

Figure 9.9
Each pattern piece is traced onto a large sheet of paper to make the production marker.

marker making, include: (a) the use of miniaturization of pattern pieces combined with enlargement photography to produce a full-size marker, (b) the use of light sensitive paper in which the paper areas covered by the tagboard pattern pieces remain white while exposed areas darker to show the silhouette of pattern pieces, and (c) water soluble dye sprayed over the pattern pieces while laying on the fabric, leaving the fabric uncolored in the areas covered by the pattern pieces.

COMPUTER MARKER MAKING

Whereas various marker-making methods are in use in today's industry, computer marker making is the method most companies prefer. With CGMM, the marker making function is tied to the pattern grading function. Thus, a company that grades by computer also makes markers by computer. The CGMM system is purchased as a package, including the plotter that draws the marker.

Once the pattern pieces have been graded by computer and stored in the computer's memory, the marker maker can retrieve all of the pattern pieces needed in the size range. The fabric width is displayed on the monitor, along with markings for stripes or plaids if necessary. With the use of the cursor, each pattern piece is moved one by one into the fabric area, creating the layout plan. The computer is programmed to keep all pattern pieces aligned "on grain," to avoid skewing pattern pieces. Accidental overlapping of pattern pieces is avoided, for the pattern piece signals the marker maker by blinking if one piece overlaps another.

ADVANTAGES OF COMPUTER MARKER MAKING

The marker program calculates the fabric utilization, and this figure appears as a percentage on the monitor. This helps the marker maker attain the high-

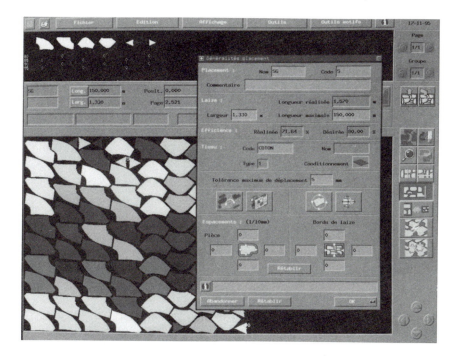

Figure 9.10
A production marker is displayed on the computer screen, showing the tight layout on the left and the utilization percentage on the right.

est utilization. An article in *Apparel Industry Magazine* discussed the complexity of marker making variables:

> Your greatest single cost is cloth. The management of cloth is unconditionally crucial to the successful management of your business and your profits. As you can see, finding the ideal approach to the many variables requires elaborate mathematical calculations using sophisticated computer programs. There is just no other practical way to arrive at an optimal solution. The variety of factors make the standard approach (based on human experience) far too unreliable. (Dennison, 1993, pp. 82–84)

Some manufacturers have estimated that the cost savings in better fabric utilization has paid for the equipment in less than two years. According to a study conducted at Clemson Apparel Research (Hill, 1994), for a CAD system used for grading and marking "The investment required is $95,000. . . . In the area of direct labor, savings amount to $87,330 a year. . . . Finally, a CAD system will result in a 2% fabric savings per year for a total of $36,750" (p. 38). A fifteen-month payback period is cited, with a 377% return on investment (ROI).

Another advantage of computer marker making is that the layout plan can be stored for future reference. Multiple copies can be plotted whenever they are needed. To begin a new marker, a similar marker from a previous season can be viewed as a reference to speed the decision-making process. Accuracy is extremely high with CGMM, as each copy is exactly the same as the original. No accidental growth during tracing occurs.

Some companies that began their "computerization" with CGMM systems have integrated CGMM with other stages in design, development, and production. Design integration was discussed in Chapter 6 and development integration in Chapter 7. Production integration will be covered in Chapter 11. Complete integration of computer systems throughout the entire process provides advantages to all parties in the fiber-textile-apparel-retail chain.

As the cost of some CGMM systems decreases and their "user-friendliness" increases, more companies are purchasing these systems. Some systems are in a price range affordable to small apparel companies. Other small companies will use the CGMM service of a larger company. Some contractors in foreign production centers as well as in the United States have CGMM equipment. With a modem, the apparel company's PDS can be linked directly to the contractor's CGMM system. This saves time and increases accuracy.

COMPUTER AIDED DESIGN/COMPUTER AIDED MANUFACTURING

Computer aided design, pattern making, marker making and grading combined with computerized cutting are an important part of Quick Response. These strategies, commonly referred to as **CAD/CAM,** can increase the speed and accuracy of pattern making, marker making, grading patterns, cutting fabric, and sewing. In terms of Quick Response, CAD/CAM systems have a number of benefits. In a survey of 450 companies (Kosh, 1987), the main reasons reported for using computer aided design/manufacturing systems were: (1) improved product quality, (2) reduced sewing time, (3) reduced cutting time, (4) reduced design and sample-making time, (5) reduced pattern making and grading time, (6) reduced production marking time, and (7) diversified product line. Thus, reducing the amount of time involved in the design and pattern making stages of apparel production is an important benefit of CAD/CAM.

SUMMARY

Retail buyers' written orders in sufficient quantity to warrant production signal the chain of events that begin the process of producing a new style. These steps include ordering production fabrics, trims, and sundries, and finalizing the production pattern and written documents. To ensure quality production, the documents that accompany the pattern are as important as the pattern itself. These documents are called the garment specification sheet. They include a tech drawing of the garment style, fabric swatches, a list of all fabrics, trims, and sundries in all colorways, construction specifications (construction details and sewing steps in sequence), and measurement specifications with stated tolerances. When working with contractors, the importance of accurate documentation is essential.

In company-owned production facilities, the production pattern is graded into the specified size range and a production marker is made by the apparel company. For contracted production, either the apparel company or the contractor is responsible for the grading and marking procedures.

Computer grading and marker making systems have gained widespread use in the apparel industry. The advantages of CGMM include increased speed and improved accuracy. Integrated computer systems provide instantaneous linkage by modem or a local area network (LAN) between the PDS and CGMM, whether the two systems are separated by miles within a city (such as the design development department located at company offices and the grading and marking located at the company's factory) or by an ocean (such as the design development department located in the United States and the contractor's grading and marking department located at the factory in South Korea). The future promises continued developments in a "seamless" integration of all aspects of design, development and production.

REFERENCES

Bobbin show review. (1995, November). *Bobbin*, pp. 58–60.

Dennison, Roger. (1993, September). Optimize cloth consumption with CAD marker making. *Apparel Industry Magazine*, pp. 82–86.

Greco, Monica. (1996, February). Is on-line fabric sourcing next? *Apparel Industry Magazine*, pp. 32–34.

Hill, Thomas. (1994, March). CAR Study: UPS, CAD provide 300%+ return on investment. *Apparel Industry Magazine*, pp. 34–40.

Kosh, Kiki (1987, February). Computer systems automated design function. *Bobbin*, pp. 51–64.

Lectra demonstrates its new CAD grading package. (1995, August). *Apparel Industry Magazine*, 62.

Young, Kristin. (1996, February 2–February 8). The F word. *California Apparel News*, pp. 1, 8–9.

KEY TERMS

factoring

vendor, source, supplier

color control

commercial match

lab dip

grading

production marker

production engineer

size specification

tolerance

pattern grading

grade rules

computer grading and marker making (CGMM)

digitizer

fallout

CAD/CAM (computer aided design/computer aided manufacturing)

DISCUSSION QUESTIONS

1. Describe verbally or bring to class a product that provides an example of lack of color control with one or more components. How would you suggest that this mistake could have been avoided?

2. The quality assurance department finds that the contracted goods do not meet the stated size specifications within allowed tolerance. What are some of the problems faced by the apparel company if the shipment (or part of it) is rejected?

3. While computer grading and marker making systems are an expensive investment, what are some of the ways in which a CGMM system can quickly pay for itself?

CAREER PROFILES

Possible career opportunities in preproduction processes include specification writing, production pattern making, pattern grading and marker making, and materials manager.

PURCHASING MANAGER OR RAW MATERIALS CONTROL MANAGER, *Publicly Owned Sportswear and Athletic Shoe Company*

Job Description

Manage raw materials buyers to ensure department goals are met. Manage Sales Sample Materials Buyer to ensure timelines are met and all materials needed are ordered. Develop partnerships with vendors for supply of necessary raw materials to ensure company needs are met. Develop partnerships with contractors to be sure best possible service is provided for our company. Ensure billing and payment issues regarding raw materials sold to contractors are meeting the best interest of our company. Develop, monitor, and update systems to ensure efficiency in the department and to provide necessary information exchanges with other departments and liaison offices.

Typical Tasks

▌ Prepare annual department budget and action plan.

▌ Determine greige commitments and/or forecast of company-developed styles, have contracts issued, work with off-shore liaison offices to provide accurate and timely reports, updates, and information as requested to make ongoing greige commitments with vendors.

▌ Color assort and preorder raw materials as needed, keeping excess to a minimum and maintaining a program to dispose of excess raw materials.

▮ Monitor lab dip and first production submit information from the Apparel Lab to ensure materials will meet production timelines. Monitor deliveries to contractors. Troubleshoot quality problems.

▮ Generate computer reports using a variety of different systems

▮ Heavy use of telephone to communicate with vendors/contractors/other company departments/off-shore liaison offices

▮ Heavy use of fax machine and computer E-mail system to communicate in writing

▮ Constant on-going "coaching" of buyers to meet department goals

What Do You Like Best About Your Job?

Working with a variety of people: within my company, with vendors, sewing contractors, and off-site company personnel

PATTERN DEPARTMENT MANAGER,
Publicly Owned Sportswear and Athletic Shoe Company

Job Description

Manage apparel pattern making and grading and marker making process, including providing leadership, delegating assignments, managing workload, assisting staff, administrative duties, and development and integration of CAD/CAM. Supervise staff of 20. Establish fit and quality standards on a global basis based on manufacturing capabilities. Collaborate with appropriate departments to ensure our apparel is developed in a manner consistent with established global guidelines.

Typical Tasks

▮ Produce and maintain globalized standardizations of patterns, specs, fitting, body types, and grading information to ensure our company's apparel construction is clear and understandable in every country

▮ Monitor and track workload of approximately 1,400 styles per year, 300 to 400 custom patterns, 700 to 900 grading requests, and 50 to 70 special promo projects

▮ Select, train, manage, and develop staff. Duties include hiring, performance management, salary administration, training, and separation decisions. Maintain familiarity with and an understanding of applicable federal and state human resource regulations. Plan, monitor, and adjust staffing needs according to project workload. Design and implement training programs for staff including state-of-the-art computerized pattern making using CAD/CAM applications, and cross-training all personnel in the areas of marker making, grading, and pattern and computer operations

- Oversee the selection of pattern department capital expenditures in collaboration with manager. Negotiate contracts, warranties, and training programs for new equipment. Develop space planning strategies as department grows and changes
- Collaborate with Design and Development to ensure interpretation of design concepts are upheld, products are manufacturable and timelines are met. Offer suggestions that provide most economical method for production
- Oversee development of grading standards and maintenance of Grading Silhouette Book

What Do You Like Best About Your Job?

The people I work with, the variety of responsibilities, having a job where I make a significant contribution to the company and provide opportunities for my staff to develop and grow.

TRIM BUYER, *Privately Owned Suit and Dress Company*

Job Description

Write garment specifications, source vendors. Order trims, buttons, zippers, cording, snaps, interfacings and linings. Work with designers and production team on trim selection. Organize shipments to contractors in the U.S. and abroad.

Typical Tasks

- Make phone calls to vendors
- Meet with sales representatives to review lines of trims, buttons, zippers, interfacings, linings
- Fax orders and other communication
- Price and order trims and sundries
- Organize and oversee shipments of fabrics and trims to contractors
- Meet with designers and production team to select trims
- Write the garment specifications for all styles in the line

What Do You Like Best About Your Job?

There are always new things to do and remaining things to work on—never a dull moment and a wide variety of tasks.

Step 1: Research

Step 2: Design

Step 3: Design Development and Style Selection

Step 4: Marketing the Line

Step 5: Preproduction

Step 6: Sourcing
Select Production Facility

Step 7: Apparel Production

Step 8: Distribution

10

Sourcing Decisions and Production Centers

Objectives

▌ To examine the criteria used by apparel companies and retailers in their sourcing decisions.

▌ To describe the various sourcing options available to apparel companies and retailers.

▌ To outline the advantages and disadvantages of these sourcing options.

▌ To review current issues related to sourcing decisions.

▌ To describe primary domestic and international production centers.

SOURCING DECISIONS

ONE OF THE MOST important decisions made by a company is how and where goods will be manufactured. The term **sourcing** describes this decision-making process. Sourcing decisions are important to both apparel manufacturers and retailers, as they help to determine a company's competitive edge. This section outlines decision criteria, production options for companies, and issues surrounding domestic and **off-shore production** (producing outside the United States using production specifications furnished by U.S. companies). Figure 10-1 is a flowchart summarizing the sourcing process and **sourcing options** available to apparel companies and retailers.

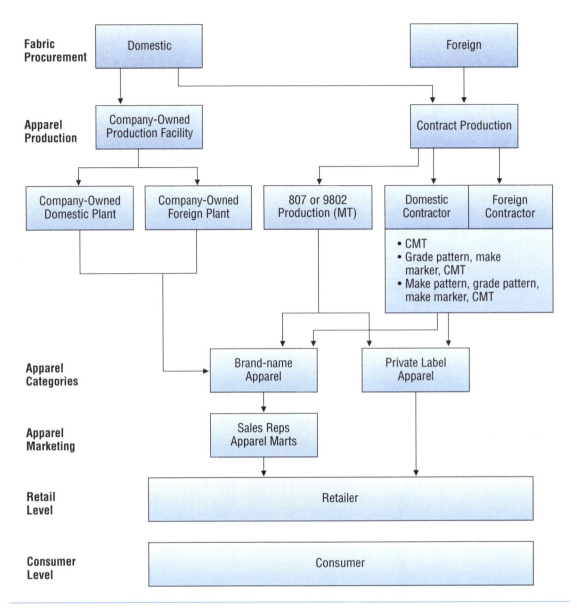

Figure 10.1
Sourcing options.

CRITERIA USED IN SOURCING DECISIONS

Before outlining the various sourcing options, the criteria companies use in making sourcing decisions will be examined. A number of criteria come into play when companies decide by what sources and where their products will be manufactured. The answers to a number of questions related to each criterion will help determine the best sourcing option for a company. These criteria include the company's sourcing philosophy, labor requirements and

Figure 10.2
For some companies
the ability to put the
"Made in the U.S.A."
logo on their products
contributes to their
sourcing decisions.

costs, fabric requirements, quality control standards, equipment requirements, plant capacities, trade barriers, and expected turn-around time. Although "cost has been and always will be a primary reason for establishing manufacturing capacity off-shore, as it is a factor of choice in country selection" (Cruz, 1995, p. 80), other factors must come into play when companies make sourcing decisions.

COMPANY'S SOURCING PHILOSOPHY. Often companies have a general philosophy towards sourcing that serves as a guideline or framework for sourcing decisions. For example, some companies are very committed to domestic production and want to be able to put "Made in the USA" labels on their products. Other companies have strong ties and positive working relations with contractors in other countries and therefore generally prefer off-shore production. Some companies have guidelines that outline their sourcing philosophies. For example, because of conflicts with human rights issues stated in the sourcing guidelines, Levi Strauss pulled their contracting out of China in the early 1990s.

LABOR REQUIREMENTS AND COSTS. Apparel production is very labor intensive, even though technological advancements are increasingly automating the process. Therefore, labor costs are an important issue in sourcing decisions. Questions companies might ask include: how many workers will be required to efficiently produce the goods? What specific skills are required to produce the product line? What is the labor cost of domestic workers compared to workers in another country? If the company owns plants, what investments in technology and personnel training need to be made? As discussed in Chapter 1, the U.S. textile and apparel industries have always been in search of cheaper labor—first within the United States and then in other countries. Because of this, during the past thirty years, U.S. apparel companies and retailers have moved a great deal of apparel production off shore where labor costs are considerably lower than in the United States. For example, the average wage (estimates are in U.S. $, including fringe benefits and social charges) for apparel workers in the United States was $6.77 per hour (1991 figures), compared to $2.22 per hour in Costa Rica, $1.88 per hour in Mexico, $1.14 per hour in Honduras (Cedrone, 1994), $3.74 in Taiwan, $2.75 in South Korea, and $3.39 in Hong Kong (1992 figures). Obviously the labor costs in these other countries are much lower than in the United States. This is the primary reason why many manufacturers are producing off shore (See Table 10-1).

To compare sourcing options according to cost, many companies have relied on comparisons of minimum wages. However, according to industry analysts, "direct labor comparative analyses, based on minimum wage, prove to be misleading for the following four reasons: (1) no one can sustain productive manufacturing operations on minimum wage, (2) not many significant manufacturers pay minimum wage, (3) not many employees will be attracted to work for minimum wage pay, and (4) employees typically cannot

TABLE 10-1

Comparisons of Apparel Manufacturing Labor Costs[1]
(Estimated Average Hourly Wages for Direct Labor Operators)

Germany[2]	$14.81	Costa Rica[3]	$ 2.22
Italy[2]	$13.50	Mexico[3]	$ 1.88
Belgium[2]	$12.57	Jamaica[3]	$ 1.54
France[2]	$12.41	El Salvador[3]	$ 1.47
Canada[2]	$ 9.53	Dominican Rep.[3]	$ 1.46
United Kingdom[2]	$ 7.99	Guatemala[3]	$ 1.27
Spain[2]	$ 7.11	Honduras[3]	$ 1.14
United States[2]	$ 6.77	Thailand[2]	$ .69
Taiwan[2]	$ 3.74	Sri Lanka[2]	$ .39
Hong Kong[2]	$ 3.39	India[2]	$ .25
South Korea[2]	$ 2.75	P.R. China[2]	$ .24
Singapore[2]	$ 2.72		

[1]In U.S. dollars including benefits and social charges
[2]1991 figures
[3]1994 figures
Note: because labor costs change frequently and are affected by other production costs, figures in this table should be used only for general comparative purposes.

be persuaded to stay at a company when receiving minimum wage pay" (Cruz, 1995, p. 80). Instead industry-specific minimums, area-specific minimums, and plant minimums have been used for comparative purposes. When comparing labor costs, fringe benefits of workers must also be taken into account. Again industry analysts suggest that labor cost include earned pay and that all other labor costs be included in fringe benefits (Cruz, 1995).

FABRIC REQUIREMENTS. Whether the fabric will be procured in the United States or from a foreign supplier is also an important sourcing decision. If fabric is procured in the United States, companies may also want to manufacture the goods in the United States. If foreign fabric is used, typically the products are also produced off shore. This reduces costs by eliminating fabric shipping expenses. Another important question regarding the fabric is whether the fabric will be cut in the United States. If fabric is cut in the United States, even if the garments are sewn in another country, companies can take advantage of certain tariff allowances. This and other trade issues will be discussed later in the chapter.

QUALITY CONTROL STANDARDS. One question asked by companies in their sourcing decision is how important is maintaining specific quality control standards? Because quality is most effectively controlled in com-

Figure 10.3
The ability to ensure that garments meet quality specifications is often a criterion in sourcing decisions.

pany-owned facilities, a company's response to the importance of quality control may be the primary reason for using company-owned plants for production or for selecting a contractor the company knows to produce high-quality products (although they may be at a higher cost).

EQUIPMENT REQUIREMENTS. Depending on the product line, equipment needs will vary. Therefore, companies will ask questions such as: what equipment is needed to efficiently produce the goods? How specialized are these equipment needs? Will different equipment be needed next season or next year to produce goods for the company? Are we as a company in a financial position to invest in new equipment? Depending on the current and future equipment needs of a company, as well as it's financial capabilities, a company will decide to contract or use it's own factories.

PLANT CAPACITIES. Another sourcing decision criterion is to determine plant capacities in light of production needs. Companies will want to know what the production capabilities of company-owned plants as well as contractors are, and whether these are sufficient to meet production needs. If they are found to be insufficient, the company may decide to hire (additional) contractors, expand current plants, or build new plants. If plant capacities are found to be greater than needed, then downsizing strategies

Figure 10.4
When specialized production equipment is required, companies work with contractors that have the needed equipment.

are in order. Facility costs will vary across countries, as will the terms of leasing. It is important for companies to read the fine print of leases to determine what is included.

TRADE BARRIERS. Under current international trade policies, textile and apparel goods imported into the United States from many countries are subject to trade barriers, such as tariffs and quotas. **Tariffs** are taxes assessed by governments on imports; **quotas** are numerical limits on the number of products in specific categories that can be imported. Therefore, if off-shore production is an option, the company must decide if and how these trade barriers may affect importing the goods they produce into the United States (or other countries)? Because both tariffs and quotas add to the cost of production, companies that produce off shore must weigh these additional costs against the lower costs of labor in these countries.

EXPECTED TURN-AROUND TIME. Another question asked by companies is how fast can goods be produced, shipped, and distributed to retailers? Would turn-around time be faster if production location changed? In an era when getting products to the consumer as quickly as possible is important to the success of a company, production, shipping, and distribution times need to be determined and compared. Companies should consider the distance and shipping time between the sewing factory and the company's distribution center. For example, a company whose distribution center is in New York may choose a contractor in Costa Rica over a contractor in Thailand because of shipping time and costs. Strategies associated with Quick Response are designed to shorten the time between fiber and finished product through increased use of technology. Turn-around time is particularly important for products such as swimwear. It is estimated that two-thirds of all swimwear is sold from May through July. Therefore, for reorders, swimwear companies need the fastest turn-around possible. Because of this, many swimwear companies manufacture their goods domestically. For example, Authentic Fitness, maker of Speedo swimwear estimates that their swimwear, which can be produced in 5 weeks domestically, would take 16 weeks if produced off shore (Brown, 1995). Thus, because of the shorter turn-around time, domestic production is preferred over off-shore production.

SOURCING OPTIONS

Based on these factors, a number of sourcing options are available to apparel companies and retailers. In general, major sourcing decisions focus on whether production will be domestic or off shore and whether production will take place in a company-owned facility or will be contracted to others. Advantages and disadvantages of each option must be weighed by companies in light of their product line, operational strategies, and organizational philosophy. For some companies, the flexibility afforded by using contractors is necessary; other companies believe they have greater quality control by producing products in their own plants. Some companies produce off shore to take advantage of lower labor costs. However, just because labor costs are lower in another country does not necessarily mean that overall production costs are lower or that producing off shore is the right decision for a company. What follows are the basic sourcing alternatives available to apparel manufacturers and retailers. Tables 10-2 and 10-3 outline the primary advantages and disadvantages of these sourcing options.

TABLE 10-2

Advantages and Disadvantages of Domestic and Off-Shore Production

	ADVANTAGES	DISADVANTAGES
Domestic Production	▮ trade barriers not a concern ▮ supported by consumers who desire products "Made in the USA"	▮ labor costs higher than in some other countries
Off-Shore Production	▮ labor costs lower than in the United States. barriers ▮ can take advantage of 807 (9802) production	▮ differences in cultural norms and language ▮ possible trade barriers

TABLE 10-3

Advantages and Disadvantages of Owned-Facility and
Contractor Production

	ADVANTAGES	DISADVANTAGES
Owned-Facility Production	▌ quality control ▌ greater control over production timing	▌ financial requirements associated with equipment and personnel ▌ need to assure continuous production ▌ higher labor costs ▌ foreign ownership creates additional financial risks
Contractor Production	▌ greater flexibility to changing equipment or production needs ▌ no investment in factories, equipment, or training needed	▌ less control over quality or production timing

DOMESTIC FABRIC, DOMESTIC PRODUCTION IN OWNED FACILITY

In this case, fabric produced in the United States is shipped to a company-owned plant in the United States for production. This option allows for the greatest control over quality and timing of production. To be competitive, companies who own their own facilities need to (and have the control to do so) invest in technology to increase productivity and reduce sewing costs. Companies that choose this option typically produce similar types of goods each year so that equipment requirements do not change drastically. Companies must also invest in training personnel. It is estimated that the cost of training new sewers can be as high as $5,000 per sewer (Ratoff, 1994). Companies must also plan to maintain consistent and continuous production so that personnel are not continually laid off during slow periods and then rehired during busy periods. To maintain continuous production, these companies will sometimes serve as contractors for other companies. Labor costs are generally higher for companies that own their own plants, but many companies are dedicated to making domestic production competitive through increased productivity. Generally, companies who have chosen this option are proud to put the "Made in the USA" label on their product and are committed to domestic production. In recent years, the implementation of Quick Response strategies in apparel production have been common for companies that produce domestically in their own plants. Other advantages

Figure 10.5
Company-owned factories, such as this Jantzen plant, allow the greatest control over quality and production timing.

of this option are that companies do not have to worry about trade barriers, and shipping costs and time may be less than for products produced off shore. As one industry consultant stated "owning a sewing factory requires a long-term view, commitment and deep pockets" (Ratoff, 1994, p. 7).

DOMESTIC FABRIC, DOMESTIC CONTRACTOR PRODUCTION

Under this option, fabric is procured domestically and production is contracted to a domestic company (contractor) that specializes in the type of production required. By using a contractor, the company loses some control over quality and timing of production. However, with contractor production, the company does not have to invest in factories, equipment, or training personnel. This is important for small companies that may not have the financial resources to build a production plant. By using contractors, companies have increased flexibility in production methods. This is important for companies whose product lines—and therefore equipment needs—vary from year to year. Sometimes manufacturers that typically produce in their own plants choose this option when orders have outpaced their production capacity. For those who believe producing in the United States is important, companies can still put "Made in the USA" on their labels. As with the previous sourcing option, trade barriers are not a concern under this option, and shipping costs and time may be an advantage. Contractors can be located in several ways. Sourcing fairs are trade shows that bring contractors and companies together. At these fairs, contractors have booths with samples of their merchandise and information regarding their expertise and capacities. Sourcing fairs are also held in conjunction with other trade shows, such as the Bobbin Show or the American Apparel Contractors Association convention. Both domestic and foreign contractors use sourcing fairs to connect with companies, and companies use them to find appropriate domestic and foreign contractors. Contractors and companies also use classified advertisements in trade papers such as *Women's Wear Daily* or *Daily News Record* to advertise their need or availability. The Internet is also being used as a vehicle to connect companies (see, for example, the "Apparel Exchange" at http://www.apparelex.com).

DOMESTIC OR FOREIGN FABRIC WITH 807 (9802) PRODUCTION

Using fabric produced either in the United States or elsewhere, companies choosing this option combine domestic production with a special type of offshore production known as **807 or 9802 production.** Under Harmonized Tariff Schedule number 9802 (formerly number 807) of the U.S. tariff regulations, for garments whose pieces were shipped to another country for assembly, tariffs are only on the "value-added" (typically the cost of assembly) to the garment. For example, hypothetically speaking, suppose the value of the garment pieces was $20,000 when they were shipped to Indonesia for assembly. After assembly, the garments were worth $50,000. Under this tariff regulation, the import tax would be on $30,000, the value added to the garment pieces. This option provides the manufacturer with control over the design and cut of the garments, while taking advantage of lower labor costs in other countries. With this option, however, companies must be concerned with any quota requirements that are the same as with other garments. Companies also must be able to handle possible language and cultural differences when working with contractors in other countries. The 807(A) program, begun in 1986, furnishes duty breaks and unlimited quotas for apparel assembled in Caribbean Basin nations using fabric produced and cut in the United States. The phrase **maquiladora operations** is used to describe "assembly plants, mostly along the U.S.-Mexico border, in which garments are assembled from U.S.-cut parts and shipped back to the United States" (Dickerson, 1995, p. 189).

DOMESTIC OR FOREIGN FABRIC, FOREIGN CONTRACTOR PRODUCTION

This option is similar to the previous option, except that garments are not cut in the United States. The primary advantage is the lower labor costs found in other countries. Disadvantages are similar to the previous option: possible trade barriers and language and cultural differences in other countries. When using domestic fabric, shipping time and costs may be higher than if fabrics were produced closer to the production facilities.

FOREIGN FABRIC, FOREIGN PRODUCTION IN OWNED FOREIGN FACILITY

In some cases, companies may own production facilities in other countries. Although this option allows companies to have control over quality and timing of production while taking advantage of lower labor costs in other countries, the financial risks associated with building and running a production facility outside the United States are great. Government policies, personnel expectations, and cultural norms regarding business operations in another country may be very different from those in the United States. In fact, under some countries' policies, foreign ownership of plants is prohibited. Similar to contracting off shore, companies that own their production facilities must also abide by the laws governing international trade regarding tariffs and quotas.

COMBINATION OF ALTERNATIVES

Many companies use a combination of options depending on their production requirements at any point in time. Many companies are diversifying their sourcing. Using a variety of sourcing options provides companies with the flexibility needed to change production in response to consumer demand, production requirements, and international relations. The American Apparel Manufacturers Association can provide companies with effective models related to sourcing options.

Sourcing decisions are complex and companies must examine both fixed and variable costs associated with manufacturing in the various options in order to accurately assess the financial benefits of any one option (Brooks, 1992). Table 10-4 compares the costs of manufacturing a sports jacket using off-shore contract production with domestic production. Note that although the cost to purchase the jacket from an off-shore contractor is less than total manufacturing costs using domestic production, transportation, credit, and administrative costs substantially raise the total buying costs.

Sourcing decisions may also change over time. In some cases, manufacturers who once produced in the United States have moved production off shore. For example, Timberland, the producer of hiking boots and outerwear, contracted only 5 percent of its production in 1990. However by the end of 1995, 60 percent of its production was off shore. By 1996, virtually all of its production had been shifted to off-shore contractors. Sourcing decisions for some companies are changing to take advantage of reforms in trade regulations. For example, Pendleton Woolen Mills, the all-American producer of men's and women's wool and nonwool apparel, blankets, and piece goods moved some production of women's blouses to Mexico to take advantage of duty-free imports under the North American Free Trade Agreement. Other companies have turned "to nearby Central American and Caribbean countries for their production needs, where labor costs are still lower than they are in the U.S., and where proximity helps improve quality control and shipping times" (Friedman, 1996, p. 6). Such shifts in production have con-

TABLE 10-4

Domestic and Off-Shore Contract Production of a Sports Jacket

| | PRODUCTION | |
COST ELEMENT (PER JACKET)	DOMESTIC	OFF-SHORE CONTRACTOR
Materials, including fabric lining and trim	$ 18.50	
Direct labor, including cut, make, trim, taxes, and fringe benefits	$ 13.40	
Factory Expenses		
Supervision/Indirect	$ 2.50	
Facilities	$ 2.00	$ 2.00
Insurance	$ 2.50	$ 2.50
Depreciation	$ 3.00	$ 3.00
Total Manufacturing Costs	$ 41.90	$ 7.50
Cost to Purchase		$31.00
Other Assignable Costs		
Letters of credit (2%)		$ .62
Interest on higher inventory		$ .26
Transportation (5%)		$ 1.55
Procurement and administration		$ .31
Total Transaction Cost	**$41.90**	**$41.24**

tributed to declines in employment in domestic apparel production. In fact, according to the Labor Department, the number of jobs in apparel manufacturing has steadily declined since 1991 (it should be noted that job losses can also be attributed to sluggish apparel sales in the United States).

PRODUCTION CENTERS

DOMESTIC PRODUCTION CENTERS

Apparel production facilities can be found in every state, although the greatest number are in California, New York, North Carolina, Texas, Florida, Georgia, Pennsylvania, and Alabama. This distribution reflects the historical concentration of apparel manufacturing in the New York City and Los Angeles areas and the lower wages found in the southern states compared to other states. Tables 10-5, 10-6, and 10-7 list the top ten apparel manufacturing areas in the United States. With more than 100,000 people employed in apparel production, apparel manufacturing accounts for approximately 15

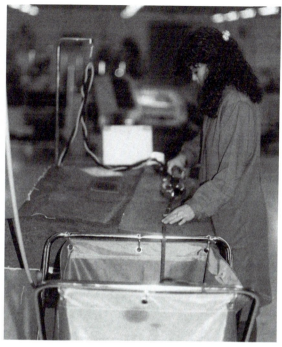

Figure 10.6
Apparel production can
be found in every state,
although the highest
concentration is in New
York and California.

percent of Los Angeles's total manufacturing base (Moore, 1995). In New York City, nearly one-half of all manufacturing workers are in the apparel industry, with 100,000 employed. New York's industry consists of approximately 4,500 companies—4,000 contractors and 500 designer/manufacturers. In addition, New York produces approximately 28 percent of all dresses manufactured in the United States. Through the Garment Industry Development Corporation of New York City (GIDC), training and educational programs have been established to improve the skills of apparel workers. The third largest production area is Georgia, with 57,607 employees working in 669 companies. Apparel production accounts for approximately 10 percent of Georgia's manufacturing workforce behind textiles (20 percent) and food products (12 percent). Miami employees almost 20,000 people in apparel manufacturing. Miami's apparel production is centered on "807 and 807(A) production" in which garments are cut in Miami and sewn in the Caribbean Basin (Moore, 1995).

Within the United States, Texas and California have seen the greatest growth in apparel production jobs in the last decade (DesMarteau, 1994; Southern California Edison Company, 1995). In Southern California this

TABLE 10-5

The Top 10 U.S. Apparel Manufacturing Areas Ranked by Number of Employees

1.	Los Angeles	101,000°°
2.	New York City	100,000°
3.	Georgia	57,607°°°
4.	Miami	19,642°°
5.	San Francisco	15,000°°
6.	Greenville Area	13,700°
7.	Dallas	9,766°
8.	Greensboro Triad	9,700°
9.	LeHigh Valley	8,400°
10.	Charlotte	8,000°

° 1995 figures
°° 1994 figures
°°° 1993 figures

TABLE 10-6

Top 10 U.S. Apparel Manufacturing Areas Ranked by Number of Facilities

1.	New York City	4,500°
2.	Los Angeles	4,024°°°°
3.	Miami	670°°
4.	Georgia	669°°°
5.	Dallas	460°°
6.	San Francisco	417°°°°
7.	LeHigh Valley	200°
8.	Greenville Area	150°
9.	Greensboro Triad	140°
10.	Charlotte	107°°

° 1995 figures
°° 1994 figures
°°° 1993 figures
°°°° 1992 figures

TABLE 10-7

Top 10 U.S. Apparel Manufacturing Areas Ranked by Average Hourly Wages

1.	San Francisco	$11.58°°°^
2.	Los Angeles	$ 8.30°°°^
3.	Charlotte	$ 7.96°°^
4.	Greensboro Triad	$ 7.48°°
5.	Dallas	$ 7.42°
6.	Miami	$ 7.25°°
7.	Greenville Area	$ 7.23°^
8.	New York City	$ 7.00°
9.	LeHigh Valley	$ 6.48°^
10.	Georgia	$ 6.45°°°^

° 1995 figures
°° 1994 figures
°°° 1993 figures
^ based on weekly or yearly averages

growth has been attributed to the pool of skilled labor, primarily from the Latino and Asian populations in the area. Growth in apparel production facilities in states that border Mexico can also be attributed to the increased trade with Mexico as a result of the North American Free Trade Agreement. For example, many companies are moving production to Texas in order to be closer to Mexico, without actually moving production to Mexico. Criteria used by companies in opening or expanding production facilities include "proximity to headquarters, affordability of utilities, availability of skilled labor and an appropriate existing building" (DesMarteau, 1994, p. 80).

FOREIGN PRODUCTION CENTERS

From a global perspective, apparel production facilities can be found in developed countries (industrialized countries) such as Canada, Japan, and countries in Western Europe; newly industrialized countries (NICs) such as Mexico, Brazil, Hong Kong, South Korea, and Taiwan; developing countries such as Bangladesh, Costa Rica, and Guatemala; and countries governed by single-party communist regimes such as China and Vietnam. Many of the newly industrialized countries have large textile and apparel industries. For example, apparel production is Hong Kong's largest industry.

Figure 10.7
Production facilities for apparel and accessories can be found world-wide.

Hong Kong, Taiwan, and South Korea are sometimes referred to as the "Big Three" in textiles and apparel trade because of their importance in the global production of textiles and apparel. Because China is currently the world's largest apparel exporter, it is often added to this list, which becomes the "Big Four." In 1997, sovereignty of Hong Kong will transfer from Great Britain to China. At this point, no one is sure what this change will mean to Hong Kong producers. Some U.S. companies have chosen to find contractors elsewhere, whereas others are confident that policies will remain favorable for companies located there.

As with the newly industrialized countries, many developing countries rely on textile and apparel manufacturing for their economic development. Several characteristics of textile and apparel manufacturing account for this. Because textile and apparel production is highly labor intensive, the industry provides work for many people. Compared with other manufacturing industries, apparel production is fairly inexpensive to establish. Essentially all that is needed are industrial sewing machines, pressing equipment, and a building. In addition, because of continuously changing fashion trends, there is a constant demand for textile and apparel products. Thus the textile and apparel industry is often the first rung on the ladder of economic development for individuals as well as for countries. Therefore, developing countries in Southeast Asia, Africa, the Caribbean basin, and South America greatly contribute to the global production of textiles and apparel.

Spurred by the North American Free Trade Agreement, in 1995 Mexico surpassed China as the U.S.'s leading supplier of imported apparel and textiles. Although analysts predict that China will again surpass Mexico once quotas are entirely phased out worldwide in 2005, Mexico has gained popularity as a sourcing option because of the reduced or zero duties and the shorter turnaround time as compared to Asian countries (Ostroff, 1995). Indeed, from 1994 to the year 2000, apparel exports from Mexico are expected to grow at a rate of 10.5 percent per year (Southern California Edison Company, 1995). However, this growth will depend on U.S textile and apparel design companies. Because most of the apparel produced in Mexico is made with fabrics produced and cut in the United States, U.S. textile producers have benefited from the arrangement. Design leadership and other services for the Mexican industry will also come from the United States. Thus increased partnerships with Mexican companies may provide new opportunities for the U.S. industry.

CURRENT ISSUES IN DOMESTIC AND FOREIGN PRODUCTION

CHANGES IN INTERNATIONAL TRADE LAWS

Currently, one of the greatest disadvantages to foreign production is international trade restrictions, including tariffs and quotas. However, several recent developments in international trade laws have affected how apparel manufacturers and retailers view off-shore production. The North American Free Trade Agreement (NAFTA), which took effect on January 1, 1994, phases in duty-free trade among Canada, Mexico, and the United States. In addition, the new World Trade Organization (WTO) Agreement on textiles and clothing went into effect on January 1, 1995. According to the WTO, the Multi-Fiber Arrangement (MFA) and quotas on textiles and apparel will be phased out and tariffs will be reduced by the year 2005. With these changes, there will undoubtedly be increased use of foreign contractors as a sourcing option.

SWEATSHOPS IN THE UNITED STATES

Although sweatshops have been around since the turn of the century, the prevalence of sweatshops in the apparel industry has grown in recent years. A number of factors have contributed to this problem. Until the 1960s, a majority of U.S. apparel companies owned large factories whose workers were usually unionized. Federal and state agencies could easily inspect the

Figure 10.8
Sweatshop conditions in apparel manufacturing still exist despite government and industry pressure to maintain safe and healthful working conditions.

facilities and enforce laws. However, as more companies are moving away from owning their own facilities to using contractors to handle the assembly part of production, there has been a shift in apparel production from large company-owned factories to a vast array of small specialized contractors. Along with this shift, the industry has seen a growth in and proliferation of sweatshops. At the same time, there has been a decrease in government agencies' ability to regulate working conditions with the sweatshops. As reported in the *New York Times* (Finder, 1995, p. B4), sweatshops "generally employ 20 to 50 workers, many of them illegal immigrants, willing to suffer long hours, low pay and miserable working conditions, just to have a job. . . . [Owners] pay their workers in cash and often deny them the minimum wage, overtime, holidays or any other benefits." It is estimated that more than 2,000 sweatshops operate in the New York City area alone, with Los Angeles being the other mecca for such establishments (although sweatshops can most likely be found in any city with contract sewing shops). Reminiscent of the early 1900s, stories have emerged of lurid working conditions, piecework pay below the minimum wage (e.g., 65 cents per hour), and children working and playing alongside their mothers in factories (Lii, 1995).

Rather than attempting to inspect the vast numbers of production facilities, government agencies are asking manufacturers and retailers to take greater responsibility for monitoring the working conditions of their contractors and subcontractors. Some manufacturers are already auditing the wages and working conditions of their contractors to assure that they meet the legal standards. In an effort to increase consumer awareness of the problem and to put pressure on companies, in 1995, the U.S. Labor Department (headed by Labor Secretary Robert Reich) published an honor roll or "Trendsetter List" of companies (including retailers) that take responsibility for monitoring the practices of contractors that produce goods for their company (Raney, 1995). Manufacturers and retailers are also engaged in self-policing practices of manufacturers to help curb the problem.

HUMAN RIGHTS ISSUES IN OFF-SHORE PRODUCTION

In recent years, many apparel manufacturers and retailers have been admonished for owning factories or using contractors in countries that violate human rights by using child labor, tolerating poor working conditions, and accepting violence against union groups. The government, as well as labor, human rights, and religious groups have put pressure on apparel manufacturers and retailers not to use foreign suppliers that violate human rights or hire contractors in countries whose political policies violate human rights. However, simply boycotting such contractors or countries is not necessarily the answer to this complex problem. In many developing countries, apparel production provides much-needed jobs for thousands of workers. In many cases the wages of working children are essential for providing basic necessities for themselves and their families. Therefore, rather than punishing these individuals by boycotting the country or contractor and leaving them without needed jobs, some companies have responded by attempting to reform working conditions and make sure that workers are not abused. Many large retailers and mass manufacturers have adopted sourcing guidelines and regularly inspect foreign contractors to assure that workers are not being exploited.

One of the first companies to implement such guidelines was Levi Strauss and Co. In 1992, it established guidelines for its hired contractors covering such issues as the treatment of workers and the environmental impact of production (Zachary, 1994). Levi Strauss, which works with contractors in more than sixty countries outside the United States, regularly inspects plants and will cancel contracts with companies that breach these rules. These guidelines ban the use of child and prison labor, establish a maximum work week of 60 hours, with at least one day off in seven, confirm that workers have the right to free association and a nonexploitive environment, require that wages (at a minimum) comply with the law and match prevailing local practice, require that business partners comply with legal business requirements, and insist that certain environmental requirements must be met. Levi Strauss will not source in countries where conditions violate certain human rights (Haas, 1994). Other companies such as Wal-Mart, Nordstrom, and Reebok have established similar guidelines. Some companies require that contractors pay for the cost of any necessary improvements; others help pay some of the costs. For example, Timberland has provided money for educational purposes and water treatment systems in communities in China, where its products are manufactured. When Levi Strauss & Co. discovered a group of underage workers at two contractor factories in

TABLE 10-8

**Levi Strauss and Company
Country Assessment Guidelines**

The diverse cultural, social, political, and economic circumstances of the various countries where Levi Strauss & Co. has existing or future business interests raise issues that could subject our corporate reputation and therefore, our business success, to potential harm. The Country Assessment Guidelines are intended to help us assess these issues. The Guidelines are tools that assist us in making practical and principled business decisions as we balance the potential risks and opportunities associated with conducting business in a particular country.

In making these decisions, we consider the degree to which our global corporate reputation and commercial success may be exposed to unreasonable risk. Specifically, we assess whether the:

1. **Brand Image** would be adversely affected by a country's perception or image among our customers and/or consumers;
2. **Health and Safety** of our employees and their families, or our Company representatives would be exposed to unreasonable risk;
3. **Human Rights Environment** would prevent us from conducting business activities in a manner that is consistent with the Global Sourcing Guidelines and other Company policies;
4. **Legal System** would prevent us from adequately protecting our trademarks, investments or other commercial interests, or from implementing the Global Sourcing Guidelines and other Company policies; and
5. **Political, Economic And Social Environment** would threaten the Company's reputation and/or commercial interests.

In making these assessments, we take into account the various types of business activities and objectives proposed (e.g., procurement of fabric and sundries, sourcing, licensing, direct investments in subsidiaries) and, thus, the accompanying level of risk involved.

Bangladesh, the company convinced the contractors to take the children off the production lines so they could attend school. Levi Strauss & Co. paid for the children's school fees, books, and uniforms, while the contractors agreed to continue their wages while they attended school. The contractors also agreed to stop employing child labor.

Even if companies adopt guidelines, however, it is difficult to improve working conditions in overseas factories, particularly if companies do not inspect and enforce their codes (Ortega, 1995) and if the governments do not enforce certain standards. In many cases, countries have resisted adopting certain guidelines, which they view as "western standards" of business. Large companies that may contract in more than 50 different countries and work with hundreds of different contractors are also finding it difficult to inspect and regulate working conditions in every factory. In addition, according to some critics, some companies are interested in the public relations appeal of sourcing guidelines, but do very little to enforce the rules (Ortega, 1995).

TABLE 10-9

Levi Strauss and Company
Business Partner Terms of Engagement

1. Ethical Standards

We will seek to identify and utilize business partners who aspire as individuals and in the conduct of all their businesses to a set of ethical standards not incompatible with our own.

2. Legal Requirements

We expect our business partners to be law abiding as individuals and to comply with legal requirements relevant to the conduct of all their businesses.

3. Environmental Requirements

We will only do business with partners who share our commitment to the environment and who conduct their business in a way that is consistent with Levi Strauss & Co.'s Environmental Philosophy and Guiding Principles.

4. Community Involvement

We will favor business partners who share our commitment to contribute to improving community conditions.

5. Employment Standards

We will only do business with partners whose workers are in all cases present voluntarily, not put at risk of physical harm, fairly compensated, allowed the right of free association and not exploited in any way. In addition, the following specific guidelines will be followed:

SUMMARY

The term sourcing is used to describe the decision process of companies in determining how and where the textile and apparel products or their components will be produced. In making sourcing decisions, companies take into consideration their general sourcing philosophy, labor requirements and costs, fabric requirements, quality control standards, equipment requirements, plant capacities, trade barriers, and expected turn-around time. Based on these criteria, a number of sourcing options are available to apparel companies and retailers. Major sourcing decisions focus on whether

WAGES AND BENEFITS. We will only do business with partners who provide wages and benefits that comply with any applicable law or match the prevailing local manufacturing or finishing industry practices.

WORKING HOURS. While permitting flexibility in scheduling, we will identify prevailing local work hours and seek business partners who do not exceed them except for appropriately compensated overtime. While we favor partners who utilize less than sixty-hour work weeks, we will not use contractors who, on a regularly scheduled basis, require in excess of a sixty-hour week. Employees should be allowed at least one day off in seven.

CHILD LABOR. Use of child labor is not permissible. Workers can be no less than 14 years of age and not younger than the compulsory age to be in school. We will not utilize partners who use child labor in any of their facilities. We support the development of legitimate workplace apprenticeship programs for the educational benefit of younger people.

PRISON LABOR/FORCED LABOR. We will not knowingly utilize prison or forced labor in contracting or subcontracting relationships in the manufacture and finishing of our products. We will not knowingly utilize or purchase materials from a business partner utilizing prison or forced labor.

HEALTH & SAFETY. We will only utilize business partners who provide workers with a safe and healthy work environment. Business partners who provide residential facilities for their workers must provide safe and healthy facilities.

DISCRIMINATION. While we recognize and respect cultural differences, we believe that workers should be employed on the basis of their ability to do the job, rather than on the basis of personal characteristics or beliefs. We will favor business partners who share this value.

DISCIPLINARY PRACTICES. We will not utilize business partners who use corporal punishment or other forms of mental or physical coercion.

production will be domestic or off shore and whether production will take place in a company-owned facility or will be contracted to others.

Domestic apparel production is primarily found in New York, California, and in southern states. Foreign production is concentrated in several areas, although Hong Kong, Taiwan, South Korea, and China are primary contributors to global production. Current issues surrounding apparel production are sweatshops in the United States, changes in international trade laws that will reduce trade barriers, and human rights issues in off-shore production facilities.

REFERENCES

Brooks, Gary. (1992, September). Make domestically or import: How to avoid costly mistakes. *Apparel Industry Magazine,* pp. 180–184.

Brown, Christie. (1995, September). The body-bending business. *Forbes,* pp. 196–204.

Cedrone, Lisa. (1994). 11th Annual Caribbean and Latin American comparative analysis. *Bobbin,* special report.

Cruz, Sergio. (1995, November). Site selection: Straight talk about costs. *Bobbin,* pp. 80–84.

DesMarteau, Kathleen. (1994, October). Need plant, will travel. *Bobbin,* pp. 80–86.

Dickerson, K.G. (1995). *Textiles and Apparel in the Global Economy.* (2nd ed.). Englewood Cliffs, NJ: Prentice-Hall.

Finder, Alan. (1995, February 6). Despite tough laws, sweatshops flourish. *New York Times,* pp. A1, B4.

Friedman, Arthur. (1996, March 26). Sourcing now: The proximity factor. *WWD,* p. 6.

Haas, Robert D. (1994, May). Ethics in the trenches. *Across the Board, 31,* 12–13.

Lii, Jane H. (1995, March 12). Week in sweatshop reveals grim conspiracy of the poor. *New York Times,* pp. 1, 40.

Moore, Lila. (1995, September). Home is where you sew it. *Apparel Industry Magazine,* pp. 38–54.

O'Rourke, Mary T. (1992, September). Labor costs—From Pakistan to Portugal. *Bobbin,* pp. 116–122.

Ortega, Bob. (1995, July 3). Broken rules: Conduct codes garner goodwill for retailers, but violations go on. *Wall Street Journal,* pp. 1, A4.

Ostroff, Jim. (1995, December 12). Mexico's fast trip to the top. *WWD,* pp. 7, 11.

Raney, Joanna. (1995, October 10). Reich: Inside the sweatshop war. *WWD,* p. 32.

Ratoff, Paul. (1994, May 27–June 2). To manufacture in-house—Yes or no? *California Apparel News,* p. 7.

Southern California Edison Company. (1995, February). *Southern California's apparel industry: Building a path to prosperity.* Rosemead, CA: Author.

Zachary, G. Pascal (1994, July 28). Levi tries to make sure contract plants in Asia treat workers well. *The Wall Street Journal,* pp. A1, A9.

KEY TERMS

sourcing
off-shore production
sourcing options
tariffs

quotas
807 or 9802 production
maquiladora operations

DISCUSSION QUESTIONS

1. Many apparel companies have shifted production from company-owned facilities to contractors. Why has this shift occurred? What problems in domestic and foreign production are associated with this shift?

2. What are the advantages and disadvantages for an apparel company in its developing and implementing sourcing guidelines related to human rights and environmental issues?

CAREER PROFILE

SOURCING ANALYST, *Publicly Owned Sportswear Company*

Job Description

Develop source plans and costing worksheets taking into consideration quotas, capacities, pricing, competitiveness, and quality.

Typical Tasks

▪ Determine source for garments and negotiate terms

▪ Determine the effect of quotas, duties, freight, and other miscellaneous charges on the landed cost of garments and margin analysis

▪ Communicate with other departments (marketing, product development, forecasting and scheduling, customs, cost accounting)

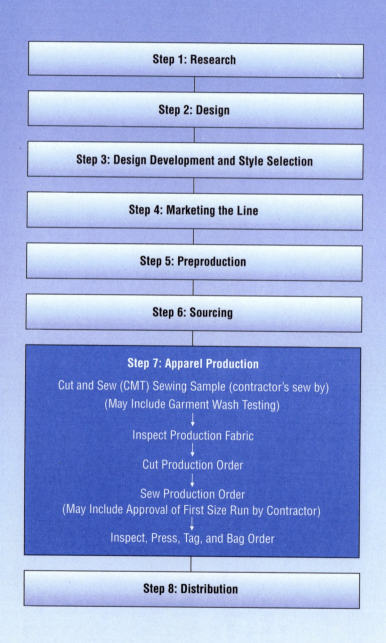

Step 1: Research

Step 2: Design

Step 3: Design Development and Style Selection

Step 4: Marketing the Line

Step 5: Preproduction

Step 6: Sourcing

Step 7: Apparel Production

Cut and Sew (CMT) Sewing Sample (contractor's sew by)
(May Include Garment Wash Testing)

Inspect Production Fabric

Cut Production Order

Sew Production Order
(May Include Approval of First Size Run by Contractor)

Inspect, Press, Tag, and Bag Order

Step 8: Distribution

11

Production Processes and Quality Assurance

Objectives

▌ To describe the types of equipment used for fabric inspection, spreading, cutting, and bundling.

▌ To identify and describe the production systems used in the industry.

▌ To describe production processes used in the manufacture of apparel.

▌ To examine the components of quality assurance and explain the importance of quality assurance in delivering on-time acceptable merchandise to the retailer.

▌ To explore the nature of future plans for improved productivity within the textile and apparel industries.

▌ To identify agents who assist apparel manufacturers move products produced off shore into the United States.

PRODUCTION CONSIDERATIONS

THE PREVIOUS CHAPTERS discussed the development of a product line from market research, creation, design development, pattern development, and preproduction through sourcing options. The product line is now ready for production. **Production** is the construction process by which the pattern pieces, materials, and trims are merged into a finished apparel product or accessory. The cost to produce the product is affected by the product design and pattern as well as by the production processes. Therefore, it is essential to the success of the company that the designer and pattern maker be well versed in the production systems used to manufacture the product. Some of the decisions regarding the relationship between design, pattern, and production occur during the planning and review meetings. However, if difficulties arise during production, the designer and pattern maker may be consulted in addition to the production engineer.

Production methods vary greatly depending on factors such as available technology, wholesale price zone, and geographic location of production. Production is one of the areas in the apparel industry that changes quickly, especially with advances in new computer technology. Therefore, this chapter will provide an overview of the methods of cutting, producing, assuring product quality, and importing goods.

FABRIC INSPECTION

The preproduction steps discussed in Chapter 9 included ordering production fabrics and trims. A part of this process involves approving fabric and trim colors and the quality of components. Samples are submitted by suppliers (vendors) and approved by the apparel or accessory manufacturer. It is assumed by the apparel manufacturer that the production fabrics and trims will accurately match (called a commercial match) the samples submitted and used for the production of the sample garments. The retailer's orders are written based on the materials, trims, and construction quality seen in the sample garment. If the quality or color match of any part of the production goods is inferior, the retailer may reject an entire order. Fabric inspection can be the responsibility of the apparel producer or the textile producer.

FABRIC INSPECTION BY THE APPAREL PRODUCER

To avoid problems arising from inferior fabric quality, some apparel manufacturers inspect fabrics on their arrival from the textile manufacturers. Various types of machinery are used to speed this process, including computerized equipment that scans across the fabric along the entire length to note any shade variation from beginning to end of fabric roll. Other equipment checks the density of the weave or knit. Some companies, however, rely on visual inspection. On occasion, it has been necessary to reject fabric orders because of color or quality problems. Ordering replacement fabric can delay production by weeks. At times, a textile manufacturer may be unable to replace rejected goods. The production schedule for the contracted arrival date of the goods at the retailer can be jeopardized because of fabric problems.

If the apparel producer is responsible for inspecting fabrics, the fabric goods must arrive at the cutting facility in time to allow for inspection before cutting begins. This requires a crew of workers paid by the apparel facility to inspect the goods. In addition, costs of production increase any time the fabric is in storage or in inventory and not being processed, as when the fabric is waiting to be cut and sewn. As the apparel industry moved toward faster turn-around time, it became obvious that several processes would need to change. Among them is fabric inspection at the textile mill.

FABRIC INSPECTION BY THE TEXTILE PRODUCER

Through Quick Response strategies: (a) partnerships in trust have been formed between the textile manufacturer and the apparel manufacturer ensuring that the textile manufacturer inspected the goods and that they were of the quality shown by the sample, and (b) goods would arrive at the production facility just in time to cut and sew, as set forth by the apparel manufacturer's schedule. Therefore, QR apparel manufacturers no longer routinely inspect fabric. Instead, textile manufacturers inspect the goods before they leave the textile mill. At the textile mill, flaws in weaving or knitting are marked along the selvage edge of the fabric, so that the apparel producer knows where the flaws are and can cut around them. Once inspected, the fabric ordered for production is sent in large rolls from the textile manufacturer or fabric wholesaler to the apparel manufacturer or cutting facility.

Currently, many smaller apparel manufacturers do not have the production volume to participate in this aspect of Quick Response. They continue to inspect the fabric and trims prior to sending them to cutting. Even with Quick Response participants, fabric flaws can occur. It is important for all workers to be alert to flaws, such as off-grain stripes, that could cause the rejection of an order.

For apparel companies that own their factories, the fabric and trims are usually sent from the supplier (vendor) either directly to the company's production plant or to the apparel company's warehouse (where inspection may occur if it is not a QR company) and then on to the production plant. For companies that use contractors for the cutting and sewing operations, the fabric might be ordered, received, and inspected by the apparel manufacturer, which then sends the fabric rolls to the cutting facility. In other cases, the fabric is ordered by the production facility, which assumes the responsibility for the quality of the fabrics and trims. This is typically done when the fabric is manufactured off shore and the cutting and sewing occurs off shore.

PRODUCTION SPREADING, CUTTING, AND BUNDLING

SPREADING

Spreading is the process of unwinding the large rolls of fabric onto long, wide tables. The fabric is stacked, layer upon layer, depending on the size of the cut order. For **production cutting,** the fabric is laid flat across its entire

Figure 11.1
Fabric is spread carefully and stacked layer upon layer in preparation for production cutting.

width from selvage to selvage. For large cuts, thin sheets of paper may be laid between every 10 or 12 layers of fabric, in order to count layers more quickly. This saves a great deal of time after cutting, when the stacks of cut pieces need to be assembled into different groups (bundles) for sewing. When a style will be produced in several colors, the fabric layers will reflect the correct number of layers for each color needed.

Fabrics that have a directional print or napped fabrics such as corduroy and velvet need to be laid so that all layers face the same direction (called face-up). This is a more time-consuming process than face-to-face spreading (two-directional) and is reflected in the labor cost to cut. Fabrics such as stripes and plaids also take more time to lay up, and therefore cost more to cut. Stretch fabrics, such as swimwear fabrics, require great care during lay-up to avoid distorting the fabric.

A variety of equipment speeds the fabric laying process. **Spreading machines** guided on tracks along the side edges of the cutting table carry the large rolls of fabric, spreading the fabric smoothly. A cutting knife is sent across the fabric at the desired length. Other systems utilize spreading machines that roll along the floor beside the cutting table. Some spreading machines require operators, but automatic and robotic spreaders are an option. In 1995, Saber Industries introduced the first robotic, digitally controlled spreader in the apparel business ("Saber introduces," 1995).

CUTTING

The marker made during preproduction (see Chapter 9) is laid onto the top layer of fabric, serving as a cutting guide if the fabric will be cut by one of several hand processes. There are several types of specialized hand-guided knives and rotary cutters used for cutting the multiple thicknesses of fabric.

Figure 11.2
An industrial knife is used to hand-cut fabric layers with the marker resting on the top layer of fabric.

Die cutting is another type of cutting process used for specific purposes. For very small pieces that will be cut repeatedly, season after season, it is more precise and more economical in the long run to use a die. The die is similar to a cookie cutter—a piece of metal with a sharp edge, tooled to the exact dimensions of the shape of the pattern piece. The die is positioned over several layers of fabric. Then, a pressurized plate is applied to the die to cut through the thicknesses of fabric. A fabric appliqué that might be used season after season is an example of a pattern piece that would be economical to cut using a die. The original cost of the die is expensive, but its continued use reduces the effect of the initial cost and increases the cutting accuracy compared to hand cutting the same piece.

For facilities that have computerized cutting, special tables are required to accommodate the cutting equipment. The table surface is covered with bristles that allow the cutting blade to slide between them. The fabric layers are compressed with air to provide a more compact cutting height, thereby increasing the accuracy of the cut. The table surface is designed to accommodate the required suction. The computer-generated marker is laid onto the top layer of fabric. The cutting equipment is guided by computer coordinates, not by "seeing" the pattern piece outlines on the marker. The plotted marker is used for several purposes: (1) to ensure that the marker is laid properly onto the fabric, especially when plaids or stripe notations must be aligned, and (2) to indicate the sizes of the pattern pieces and styles for the workers who will bundle the pieces after cutting. Computerized cutting is much faster and generally more accurate than hand cutting or even die cutting.

In some cases, apparel manufacturers are responsible for making the production marker; in other cases the contractor is responsible. The marker, whether drawn by hand or plotted by computer, is sent to the cutting facility or contractor for the cutting process. Computerized cutting and sewing facil-

Figure 11.3
A cutting protocol system interfaces with computer cutting equipment to enhance cutting efficiently.

Figure 11.4
The computerized cutter requires a special table surface to accomodate the knife blade requirements.

ities may be linked by modem to the apparel manufacturer's computer, so that the marker file can be downloaded using the modem. This increases the speed of delivery of the marker to the cutting facility or contractor. Other sewing contractors may have CGMM equipment and may be responsible for making the marker. As mentioned in Chapter 9, the style's pattern file might be sent by modem from the apparel manufacturer to the sewing contractor, which will use CGMM equipment to make the marker and cut the style.

Laser cutting is also driven by computer. It offers many of the same advantages as knife-blade computer cutting, including high speed and accuracy. Laser cutting can be economically done with one or several layers of fabric (low-ply cutting) compared to the many stacked layers used with computer cutting. This provides greater flexibility so that small production runs become more economical.

Although the marker's layout utilizes the fabric in the most efficient plan possible, there is still a substantial quantity of **fallout,** or waste material. In the past, the waste goods commonly were delivered to landfills. This procedure has become more expensive, in part because of the reduction in available landfill space. Today's society expects responsible recycling as well. Textile and apparel waste recyclers provide a market for some of this waste. The payback varies according to several categories. For example, cotton fabric byproducts are very marketable, especially if they are white. Remnants large enough to be used as wiping cloths have a good market (Kron, 1992, p. 74). While there are no official figures reflecting the size of the textile and apparel waste industry, a textile and apparel waste recycler estimated that in 1992 between 1.5 billion and 1.9 billion pounds of new fiber and fabric wastes were produced annually in the United States.

As reported in *Apparel Industry Magazine* (Kron, 1992) the Council for Textile Recycling Inc. was formed by the International Association of Wiping Cloth Manufacturers (IAWCA) with the mission of increasing the amount of waste that can be recovered. At the same time, IAWCM seeks to develop new uses, products, and markets for products derived from preconsumer and postconsumer textile waste, as well as to inform manufacturers of this industry.

BUNDLING

After cutting, the component pieces for each size and color must be grouped together in some way. **Bundling** is the process of disassembling the stacked and cut pieces and reassembling them grouped by garment size, color dye lot, and quantity of units in which they will proceed through production. Bundling is done by hand, with one or more workers picking the required garment parts from the stacks and grouping them ready for production.

PRODUCTION SEWING SYSTEMS

Although new production systems have been developed, older, traditional mass-manufacturing systems are still used in some facilities. It is important to understand a variety of production systems in order to make informed decisions about the production system most suitable for the garment style, price range, and sourcing option.

SINGLE-HAND SYSTEM OF PRODUCTION

As discussed in Chapter 7, the prototype product is produced by a single individual. The sample maker (also called sample hand) completes all the

Figure 11.5
With the bundle system, a sewing operator quickly unties a bundle of garment pieces to perform one or several sewing steps on each garment in the bundle.

steps required in production, moving from one type of specialized equipment to another as needed based on the garment or product style's requirements. Some apparel and accessory goods are produced in limited quantity using a system similar to that used to sew the prototype. In a **single-hand system** one individual is responsible for sewing an entire garment. The bundle for this production system would include all the garment parts for one style in one size. In today's market, the single-hand system is used for couture and in some very high-priced apparel produced in a limited quantity. This system is slower than "mass-produced" systems, and may include considerable detail or handwork during production.

Most apparel is manufactured using one of several production systems of large-quantity or "mass manufacturing." The most common categories of production systems are bundle systems, unit production systems, and flexible manufacturing systems.

PROGRESSIVE BUNDLE SYSTEM

Before the implementation of QR strategies, the **progressive bundle system** was the most common production system used by apparel manufacturers. With the bundle system, garment parts are bundled together and put in carts that are rolled from one sewing machine operator to another. Machine operators open the bundle of the garment parts, perform one or two construction steps on each garment in the bundle, and rebundle the garment parts for transport to the next operator. The operator's pay is calculated by the number of pieces completed per day (piece-rate wage). Sometimes referred to as a "batch" or "push" system, the progressive bundle system tends to generate high levels of **work-in-process (WIP)** and often creates bottlenecks in the production line as some operators outperform others (Hill, 1992).

In the past few years, a number of systems have been implemented that create more efficient and effective short-cycle manufacturing (Colgate, 1989). In a study conducted by researchers at Columbia University (Bailey, 1993), about 75 percent of 343 apparel companies surveyed reported using some sort of program to speed up production time, but few companies used these programs for more than half of their direct labor.

UNIT PRODUCTION SYSTEMS

To achieve efficient and effective short-cycle manufacturing, some companies have focused on investment in technology. This type of investment is often in the form of **unit production systems (UPS)** and other computerized overhead transport systems. With UPS, garment parts are fed on overhead conveyors, one garment at a time, to sewing machine operators. Gar-

Figure 11.6
With a Unit Production System, the pieces of each garment are delivered to the sewing operator. She may not need to remove the garment from the conveyor while performing the sewing step.

ment parts are delivered directly to the operators' ergonomically designed workstations. This dramatically reduces operator handling time during production. Workstations can be easily moved to accommodate different equipment needs for various garments. Similar to modular manufacturing (discussed below), operators are cross-trained in a number of procedures in the manufacturing cycle. The transport system is designed to include bar codes to track WIP.

A study by Clemson Apparel Research (Hill, 1994) determined that UPS would provide the hypothetical apparel manufacturing plant a 329 percent return on its investment and would pay for itself in 11 months. The primary savings to the company would be in the areas of reduced direct labor costs (shorter waiting periods, less overtime, improved ergonomics) and reduced work-in-process inventory levels. Many production facilities have shown substantial increases in production with UPS systems. According to the general manager of F. Fashions (a San Diego golf shirt contractor), "the workers on the UPS routinely generate 20 percent to 25 percent more garments than F. Fashions' bundle lines" (DeWitt, 1995, 54).

Although UPS is considered an improvement over bundle systems, practitioners have identified a number of disadvantages in UPS systems: (1) UPS requires a significant investment in equipment, (2) UPS systems are difficult and expensive to expand, (3) differences in operator performance will affect overall productivity with UPS, (4) repetitive movement of the operators can be problematic, (5) the development of teamwork with UPS systems is difficult, if not impossible, (6) UPS includes some added operations, such as loading hangers, unhanging, and rehanging for certain proce-

Figure 11.7
Computerized production systems permit computer tracking of work-in-process as well as increased efficiency compared with the bundle system.

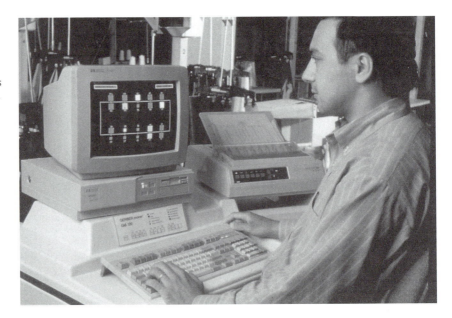

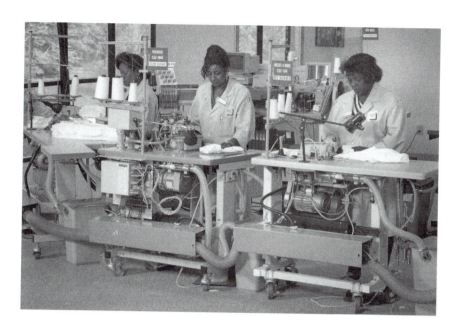

Figure 11.8
New sewing equipment
has been developed to
facilitate operators in the
standing position.

dures, (7) training and "inserting" new operators on an established UPS line
is difficult, and (8) UPS setup requires new software, computers, and controls (Egan, 1994). Advantages and disadvantages of UPS systems are evaluated by management in its decision to invest in this technology.

FLEXIBLE MANUFACTURING SYSTEMS

Whereas UPS requires an investment in equipment, some companies have
focused on an investment of resources in personnel training and team building to increase productivity. **Flexible manufacturing (FM)** is defined as
"any departure from traditional mass production systems of apparel toward
faster, smaller, more flexible production units that depend upon the coordinated efforts of minimally supervised teams of workers" (AAMA, Technical
Advisory Committee, 1988, as cited in Hill, 1992). Although FM systems are
known by many names, including modular manufacturing, self-directed
work teams, compact production teams, or flexible work groups, the emphasis of the strategy is on group effort, employee involvement, and employee
empowerment. In FM systems, a shift is made in manufacturing management away from emphasizing high individual productivity and low cost to
shortening the manufacturing cycle and quick delivery of the finished product. The term **modular manufacturing** is most often used in the U.S.
apparel industry to describe flexible manufacturing (Hill, 1992).

   With modular manufacturing, the sewing factory is organized into teams
of 7 to 9 operators. Operators are cross-trained in all areas of garment construction. Every team is responsible for the production of entire garments,

instead of one operator sewing a single operation such as a setting in a sleeve or a zipper. Equipment is arranged so that work can be passed from one team member to another, who may be either in a standing or sitting position. Often referred to as a "pull" system, the number of units within each operation may vary from one to as many as ten. In a module, operators work as a team and solve problems as a team, thus creating a more productive environment. The team rather than individuals is responsible for the construction of the entire garment. Flaws in production are handled as a team; if a mistake is found, the entire garment is returned to the team where the operators decide how best to fix it. Therefore, the traditional piece-rate wage is not applicable. The team is paid not only according to the quantity it produces, but also by the quality of its work. Pay is based on a collective effort. In theory, if an apparel factory was completely "modular," it would be redesigned into modular units, with each producing complete garments in a few hours. "Modular manufacturing enables a group of operators to take raw materials, assemble, package and ship the final product in minutes, instead of days" (Bennett, 1988, p. 51). For mass-manufactured products, the bottom line is cost containment. This is affected by: (1) the length of time that is required to produce the style, and (2) the length of time the style is in progress (work-in-process, or WIP). Reduction in one or both of these areas will result in a lower production cost. Modular manufacturing has shown its cost benefits by containing costs on both accounts.

However, despite the advantages of modular manufacturing, a number of factors must be taken into consideration before a company decides to change to this system of manufacturing. Downtime is particularly critical with modular methods. With modular manufacturing, each minute a machine is down can cost $3 to $5 (Bennett, 1988). Converting to a modular manufacturing system requires the involvement of all employees, an investment in education and training, a shift of management responsibilities from a few people to the team as a whole, and support from management (Bennett, 1988).

COMBINATION OF SYSTEMS

Most sewing facilities utilize more than one type of production system. For example, a contractor may use UPS for certain garment styles that suit this production system, while using a progressive bundle system for other styles. The quantity of production influences the production system. For example, it may not be economical to set up a UPS module for a small production run.

DEVELOPMENTS IN APPAREL PRODUCTION EQUIPMENT

The industrial machines used in sewing facilities are designed to sew much faster than home sewing machines, which are driven by a motor. Industrial machines have engines, with a clutch, brake, and continuous oil feed. Home sewing machines can perform many different functions (sew straight seams, zigzag, overcast, blind hem, and make buttonholes), whereas industrial machines perform very specialized functions (sew buttonholes or sew straight seams or sew blind hems). The specialized equipment may be fitted with additional devices or guides to further customize an operation. For example, a metal plate can be added to the sewing bed to guide elastic evenly under the needle.

The production system represents the path the garment takes at it moves through production. The same piece of sewing equipment could be used for a progressive bundle system or a flexible manufacturing system. This fact also provides the flexibility to move equipment from one system to another, depending on the equipment requirements, to produce current styles.

Equipment maintenance is a critical concern for production sewing. Any breakdown of equipment can stall production. This can be of great concern to an entire team on a UPS line. Maintenance personnel must be ready to troubleshoot, repair, or replace equipment rapidly. In some countries, machine parts are not immediately available, causing delays in the production schedule. The noise level and airborne fiber particles in sewing facilities are concerns that are being addressed as we have become more aware of their harmful effects. Workers wear protective clothing, air filtration systems in factories are used, and other environmental controls have been developed.

High-technology systems will continue to play an increasingly important role in cost reduction efforts. Regardless of the production system used, new equipment will be developed to enhance production. These developments include new types of computerized, programmable sewing machines, robotic sewing equipment, and laser cutting equipment. Just as the cost of personal computers has declined over time, high-tech equipment costs have also declined, making it more affordable to apparel manufacturers. According to an executive of Spring Ford Knitting Company (Easley, 1994, p. 42), "Over the past five years, $11 million investments in sewing, cutting and unit production systems have helped the company grow into a $75 million operation. Sales have increased 15% to 20% each of the past five years."

COMPUTER INTEGRATED MANUFACTURING

Computer integrated manufacturing (CIM) is the "integration of various computerized processes to form a common linkage of information and manufacturing equipment to produce a finished product" (Kron, 1988, p. 52). Although computers are used at every stage in the apparel production process, often data must be reentered at each step. The CIM concept is to allow the computer systems within an organization to communicate, thus reducing the time needed to enter data and minimizing the opportunities for human error in data entry. Whereas Electronic Data Interchange (EDI) focuses on communications between companies (see Chapter 12), CIM focuses on communications within companies.

In the apparel industry, the most common CIM linkages are the computer aided process for pattern making, grading, and marker making, which are electronically linked to cutting equipment. Other CIM linkages include interfaces between CAD systems and other computers for the preparation of costing models, specification sheets, and cut order planning. Some companies also use CAD data to drive numerically controlled stitching machines. In theory, every piece of equipment that is automated or semiautomated could be part of a CIM system.

One of the first companies to make extensive use of CIM was Girbaud, a Greensboro, North Carolina-based producer of trendy men's, women's, and boys' apparel. In the early 1990s, Girbaud, a subsidiary of VF Corporation, developed one of the most completely integrated computer information systems in the apparel industry (DeWitt, 1992; Hasty, 1994). The Girbaud Business Information System (GBIS) provides business data to employees in every department—design, finance, sales, production—immediately (i.e., in "real time") and at every company location, including the Greensboro business and distribution facilities, the New York sales office, and account managers' home offices. In addition to the integration of business and apparel applications, such as CAD, GBIS also includes automatic stock replenishment based upon weekly collection of point of sale (POS) data, advance shipping notices, and electronic funds transfer payments to Girbaud from retailers. Also included in the initial implementation (but subsequently abandoned for technological reasons) were computer-generated sales presentations to retail customers and graphical links to sales data (allowing garment drawings and sales data to appear on the same computer screen in full color). CAD systems are used extensively in product development, including pattern grading and marker making. Girbaud's goal was to integrate its suppliers (such as fabric vendors) into the system to a greater degree, with the concept of suppliers and contractors altering production based on the rate that merchandise is purchased by consumers.

PRODUCTION PROCESSES

An important aspect of production is planning the sequence of operations required to produce the garment style. Production processes include the sewing sequence, as well as other tasks performed at the sewing facility related to completing the product. Different categories of products may require very different processes and types of equipment. For example, men's tailored suits require many more steps in production than men's casual sportswear. The types of sewing and pressing equipment are quite different for tailored apparel versus sportswear. Chapter 4 discussed how the classifications of apparel relate to the sewing processes and the types of equipment. Boys' and girls' clothing requires similar sewing processes and equipment and could be manufactured by the same facility, whereas men's tailored clothing and men's sportswear production need to be handled by different factories.

As discussed in Chapter 9, the sequence of sewing operations may have been determined at the time the style's cost was calculated. The production processes used to sew the sales representatives' samples (made to sell the style to retail buyers) are frequently the same processes used to sew the production orders. Any problems in production might be corrected during the production of the sales samples.

Determining the most efficient production process depends on many factors such as:

▮ the equipment capabilities of the specific sewing factory (e.g., the availability of a pocket-setting machine can greatly speed production of a style with a welt pocket)

▮ the labor cost of the sewing team (in some factories where labor is very inexpensive, more work may be done by hand than by expensive equipment)

▮ whether certain steps should be subcontracted (for example, a shirt with a pleated front inset might be less expensive to produce if the fabric for the front inset were sent to a pleating contractor, then returned to the sewing factory for cutting and sewing into the shirt)

Some operations, such as fusing interfacing to garment sections, may be performed prior to the sewing process. The pieces to be fused are laid on conveyor belts and moved through large fusing "ovens" to adhere the interfacing. Patch pockets, such as those sewn to the back of jeans, are prepared for sewing by prepressing the raw edges to the inside. A metal template of the finished pocket dimensions might be used to aid in accuracy as the edges are turned under around the metal template. A fusing agent might be applied to help the seam allowances adhere to the inside of the pocket. Hundreds of pockets are prepared, then delivered to the site where they will be attached to the pants. This process is most efficient for one-size pieces. Since garment pieces may be cut from dye lots with varying color, care must be taken to match pocket pieces to identical dye lot garment sections. If the pockets were sized as small, medium, and large, care must be taken to attach the prepared pockets to the correct pant size. Belt loops might be made as a long continuous strip for the entire production run. Yards of the strips are wound onto holders attached to the sewing station. The belt loops are cut to length one at a time and sewn sequentially around the pant waistband. Many processes are streamlined to provide the most labor-effective production.

Sometimes several different factories are used to produce a large order. In these cases, the production processes may not be exactly the same for the different factories producing the same style. Each contractor submits a sample sewn at its factory to the apparel manufacturer for approval. The same process is followed for the samples sewn for sales representatives by contractors. The contractor's sample might be called a **sew by** or a **counter sample.** After approval, this sample is used as the benchmark against which to check the sewn production goods.

Although great effort is expended to plan a smooth production run, many problems can stall production. Some problems that can occur with the procurement of materials have been discussed. Production problems include complications due to delays in receiving a shipment of zippers or late arrival of subcontracted work. Troubleshooting is an integral part of production. When sourcing off shore, unexpected problems can be difficult to solve. A flood in Bangladesh, a hurricane in the Dominican Republic, a rail workers' strike in France, or a teamsters' strike in the United States can cause production delays that could not be planned for or avoided. Management personnel of apparel manufacturers often travel to production facilities (whether company owned or contractor owned) to check on production or help solve production problems.

FINISHING

At the end of the production line, the goods await various finishing steps. Pressing may occur only at this stage in production. Edge stitching or top stitching may be used to reduce the need to press during production, thereby reducing labor costs. Specialized pressing equipment produces excellent results on finished goods very quickly. Other types of specialized equipment perform other functions, such as turning pant legs right side out (pants come off the production line inside out).

Whereas labels placed in highly visible locations as a part of the brand identity of the goods are attached to the product during production, other labels might be attached during finishing. Labels might include identifying characteristics hidden to the eye. A bar code "fingerprint" visible to a scanning device can be included in the sew-in label to identify the product's pro-

Figure 11.9
Finishing processes, such as stonewashing, require specialized equipment that meets environmental safety standards.

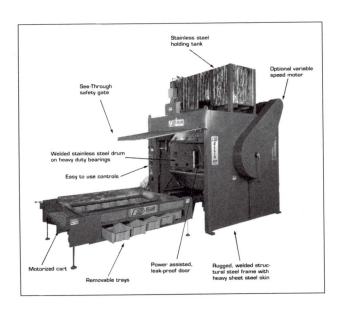

duction facility or retail destination. This technology can reduce the possibility of counterfeit goods and can also be used by the retailer to verify the origin of customer-returned goods. Providing goods with floor-ready labels and hangtags are features that utilize the advantages of Quick Response as well.

Finishing steps can include such operations as buttons and buttonholes and snap-setting in some facilities. Other types of finishing operations include a variety of fabric treatments. Garments might be laundered before shipping. Laundering might be performed to enhance the hand or visual appeal of the fabric. For example, stone washing has been used to soften denim fabric. Another reason for laundering is to shrink a product prior to shipping. While we are familiar with purchasing some products large enough to "shrink-to-fit," many consumers find it advantageous to know that the garment has been preshrunk, that the way it fits when it is tried on is the way it will fit after washing at home. For garments that will be laundered after production and before shipping, the pattern pieces for the garment had to be created very carefully with the exact shrinkage factor incorporated into each pattern piece.

Special finishes might be incorporated during finishing of the garments, rather than to the textile goods at the textile mill. For example, a wrinkle-resistant finish might be applied to apparel goods, such as 100 percent cotton trousers. Technological developments will continue to improve the garment-applied finishes.

Many apparel manufacturers purchase dyed products in color allotments based on the quantity of orders for each color. Other manufacturers produce "colorless" garments, then dye the garments during finishing. The term used to describe this is a **garment dyed** process. The procedure of dyeing finished goods has several advantages. It can provide quick delivery of the goods to the retailer, for production can begin on the "colorless" garments while the sales force is accumulating the sales totals by color. For the same reason, it represents a reduced risk to the manufacturer. Garment dyeing can be considered one of the Quick Response strategies. Care must be taken to select buttons and other trims that can accommodate the dyeing operation.

Since concern was first raised about the environmental consequences of some finishing operations, much has been done to minimize the negative environmental impact of finishing operations. As reported in a December 1995 article in *Apparel Industry Magazine*: "A new 65,000-sq.-ft. laundry facility located in Hickman, Kentucky, has doubled Chic's processing capacity from 200,000 units a week to 400,000. The facility, which utilizes Milnor 450 lb. and 550 lb. washers and dryers, has a heat reclamation system, a primary water treatment system and its own waste water treatment plant" (Moore, 1995, p. 5). New developments will continue to improve environmental protection.

Goods are prepared for shipping by being either folded or hung. At some facilities, folding might be accomplished by hand, with cardboard, tissue, straight pins, and plastic bags. At other facilities, machines are used to fold the goods. For garments placed on hangers, overhead tracks bring the garment to equipment that may cover each item with a plastic bag. Depending on the channel of distribution, the finished goods may be boxed and sent to: (a) the manufacturer's distribution center, (b) the retailer's distribution center, or (c) directly to the retailer (see Chapter 12).

QUALITY ASSURANCE

Quality assurance refers to the product meeting the standards of acceptance set forth by the contracting party. The contracting party could be the apparel manufacturer for goods produced by a contractor. The contracting party could also be a retailer for private label goods. Many of the fabric and sewing operations are specified in detail on the garment specification sheet and are an important part of quality assurance. Visual inspection—for loose threads, for example—forms another important part of quality assurance.

The fabric inspection component of quality assurance was discussed earlier in this chapter. The spreading and cutting operations include areas such as on-grain garment parts and dye lot color matching. The sewing and finishing operations are also important aspects of quality assurance. Garments are inspected during the sewing operation to assure the specified quality of production. Inspectors can include sewing operators, team quality auditors, plant supervisors, or quality auditors sent by the contracting party (apparel manufacturer or retailer).

Quality assurance includes use of quality products such as thread, buttons, zippers, snaps, elastic, and hem tape, as well as sewing operations such as stitch type and length, seam type, edge finish, top stitching, turned edges, buttonhole stitching, hem stitching, and plaid matching. Finishing operations include thread trimming, button and snap attachment, shoulder pad and lining tacking, pressing, and buttoning the garment.

Another component of quality assurance is the consistency of the size specifications for all products produced in each size. All of the finished products must conform to the specified tolerances—that is, the amount the product can deviate (plus or minus) from the garment dimension—stated on the spec sheet (see Chapter 9). Many apparel manufacturers check a specified number of garments in each shipment received from the contractor to determine whether the size standards have been met.

The difficulty lies in deciding what to do with any products that do not meet the quality standards. It may not be possible to cut and sew a replacement order of garments if a group of finished goods do not meet the size specifications. The textile manufacturer may not have replacement fabric, or the time necessary to produce replacement garments may exceed the deadline established by the retailer. Some garments end up as seconds at company employee stores and outlet malls, may be purchased by jobbers, or are given to charities. In addition to the loss to apparel manufacturer and contractor, the retailer expecting the goods may suffer if an order cannot be filled. Therefore, it is to everyone's benefit to assure quality production.

TABLE 11-1

Comparisons of the Old Inspection-Based Quality Control Methods with More Successful Production-Based Quality Assurance Methods

OLD WAY 100% Inspect/Quality Control	NEW WAY Quality Assurance/Empowerment
Acceptable Quality Level (AQL)	Zero defects
Inspector dominant	Associate responsibility
Attempt to *inspect* quality into the product	*Build* quality into the product
Justification for equipment investment based solely on reduction in labor content	Justification for equipment investment based on quality improvement
Need to produce volume first priority	Need to make a quality product first priority
Quality inspector given responsibility for product quality	Associate accepts ownership of quality process
Operator punishment for creating defects	Associate reward for recognizing and correcting the cause of defects
No incentive for quality production—inspector paid based on pieces processed	Incentive for quality production—associates paid based on number of first quality products produced
Inspectors paid for finding defects (nonvalue-added activity)	No need for inspectors, as associates paid for producing quality the first time (value-added activity)
Limited after-the-fact reporting	Causal analysis by statistical process control and other measurement tools (reporting of defects by type, quantity, area, associate)
Repair an integral part of the process	Low or no need for repair and cost of repair not justifiable
Standards are what the supervisor says they are	Standards are based on specifications developed with consideration for process capability

In developing quality assurance programs, companies are relying less on after-the-fact inspection and more on building quality into the products during production. Through flexible manufacturing methods, operators are responsible for the quality of the product throughout production. Table 11-1 compares the old way of using inspections for quality control with the new way of assuring quality products. Another aspect of Quick Response related to quality assurance is called **floor ready merchandise (FRM)**, a partnership between the apparel manufacturer and the retailer. The FRM policy at Haggar Apparel Company requires that the apparel manufacturer ship the goods to the retailer's distribution center or retail store with bar coded price ticketing, carton labeling, shipping documentation, hanger application, and shipment accuracy. "If FRM can only remove two days of delay associated with a retailer's distribution center, and if the DC [distribution center] is typically receiving goods every two weeks, then it is possible to get 52 additional selling days per year." (Swank, 1995, p. 106) Providing floor ready merchandise adds to the apparel manufacturer's cost (wholesale cost), which in turn, is reflected in the wholesale price (price retailer pays to manufacturer), and may be reflected in the retail price paid by the consumer.

EXPORT AGENTS, FREIGHT FORWARDERS, AND CUSTOMS BROKERS

Because a substantial portion of the apparel and accessories industries relies on off-shore factory production, it is important to discuss some of the aspects related to shipping goods out of the production country and into the United States. Many foreign countries have export regulations for shipping goods out of the country. It can be helpful for the U.S. apparel manufacturer who contracted the goods (the importer) to appoint an **export agent** in the exporting country to assist with exporting the products.

A **freight forwarding company** arranges to move a shipment of goods from the country where the goods were produced to the United States. Tariffs and quotas (regulations affecting apparel manufacturers who import apparel and textile products into the United States) were discussed in Chapters 2 and 10. The U.S. Customs, a part of the federal government, is the regulatory agency. A licensed customhouse broker in the United States is an agent hired by the U.S. apparel manufacturer to assist the company in importing products. The **customs broker** (licensed by the Customs office) is familiar with the complex U.S. Customs regulations concerning importing textiles and apparel and will assist the apparel manufacturer to gain customs clearance. The apparel manufacturer is charged a fee by the customs broker on a transaction basis, not by the number of items in a transaction. A consolidator might also be hired by the apparel manufacturer to serve as an intermediary for the freight forwarder and the customs broker. Whereas using a customs broker is optional, it can be very helpful to the apparel manufacturer. Sometimes, a shipment of goods is stalled by customs or sent back to the country of origin to correct the documentation. Not only does the apparel manufacturer face losing the retailer's business, but it may also face a fine by the shipping company that cannot unload the shipment.

SUMMARY

This chapter examined some of the important aspects of production. With the background of the previous chapters, the interrelationship between research, design, pattern development, preproduction, and production should be clear. All systems must work together for production to flow smoothly. Any problem along a style's path may slow production. Delays to the contracted delivery date can cost the manufacturer not only the loss of the style's profit, but the loss of future business by retailers.

A large portion of the cost to produce apparel and accessories is consumed by the labor required to cut and sew the goods. Reducing labor costs can help retain reasonable prices for finished goods. Specialized equipment has been developed to speed production and improve accuracy. New technology in equipment and manufacturing systems has dramatically changed apparel production and provided a more efficient use of the labor team. Workers are more actively involved in providing an efficient production system and in team responsibility for the quality of the goods produced. It is remarkable to learn that, given the high cost of new, technologically advanced equipment, the increase in production efficiency rapidly pays for the cash outlay to purchase new equipment. The vice president of manufacturing for K-Products stated, "So far the change to modular manufacturing has gained the company a 15% to 60% increase in efficiency, depending on which product we're talking about" (Moore, 1995, p. 66). These changes in production systems have required changes in the manner in which employee compensation is determined. Pay based on the team's performance, group incentives for high performance and quality, and straight hourly wages have replaced traditional piece rates at many facilities. Workers are cross-trained on various equipment and in a variety of skills to provide greater flexibility to the workforce.

The number of different garment styles produced per season has increased for many production facilities. This makes it more difficult for production to flow smoothly. Flexibility in production systems will continue to be an important cornerstone of increased efficiency and decreased labor costs. Concern for worker's ergonomic needs is another trend that has changed the look of production facilities. We no longer see banks of seated sewers bent over sewing machines. Workers stand, walk from point to point, and sit on stools to provide better body positioning, circulation, and muscle relaxation.

Finishing operations performed at the end of production include laundering, garment finishes, and garment dyeing, as well as packaging products ready for distribution. Although some apparel manufacturers ship goods from their distribution centers to the retailers' distribution centers, new channels of distribution include shipping goods directly from the factory to the retailer's distribution center or shipping the goods directly to the specific retail store. Providing floor ready merchandise for the retailer with bar coded hangtags improves the efficiency of the entire flow of goods.

Quality assurance is an integral part of the product, from its inception to arrival in the customer's hands. Quality assurance includes all aspects of the product: the textile goods, component parts such as buttons and zippers, sewing, size specifications, and finishing.

In the future, it is likely that more retailers, including mail order companies, will be involved in off-shore apparel manufacturing. It is increasingly important to understand the various processes, agencies, and personnel involved in these complex business transactions. Changes in regulations as well as in political and economic conditions and environmental considerations can affect the production of goods.

REFERENCES

Bailey, Thomas. (1993, August). *The Spread of Quick Response and Human Resource Innovation in the Apparel Industry.* Institute on Education and the Economy, Teachers College, Columbia University.

Bennett, Billy. (1988, October). It's a mod, mod, mod environment. *Bobbin,* pp. 50–55.

Colgate, Anne Imperato. (1989, April). Short and quick: The trick. *Bobbin,* pp. 64–70.

DeWitt, John W. (1992, September). The ultimate consumer connection. *Apparel Industry Magazine,* pp. 56–62.

DeWitt, John W. (1995, June). F is for fine—and fast. *Apparel Industry Magazine,* pp. 52–58.

Easley, Kimberly. (1994, June). Spring Ford's niche blooms. *Apparel Industry Magazine,* pp. 42–44.

Egan, Leonard. (1994, May). Letter to the Editor. *Apparel Industry Magazine,* pp. 18–20.

Hasty, Susan E. (Ed) (1994, March). *The Quick Response Handbook.* Supplement to *Apparel Industry Magazine.*

Hill, Ed. (1992, February). Flexible manufacturing systems, Part 1. *Bobbin,* pp. 34–38.

Hill, Thomas. (1994, March). CAR study: UPS, CAD provide 300 percent+ return on investment. *Apparel Industry Magazine,* pp. 34–40.

Kron, Penny. (1988, May). The CIM search. *Apparel Industry Magazine,* pp. 52–64.

Kron, Penny. (1992, September). Recycle—If you can! *Apparel Industry Magazine,* pp. 74–82.

Moore, Lila. (1995, January). K-Products walks fine line of modular production. *Apparel Industry Magazine,* pp. 64–70.

Moore, Lila. (1995, December). Master of just-in-time. *Apparel Industry Magazine,* pp. 4–8.

Quick Response: America's Competitive Advantage [slide set program guide] (1988). Washington, D.C.: American Textile Manufacturer's Institute.

Saber introduces first truly robotic spreader. (1995, August). *Apparel Industry Magazine.* pp. 46–48.

Swank, Gary. (1995, January). QR Requires floor-ready goods. *Apparel Industry Magazine,* p. 106.

KEY TERMS

production

spreading

production cutting

spreading machines

die cutting

fallout

bundling

single-hand system

progressive bundle system

work-in-process (WIP)

unit production system (UPS)

flexible manufacturing (FM)

modular manufacturing

computer integrated manufacturing (CIM)

sew by (counter sample)

garment dyed

quality assurance

floor ready merchandise (FRM)

export agent

freight forwarding company

customs broker

DISCUSSION QUESTIONS

1. Give several examples of problems that may occur with fabric quality. Discuss options available to the apparel manufacturer to correct the problem and explain how this affects production and delivery to the retailer.

2. Compare and contrast the advantages and disadvantages of the progressive bundle, unit production, and flexible manufacturing systems of apparel production.

3. Describe an example of a quality assurance production problem you have experienced with an apparel product or accessory. How might this problem have been avoided?

CAREER PROFILES

Careers in the production area include positions as production cutters, sewing operators, production supervisors, plant managers, and quality assurance coordinators. If you are considering a career in the production arena, what would your job description entail and what are some typical tasks that you would perform?

PRODUCTION MANAGER,
Private Label Manufacturer of Intimate Apparel

Job Description

Manage production of in-house sampling requirements (market, first fit, sew by, and photo samples), technical development, standards, and quality control, price negotiations and order placement with suppliers and subcontractors, development and implementation of production procedures and controls from order placement to shipment, automation of production procedures and controls, and production personnel. Manage contracted production in Hong Kong, Taiwan, UAE, Sri Lanka, Bangladesh, India, Hungary, and Turkey.

Typical Tasks

- Liaise with design, sales, and sample room as well as factories
- Visit factories for preproduction review on new styles and to check production in process as well as approve production for shipment
- Review samples from factories to check for spec, approve fabric, trims, color
- Organize labels, packaging
- Prepare cost sheets
- Fax communication

What Do You Like Best About Your Job?

The diversity of tasks, the challenge of delivering garments on time and to specification, and crisis management

ASSISTANT PLANNER, *Athletic Sportswear Company*

Job Description

This position involves planning responsibilities for custom team orders and basic team orders, warehouse inventory responsibilities, clerical responsibilities to maintain files on forecasting, purchasing, and sales history, and quality control assistance during peak times.

Typical Tasks

- Write up weekly orders, manage flow of finished goods, approve inventories, keep weekly sales history
- Maintain bill of materials on Stylemaster (software program)
- Enter production receipts and matching invoices, packing slips and purchase orders for accounting department
- Maintain excess fabric inventory and keep swatch book up-to-date
- Maintain inventory of finished goods closeouts and excesses

What Do You Like Best About Your Job?

Because my tasks are so varied, I am not only becoming very versatile, but I am learning how my efforts affect others in the company and vice versa.

APPAREL QUALITY ANALYST, *Department of Quality Assurance, Large Publicly Owned Athletic Clothing Manufacturer*

Job Description

Investigate and prepare reports on all apparel quality issues working toward a resolution. Recommend action to and follow up with affected parties (development, marketing, sales, production). Develop and maintain a strong working relationship with related departments. Conduct meeting with departments to inform and reach a joint decision. Arrange for component, fabric, and finished product tests and inspections as necessary. Communicate with Quality Assurance (QA) managers in Asia, Europe, and other locations in the United States. The apparel quality analyst position functions as a global position.

Typical Tasks

- Communicate daily with related departments throughout the entire life of the quality issue via E-mail and phone

- Prepare weekly quality logs for the QA department
- Investigate the scope, nature, probable cause, and resolution of quality issues. Samples from the field and distribution center come to me. I am the "center fielder"; most communication comes directly to me and I will respond with the final decision and direction on each issue
- Prepare reports and submit samples to the textile testing lab when the quality issue involves fabric development
- Perform inspections/audits at three factories once a month. Being a field auditor is a small part of my responsibility. We have field auditors who inspect/audit factories.

What Do You Like Best About Your Job?

I enjoy the challenge of my position. It is always changing. Quality Assurance is a fairly new department for apparel in this company. I enjoy being part of a growing department. I am learning much about the production end of the company. I work closely with factories in Asia and the United States, with production, sourcing, scheduling, sales, marketing, and development. I also can relate to how important development is to the success of a product. Trying to solve the mystery work by locating the problem is very interesting. QA is becoming a more proactive department. Solving problems before they go into production is a key goal. It will not only make the company's brand a stronger and better apparel brand for quality, but it will also shorten our time lines and give retailers their product faster.

QUALITY ASSURANCE MANAGER, *National Direct Mail Retailer*

Job Description

To establish an effective quality assurance program for the company through development of quality guidelines, sizing standards, product testing program, and work flow process between the distribution center and the corporate office.

Typical Tasks

- Monitor product return rate by style
- Review products with merchandisers to ensure that they meet corporate guidelines
- Work with vendors who take issue with our corporate guidelines
- Monitor arrival of products at distribution center and oversee inspection of specified quality and size standards
- Meet with inventory planners
- Conduct product training such as fit sessions so sales force understands each product's wearing and design ease

What Do You Like Best About Your Job?

Support from management to develop and enforce a quality assurance program with vendors in order to provide the highest quality to our customers; satisfaction that this department has made a positive impact on the bottom line of the company, that one always takes the viewpoint of the customer in terms of product satisfaction, and being able to establish a new division from the ground up.

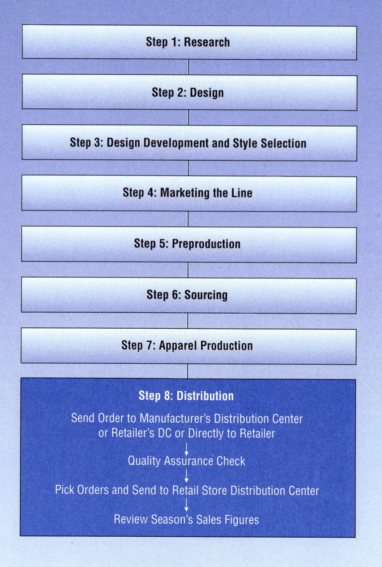

Step 1: Research

Step 2: Design

Step 3: Design Development and Style Selection

Step 4: Marketing the Line

Step 5: Preproduction

Step 6: Sourcing

Step 7: Apparel Production

Step 8: Distribution

Send Order to Manufacturer's Distribution Center
or Retailer's DC or Directly to Retailer

Quality Assurance Check

Pick Orders and Send to Retail Store Distribution Center

Review Season's Sales Figures

12

Distribution and Retailing

Objectives

▌ To outline and describe the primary marketing channels used in the distribution of apparel.

▌ To discuss the distribution strategies and distribution methods for apparel products.

▌ To describe the partnerships between apparel companies and retailers in carrying out Quick Response efforts.

▌ To define and describe the various categories of retailers.

MARKETING CHANNELS

WE HAVE FOLLOWED apparel products from their design through their production. The next stage is distribution to the ultimate consumer. The process of products moving from the manufacturer to the ultimate consumer is referred to as a **marketing channel.** Marketing channels consist of businesses that perform manufacturing, wholesaling, and retailing functions in order to get merchandise to the consumer. Marketing channels can be composed of several structural designs including (see Table 12-1):

TABLE 12-1

Marketing Channels

DIRECT MARKETING CHANNEL
Manufacturer ─────────────────────────────▶ Consumer

LIMITED MARKETING CHANNEL
Manufacturer ─────────────▶ Retailer ──────────▶ Consumer

EXTENDED MARKETING CHANNELS

Manufacturer ──▶ Wholesaler ──────▶ Retailer ───────▶ Consumer
Manufacturer ──▶ Wholesaler ──▶ Jobber ──▶ Retailer ──▶ Consumer

▌ Direct Marketing Channel
▌ Limited Marketing Channel
▌ Extended Marketing Channel

A **direct marketing channel** involves apparel manufacturers selling directly to consumers. For example, consumers may purchase goods directly from the manufacturer through catalogs or over the Internet. Although some apparel products are available to consumers in this direct manner, consumers do not have the resources to deal directly with manufacturers for all of their apparel purchases (nor do manufacturers have the resources to deal directly with individual consumers). Therefore, consumers must rely on retailers to search for and screen manufacturers and products for them.

In a **limited marketing channel** retailers survey the various manufacturers and select (i.e., buy) merchandise they believe their customers will want and thus perform an important service to consumers. Retailers may also arrange for the production of specific goods (e.g., private label merchandise) that they then make available to their customers. Retailers also serve as a gatekeeper, by narrowing the choices for consumers and providing them with access (through retail outlets) to the merchandise. In some cases, apparel manufacturers sell merchandise through their own retail stores (e.g., Ralph Lauren, NIKE, Jantzen). Because of the use of a retail store in the distribution process, this format is also considered a limited marketing channel. The limited marketing channel is the most typical marketing channel for apparel products.

Extended marketing channels involve either wholesalers that acquire products from manufacturers and have them readily available to retailers or jobbers that buy products from wholesalers at special rates and make them available to retailers. Extended marketing channels are used in the distribution of many basic items, such as T-shirts, underwear, and hosiery. For example, a company may produce white T-shirt "blanks" and sell them to wholesalers. The wholesalers will sell the T-shirts to manufacturers that will have designs screen printed on the shirts (using a textile converter for the screen printing process). The shirts are then sold to retailers. However, because of the increased time involved in this marketing channel, it is seldom used for fashion goods that companies want to get to the consumer as quickly as possible.

MARKETING CHANNEL INTEGRATION

Marketing channel integration is the process of connecting the various levels of the marketing channel so that they work together to provide the right products to consumers in the right quantities, in the right place, and at the right time. Integration can be created through conventional marketing channels or through vertical marketing channels.

Conventional marketing channels consist of independent companies that separately perform the manufacturing, distribution, and retailing functions. **Vertical marketing channels** (vertical integration) consist of companies that work as a united group. For example, when a manufacturer sells merchandise only through its own (or franchised) retail stores, this is a vertical marketing channel. Private label merchandise produced specifically for a retailer would also be a type of vertical marketing channel (e.g., The Limited, The Gap). In some cases, manufacturers will sell their merchandise through their own stores as well as through other retailers. This distribution strategy is known as **dual distribution** or **multichannel distribution.** Many manufacturers, such as Liz Claiborne, Esprit, Pendleton, and NIKE, have opened their own stores while at the same time distributing their merchandise through other retailers as well. Thus, they are engaged in dual distribution.

MARKETING CHANNEL FLOWS

Companies that are part of marketing channels are connected on several levels, including physical flow, ownership flow, information flow, payment flow, and promotion flow. Each relates to specific functions that companies perform throughout the marketing channel.

- **Physical flow** involves the trafficking of merchandise from the manufacturer to the retailer or ultimate consumer. It includes warehousing (or storing), handling, and transporting merchandise so that it is available to consumers at the right time and at the right place.

- **Ownership flow** or **title flow** involves transferring of ownership or title from one company to the next. For example, does the retailer own the merchandise when it leaves the manufacturers' distribution center or when the retailer actually receives the merchandise? The point at which the title is transferred is negotiated between the manufacturer and retailer.

- **Information flow** involves communication among companies within the marketing channel pipeline. Increased information flow between manufacturers and retailers has resulted from many QR strategies that will be discussed later in the chapter.
- **Payment flow** involves the transfer of monies among companies as payment for merchandise or services rendered. This includes both the methods used for payment and to whom payments are made.
- **Promotion flow** involves the flow of communications designed to promote the merchandise to either other companies (trade promotions) or to consumers (consumer promotions) in order to influence sales.

DISTRIBUTION STRATEGIES

Companies must decide how their merchandise will be distributed to the ultimate consumer. Distribution strategies are based on the type of marketing channel to which the company belongs (direct, limited, or extended), the buying characteristics of the target market, product type, and wholesale price zone of the merchandise. Distribution strategies include intensive or mass distribution, selective distribution, and exclusive distribution.

- **Intensive Distribution** or **Mass Distribution.** Under this strategy, products are made available to as many consumers as possible through distribution at a variety of retail outlets, including supermarkets, convenience stores, and mass merchandisers or discount stores. L'eggs, Hanes, and No Nonsense hosiery brands use this type of distribution strategy.
- **Selective Distribution.** In selective distribution, manufacturers only allow their merchandise to be distributed through certain types of stores. Some manufacturers require a minimum quantity to be purchased; others limit their products' distribution to retailers in noncompeting geographic areas. Esprit, for example, has set criteria as to the image and geographic location of stores in which its merchandise can be sold.
- **Exclusive Distribution.** In exclusive distribution, manufacturers limit the stores in which their merchandise is distributed in order to create an "exclusiveness" image. Companies that produce merchandise in the designer wholesale price zone often use an exclusive distribution strategy by selling goods only through a few stores or boutiques. Private label merchandise produced for a specific retailer is also considered a type of exclusive distribution because the brands are only available at specific stores.

THE DISTRIBUTION PROCESS

MANUFACTURER DISTRIBUTION

For some apparel companies, shipments to their retail accounts are made directly from the production facility. For other apparel companies, the flow of goods from production facilities to retailers involves the use of **distribution centers (DCs).** Apparel manufacturers will use distribution centers when shipments to retailers consist of goods produced in more than one location (especially when contractors are used). In these cases, merchandise from the various locations are brought to a centralized location for quality assurance, picking (selecting the appropriate assortment of goods to fill a specific retailer's order), packing of the merchandise, and distribution to the retail store accounts. To speed up the process, in recent years many companies have reduced the use of distribution centers and are shipping to retailers directly from the production facility (Moore, 1994). Others are changing the focus of their distribution centers away from being a warehouse of inventory to being a location where merchandise is stored for only a short period of time. Such a "flow-through" facility involves the movement of merchandise from receiving to shipping out to stores with little, if any, time in storage (Nannery, 1995). There is also a trend among apparel companies to use DCs for adding value (process by which products gain additional value or worth to the manufacturer, retailer, or consumer) to the merchandise by affixing hangtags, labels, and price information in order to make the goods floor ready (Moore, 1994). When manufacturers preticket merchandise, retailers do not have to spend extra time ticketing the items before the apparel hits the selling floor. This process, known as **vendor marking**, results in floor ready merchandise (see also Chapter 11).

RETAIL DISTRIBUTION

Retailers will also use distribution centers to facilitate distribution of merchandise from a variety of apparel companies (vendors) to a number of stores. Goods are shipped from the manufacturers to a centralized retail distribution center, where merchandise for the retailer's stores are combined

Figure 12.1
The distribution process includes shipping merchandise to retail accounts.

and shipped to the individual stores. If merchandise has not been vendor marked, then hang tags, including stock-keeping unit and price information, are affixed to the merchandise at the retailer DC. Retail distribution centers are often centrally located to speed delivery to stores.

QUICK RESPONSE: PARTNERSHIPS BETWEEN MANUFACTURERS AND RETAILERS

One of the primary goals of Quick Response strategies is to increase the speed by which merchandise gets to the consumer. The establishment of partnerships between manufacturers and retailers was imperative for this goal to be achieved. These partnerships have been critical to the success of Quick Response since the program's inception. These partnerships depend on several distribution strategies, including UPC bar coding, vendor marking, and electronic data interchange.

UPC BAR CODING AND VENDOR MARKING

The **Universal Product Code (UPC)** numbering system is one of several bar-code symbologies used for the electronic identification of merchandise. The use of UPC bar coding is often seen as the foundation of many QR strategies, because it is considered necessary for communications between manufacturer and retailer. A UPC number is a twelve-digit number that identifies manufacturer and merchandise items by stock-keeping unit (SKU): vendor, style, color, and size. It is represented by a bar code made up of a pattern of dark bars and white spaces of varying widths. A group of bars and spaces represents one character. UPC bar codes are electronically scanned and "read" by scanning equipment. The scanning equipment provides a source of intense light that illuminates the symbol. The dark bars tend to absorb the light back to the scanner. The scanner collects the reflected pattern of light and dark and converts it into an electrical signal that is sent to a decoder. The decoder, which may be part of the scanner unit or may be a separate device, translates the electrical signal to binary numbers for use by the point-of-sale terminal or computer. Scanners can be categorized as either: (1) contact readers, which must touch or come in close proximity to the symbol, or (2) noncontact readers, in which case the bar code is moved past a fixed beam or moving beam scanner.

The twelve-digit UPC number consists of (see Figure 12-2a):

▌ A one-digit number system character (NSC) that identifies the general category of merchandise and is assigned as follows:

0: 92,000 manufacturer ID numbers, 8,000 locally assigned numbers

1: reserved

2: items sold by unit of measure or random weight items, such as meat and produce

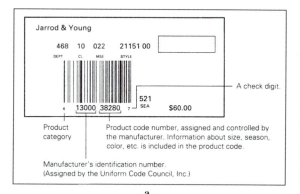

a.

b.

Figure 12.2
a. Universal Product Code (UPC) or bar code ticket. **b.** UPC bar codes are found on apparel hangtags to facilitate the collection of point-of-sale information.

3: health-related and drug items

4: retailer use only (internal use by retailer)

5: coupons

6: 100,000 manufacturer ID numbers

7: 100,000 manufacturer ID numbers

8: reserved

9: reserved

In the sewn products industry 0 and 7 are typically used.

- A five-digit manufacturer identification number. Manufacturer identification numbers are controlled and distributed by the Uniform Code Council (UCC). The UCC is the administrative council that oversees the issuing of UCC numbers and provides assistance in implementing the use of bar codes. To obtain a manufacturer identification number, manufacturers must become a member of the UCC with their membership fee based on their sales volume.

- A five-digit item code number. The item code number includes SKU information, including style, color, and size. This code number is controlled by the company. One fallacy is that this five-digit code includes all SKU information. Typically, it contains only a reference code that tells the computer where to find information about the garment (Drori, 1992).

- A check sum digit. The check digit is included at the far right of the bar code and is used for error detection. The company that prints the bar code tickets assures the accuracy of the bar code by performing a series of arithmetic operations on the first 11 numbers of the code and obtaining a single digit result, the check sum digit.

Both vendor-marked merchandise and retailer prepared bar codes are being used to increase the accuracy of inventories and the speed of checkout. There are a number of benefits of UPC bar coding and point-of-sale (POS) scanning, including maximizing the efficiency of store personnel, speeding up the check-out process, improving the accuracy of pricing, providing accurate sales information, and providing accurate on-going inventory counts.

One of the most obvious benefits of using bar codes is the reduction in time needed to complete a transaction at point of sale. In some early tests, UPC technology reduced checkout time by 49 percent (Specht, 1987). An even more important benefit of scanning bar codes is that accurate SKU information is retrieved at the point of sale. This means that product sales and retail inventory are automatically tracked. With this accurate and timely sales information, retailers and manufacturers can plan inventory needs to more closely match sales or projected consumer demand. For example, with accurate sales data, retailers are able to track sales trends and thereby avoid overstocking merchandise (thus reducing markdowns). Correct point-of-sale information can also be used to more efficiently reorder merchandise and thereby reduces the possibility of a retailer being out-of-stock in a particular style, size, or color of merchandise. Automatic reordering of merchandise is dependent upon the use of point-of-sale information provided by UPC bar codes. Generally UPC bar codes are attached to the merchandise by the manufacturer/vendor (vendor marking).

In addition to these point-of-sale (POS) benefits, retailers are also using bar codes to scan inventory in their distribution centers and to facilitate the movement of shipping cartons in distribution centers. These bar codes identify each shipping container's contents and are used for tracking and sorting merchandise at the DCs. Code 39 or Code 128, two other types of bar code formats that can include both numbers and letters, are often used for this purpose. L.L. Bean is an example of a company that successfully uses bar codes to improve the efficiency and accuracy of its merchandise distribution. L.L. Bean, headquartered in Freeport, Maine, is known for sensible, quality merchandise distributed primarily through mail order. The company has built its reputation on the fact that it can deliver virtually any item almost anywhere in the United States or Canada within 72 hours and that orders are filled correctly 99.8% of the time (Olive, 1988). The L.L. Bean Distribution Center is the core of this direct marketing effort. Incoming merchandise cases are marked with a bar code (Code 39) label that includes information regarding stock number and case quantity. This "automatic identification" information is used to improve the accuracy and speed of the processing of merchandise and inventory control.

ELECTRONIC DATA INTERCHANGE

Electronic data interchange (EDI) focuses on improving computer-to-computer communications between the manufacturer and retailer. In the past, purchase orders, invoices, and any other type of written communication generated by one company were sent to another company by mail or fax. The receiving company would then enter the data into its computer (see Figure 12-3). With EDI technology, business data are transmitted electroni-

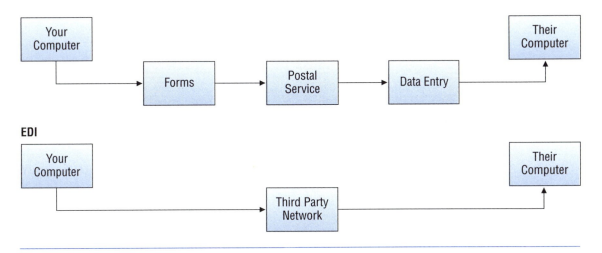

Figure 12.3
Electronic data interchange (EDI) improves the efficiency of computer-to-computer communications between manufacturers and retailers.

cally. In other words, computers from one company "talk" directly to computers from other companies or through a third party's computer system called a value-added network (VAN). This eliminates the processing of much of the paperwork and, in effect, creates a "paperless office." Not only are paper documents replaced by electronic documents, but the time delays associated with using mail services and handling paper are eliminated. Currently the most common EDI transactions used in the apparel industry are purchase orders, invoices, packing slips, advance shipping notices (ASN), reporting inventory counts, reporting changes to inventory such as sales and returns data, and price/sales catalog. A goal of some retail distribution centers is to deal with cross dockable shipments. This means that goods are received from the manufacturer as floor ready merchandise (preticketed with UPC and retail price and hanging goods are prehung), so that they can be sorted for store distribution without the need for additional processing (Robins, 1994). For cross docking to happen, advanced shipping notices must be requested and received by the retailer from the manufacturer and the goods must be received "floor ready."

The EDI capabilities of the manufacturer have become increasingly important to large retailers. In some cases, retailers are requiring that their suppliers establish EDI links (Bert, 1989). Others charge manufacturers a fee if EDI is not used for invoices or advance shipping notices. Many companies are moving to more sophisticated communications protocols that allow EDI transactions to be combined with other electronic data, including electronic mail, graphics, and video (DeWitt, 1993). Electronic funds transfers are also being used to replace manual check payments. However, as Alan Brooks, president of New Generation Computing, states, "EDI is not a technical issue as much as it is an area for management to control. We can have all the numbers and standards, but those will never bring good business judgment to the table. In the garment industry, you have to keep a *feel* for what is going on everywhere—especially in this electronic age" (DeWitt, 1993, p. 41).

Large manufacturers and retailers are the primary users of EDI; many small companies have not yet adopted EDI technology, but reduced costs and improvements in the technology are allowing more small companies to become involved. Bailey (1993) surveyed 343 apparel firms. Although approximately one-third of the plants received at least 60 percent of their orders through direct computer links, close to one-half still received none of their orders through computer links. However, each year additional companies, large and small, are investing in EDI technology. Indeed, according to a survey conducted by the National Retail Federation (National Retail Federation, 1993), a growing number of retailers are committed to Quick Response, primarily through the use of bar coded marked goods and the use of electronic data interchange.

VENDOR-MANAGED RETAIL INVENTORY

An outcome of UPC vendor marking, EDI, and tracking of goods at the retail level is the potential for **vendor-managed retail inventory.** One of the most beneficial strategies to improve the efficiency in the apparel supply pipeline between the manufacturer and retailer has been to establish programs whereby sales/stockout data are reviewed by the manufacturer and replenishments are ordered as often as required. In some cases, data are reviewed daily rather than monthly or bimonthly as was done in the past (Robins, 1993). Many large apparel retailers have incorporated this type of technology into their way of doing business. For example, in 1992, JCPenney estimated that approximately one-third of its menswear merchandise was on automatic electronic replenishment (Abend, 1992). Obviously, this type of

Figure 12.4
Manufacturers of lingerie typically deliver preticketed floor-ready merchandise as part of vendor-managed retail inventory strategies.

strategy would not be possible without POS data being sent from the retailer to the manufacturer. "While retailers early in the QR movement showed some apprehension about sharing POS data, this apprehension has all but disappeared, and the sharing of POS data is now an accepted cornerstone of QR partnerships" (Robins, 1993, p. 22). Although the number of companies involved with vendor-managed retail inventory is small, those companies tend to be the larger, more advanced retailers and manufacturers. As part of vendor-managed inventory, some manufacturers are delivering floor ready merchandise.

Wrangler, a subsidiary of VF Corporation that manufactures men's and women's jeans, is an example of a company that has been very successful in managing retailer inventories (Hasty, 1994). Wrangler salespeople work closely with retail buyers in determining product mix and appropriate stock levels for specific stores. Wrangler sends new orders anytime the store's stock falls below a specified minimum. Wrangler receives POS information from more than 5,000 stores either daily or weekly and each order is customized for a specific store depending upon the store's stock levels of various SKUs. Wrangler's goal is to receive POS information in the morning and ship jeans the same day.

MODULAR METHODS

Although modular methods have primarily been seen in production facilities (see Chapter 11), some companies have introduced the same philosophies in their distribution centers to improve the efficiency of their DCs. One such company is Columbia Sportswear Inc., headquartered in Portland, Oregon (Gilbert & Carlson, 1995), which has initiated modular concepts in its customer returns processing and quality assurance areas of the distribution center. Similar to modular (or flexible) manufacturing practices, teams of workers move products from one operation to the next rather than one person performing the same function on a continual basis. Pay for the employees depends on overall facility performance rather than on individual performance. Columbia has found that the implementation of these concepts has increased the speed for the processes and improved the quality of the work performed.

IMPLEMENTING QUICK RESPONSE

This book has focused on Quick Response strategies implemented throughout the textile, apparel, and retailing industries (see Table 12-2 for a summary of the most common QR strategies at each stage). Now the focus will shift to the systematic implementation of QR strategies among textile, apparel, and retailing companies. The implementation of Quick Response strategies involves a shift in a company's management style, in addition to an investment of a company's resources in increased technology, training, and

TABLE 12-2

Most Common QR Strategies Grouped by Manufacturing Area

TEXTILE TO APPAREL	PRODUCTION (Continued)
Reduction in inventory	Overhead conveyor for handling
Small lot fabric orders	Garment dyed products
EDI confirmation with suppliers	
Shade sorting of fabric rolls	**APPAREL TO RETAIL**
Reduction of wait time	Garment design—CAD
Elimination of redundant tests	Bar coding of finished garments
	Product information with customer
PRODUCTION	EDI confirmation with customers
Flexible manufacturing	Receive POS information
Automated sewing operations	Forecasting with retailer
Scan bar coding of fabric	

evaluation. Therefore, a company typically phases in strategies that are most consistent with its strategic plans. Typically, strategies have been most readily adopted by large manufacturers and retailers that produce and sell basic and seasonal merchandise. However, small companies that produce and sell fashion goods have begun to adopt at least some QR strategies.

According to "The Quick Response Handbook" (Hasty, 1994, pp. 5–6), Quick Response implementation can be described in terms of six stages that build upon one another:

Stage One enables QR by installing bar coding and EDI, which provide accurate sales data and speed communications.

Stage Two starts QR replenishment. Apparel firms ship reorders more frequently and faster, which increases sales by keeping stores in stock.

Stage Three streamlines replenishment. Retailers and suppliers jointly review sales data, develop plans and forecasts for future demand, and reduce inventory while keeping stores fully stocked.

Stage Four involves customizing assortments and replenishment, not only for each retailer but for each store unit in a retail chain. In many instances, apparel firms participate in or even make decisions regarding product assortment, quantities, sales floor displays/fixtures, and sales floor customer service (training/motivating associates).

Stage Five adds fashion goods to the basic and seasonal goods most common in QR alliances. New products are created jointly by the manufacturer and retailer, bypassing the traditional buyer-salesperson process and shortening the time from concept to new product on the shelf. In-store testing of new products is part of this stage.

Stage Six integrates all of the stages and QR capabilities with the apparel firm's total business processes in support of its strategy.

THE RETAIL LEVEL WITHIN THE MARKETING CHANNEL

By definition, **retailing** is the "business activity of selling goods or services to the final consumer," and a **retailer** is "any business establishment that directs its marketing efforts toward the final consumer for the purpose of selling goods and services" (Lewison, 1994, p. 5). Retailers range in size from small sole proprietorships that cater to a local market to large corporate store ownership groups. Table 12-3 is a listing of some of the primary retail corporations and the stores owned and operated by these corporations.

Retailers can be classified according to many of their characteristics, including their ownership, merchandise mix, size, location, and organizational and operational characteristics. One typical way of classifying retailers is on the basis of their merchandising and operating strategies, which results in the following categories: department stores, specialty stores, chain stores, discount retailers, off-price retailers, supermarkets, convenience stores, contractual retailers, warehouse retailers, and nonstore retailers. Because of the diversity found among retailers, these categories are not mutually exclusive. For example, a specialty store retailer may also be a chain store operation; a department store may also engage in nonstore retailing by sending mail-order catalogs to their credit-card customers. Table 12-4 lists the dollar share percentage among various apparel retail categories.

DEPARTMENT STORES

Department stores are large retailers that departmentalize their functions and their merchandise. Department stores are characterized by a fashion orientation, full markup policy, and operations in stores large enough to be shopping center anchors. These include traditional department stores such

Figure 12.5
Department stores such as Dillard's often serve as a shopping center anchor.

TABLE 12-3

Selected Major Retail Corporations

CARSON PIRIE SCOTT & CO

P.A. Bergner
Carson Pirie Scott
Boston Stores

DAYTON HUDSON CORPORATION

Target
Mervyn's
Dayton's Minneapolis
Hudson's Michigan
Marshall Field

DILLARD'S

Dillard's

FEDERATED DEPARTMENT STORES INC.

Bloomingdales
The Bon Marché
Burdines
Rich's/Lazarus/Goldsmith's
Stern's
Macy's East
Macy's West

THE GAP, INC.

The Gap
Banana Republic
Gap Kids
Old Navy Clothing

HARCOURT GENERAL, INC.

Neiman Marcus
Bergdorf Goodman

KMART

Kmart
SuperKmart
Builders Square
Borders-Waldenbooks

THE LIMITED, INC.

The Limited
Limited Too
Express
Structure
Victoria's Secret
Victoria's Secret Bath Shops
Lane Bryant
Lerner New York
Henri Bendel
Abercrombie & Fitch
Cacique
Bath & Body Works
Galyan's Trading Co.
Bath and Body Works at Home

MAY DEPARTMENT STORES

Meier & Frank
Robinson-May

Famous-Barr
Foley's
Kaufmann's
Hecht's
Lord & Taylor
Filene's
Payless ShoeSource

MELVILLE CORPORATION

Marshall's
Thom McAn
Wilson's
Kay-Bee
Linens 'N Things
This End Up
Foot Action
Meldisco

NORDSTROM

Nordstrom
Nordstrom Rack

J.C. PENNEY

JCPenney

SEARS

Sears

SPIEGEL, INC.

Eddie Bauer
Honey Bee
Spiegel

TOYS "R" US

Toys "R" Us
Kids "R" Us

US SHOE CORPORATION

Casual Corner
Petite Sophisticate
Career Image
Capezio
August Max
Lenscrafter
Footwear
Cabaret
Caren Charles

WAL-MART STORES, INC.

Wal-Mart
Sam's Club
Hypermart USA
Super Saver Warehouse Club

F.W. WOOLWORTH

Woolworth
Kinney/Footlocker
Richmond Brothers/Susies
Kids Mart/Little Folks

ZCMI

ZCMI

as Macy's, Dayton Hudson, and May Co., as well as limited line department stores such as Nordstrom, Saks Fifth Avenue, Mervyn's-California, and Neiman Marcus (which were once classified as specialty stores).

With the goal of catering to a broad range of consumers, department stores carry a wide variety of merchandise lines with a reasonably wide selection within each category. Department stores typically carry national brands

TABLE 12-4

Apparel Retail Categories: Dollar Share Percentage

RETAIL CHANNEL	DOLLAR SHARE %
Department Stores	22.5%
Specialty Stores	17.9%
Major Chains	14.6%
Discounters/Warehouse Clubs	22.5%
Off-Price	6.7%
Nontraditional°	9.9%
Nonstore (direct mail, TV)	6.0%

° factory outlets, food & drug, variety, other

TABLE 12-5

Top 10 Department Store Groups by Sales Volume

STORE OWNERSHIP GROUP	SALES VOLUME (000) 1994
May	$11,877,000
Federated	$ 8,315,877
Dillard	$ 5,545,803
Nordstrom	$ 3,894,478
Dayton Hudson	$ 3,150,000
Mercantile	$ 2,819,837
Neiman Marcus	$ 2,092,906
Broadway Stores	$ 2,086,804
Belks	$ 1,785,000
Saks Fifth Avenue	$ 1,390,000

and private label merchandise. Depending on their price assortment, they may also carry merchandise in the designer price zone. Although department stores have been criticized for being boring, confusing, and "dinosaurs" of retailing, they continue to have the largest share of the apparel market (Schneiderman, 1995). However, faced with increased competition, department stores are refocusing, with a new emphasis on presentation, customer service, and having the right products for their target market that are different than the products carried by other stores. This type of merchandising strategy, known as **relationship merchandising,** addresses the needs of individual customers (Retailing 2000). Nordstrom has been cited as the prototype of this type of merchandising strategy. Table 12-5 is a listing of the top ten department stores groups, ranked by 1994 sales volume.

TABLE 12-6

Top 10 Apparel Specialty Chains by Sales Volume

STORE CHAIN	SALES VOLUME (000) 1994
The Limited	$7,320,792
Melville Specialty	$5,674,747
Woolworth Specialty	$3,977,000
TJX	$3,842,818
The Gap	$3,722,940
US Shoe	$2,598,308
Payless ShoeSource	$2,116,000
Burlington Coat	$1,480,676
Petrie Stores	$1,480,071

SPECIALTY STORES

A **specialty store** focuses on a specific type of merchandise by carrying one category of merchandise or a few closely related categories of merchandise (e.g., jewelry, shoes, eyeglasses, intimate apparel), by focusing on merchandise for a well-defined target market (e.g., men, women, bicyclists, large-size consumers), or by carrying the merchandise of one manufacturer or brand (e.g., Nine West, Ralph Lauren, Baby Guess/Guess Kids). Specialty stores carry a limited but deep assortment (i.e., excellent selection of brands, styles, sizes) of merchandise. Specialty stores carry national brands and private label merchandise; some will also carry merchandise in the designer price zone. Specialty stores that concentrate on designer price zone merchandise

Figure 12.6
The Gap is an example of a specialty store chain that focuses on a limited number of apparel and accessory categories.

or unique merchandise distributed exclusively to only a few stores are sometimes referred to as **boutiques.** Two of the largest apparel specialty stores chains in the United States are The Limited and The Gap (see Table 12-6 for a listing of specialty stores ranked by 1994 sales).

CHAIN STORES

Chain store organizations own and operate several retail store units that sell similar lines of merchandise in a standardized method and function under a centralized form of organizational structure. Chain stores are characterized by centralized buying, no one main or flagship store (as is typically the case with multiunit department stores with branches), centralized distribution, and standardized store décor and layout. All management and merchandising decisions and policies are made by managers at a central headquarters or home office. Chain store operations include large chains (defined as 11 or more units), which may be national or international in scope, such as JCPenney, Sears, Wal-Mart, Target, and The Limited, or they can be small chains (two to ten retail units) within a local or regional area. Although chain stores benefit from the "economies of scale" that comes with purchasing merchandise for a number of stores, they also carry merchandise that caters to the wants and needs of more localized target markets. Private label merchandise is an important part of the merchandise mix for chain store retailers (e.g., JCPenney's private label lines include Worthington and Stafford).

DISCOUNT RETAILERS

A **discount store** is one that sells brand name merchandise at below traditional retail prices and includes apparel merchandise at the budget wholesale price zone. Discounters also carry private label merchandise (e.g., Kmart's Jaclyn Smith and Hunter's Glen apparel lines, Target's Greatland

Figure 12.7
Wal-Mart, a national discount chain, sells a variety of merchandise including family apparel and accessories.

TABLE 12-7

Top 10 Discount Stores by Sales Volume

STORE CHAIN	VOLUME (000) 1994
Wal-Mart	$58,000,000
Kmart	$28,632,277
Target	$13,622,000
Miejer	$ 6,000,000
Fred Meyer	$ 3,128,432
Caldor	$ 2,748,634
Ames	$ 2,142,827
Venture	$ 2,017,283
Bradlees	$ 1,916,555
Hills	$ 1,872,021

line). Through mass-merchandising strategies, discounters are able to keep prices lower than other retailers. Quantity discounts from manufacturers and high turnover rates on products contribute to discount retailers' ability to offer lower prices to consumers. Other strategies include limiting brands and styles to only the most popular items, self-service, lower overhead costs, and promotions that cater to a broad target market. National discount chains such as Wal-Mart, Kmart, and Target buy huge quantities of merchandise from manufacturers and can operate on smaller profit margins than can department stores. Stores such as Target are sometimes referred to as "upscale discounters," because the stores have a "department store feel" and apparel accounts for 45 percent or more of total sales. Table 12-7 lists the top ten discount stores by sales volume in 1994.

OFF-PRICE RETAILERS

Off-price retailers specialize in selling national brands, designer apparel lines, or promotional goods at discount prices. Off-price retailers are characterized by buying merchandise at low prices, carrying well-established (including designer) brands, and having merchandise assortments that change and may be inconsistent. Off-price retailers include:

▌ **Factory outlet stores:** manufacturers' outlets that sell their own seconds, irregulars, or overruns (merchandise produced in excess of their orders). In some cases manufacturers will use their outlet stores as test markets for styles, colors, or sizing of merchandise. Once located primarily near production or distribution centers, factory outlet stores comprising entire shopping centers are now common throughout the United States,

Figure 12.8
Independent off-price retailers, such as Ross Dress for Less, sell national brands and promotional goods at discount prices.

although they are typically located at a distance from full-price retailers who carry their goods.

- **Independent off-price retailers:** these stores buy irregulars, seconds, overruns, or leftovers from manufacturers or other retailers, e.g., Ross, T.J. Maxx, Burlington Coat Factory.
- **Retailer-owned off-price retailers:** some retailers operate their own off-price stores, e.g., Nordstrom Rack, Filene's Basement.
- **Closeout stores:** retailers who specialize in buying a variety of merchandise through retail liquidations, bankruptcies, and closeouts.

SUPERMARKET RETAILING

Conventional **supermarkets** are large self-service grocery stores that carry a full line of foods and related products with at least $2 million annual sales. Some supermarkets have broadened their merchandise and service offerings. **Superstores** are upgraded supermarkets with at least $8 million in annual sales and are at least 30,000 square feet in total area. Only a limited number of apparel products are distributed through these various types of supermarkets. Typically these include basic items such as mass-merchandised hosiery, packaged undergarments, T-shirts, and inexpensive eyewear.

These items must accommodate a self-service merchandising strategy, so visual displays that assist consumers in selecting the right style and size are common. These items are also most likely to use an extended merchandising channel that facilitates supermarkets' buying of these goods.

CONVENIENCE STORES

Convenience stores are small stores that offer fast service and a convenient location, although they carry a limited assortment of food and related items. Similar to supermarkets, the most typical apparel products carried by convenience stores are basic items such as mass-merchandised hosiery (e.g., L'eggs, No Nonsense).

CONTRACTUAL RETAILERS

Retailers may enter into **contractual** agreements with manufacturers, wholesalers, or other **retailers** in order to integrate operations and increase market impact. Such contractual agreements include retailer-sponsored cooperatives (e.g., organization of small independent retailers), wholesaler-sponsored voluntary chains (e.g., wholesaler-developed program for small independent retailers), franchises, and leased departments. Franchises and leased departments are the most typical of the contractual retailers for the distribution of apparel.

FRANCHISE. In a **franchise** agreement, the parent company provides the franchisee with the exclusive distribution of a well-recognized brand name in a specific market area, as well as assistance with organization, visual merchandising, training, and management in return for a franchise payment. The franchisee also agrees to specific standards in-store design, visual presentation, pricing, and promotions specified by the parent company. Examples of franchises include Ralph Lauren's Polo Shops and Yves St. Laurent's Rive Gauche boutiques.

LEASED DEPARTMENTS. Some retailers will lease space within a larger retail store to operate a specialty department. The larger retail store provides space, utilities, and basic in-store services. The specialty department provides the stock and expertise to run the department and adds to the service or product mix of the larger store. Typical **leased departments** are beauty salons, fine jewelry, furs, and shoes. You will note that in each case specific expertise and investment in stock is needed. With this type of arrangement, the primary advantage for the larger retailer is that they can offer their customers products and services that they may not be able to offer otherwise. The primary advantage for the specialty department is their association with the larger retailer.

WAREHOUSE RETAILERS

Warehouse retailers reduce operating expenses and offer goods at discount prices by combining showroom, warehouse, and retail operations together. These include stores such as catalog showrooms (e.g., Service Merchandise, Best Products), home centers (e.g., Home Depot, Builder's Square), hypermarkets (e.g., Wal-Mart's Hypermarket USA), and warehouse clubs (e.g., Costco Wholesale, Price Club, and Sam's Club). Few apparel products are sold through warehouse retailers, although one can find basic items such as underwear and casual sports clothes. Merchandise is obtained through an extended marketing channel in these types of stores.

NONSTORE RETAILERS

A **Nonstore retailer** distributes products to consumers through means other than traditional retail stores. In the last 15 years nonstore retailing has grown tremendously. This trend is due to a number of social, economic, and lifestyle changes, including:

- the increased demand by consumers for convenience, product quality, and selection,

- a highly fragmented market that demands products to fulfill special needs and interests,

- the continued growth in the number of women in the workforce and dual-income families, which creates increased time pressures for shopping by household members,

- the expanding use of credit cards, such as VISA, Mastercard, American Express, and Discover,

- increased speed of delivery by package carriers (e.g., Federal Express, UPS), and

- technological advancements in interactive shopping.

Nonstore retailing methods include at-home, mail-order, electronic, telephone/television, machine and vending machine formats.

AT-HOME RETAILERS. At-home retailers use the marketing strategy of making personal contacts and sales in consumers' homes. This may include door-to-door sales or party plan methods. The party plan method involves a salesperson giving a presentation of merchandise at the home of a host or hostess who has invited potential customers to a "party" (e.g., Doncaster). Accessories and lingerie are typical types of apparel products sold using this retail method.

Figure 12.9
Mail-order retailers, such as Lands' End, provide a number of services to facilitate consumer purchasing of merchandise from a catalog.

MAIL-ORDER RETAILERS. Mail order companies sell to the consumer through catalogs, brochures, or advertisements, and deliver merchandise by mail or other carrier. Customers can order by mail, over the phone, or by fax. Some companies focus almost entirely on the use of catalogs (e.g., L.L. Bean, Lands' End, Orvis, Spiegel). All types of retailers may operate mail order businesses, some of which offer merchandise through their catalogs that is not available in their stores (e.g., J. Crew, Victoria's Secret).

ELECTRONIC RETAILERS. Taking advantage of the growth in computer and television technology, electronic retailers sell goods and services through electronic and video systems. These may involve videotape catalogs or interactive electronic systems in which product information and graphics are transmitted over telephone or cable television lines and displayed on a potential customer's computer or television screen. Currently the two most common ways of shopping by computer are (1) the use of on-line services such as America On-line or other access to the Internet (through independent access companies) whereby you can scan electron catalogs and place an order directly by typing in your credit card number, and (2) CD-ROM shopping whereby electronic catalogs are available on CD-ROM disks and orders are made on forms, generated by the program, which can be phoned, mailed,

Figure 12.10
Electronic retailing
outlets such as World
Wide Web sites are
creating new forms of
retail environments.

or faxed to the company. According to industry analysts, retailing on the Internet (and World Wide Web) has the potential to become an important vehicle for selling and purchasing goods (Mastercard International, 1996).

TELEPHONE/TELEVISION RETAILERS. Some retailers use telemarketing and home shopping methods. In telemarketing, retailers use the telephone to supply customers with information or receive merchandise or lay-away orders. Home shopping formats include the presentation of merchandise on the television and customers ordering the merchandise over the telephone (usually using a toll-free number), with payment by credit card, C.O.D., or check. Merchandise is delivered through the mail or by another carrier. Home shopping has become big business. Home Shopping Network (HSN) and QVC are the largest of these retailers, both of whose sales are just over $1 billion per year. Once focusing on budget price zone items, TV home shopping has expanded to include designer lines. Some retailers, such as Saks Fifth Avenue and Bergdorf Goodman, have also experimented with television shopping, although few have developed on-going ventures into this type of retailing venue.

VENDING MACHINES. Vending machines are coin-operated machines used to meet the needs of consumers when other retailing formats are unavailable. Although vending machines are seldom used for the distribution of apparel products, vending machines have been used to sell hosiery, T-shirts, and even men's dress shirts.

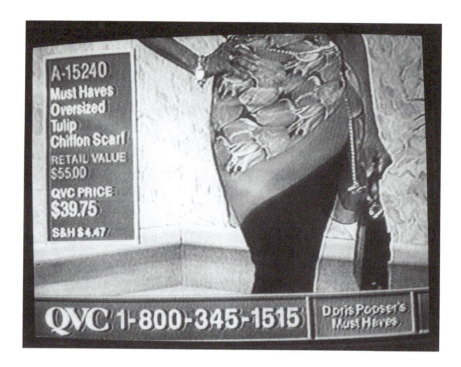

Figure 12.11
Growth in nonstore retailing, such as television retailing, is expected to continue.

In a 1994 survey sponsored by *Women's Wear Daily*, 800 female consumers from major markets around the United States were asked to name their favorite stores for women's apparel (Nardoza, 1994). The responses consisted of a wide variety of retailers, including department stores, specialty stores, discounters, and off-price stores (see Table 12-8 for a complete listing of the top 25 stores). For specific categories, The Gap rated highest for jeans, Victoria's Secret rated the highest for intimate apparel, and JCPenney topped the list for dresses, careerwear, and activewear.

TRADE ASSOCIATIONS AND TRADE PUBLICATIONS

Table 12-9 lists some of the primary retail trade associations. The National Retail Federation (NRF) is the largest trade association for retailers in the United States. It represents 27 national retail associations, all 50 state associations, and stores from 50 different nations. The NRF Annual Convention and Expo is held in New York each January. The NRF publishes *Stores* magazine, a monthly trade publication that addresses the interests of those in the retailing industry. A number of other trade publications cater to those involved with distribution and retailing. Table 12-10 includes a listing of some of these publications.

TABLE 12-8

WWD's Best Stores Survey

TOP 25 STORES

1. JCPenney	14. Lane Bryant
2. Macy's	15. Ross
3. Mervyn's	16. Rich's
4. Wal-Mart	17. Lerner Stores
5. Dillard	18. Emporium-Capwell
6. Nordstrom	19. Target
7. Kmart	20. Casual Corner
8. Sears	21. Robinson's May
9. Burdines	22. Foley's
10. Dayton Hudson	23. Marshall Field's
11. Fashion Bug	24. Abraham & Straus
12. Marshalls	25. Carson Pirie Scott
13. Lord & Taylor	

A LOOK TO THE FUTURE

Change has become the norm in the textile, apparel, and retailing industries. Faced with increased global competition, rapid changes have been made by textile, apparel, and retailing companies in order to survive. The belief has been that the strongest advantage the United States could offer is time. If we could produce the goods faster, we could have them at market sooner. If we could produce goods closer to the delivery date, we could predict more accurately what would sell, and we would pay less interest on borrowed money needed for inventory and business operations. If we could automatically replenish goods sold by the retailer, then consumers would be more likely to find the goods they want when they wanted them.

How could we increase speed without decreasing product quality? The answer was technology. It was to become our most valuable competitive edge. Though the initial cost of computer technology was high, management pushed forward. Computers invaded every aspect of the industry. It was clear that the investment paid for itself, both in speed and in accuracy. In time came integrated computer systems. Now, every phase of the fiber-textile-apparel-retail complex can be linked with data interchange and data management. Ordering can be transacted on-line. A computer screen has replaced most of the paper trail. Such dramatic changes in ways of doing business have been dependent on increased partnerships among companies within the textile-apparel-retailing marketing channel.

TABLE 12-9

Selected Retail Trade Associations

AMERICAN MANAGEMENT ASSOCIATION

135 West 50 Street
New York, NY 10019
(212) 586-8100

FOOTWEAR INDUSTRIES OF AMERICA

1420 K Street NW
Washington, D.C. 20005
(202) 789-1420

NATIONAL MASS RETAIL ASSOCIATION

1901 Pennsylvania Avenue NW
10th Floor
Washington, D.C. 20006
(202) 861-0774

NATIONAL RETAIL FEDERATION

100 West 31st Street
New York, NY 10001
(212) 244-8780

NATIONAL SHOE RETAILERS ASSOCIATION

9861 Broken Land Parkway
Columbia, MD 21046
(410) 381-8282

SHOE RETAILERS LEAGUE

275 Madison Avenue
New York, NY 10016
(212) 889-7920

Some said that computer technology was only for the "big" companies. While many large companies were the first to use computer technology, small companies began to embrace technology as well. Costs have decreased and technology has improved to the point where very small apparel companies and retailers cannot afford to *not* use computers.

TABLE 12-10

SELECTED TRADE PUBLICATIONS RELATED TO BUSINESS, DISTRIBUTION, AND RETAILING

Advertising Age, the international newspaper of marketing: Published by Crain Communications, this trade publication includes articles on domestic and international advertising news and trends.

Chain Store Age Executive: A Lebhar-Friedman publication, this trade magazine focuses on information of interest to managers and executives of chain stores, such as finance, sales, new products, and chain store news.

Discount Merchandiser: Published by Schwartz Publications, this publication addresses all aspects of discount merchandising including manufacturing, retailing, advertising, and other industry information.

Discount Store News: the international journal of retailing: Published by Schwartz Publications, this trade newspaper focuses on timely news related to discount stores. Articles cover new products, licensing, visual merchandising, and industry trends.

Marketing News: reporting on the marketing profession and its association: A publication of the American Marketing Association, this newspaper covers information and news of interest to marketing professionals including marketing strategies, retailing, market research, and trends.

Retail Control: retail business review: A publication of the National Retail Federation and National Retail Dry Goods Association, this bimonthly magazine focuses on retail trade and accounting issues in retailing.

Retailing Today: Published by Robert Kahn & Associates, a monthly newsletter for retail managers focusing on trends, sales, and issues in the retail industry.

Stores: A publication of the National Retail Federation, this monthly trade magazine includes information of interest to retailers in general. The July issue includes a ranked listing of department stores; the August issue includes a ranked listing of specialty stores.

Supermarket Business: Published by Howfrey Communications, this publication focuses on information of interest to supermarket managers, such as marketing, finance, store layout, and advertising.

At the same time the industry increased its emphasis on technology, the traditional assembly-line approach to production was examined. A trend developed that centered on a team approach compared to individual units of workers. Teams became responsible for work flow and were given group responsibility for the quality of the product.

Although segments of the manufacturing process continued to make advances in technology, many companies chose to manufacture off shore. For a while, labor was cheap. Then, as developing countries advanced economically, labor costs increased. New countries were selected for inexpensive labor. Many of the off-shore contractors realized that they also needed computer technology for the same reasons the United States needed it a decade before. Contractors in the more developed countries are beginning to utilize computers, not only for increased speed and accuracy in their facilities, but also to communicate with apparel companies in the United States. How much longer will the United States have its competitive edge in technology? What is coming next?

A number of issues will shape the future of the U.S. textile, apparel, and retailing industries: global competitiveness, consumers' increased desire for hardgoods (i.e., computers) relative to softgoods, changes in the way consumers buy goods, and changes in the way companies conduct their business. James Oesterreicher, CEO of J.C. Penney Company Inc., identified five elements needed to create and retain a competitive advantage within a global industry (Oesterreicher, 1995):

1. Creating a "point of difference" in the product offered. In order to compete for the consumer's dollar, companies must create products that are perceived as having a relative advantage over competing products. This relative advantage may be in terms of function, style, image, price, service, or a combination of factors. Licensed goods and private label merchandise are two ways in which companies will create perceived difference.

2. Determining sourcing options, either domestic or abroad, that provide products that meet consumers' expectations in terms of quality, fashion, style, and price. Sourcing decisions must be based on a number of factors, not simply labor costs.

3. Defining a cost structure that gives consumers the style, size, and color they want when they want it. Consumers' desire for quality and value will continue in the future. This has led to increased vertical integration; retailers will continue to source their own private labels and manufacturers will continue to get into the retail business. Direct distribution strategies through avenues such as the Internet will continue to grow.

4. Using technology to make the company more efficient and effective. Technology must be used to increase productivity and facilitate better management of businesses. QR strategies are dependent upon appropriate use of technology in designing, manufacturing, and distributing goods more effectively and efficiently. According to an industry analyst (Barnes, 1996, p. 78), "the electronic data interchange (EDI) technology used in the last decade to shift the apparel supply complex from a push to a pull system now is being used to get closer to both retail customers and consumers—the ones who exercise power over our market." Indeed, sales information is not only being used to quickly replenish desired goods, but these databases are being used to plan future lines and design marketing strategies.

5. Investing in well-trained and motivated people to carry on the company's business. The company's greatest asset is its employees. Teamwork among employees will continue to be a necessity.

Thus, as we move into the twenty-first century, the strength of the domestic textile, apparel, and retailing industries will depend on our ability to change and respond to the wants and needs of consumers.

SUMMARY

The function of moving apparel products from the manufacturer to the consumer is known as a marketing channel. The form of marketing channel in which a company participates relates to the product type, consumer target market, company affiliations, and size of the company. Direct, limited, and extended marketing channels are all used for the distribution of apparel, although limited channels are the most common. In addition, both conventional and vertical marketing channels can be seen throughout the apparel industry. Companies must decide how widely their merchandise will be distributed; some will focus on mass distribution, whereas others will decide on a selective or exclusive distribution strategy. Apparel companies will distribute their goods either directly to their retail accounts or through the use of distribution centers. Retailers with many stores may also use distribution centers as a centralized location for merchandise to be shipped to the various stores.

Quick Response strategies are important in the distribution process, and partnerships between apparel companies and retailers are important for these strategies to be effective. These strategies include the use of Universal Product Code bar coding on product labels and shipping cartons, vendors (manufacturers) assuming responsibility for affixing labels and price information on products, and the use of electronic data interchange for the electronic transmission of invoices, advance shipping notices, and other forms. In some cases, using these strategies, programs have been established whereby the vendor (manufacturer) manages retail inventory and automatically replenishes the retailer's stock when needed.

The retailing level of the marketing channel focuses on selling the merchandise to the final consumer. Retailers are often classified according to merchandising and operating strategies into the following non-mutually exclusive categories: department stores, specialty stores, chain stores, discount retailers, off-price retailers, supermarkets, convenience stores, contractual retailers, warehouse retailers, and nonstore retailing. Each type of retail category is used for the final distribution of apparel products to the ultimate consumer, although some are used more than others (e.g., department stores, specialty stores, discount stores).

REFERENCES

Abend, Jules (1992, February). Retail replenishment demands rising. *Bobbin*, pp. 80–83.

Bailey, Thomas (1993, August). *The Spread of Quick Response and Human Resource Innovation in the Apparel Industry*. Institute on Education and the Economy, Teachers College, Columbia University.

Barnes, Mike (1996, January). Techology's Role in the '90's. *Apparel Industry Magazine*, p. 78.

Bert, Jim (1989, March). The EDI link. *Connections* (Supplement to *Apparel Industry Magazine*), pp. 4–5.

DeWitt, John W. (1993, June). EDI's new role: Electronic commerce. *Apparel Industry Magazine,* pp. 36–41.

Drori, Neil (1992, February). Taking the bull out of bar codes. *Bobbin*, pp. 14–18.

Gilbert, Charles, and Carlson, Dave. (1995, October). Making the modular pay in the DC. *Bobbin*, pp. 84–88.

Hasty, Susan E. (Ed) (1994, March). *The Quick Response Handbook.* Supplement to *Apparel Industry Magazine.*

Lewison, Dale M. (1994). *Retailing.* (5th ed.). New York: Macmillan.

Mastercard International (1996, February). Internet shopping: New competitor or new frontier? Supplement to *Stores,* MC1–MC24.

Moore, Lila. (1994, September). DCs face uncertain future. *Apparel Industry Magazine,* pp. 58–62.

Nannery, Matt. (1995, March 15). Fred Meyer bets the warehouse on QR. *WWD*, p. 25.

Nardoza, Edward (1994, October). The best stores. Supplement to *WWD.*

National Retail Federation. (1993, January). *Fifth Annual Bar Code/EDI/Quick Response Survey Results.* New York: Author

Oesterreicher, J. (1995, April). Meeting the global challenge. *Apparel Industry Magazine*, p. 114.

Olive, Robert (1988, February). L.L. Bean: Rapid receiving. *Apparel Industry Magazine,* pp. 56–60.

Robins, Gary (1993, March). Quick Response. *Stores,* pp. 21–22.

Robins, Gary (1994, March). Less work, more speed. *Stores,* pp. 24–26.

Schneiderman, I. P. (1995, October 5). Lost in a maze. *WWD*, pp. 1, 8–10.

Specht, Diane (1987, November). Preparing for the future. *Earnshaw's Review,* pp. 62–65.

KEY TERMS

marketing channel

direct marketing channel

limited marketing channel

extended marketing channel

conventional marketing channel

vertical marketing channel

dual distribution
   (multichannel distribution)

physical flow

ownership flow (title flow)

information flow

payment flow

promotion flow

intensive distribution
   (mass distribution)

selective distribution

exclusive distribution	chain store
distribution centers (DCs)	discount store
vendor marking	off-price retailer
Universal Product Code (UPC)	supermarket
electronic data interchange (EDI)	superstore
vendor-managed retail inventory	convenience store
retailing	contractual retailer
retailer	franchise
department store	leased department
relationship merchandising	warehouse retailer
specialty store	nonstore retailer
boutique	

DISCUSSION QUESTIONS

1. Describe the role of distribution centers for apparel manufacturers and retailers. How and why has the role changed?

2. Bring in several apparel merchandise hangtags or packages that have UPC bar codes. What information does the bar code provide to the manufacturer? To the retailer? To the consumer? What other information is on the ticket or package that is helpful to the consumer?

3. If you were the president of a small apparel manufacturer of trendy sportswear, what QR strategies would you implement first? Why?

4. Name and describe your three favorite stores. What type of retail store is each? What are characteristics of the types of retail stores you named?

CAREER PROFILES

Careers in retailing are as varied as the stores themselves. Some of the career possibilities include store management, merchandise buying, private label merchandise development, catalog and nonstore retailing, and promotion and advertising, to name just a few.

**ASSISTANT RETAIL MANAGER FOR A CHAIN
SPECIALTY STORE** (*Women's Apparel*)

Job Description
Work in partnership with the store manager and sales associates in running the store.

Typical Tasks

- In-store customer service
- Visual merchandising activities on an ongoing basis
- Payroll, operations
- Working with and managing the sales associates

What Do You Like Best About Your Job?

The diversity that each day brings, working with a variety of people and customers.

DISTRICT MANAGER FOR A CHAIN SPECIALTY STORE
(*Accessories/sunglasses*)

Job Description

Oversee the performance of 15 to 25 stores. Motivate people to sell and service customers to reach the goals set. Monitor the business cost of each store and keep within the company's guidelines. Open new stores and staff them. Train and monitor the merchandising at each store.

Typical Tasks

- Balance and determine budgets for each store
- Visit stores on a regular rotation to monitor performance
- Merchandise stores to meet guidelines and increase sales

What Do You Like Best About Your Job?

Managing people effectively and watching them grow and become the best they can be under this supervision. Freedom to improve stores and affect their sales as I see necessary.

MERCHANDISING MANAGER/HEAD BUYER,
International Specialty Store Retailer

Job Description

To ensure merchandise mix, availability, distribution to all stores, inventory management, pricing, market development and trends for the future, and purchase target allocation for all stores.

Typical Tasks

- Select merchandise mix to be carried throughout the stores
- Work with local suppliers and negotiate terms and conditions for each line of merchandise
- Control inventory levels of merchandise (maximum three months inventory levels)
- Keep informed about the latest trends and developments (competitors, etc.)
- Set up target purchase budget on a yearly basis

What Do You Like Best About Your Job?

I like my job because I get a chance to select and see the upcoming range of merchandise. It is also challenging work (to be able to maintain three months inventory levels).

CUSTOMER SERVICE SUPPORT, *Catalog Retailer*

Job Description

Update representatives about back order products. Contact customers either by phone or by mail with current back order status. Cancel products whenever necessary. Try to find comparable products for possible substitutions.

Typical Tasks

- Write lots of letters
- Phone contact with customers

What Do You Like About Your Job?

Flexibility to do what is necessary and take whatever measures I need to take to help the customer.

Part Four

ORGANIZATION AND
OPERATION OF THE
ACCESSORIES AND HOME
FASHIONS INDUSTRIES

13

Accessories

Objectives

▌ To discuss the relationship between fashion apparel and accessories.

▌ To compare similarities and differences in the design and manufacturing of accessories and fashion apparel products.

▌ To compare similarities and differences in the past, current, and future marketing and distribution strategies for fashion accessories.

RELATIONSHIP OF ACCESSORIES TO THE APPAREL INDUSTRY

JUST THINK ABOUT any "new" fashion look and how important the shoe style, leg covering, or jewelry is to creating this fashion look. The accessories industries comprise a vital component of the total fashion industry. Primary accessory categories include footwear, hosiery/legwear, hats and headwear, scarfs and neckwear, belts, handbags, gloves, and jewelry. Other accessories include sunglasses, handkerchiefs, hair accessories, and umbrellas. Each season, changes occur in accessories that relate directly to the changes occurring in fashion apparel. For example, the styling, colors, textures, and scale of jewelry will be similar to the type of apparel with which it will be worn. For example, when shoulder pads and large-scale lapels and collars are in fashion, then the jewelry will be large in scale as well. Fashion trends

357

are so closely linked between apparel and accessories that one can purchase a sweater, belt, and shoes in the same "hot new fashion color" at the same time in the market. It is clear that these industries must work together.

Yet fashion apparel products and accessories are distinctly different in some respects. Some accessories can be manufactured very quickly, developing from a new trend in apparel. For example, belt manufacturers began to produce southwestern-style conch belts as soon as the "Santa Fe" fashion look began to develop. And just as quickly, neckwear producers added bolo ties to their collections. According to the national sales manager for a hosiery company, "In developing a product mix, the hosiery industry really has to follow other market segments. We can't set the trends, but we can accessorize them" (Rabon, 1995, p. 66).

Other accessories take much longer to produce. The footwear industry needs time to design and produce the product, including time to procure materials. The design phase for shoes may even begin before the design phase for an apparel product, especially if specialty leather materials are required. Therefore, forecasters in the shoe industry must be keenly aware of market and fashion trends so that they can accurately predict appropriate shoe fashions that complement and coordinate with fashion apparel.

ACCESSORIES CATEGORIES

Accessories manufacturers are grouped into categories. These include:

- footwear;
- hosiery and legwear;
- hats and headwear;
- scarfs and neckwear;
- belts, handbags, and small leather goods;
- gloves;
- and jewelry.

Many accessory companies specialize in manufacturing only one type of product; that is some shoe companies may manufacture only shoes; some neckwear companies produce only neckwear. Some companies prefer to diversify into more than one accessory category. Other companies manufacture both accessories and apparel. Hermès, a French company that began as a saddlemaking business in 1837, currently produces high end purses, bags, belts, footwear, saddles, scarfs, neckties, fragrances, and apparel. Hermès "has grown and prospered because of a rigid adherence to original stands of quality, combined with a willingness to move with the times by replacing a declining demand for saddles and harnesses with broader merchandise selections" (Marcus, 1979, pp. 88-89). Dooney & Bourke, a handbag manufacturer, has diversified into footwear. Some apparel manufacturers produce

Figure 13.1
Some manufacturers, such as Ferragamo, produce goods in more than one accessory category.

their own accessories to coordinate with their apparel lines. For example, NIKE produces a line of backpacks and sports equipment bags in collaboration with its footwear and apparel lines. Columbia Sportswear also produces coordinating hats and bags for their apparel lines.

Other companies form agreements to produce coordinating apparel and accessories. For example, in skiwear, Roffe Skiwear produces the outerwear apparel products and Demetre produces the coordinating knit sweaters, headwear, and handwear. Thus, the expertise required to manufacture each type of product rests in the hands of the company best qualified to produce it.

Many "name designers" use licensing agreements with accessory manufacturers to produce the specific style of accessory that completes the total fashion look desired by the designer. Designers such as Liz Claiborne, Donna Karan, and Calvin Klein have their names linked to belts, hosiery, shoes, or eyewear. As discussed in Chapter 2, licensing agreements can be beneficial to both the accessory manufacturer and the designer. For the accessory manufacturer, the designer name provides immediate brand recognition among consumers. For the designer, he/she can expand into a variety of product lines through licensing arrangements.

Due to the current buying patterns for retailers, the number of market weeks varies. Groups involved in market week issues include the Accessories Council and the National Fashion Accessories Association (NFAA). For reference, Table 13-1 lists selected trade publications, Table 13-2 lists selected trade shows, and Table 13-3 lists selected trade associations for accessories.

Although there are differences in production processes within the accessories industry, most lines are produced following procedures similar to

TABLE 13-1

Selected Trade Publications for Accessories

Footwear News
Footwear Plus
Hosiery News (published by the National Association of Hosiery Manufacturers)
Women's Wear Daily, including special accessories supplements, Monday issues feature accessories/innerwear/legwear industry news

TABLE 13-2

Selected Trade Shows for Accessories

Accessorie Circuit held in NYC three times a year

Fashion Accessory Exposition held in NYC twice a year

Fashion Footwear Association of New York (FFANY) sponsors four trade shows a year in NYC

International Hosiery Exposition (IHE)

International Shoe Fair (GDS) held in Dusseldorf, Germany, twice a year

Shoe Fair held in Bologna, Italy

United Jewelry Show held in Providence, RI, four times a year

Western Shoe Association sponsors two trade shows a year in Las Vegas

TABLE 13-3

Selected Trade Associations for Accessories

American Leather Accessory Designers (ALAD)

Fashion Footwear Association of New York (FFANY)

Fashion Jewelry Association of America

Headwear Institute of America

Jewelers of America

National Association of Fashion and Accessory Designers

National Association of Hosiery Manufacturers (NAHM)

National Association of Milliners, Dressmakers, and Tailors

National Fashion Accessories Association

National Glove Manufacturers Association

National Shoe Retailers Association

Neckwear Association of America, Inc.

North American Hosiery Council

Sporting Goods Manufacturers Association (SPMS), and a subcategory, Athletic Footwear Association (AFA)

Sunglass Association of America

Western Shoe Association (WSA)

the steps in the research, design, production, and distribution of apparel. These steps include:

▌ researching (including color, material, trend, and market research),

▌ designing sketches,

▌ pattern making (or creating molds in the jewelry industry),

■ developing prototypes,

■ costing,

■ marketing, including presenting a minimum of two lines per year,

■ production, and

■ distribution and retailing.

We will discuss some of the important aspects of the design, marketing, and merchandising of the accessories industries in the following sections.

FOOTWEAR

During the past few decades, the footwear industry has changed in a number of ways. First, footwear sold by U.S. manufacturers has shifted from domestic to global production (see Tables 13-4 and 13-5). This is primarily because of rising labor costs in the United States; shoe production can be very labor intensive. Second, the production of leather footwear has been augmented by the production of footwear using a variety of manufactured materials. The types of shoes most frequently purchased have shifted as well. Athletic shoes have gained a tremendous market share of the footwear industry. In 1993, of the 965,485,000 total pairs of adults' and children's shoes purchased in the United States, 38 percent were athletic shoes, 22 percent were dress shoes and boots, and 20 percent were casual shoes. The remaining figures included: sandals, 7 percent; work shoes and boots, 4 percent; Western/casual boots, 2 percent; hiking, hunting, and fishing boots, 2 percent; and all others, 5 percent (*The U.S. Athletic Footwear Market Today*, 1994, p. 8).

TABLE 13-4

U.S. Footwear Imports by Country of Origin (in thousands of pairs)

	1978	1981	1991	1992	1993	1994
TOTAL IMPORTS	**373,515**	**375,408**	**936,991**	**974,179**	**1,065,268**	**1,101,268**
China	N.A.	7,105	424,542	506,058	622,240	680,719
Brazil	27,427	43,027	93,601	106,123	130,002	121,239
Indonesia	428	N.A.	51,014	76,807	84,276	79,017
Italy	62,934	50,163	33,115	34,799	35,446	42,395
Taiwan	117,237	118,816	117,886	75,347	46,716	32,705
Thailand	1,580	5,822	24,522	25,500	25,465	24,509
South Korea	30,591	43,972	113,671	70,704	36,490	24,294
Spain	37,458	18,995	17,500	15,477	15,080	24,256

TABLE 13-5

U.S. Footwear Consumption (in thousands of pairs)

	1968	1978	1981	1991	1992	1993	1994
Production	642,400	418,938	371,997	168,992	164,833	171,733	161,711
Exports	2,400	6,935	11,179	17,930	20,790	20,684	22,505
Imports	175,300	373,515	375,408	936,991	974,179	1,065,268	1,101,268
Consumption	815,300	785,503	736,226	1,088,053	1,118,222	1,216,317	1,240,474
Percent of import penetration	21.5	47.5	51.0	86.1	87.1	87.6	88.8

Although the majority of shoes purchased are for the adult market, it is worthwhile to survey the size of the children's market. "The children's shoe market accounted for nearly 12 percent ($1.5 billion) of athletic/casual shoe sales in 1994" (Girone, 1995, p. 113). Although fewer children's shoes were sold in the early 1990s compared to the recent past, the children's shoe market represents a large market and potential growth area for the industry.

FOOTWEAR PRODUCERS

In the United States, several large shoe manufacturers produce the vast majority of shoes. The largest shoe manufacturers in the United States are no longer fashion shoe companies. NIKE and Reebok, two companies that produce primarily athletic shoes, are the top U.S. producers of footwear. According to *Hosiery News* ("Athletic footwear," 1995, p. 25), "Consumers reported purchasing 254.6 million pairs of athletic footwear during the first 8 months of 1994. They reported spending $7.695 billion for the shoes." Several large companies also dominate the fashion footwear business. Among them are the United States Shoe Corporation and Brown Shoe Company.

From an international perspective, Italy has a reputation for leading trends in fashion footwear. Stanley Marcus, former chairman of Neiman Marcus stated, "Europe, and particularly Italy, always has had great shoe designers whose greatest strength has been their willingness to experiment" (Marcus, 1979, p. 87). In addition to its design reputation, Italy has for centuries produced fine leathers for apparel as well as for footwear. The handcrafting of Italian leather products has maintained a worldwide reputation for centuries as well. Salvatore Ferragamo shoes and handbags, Bruno Magli shoes, and Gucci handbags epitomize quality Italian leather materials and workmanship.

Some of the high-end footwear producers continue to utilize handstitching and other handwork. Hermès (France), Ferragamo (Italy), and Dooney &

Bourke (United States) are examples of companies that feature handwork. There still exists a market for handmade shoes and boots, perhaps most evident on Saville Row in London, where custom shoemakers such as Lobb are neighbors to custom shirt makers and **bespoke** (custom) tailors.

DESIGN AND PRODUCTION

Shoe designers research fashion trends in much the same way as do apparel designers. Many shoe designers throughout the world attend the Italian leather shows as well as various shoe trade shows to view the latest developments in leather and shoe design. The shoe designers work in conjunction with the merchandisers and production team to develop the shoe line each season. Designers work with the shoe design components each season: the materials, trims, and styling features, as well as heel height and shape. It is remarkable that shoe designers create such a variety of innovative styles each season given the small surface area of footwear. The fabrication of prototype shoe styles and patterns is performed using steps similar to those discussed for apparel products.

Shoes are made by forming the raw materials around a **last.** The last is a wood, plastic, or metal mold, shaped like a foot. In the United States, lasts are sized in widths as well as lengths. Historically, the width of the last has

Figure 13.2
Shoes require a large number of skilled steps in production.

been different for European sizes compared to the width for American sizes. Some American footwear manufacturers produce shoes in Italy in order to take advantage of the Italian raw materials and craftsmanship. The shoes made in Italy for American manufacturers are produced using "American lasts" in order to fit the target customer's foot.

CAD technology has become an important part of the footwear industry. New developments in software allow the shoe design to be viewed three dimensionally on the screen. Some shoe manufacturers consider computer images of the styles to be sufficient to select the shoes for the line. Thus, prototypes would be made only for those styles selected for production.

The sizes of pattern pieces for shoes are small compared to the sizes of most apparel pattern pieces. Accurate cutting is vitally important to the fit and craftsmanship of shoes. Therefore, cutting footwear often utilizes a die cutting process (discussed in Chapter 11) because of its accuracy. A metal die (similar to a cookie cutter) is made to duplicate the shape of each of the pattern pieces. Its very sharp edge cuts through the layer or multiple layers of materials. Computerized cutting and laser cutting are other options (see Chapter 11) that provide extremely accurate cut pieces.

Leather hides are used for much of the fashion footwear produced worldwide. The hides are irregular in shape, and often have blemishes and thin areas as is expected of this natural product. Thus, cutting hides for the production of shoes, handbags, belts, and other leather goods requires additional time and expertise, a "waste" of some material, and often single-ply cutting to avoid blemished areas. Another factor to consider is that leather hides are a commodity traded on a market whose price varies with the supply, similar to the fur industry. Not only do prices vary based on supply, but since some of the hides sources are in other countries, the monetary exchange rate can influence the price of the raw materials.

Because shoes require a large number of skilled steps in production, labor costs tend to be high. Adding to production time and thus the labor cost is the difficulty of manipulating an awkwardly shaped product composed of many small pieces. Examine the tiny material sections of a pair of toddler's athletic or hiking shoes to imagine what it would be like to assemble the shoe sections. The development of specialized machinery has helped to keep labor costs down for those manufacturers who can afford to invest in the equipment.

Most of the domestic shoe production occurs in Pennsylvania, Maine, and Missouri. As labor costs have risen in the United States, more shoes are being produced off shore. South America (especially Brazil) and Asia produce large quantities of the shoes sold in the United States. China has become a leading manufacturer of shoes. In its 1994 Annual Report, NIKE reported that ". . . 32 factories throughout Asia produce NIKE shoes" (p. 21).

An amusing story occurred when a shipping container filled with hundreds of boxes of NIKE shoes, manufactured in the Pacific Rim and bound for the United States, broke loose from its cargo vessel near the Oregon coast. Thousands of shoes floated to shore. Eager beachcombers delighted in the loot. Unfortunately, many shoes lost their "mates" at sea. Want ads in coastal towns advertised for size mates. New friendships occurred as shoes were matched.

MARKETING AND DISTRIBUTION

New York City serves as the marketing center for footwear, with most companies having showrooms in New York. Domestic and international shoe trade shows, or markets, are held two to four times a year, similar to the apparel market shows. Fall/winter shoe lines are typically shown in January/February and spring/summer shoe lines are typically shown in August. Retail buyers, as well as manufacturers and footwear producers, attend these shows, just as the apparel trade shows are attended by people representing all aspects of the apparel industry.

Footwear is sold in many department stores, specialty stores with footwear departments, specialty shoe stores, sporting goods and athletic footwear stores, hypermarkets and discounters, and by direct retailing (mail order). Some specialty shoe stores carry products from a range of manufacturers. Foot Locker (men's) and Lady Foot Locker (women's) stores, an athletic footwear chain, carry a variety of athletic footwear brands. In addition, vertical integration is also common in the footwear industry, whereby some manufacturers own the shoe stores in which only their products are sold.

Figure 13.3
a. Almost forty percent of all footwear purchased in the United States is athletic shoes. b. Styling, color, and size variations of footwear require a large retail inventory.

a.   b.

Examples are Thom McAn, Redwing, and Stride Rite. Shoe manufacturers, such as Avia and Etienne Aigner, have stores in outlet malls. Direct retailers, such as Lands' End, L.L. Bean, Eddie Bauer, and Talbots, offer shoes in addition to apparel products. Other direct retailers, such as Masseys, focus exclusively on shoes.

Footwear retailing requires an immense inventory because of the large combination of shoe widths and lengths. When the range of seasonal colors is added to the size inventory, it is clear that shoe retailers have a challenging task to meet the consumer's need for the right product in the specific color and size. The footwear retailer requires a significant capital outlay and large inventory space. This is why some retailers lease their shoe departments to companies who specialize in shoe retailing.

The shift in location of footwear production from predominantly domestic production combined with some Western European production, to Asian and South American production was discussed earlier in this chapter. The footwear industry has also shifted its customer market from domestic consumption to a global marketplace. Canadian, Mexican, and Japanese consumers have become major markets for U.S. footwear. American branded athletic shoes are sought worldwide. In 1993, Canadians purchased 62 million pairs of U.S. shoes for a total of $1.9 billion. The athletic shoe share accounted for 25.8 percent of the total pairs, or 21 percent of the dollar market value (*The U.S. Athletic Footwear Market Today*, 1994, p. 11). The reputation for quality of the casual footwear produced by U. S. manufacturers, such as Timberland, has opened European markets for these products. For survival and expansion, footwear manufacturers must continue to seek a global market for their products.

HOSIERY/LEGWEAR

The hosiery industry is composed of companies that produce men's, women's, and children's socks, stockings, and hosiery. The hosiery industry has a long and notable history in the United States. There is evidence of stocking knitting machines in operation in New England as early as 1775. By 1875, the U.S. hosiery industry focused on the production of silk stockings, with an estimated worth of $6,000. By 1900, the industry had grown to a value of $186,413. Similar to the textile industry, hosiery production was primarily found in the northeast during this time. As with textile mills, however, production shifted to the south as labor costs increased in the northeast.

The hosiery industry has undergone major developments during the twentieth century. At the beginning of the twentieth century hosiery consisted of primarily white, "nude," and black socks and stockings in cotton, wool, silk (and later, rayon) knits. By 1928, technological advancements in knitting allowed for the production of full-fashioned men's hosiery in argyle patterns, English ribs, and cable stitches. In 1939, stockings made of

Figure 13.4
The development of framework knitting machines provided a faster way to produce hosiery.

DuPont's nylon fiber were introduced. Women loved their sheerness. Just as the demand for "nylons" soared, they were removed from the market. Nylon was needed for the war effort (World War II). During the war years, women wore socks that coordinated creatively with their suits. An amusing anecdote survives regarding women's sense of loss during the war. A group of 60 women in Tulsa, Oklahoma, were asked what they missed most during the war. Twenty said they missed men the most; forty said they missed nylons the most! In 1946, when nylon stockings became available again, the crowds waiting to purchase them created a legendary sight.

Pantyhose were developed during the 1960s when very short hemline lengths required a product to replace stockings. As the name implies, the hose, or stocking, is joined to a panty, creating an all-in-one product. This eliminated the need for garters, which are used to connect the stockings to a girdle or a garter belt. Nylon is the most prevalent fiber for pantyhose. The panty portion of pantyhose may include spandex fiber to provide some figure control and a cotton knit crotch piece. Since the 1980s, a small percentage of spandex blended with nylon in the leg portion of pantyhose has gained popularity. In the 1990s, microfiber nylon (smaller-than-usual fiber diameter) has become popular, especially for opaque pantyhose or tights. Tights are similar to pantyhose, but are made of a heavier material; they are either seamless or seamed along the center back.

Hosiery is now a dynamic, high-fashion industry for men's, women's, and children's products. Staple hosiery goods have been replaced with socks and stockings suitable for every holiday, to express one's personality, or to add extra punch to an outfit. The price of hosiery is affordable for many consumers. Therefore, this product category has strong price appeal. The consumer can update an outfit inexpensively with accessories such as hosiery. The popularity of hosiery in today's marketplace is evidenced by the specialty sock shops that have proliferated in retail and outlet malls.

HOSIERY PRODUCERS

Hosiery products include socks, stockings, pantyhose, and tights. The retail dollars spend on socks, sheer hosiery, and tights in the United States in 1994 totaled $6.9 billion (*Hosiery News*, 1995). The hosiery industry is dominated by large firms that are often part of vertically integrated companies that produce knitted fabrics as well as the finished hosiery product. Most of the domestic hosiery producers are located in the southeast, concentrated primarily in North Carolina, Alabama, Tennessee, and Pennsylvania (Table 13-6). Some of the largest U.S. hosiery manufacturers include Kayser-Roth Corporation (whose parent company is Mexico's Grupo Synkro, S.A. de C.V., the world's second largest legwear manufacturer and distributor) ("Top Mexican," 1995), Great American Knitting Mills (Gold Toe and Arrow brands), and Sara Lee Corporation whose hosiery brands include Hanes, L'eggs, and Donna Karan. In 1995, Sara Lee claimed a 47 percent share of the U.S. hosiery market (Legbeat, 1995).

TABLE 13-6

1995 Hosiery Produced by Geographic Production

	NC	AL	TN	PA
Socks	55%	18%	6%	1%
Sheers	39%	°%	5%	°%
Tights	69%	°%	5%	°%
TOTAL	50%	11%	5%	°%

° = Less than one

DESIGN AND PRODUCTION

For centuries stockings were knit by hand, using a circular knitting procedure so that no center back seam was required. The foot and leg shapes were produced by adding or subtracting stitches to control the increased or decreased circumference of the stocking. The development of framework knitting machines in England at the end of the sixteenth century ("The history of hosiery," 1974) provided a way to produce stocking blanks. However, the material was knit flat, called **flatknit.** This meant that a seam had to be sewn along the center back to create the tubular stocking. A technique, called **full-fashioned,** provided shaping of the knit goods to conform to the foot and leg shapes along the seam edges. The first full-fashioned hosiery factory in the United States was established by E. E. Kilbourn in the late 1860s.

The development of circular knitting machines in the nineteenth century provided a means to produce seamless (except for the seam used to close the toe) stockings, socks, and later tights and pantyhose. Early seamless stockings did not fit as well as full-fashioned seamed stockings. When women's hemlines were shorten during the 1920s, the better fit of seamed stockings was preferred. This is reflected in the increase in production of full-fashioned stockings from 26 percent of the market in 1919 to 60 percent of production in 1929 and more than 80 percent in the 1950s ("The history of hosiery," 1974). With the development of pantyhose during the 1960s, additional changes in production occurred.

Because pantyhose are made of manufactured fibers that are heat sensitive, the foot and leg shape of pantyhose can be built into the product during the finishing process. A heat-setting process is used to mold the foot and leg shape by placing the hosiery over a leg-shaped board. **Blocking** or **boarding** are terms used for the application of heat to create the final shape in the finishing process.

Socks are produced in varying lengths, including anklets, crew, mid-calf, and calf length. The most popular fibers for socks are cotton, wool, silk, acrylic, nylon, polypropylene, or blends of these fibers. Cotton and acrylic fibers are used frequently for ankle length socks, whereas calf length socks are often made of nylon, wool, silk, acrylic, or blends of two of these fibers. A small percentage of spandex might be added to provide some elasticity.

The size range of hosiery varies according to the type of product. Sock and stocking sizes for men, women, and children are based on a size number that is correlated to shoe size. The consumer refers to a chart that indicates the correct sock size based on the wearer's shoe size. There are fewer sock sizes than shoe sizes; each sock size fits a range of shoe sizes. For some products, the sock or stocking is available in only one size, fitting the range of the majority of the shoe sizes. Pantyhose generally are sized to fit within categories of height/weight ranges. Typical pantyhose sizes are short, average, and tall. Queen size and plus size are size categories for the larger or taller size market. Some pantyhose producers provide a petite size as well.

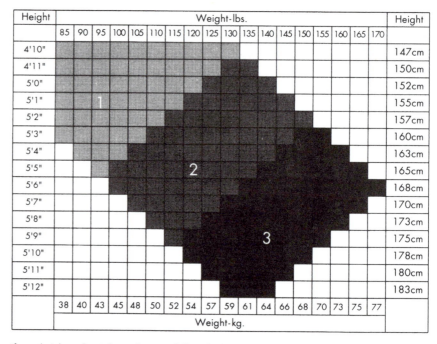

Figure 13.5
Pantyhose are sized to fit within categories of height/weight ranges.

If your height and weight combination falls in the border area, you may prefer the next larger size.

A new line of casual and athletic sock sizes was introduced in 1995 for the outsize market. The marketing manager for Adams-Millis, explained, "Just My Size socks are not simply larger versions of existing socks, but rather they are constructed with the inherent needs of tall and full-figured women in mind. Our research with plus-size women told us that fit is of paramount importance. So we made Just My Size socks with Memory Yarn, which is a combination of cotton and spandex that stretch and conforms to the individual contours of a woman's foot to ensure an unsurpassed fit and improved durability. In addition, the socks feature a knit-in arch that provides comfortable, all-day support" ("Adams-Mills launches," 1995, p. 30).

One of the strengths of the hosiery industry is the impressive variety of innovative textures, colors, and patterns available for hosiery goods. New technology continues to bring an ever-increasing array of materials for hosiery. Much of the machinery required to produce hosiery is automated or computerized, and some of it operates 24 hours a day. Innovations include the development of machinery to knit a one-piece panty hose unit ("Hosiery automation," 1995). Labor costs can be kept down by advanced technology. Thus, the hosiery industry is not threatened as much by inexpensive imports as some other industries. Another strength of the hosiery industry is that many manufacturers are vertically integrated, assisting in Quick Response programs.

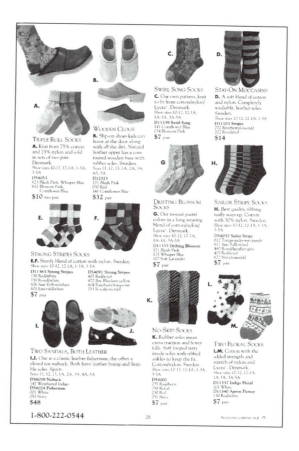

Figure 13.6
New technology brings an array of materials for hosiery.

MARKETING AND DISTRIBUTION

Market weeks for hosiery typically coincide with ready-to-wear, although much hosiery is marketed and distributed through extended distribution channels. The hosiery industry is a low-margin business. This means that the dollar amount of profit per item sold that the producer earns from the retailer is small. Similarly, the dollar amount of profit the retailer "earns" from the sale to the customer is also small. Thus, the manufacturer and the retailer need high sales volume to compensate for the low margin per item sold. A number of strategies are used to create high sales volume.

It is important to maintain a complete stock of hosiery, in the appropriate sizes, styles, and colors, to produce a large sales volume. Therefore, many large hosiery manufacturers use Quick Response with automatic stock replenishment at the retail store to ensure a complete selection of products for the customer; vendor-managed retail inventories is a common practice in the hosiery industry. The director of a hosiery association stated: "Retailers are requiring new benchmarks for product development and delivery. Just-in-time and quick turnaround are realities, and it is becoming more and more pressure driven every day. The new benchmarks are for deliveries to be shipped within 48 hours of receipt of order" (Rabon, 1995, p. 60). A casual and athletic sock manufacturer specializing in the private label business, Clayson Knitting Company, Inc., "is totally computerized with full EDI [electronic data interchange] capabilities, and all major customers send orders electronically. These orders are processed and shipped within 48 hours to 72 hours using back stocks that are maintained for these large customers" (Rabon, 1995, p. 66).

To allow for self-service retail distribution, package marketing is used by a number of companies to sell hosiery in supermarkets, convenience stores, and discount retailers. Brands such as L'eggs and No Nonsense are sold in this manner. Indeed, in 1994, discount retailers accounted for over 50 percent of the retail dollars spent for men's socks and women's socks and tights (Table 13-7). For women's sheer hosiery, the second largest percent of retail dollars was spent at discounters (the largest percent was spent at other outlets). "Consumers are refusing to pay high prices and now are purchasing the majority of hosiery items through discounters as opposed to department stores, chains and specialty stores" (Rabon, 1995, p. 60). Sid Smith, the president and CEO of the National Association of Hosiery Manufacturers (NAHM) pointed out that the domination of discount store sales "means that it is extremely price competitive both at retail and at wholesale. Hosiery manufacturers have to compete very aggressively on price" (Rabon, 1995, p. 60).

Private label hosiery is another approach used by some retailers to keep the margin low. Retailers such as JCPenney, Nordstrom, and Talbots, to name just a few, distribute private label hosiery. Fashion trends also affect the sales volume of hosiery. In the 1990s, the trend toward more casual dressing at the office may have been a stimulus for the increase seen in the sale volume of socks. Promoting hosiery as a fashion accessory rather than a staple commodity can enhance sales volume. Hosiery departments in retail stores may feature bodywear in addition to the hosiery products. Some

TABLE 13-7

1994 Percent of Retail Dollars Spent for Hosiery

	MEN'S ALL	WOMEN'S SOCKS & TIGHTS	WOMEN'S SHEER HOSIERY
Department	13.8%	9.5%	12.5%
Specialty	6.0%	10.7%	6.5%
Chains	13.1%	8.1%	7.8%
Discount	51.3%	57.0%	26.7%
Direct Mail	3.2%	3.2%	16.0%
Other Outlets	12.8%	11.5%	30.4%

retailers have found that hosiery sales increase if these products are displayed with coordinating apparel such as sportswear. This display technique is called cross-merchandising.

Licensed products is another marketing strategy that has proved successful in the hosiery industry. As with footwear and other accessories, many "name" designers license their names for hosiery. Christian Dior, Givenchy, Ralph Lauren, Calvin Klein, Donna Karan, and Liz Claiborne are examples of designers who have licensing agreements with large hosiery companies for hosiery products.

The hosiery industry relies on a close working partnership among the fiber producers, hosiery manufacturers, and retailers. By working together, the hosiery industry in the United States may be able to remain competitive with imported goods. Cooperative advertising is an example of industry partnerships used to promote hosiery products. During 1995, DuPont launched a national advertising campaign to promote its *Lycra®* brand spandex fiber. Some of the advertisements featured hosiery products utilizing *Lycra®*.

In 1995, the industry implemented a National Hosiery Week with the following objectives:

Figure 13.7
DuPont used a national advertising campaign to promote its *Lycra®* brand spandex fiber for hosiery.

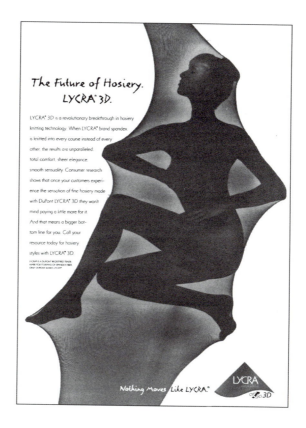

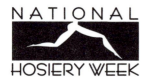

Figure 13.8
Promotions such as
National Hosiery
Week increase customer
knowledge and product
awareness.

1. Motivate consumers to look at the hosiery industry and its products positively through education.

2. Convince retailers to partner with the industry to carry messages to the consumer.

3. Encourage nonparticipating knitters and suppliers to support our communications program with money, time, and ideas.

4. Raise awareness among legislators/regulators, as necessary, regarding industry responsiveness to consumers.
   ("National hosiery week," 1995, p. 17)

National promotions such as this event benefit the producer and the retailer as well as the customer. "To help combat the decline of sheet hosiery, the NAHM used one of its new promotional efforts, National Hosiery Week, to help increase customer understanding and improve education about sheer hosiery" (Rabon, 1995, p. 63).

Although the hosiery industry will face challenges in the future, it is positioning itself for continued success. Although the North American Free Trade Agreement has prompted more imports of hosiery into the United States, the trade balance still favors the United States. For example, Mexico imported more U.S.-produced hosiery than the quantity of hosiery they exported to the United States in 1994. Canada also remains a large export market for hosiery produced in the United States.

HATS, HEADWEAR, SCARFS, AND NECKWEAR

Each of these accessory products is usually manufactured by a company that specializes in a specific item, such as hats, scarfs, or neckties.

HATS AND HEADWEAR

Men's, women's, and children's dress hats comprise a much smaller segment of the accessories category than it did several decades ago. For women, the bouffant hairstyles of the 1960s did not lend themselves to wearing most hat styles. The pillbox hat made famous by then First Lady Jacqueline Kennedy in 1961 marked the end of the hat-wearing social requirement. The custom of businessmen wearing hats began to decline during the 1960s as well. The press coverage regarding the fashion apparel and headwear of the British royal family during the 1980s renewed interest in "fashion" hats, but sales remain a small percent of the accessories area. The Paris designer shows provide a striking contrast, though, to the lack of emphasis on fashion headwear by the masses. The hats worn during the shows to compliment the fashion look of the designers are highly imaginative creations. An apparel collection shown by French designer Karl Lagerfeld included a group of hats designed by a British milliner (hatmaker) created to represent French pas-

Figure 13.9
Designer millinery,
such as this headwear
by Galliano, can be
highly imaginative.

tries—the pâtisserie collection. This type of millinery is an art form, with hat designers producing one-of-a-kind creations. The millinery provides strong visual interest to support the impact of the apparel collections.

While the popularity of wearing hats has waned in many segments of the hat industry, casual hats, sport hats, and sport caps (especially baseball caps), on the other hand, have been a growth area in the 1990s. For sports such as skiing that require head covering for functional purposes, the demand for headwear has remained at the same level as the demand for apparel in these categories.

Many hat and headwear producers specialize only in one type of product. For example, a manufacturer (sometimes referred to as an item house) will specialize in producing only baseball caps. Traditionally styled wool felt hats and straw hats are usually formed over a hat block, using steam to mold the hat into shape. Soft fabric hats and leather caps are usually sewn using construction techniques similar to those for apparel. Handwork might be required for the more expensive hats, while less expensive hats and headwear are machine made. Men's hats are produced in sizes from $6\frac{3}{4}$ to $7\frac{3}{4}$ (in $\frac{1}{8}$ inch intervals) that correspond to head circumference, or, for less structured hats, in sizes small, medium, large, and extra large. Caps may be produced in one size. Most women's hats are one size. Small children's caps and

Figure 13.10
A hat producer often specializes in one type of headwear, such as men's dress hats.

hats may be sized by age, while older children's hats may be produced in sizes extra small, small, medium, and large.

Baseball caps are used extensively as promotional items for many businesses. They can be manufactured quickly with advanced technology equipment. A large quantity of baseball caps with a company logo might be ordered for a special event. Quick delivery of the product is a necessity to meet this need. An example of the quantity of production possible with flexible manufacturing is New Era Cap Company of Derby, New York. It is a licensed official supplier of caps to Major League Baseball, the National Football League, and the National Basketball Association, as well as to hundreds of Little League teams. In its two plants, about 25,000 to 30,000 dozen caps a week are produced (Moore, 1993, p. 16).

Millinery is a term that refers specifically to women's hats, and usually denotes that handwork is involved in the hat-making process. Until the late 1960s to early 1970s, most department stores had millinery departments with millinery specialists. However, very few retailers have retained such departments. The hats sold in most retail stores are machine made and moderately priced. Only a small market for fine millinery continues to exist. Most of the fine milliners are located in New York City, although milliners can be found in Los Angeles and other major metropolitan areas.

SCARFS AND NECKWEAR

Scarfs (preferred industry spelling) represent another product whose styles follow fashion cycles and whose sales rise and fall with fashion trends. At times, large square scarfs, perhaps even shawl sizes are popular; at other times, small square scarfs or oblong scarfs might be fashionable. The scarf business is very specialized. A scarf manufacturer may specialize in only silk scarfs or only wool (or wool-blend, acrylic, or cotton) scarfs. The printing processes used to apply the fabric design are different for silk versus wool material; thus specialization in one of these materials to ensure a quality product is common. A company whose prints and printing techniques for scarfs and neckties are as famous as its leather products mentioned earlier in the chapter is Hermès. According to Stanley Marcus, former chairman of Neiman Marcus, 14 to 25 colors are used for Hermès scarfs (Marcus, 1979, p. 89), and each color requires a separate screen for printing. The scarf price reflects the complexity of the printing process.

Figure 13.11
The cost of a Pucci scarf
is reflected in the quality
of the material and the
complexity of the printing
processes.

Another luxury scarf producer is the Italian design house of Emilio
Pucci. His brightly colored, geometric print, silk scarfs became famous in
the 1960s. Pucci-styled designs are instantly recognizable and have experienced a fashion resurgence in the 1990s. In addition to these two manufacturers of very distinctive scarfs, there are many item houses in the United
States that produce scarfs in a wide variety of materials, from chiffon to cashmere, in an array of textures, colors, and prints. Echo is one of the best-
known U.S. manufacturers of moderately priced scarfs. Many of the American "name designers," such as Liz Claiborne, Oscar de la Renta, and Bill
Blass, license their names for scarfs and neckties.

Many of the scarf manufacturers use fabric manufactured in Asia and
use Asian contractors for the printing as well. The material cost may be less
in Asia, thereby making it more profitable to source off shore. The labor cost
related to the printing can be reduced by using off-shore sourcing as well.
The actual construction process for scarfs can be very rapid, with machine
rolled hemming for moderate and mass priced goods, or time consuming,
with hand-rolled hemming for luxury scarfs.

Necktie manufacturers are usually specialists, producing only neckties.
Finer quality neckties are made of silk, while lower priced neckties are poly-

ester. Wool, linen, cotton, leather, and other specialty materials comprise a small segment of production. Most necktie materials are woven; a small percentage are made of knit fabric. For neckties made of woven fabrics, the material is usually cut on the **bias,** or diagonal, to provide a more attractive knot and contour around the curve of the neck. Because a large amount of fabric is required to cut neckties on the bias, this increases the cost. It is possible to adjust the tilt of the necktie pattern as it is cut to reduce the yardage, but this adversely affects the appearance of the tie. The bias cut also produces the diagonal angle of the stripe seen on neckties as they are worn.

The fabric design for neckties is either a print, applied to the surface of the woven fabric, or a stripe, plaid, or motif woven into the fabric. Typical necktie stripes are termed **regimental stripes,** for they reflect various historical military regiments. These stripes are spaced with wider widths for the background and narrower widths for the various stripes. Many schools (private secondary schools, military schools, colleges, and universities) have a unique regimental stripe color and spacing that denotes their specific affiliation. The regimental stripe tie is considered a classic choice for conservative business attire (observe the neckties worn by a group of heads of state in a photograph). The construction process for neckties includes machine processes; some higher-priced goods require handwork as well. The price reflects the amount of time required to produce the necktie, as well as the cost of the materials. Computer aided textile design processes and new computer printing technologies provide additional ways to reduce the labor costs for the scarf and necktie industries in the United States.

Figure 13.12
The width of neckties, as well as the color and pattern, change with the fashion pendulum.

The market for neckties reflects fashion cycles. The fashion pendulum moves from narrow ties to wide ties, bow ties to no ties, bright prints to subtle stripes. The trend toward casual business dress (termed "Casual Fridays" in the 1990s) in which neckties are no longer "required" may have had some impact on the necktie business. On the other hand, specialty tie shops in retail malls are now numerous, providing consumer awareness, interest, and convenience. "Conversational" or theme necktie prints have helped to increase sales. Whether the necktie displays one's profession, hobby, or promotes a seasonal holiday, the consumer can use his necktie to "speak" to observers.

In addition to neckties, other types of neckwear include neck scarfs, or **mufflers,** often wool or silk, worn usually as an accompaniment to a wool overcoat for more formal occasions. An **ascot,** a long neck scarf worn looped at the neck, is another item of men's neckwear. While neck scarfs and ascots are not purchased as frequently as neckties, retailers such as Brooks Brothers include such items as a necessary component of a well-stocked classic men's retail store.

BELTS, HANDBAGS, AND GLOVES

Some of the unique aspects of each of the accessories categories of belts, handbags, and gloves will be discussed separately in the following section.

BELTS

The belt industry is divided into two segments:

- **cut-up trade:** belt manufacturers that produce belts for apparel manufacturers to add to their pants, skirts, and dresses and to supply as a component of the product to be shipped to retailers, and

- **rack trade:** belt manufacturers that design, produce, and market belts to retailers.

Manufacturers in the cut-up trade specialize in low-cost, high-volume items. These garment belts might be made of less-expensive materials and processes, such as the use of glue rather than stitching to attach the belt backing. Self-belts made from the same fabric as the garment might be produced by the apparel manufacturer at the same time that the garment is produced.

Belts for the rack trade often provide an important component of a fashion look, therefore this part of the accessories industry works closely with the apparel segment. Belt production is centered in New York City's fashion district. Typical materials include leather as well as numerous other materials from cording to beaded fabrics. The type of material used determines the type of construction techniques and processes.

For leather belts, cutting can be performed by hand or by the use of a strap-cutting machine that cuts even-width strips. Some leather belts are curved, or contoured, in which case the leather could be die-cut for speed

Figure 13.13
Decorative effects using buckles, stitching, and other enhancements add a lively interest to belts.

and accuracy. There are a myriad of decorative effects possible to enhance belts. Belt designers add creativity with the use of buckles, stitching, jewels, chains, metal pieces, plastics, stones, nailheads, and other embellishments. Belt backings are attached by stitching or gluing them in place.

HANDBAGS AND SMALL LEATHER GOODS

Although this category of accessories is termed handbags, a variety of products is retailed under this classification. Many of the "handbags" produced and sold today are actually shoulder bags rather than handbags. Handbags are also called purses. Women's briefcases are another product in this category, as are wallets, coin purses, eyeglasses cases, and schedule planners. (Men's briefcases are typically sold with luggage.)

Handbags can be made from a variety of materials. At least half of the handbags sold in the United States are made of leather, reptile (such as snakeskin), or eelskin. Other materials include a variety of fabrics, plastics (vinyl is the most common), and straw. For example, Judith Leiber creates beaded and metal evening bags whose retail prices begin at approximately $500.

Structured handbags are supported by a frame that provides a distinctive shape and to which hardware, such as the closure, is attached. Soft handbags, such as pouch styles, may not use a frame. Handles or straps are

WHAT HAS A STRIKING SILHOUETTE?
Venus de Milo, the Manhattan skyline,
AND THE NEW STYLES IN THE SOHO SERIES
FROM COACH.

COACH

With fall comes shorter days, cooler weather and a new selection of handbags from Coach.
New in the Soho Series are three striking silhouettes: the Soho Buckle Bag, No. 4157; the Soho Handle Bag, No. 4158; and the Soho Belted Pouch, No. 4156.
Available in a variety of classic Coach colors, these lightweight bags also come in Bottle Green, and the hottest color this fall, Red.
516 WEST 34TH STREET, NEW YORK, NY 10001

Figure 13.14
Coach bags might be sold in a separately designated retail space within a department store.

attached to carry the handbag. **Clutch** bags are designed to be held in the hand (the term is derived from clutching the bag in the hand) and may have a strap that can be stored inside the bag. Most handbags are lined in materials such as leather, suede, cloth, or vinyl. Structured bags may also have an interlining made from a stiff material to provide a firm shape.

Handbag styles range from large satchels to tiny clutches. Whereas fashion trends play an important role in handbag styling, personal choice plays a role as well. Some women prefer a very functional bag, designed to hold everything, either in a roomy tote or a compartmentalized style. Other women prefer a compact style that could range from a "wallet on a string" to a decorative evening bag to hold only a few "essentials." Although many European men carry bags, few American men have adopted this practice.

Designing handbags requires the same types of steps as many other products. Ideas are sketched and decorative trims, handles, hardware, and materials are researched. It is interesting to imagine what it would be like to be a designer for a classic handbag company such as Coach or Dooney & Bourke. How, and how much, can a designer modify a handbag? Details such as pinked edging trims a group of Dooney & Bourke bags. Colored piping in "classic" but new color combinations is added. After ideas have been generated, prototypes are made and then the line is finalized.

Leather handbags follow manufacturing procedures similar to other leather products discussed in this chapter. Fabric handbags may use die cutting and other processes similar to garment production. For all handbags, some of the assembly processes, especially adding the hardware, require handwork. Thus labor costs are an important part of the costing structure. For leather goods, the price and availability of hides is another cost consideration. There are a number of small companies that produce many of the U.S-produced handbags. Most of these companies are centered in the mid-Manhattan district of New York City. With most handbags and small leather goods sold in the United States imported, off-shore production sites in Asia, Spain, Italy, and South America are important production centers. New York City is also the primary market center for handbags and small leather goods.

Because many of the production processes are similar for various leather goods, shoe manufacturers might also make handbags and belts. Ferragamo produces coordinated handbags for some of its shoes, and Coach produces belts and other small leather goods as well as handbags. The handbag trade shows coincide with the apparel markets—generally four shows per year.

In the 1970s, several "designer" names became sought after by consumers. The Louis Vuitton vinyl handbags with the "LV" logo appeared everywhere and sold at a premium price. Gucci bags became a status symbol. French fashion designer names, such as Pierre Cardin and Christian Dior, appeared on the outside of handbags. Since then, the licensing of designer names for handbags has become a major component of this business.

Some retailers have established separate departments to feature the leather products of a specific manufacturer. Coach bags and belts often have a designated retail space, distinctively styled with shelf units and signage that the customer recognizes as being Coach. We also see vertical integration within this industry. For example, Coach also operates its own retail stores.

GLOVES

Gone are the days when a well-dressed man, woman, or child did not leave home without both hat and gloves. The popularity of dress gloves rises and falls with fashion trends. Functional gloves and mittens, such as those worn for cold winter weather remain a steady part of the industry. Sport gloves are a rising segment of the glove industry, with gloves specially designed for bicycling, weight lifting, golf, and many other sports. Women's dress gloves are produced in a variety of lengths, from wrist-length "shorties" to shoulder-length "16-button" gloves for bridal and evening wear. (The term "button" is used to designate each inch of length.)

Leather gloves and fabric gloves are the two primary categories of the glove industry. The difference in the handling of these two types of materials results in substantial differences in production. The majority of fabric gloves are made of knit fabric. Production is similar to other knit items and is located primarily in the southeast where many knitting mills are located. Knit gloves and mittens are produced quickly by using a circular knitting machine (see section in this chapter on hosiery).

Wool Blend Gloves

A warm place for ten little fingers. Choose from a riot of colors. Soft and long-wearing 50/50 blend of wool and acrylic. Sweden.

S fits 3 to 5 years
M fits 6 to 8 years
L fits 9 to 12 years

V52001
015 Black
045 Vivid Violet
031 Magenta
051 Navy
089 Harbor Green
058 Royal
030 Red $10

a.

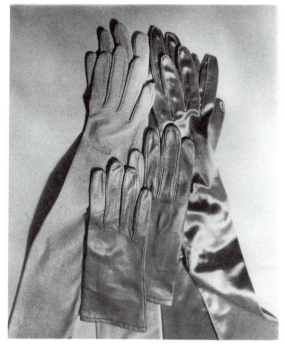

b.

Figure 13.15
a. Knit gloves are much faster to produce than leather gloves and can be made in fewer sizes or a single size.
b. Leather gloves are produced in a variety of lengths and from many different leathers.

The production of leather gloves, however, still requires many hand operations. Many glove manufacturers use off-shore contractors, primarily in Asia and the Philippines, to compensate for the cost of production labor. In the United States, a large portion of glove manufacturing is located in Gloversville, New York.

The types of leather used for gloves need to be strong, yet thin and supple. Typical glove leathers include kidskin, lambskin (cabretta is a type of lambskin), pigskin, deerskin, and sueded leathers. Among the steps in the production of better quality gloves is a process to dampen and then stretch the leather in order to improve suppleness. Some leather glove manufacturers specialize in only one part of the production process, such as cutting. This step requires careful assessment of the hide for quality and most efficient utilization. Cutting might be accomplished entirely by hand (**table cutting**) for the top quality gloves, or by less time-consuming die cutting (**pull-down cutting**) for less-expensive gloves.

The higher quality leather gloves include a number of separate sections that provide flexibility for hand movement. These sections include: a thumb section; a **trank** piece for the palm and another for the face of the hand; **fourchettes,** rectangular strips between the second/third, third/fourth, and fourth/fifth fingers to provide width; and three **quirks,** tiny triangular gussets at the base of the second, third, and fourth fingers. Each of these pieces requires painstaking care in construction in order to fit the pieces together properly.

Woven fabric gloves require similar pattern pieces and steps as described for leather gloves. Less expensive gloves might have fewer pattern pieces and are therefore not as comfortable for hand flexibility. The seams may be stitched so the raw edges are to the inside, or may be sewn with raw edges to the outside, depending on the style of glove. Gloves can be made of a combination of leather and fabric. For example, a sport glove might have leather tranks and knit fourchettes. Some leather gloves are lined with knit fabric or fur.

Knit gloves might be manufactured in one size, the fabric stretching sufficiently to fit a wide range of hand sizes. Fabric, leather, and men's knit gloves usually are produced in sizes of small, medium, large, and extra-large, or they are sized numerically, in $\frac{1}{4}$-inch intervals, corresponding to the circumference around the palm-forehand (sizes 7 to 10 for men and sizes $5\frac{1}{2}$ to 8 for women). For children, gloves and mitten sizes are related to age.

New York is the primary market center for gloves and most glove companies have showrooms in New York. Specialists called glove buyers in retail stores are of a by-gone era. Today's gloves are sold in accessory departments along with belts, scarfs, purses, and bags, and sometimes, jewelry, in department or specialty stores. Gloves are also sold by specialty accessory retailers.

JEWELRY

Jewelry is categorized as:

▋ fine jewelry,

▋ bridge jewelry, or

▋ costume jewelry.

Fine jewelry is the most expensive of the jewelry types. This category includes pieces made from precious metals, such as silver, gold, and platinum, either alone or with precious and semiprecious gemstones. Because gold is too soft to be used by itself, it is usually combined with other metals for jewelry. The gold content of a piece of jewelry is expressed in carats/karats (K) with 24K referring to solid gold; 18K and 14K gold are most often used in fine jewelry. Any alloy less than 10K cannot be labeled as karat gold. Platinum, which is heavier and more expensive than gold, is often used for rings—particularly diamond rings. Silver is the least expensive of the precious metals. Silver is often combined with other metals (usually copper). To be labeled as "sterling silver" the metal must be at least 925 parts/1000 parts silver.

Precious gemstones include diamonds, emeralds, sapphires, and rubies. All are measured in carats, with 1 carat equaling 100 points. Pearls are also included in this category even though they are not a stone, per se. Semiprecious stones include amethysts, garnets, opals, lapis, jade, topaz, and aquamarine. In recent years, semiprecious stones have gained popularity as consumer preference for colored gemstones has increased. Fine jewelry is often a vertically integrated organization whereby the designer, producer,

Figure 13.16
Pearls might be priced at either the fine or bridge price zone, depending on the quality and the manufacturer.

and retailer are often under one roof. Fine jewelry is sold through specialty jewelry stores and through upscale department stores in their fine jewelry departments.

Similar to the bridge wholesale price zone for ready-to-wear apparel which falls between designer and better price zones, **bridge jewelry** falls between fine and costume jewelry. Bridge jewelry serves as an umbrella term for several types of jewelry, including those that involve the use of silver, gold (typically 14K, 12K, or 10K), and less expensive "stones," such as onyx, ivory, coral, or freshwater pearls. One-of-a-kind jewelry designed by artists using a variety of materials is also considered bridge jewelry. Bridge jewelry is sold along with fine jewelry and costume jewelry.

Costume jewelry is the least expensive of the jewelry categories. Coco Chanel was the first prominent designer to accessorize her couture garments with costume jewelry, thus legitimizing the wearing of less expensive jewelry by women everywhere. This type of jewelry is mass produced using plastic, wood, brass, glass, lucite, and other less expensive materials. Although there are large companies in the costume jewelry industry, including Monet and Trifari, the industry is dominated by small companies that produce jewelry sold through a variety of retail outlets, including nonstore retailers.

SUMMARY

The accessories industries comprise a vital and important component to the fashion industry. Changes in accessories complement changes found in the ready-to-wear industry. Therefore, the apparel and accessories markets work together in creating total fashion looks. Accessories are grouped into the following categories: footwear; hosiery and legwear; hats and headwear; belts, handbags, and small leather goods; gloves; and jewelry. Although production processes vary, most accessory lines are created according to the following steps: research (including color, material, trend, and market research), designer's sketches, pattern making (or creating molds in the jewelry industry), development of prototypes; costing, marketing, production, and distribution; and retailing.

The footwear industry is made up of companies that produce men's, women's, and children's dress shoes and boots, athletic shoes, casual shoes, and other footwear (including work boots, Western boots, and sandals). The raw materials primarily used for footwear include leather, fabrics, and plastics. Shoes are produced by forming raw materials around a last or mold shaped like a foot. Shoe production requires a number of steps and can be very labor intensive. In an effort to reduce labor costs, production of shoes has shifted from domestic production to primarily off-shore production. New York City serves as the primary market center for footwear. Shoes are distributed through all retail channels.

The hosiery/legwear industry is comprised of companies that produce men's, women's, and children's socks, stockings, and hosiery. The hosiery industry is dominated by large firms that are often part of vertically integrated companies. Most of the domestic hosiery producers are currently located in the southeast, concentrated primarily in North Carolina. Production of hosiery is very automated and therefore, the hosiery industry is not threatened by imports as much as other industries. Hosiery companies are very involved with Quick Response strategies, including vendor-managed retail inventory, which requires consistent sales information flow between the manufacturer and retailer and allows for automatic replenishment of inventories at the retail level.

As with all accessories, hats, scarfs, neckties, belts, handbags, and gloves are affected by the apparel fashion trends of the day. Although hats and headwear companies currently comprise a much smaller segment of the accessories industries than they did decades ago, they are still an important accessory industry. Item houses that produce specialty items such as baseball caps have grown as the popularity of this type of accessory has increased. The belt industry includes the rack trade (manufacturers who design, produce and market belts to retailers) and the cut-up trade (manufacturers who produce belts for apparel manufacturers). The handbag industry includes companies that produce shoulder bags, purses, wallets, coin purses, eyeglass cases, and schedule planners. In the glove industry, leather gloves and fabric gloves are the two primary categories. Jewelry is categorized as fine jewelry, bridge jewelry, and costume jewelry. For virtually all accessories, New York City serves as the market center. Trade shows and trade associations play an important role in promoting all components of the accessory industries.

REFERENCES

Adams-Millis launches Just My Size socks for outsize market. (1995, September). *Hosiery News*, p. 30.

Athletic footwear. (1995, April). *Hosiery News*, p. 25.

Girone, J.A. (1995, October). Shoe Business. *Earnshaw's Review*. pp. 113–116.

The history of hosiery: Early industry developed slowly. (1974, November 8). *Hosiery Newsletter*, pp. 3–9.

Hosiery automation advances at F.A.S.T. show. (1995, August). *Hosiery News,* pp. 32–34.

Hosiery News, (1995, August). p. 20.

Legbeat. (1995, October 30). *WWD,* p. 35.

Marcus, Stanley. (1979). *Quest for the Best.* New York: Viking Press.

Moore, L. (1993, November). There are no caps on New Era's potential. *Apparel Industry Magazine,* pp. 16–22.

National hosiery week plans in place. (1995, August). *Hosiery News,* pp. 14–17.

NIKE, Inc. *1994 Annual Report.* Beaverton, OR.

Rabon, Lisa C. (1995, December). Makers target new benchmarks. *Bobbin,* pp. 60–63.

Rabon, Lisa C. (1995, December). Survival of the sock. *Bobbin,* pp. 65–66.

Salmon, Larry. (1976, July). The nation: Down to work American style. *Hosiery and Underwear,* pp. 14–21.

Top Mexican corporate executive tells American business delegation peso crisis offers his country opportunity to become export leader. (1995, April). *Hosiery News,* p. 29.

The U.S. Athletic Footwear Market Today. (1994, September). Athletic Footwear Association.

U.S. footwear market spread thin. (1996, February). *Bobbin,* pp. 66–71.

KEY TERMS

bespoke	**rack trade**
last	**clutch**
flatknit	**table cutting**
full-fashioned	**pull-down cutting**
blocking (boarding)	**trank**
millinery	**fourchettes**
bias	**quirks**
regimental stripes	**fine jewelry**
mufflers	**bridge jewelry**
ascot	**costume jewelry**
cut-up trade	

DISCUSSION QUESTIONS

1. Think about the accessories you are currently wearing. How do they complement the fashion apparel you are wearing? How is the design, production, and distribution of these accessories similar to and different from the fashion apparel?

2.   If you were a shoe designer, before starting your next line of shoes, what sources of information would you turn to for market and trend research? Why would this information be important in your design decisions?

CAREER PROFILES

As with the ready-to-wear industry, the accessories industries include a wide variety of career possibilities, from design to production to marketing and distribution.

COLOR AND PAINT COORDINATOR/ASSISTANT DESIGNER,
Athletic Shoe and Sportswear Company

Job Description
Create color palette for each season, decide what colors to use on each shoe taking into consideration the target customer, decide on the materials to be used in the shoe production, paint prototype shoes.

Typical Tasks
- Creating different colorways for shoes
- Using freehand and streamline applications to create the colorways
- Attend meetings to communicate with others in the department and in other departments
- Render drawings for these meetings to visually communicate designer's ideas

What Do You Like Best About Your Job?
The creativity and my coworkers.

ACCESSORY DESIGN ASSISTANT,
Privitely Owned Sportswear Company

Job Description
To provide overall basic design support to staff designers.

Typical Tasks
- Work closely with the designers to interpret consumer and market needs
- Assemble presentation materials for designers by gathering drawings/illustrations, preparing type, copying, and cutting/pasting. Assist in collecting and organizing color samples, graphics, materials, trims, and tear sheets for presentation. Assist in board layout under direction of the designer
- Maintain and update presentation materials and technical accessory illustrations throughout the design process under direction of the designer. Ensure that boards reflect accurate style lines, colorways, and graphic placement; using CAD

▌ Meet regularly with designers to set priorities and facilitate work flow. Anticipate designer needs whenever possible

What Do You Like Best About Your Job?

Creativity flow, access to the latest information, my coworkers and working environment, using CAD systems

ACCESSORIES PATTERN/SAMPLE MAKER,
Publicly Owned Athletic Shoe and Sportswear Company

Job Description

Support the design prototype process for the accessories team, including drafting patterns, interpreting design and constructing prototypes, creating specifications, technical drawings, and construction details.

Typical Tasks

▌ Draft accessories patterns from design sketches

▌ Construct, build, and/or sew accessories samples such as bags, hats, gloves, etc.

▌ Create product specifications and ensure accuracy. Create product technical drawings complete with construction details to facilitate more accurate samples from the field

▌ Review accessory samples for accuracy, color matching, durability, and function. Review construction details to ensure specifications are correct

▌ Collaborate with accessory designers, developers, and engineers to ensure the best product is produced and work out construction problems

▌ Calculate fabric utilization data and other costing factors in collaboration with engineers, designers, and developers. Evaluate new equipment with the Sample Room Supervisor and technology services manager

▌ Cut fabrics and trim. Purchase and maintain inventory of materials, supplies and notions

What Do You Like Best About Your Job?

I enjoy the variety of responsibilities I have; each day is a little different. It is as if I have several jobs. I enjoy pattern work and writing specifications (documenting construction details).

14

Home Fashions

Objectives

▮ To examine the similarities, differences, and relationships between the home fashions and the ready-to-wear industries.

▮ To describe the design, marketing, production, and distribution of textile products such as upholstery fabrics, window coverings, area floor coverings, towels, and bedding.

▮ To examine industry efforts toward sustainable design in the home fashions industry.

WHAT ARE HOME FASHIONS?

Previous chapters in this book have examined the design, marketing, and production of ready-to-wear apparel and accessories. This chapter will focus on the home fashions industry. **Home fashions** are textile products used for home end-uses such as towels, bedding, upholstery fabrics, area floor coverings, draperies, and table linens, and whose styles change over time in response to changing fashion trends. Therefore, home fashions include the home textiles, table-top, and domestics categories of the broader home furnishings industry. The home fashions industry consists of companies that design, produce, market, and distribute these home textile products.

This chapter will examine the similarities, differences, and relationships between the design, production, and marketing of home fashions and the ready-to-wear industry. There are several reasons why an understanding of the organization and operation of the home fashions industry in the broader context of apparel fashions is important. In recent years, the ready-to-wear industry and the home fashions industry have become increasingly interconnected as a growing number of apparel companies have ventured into designing, producing, marketing, and distributing home fashions. Ralph Lauren established a home fashions division soon after initiating his apparel lines. Recent entrants from the apparel arena into the home fashions market include Guess, Ellen Tracy, and Eileen West. "The crossover between apparel and home textiles is emerging as one of the hottest trends in the business today. That was the message from Linda Allard, the design force behind Ellen Tracy, a longtime apparel powerhouse. Now Allard is targeting the home" (Williams, 1995, p. 19). Her first collections for Fieldcrest Cannon debuted in 1996.

In addition, consumer demand for home fashions has been strong. This trend can be attributed to a favorable housing industry, a growing remodeling industry, consumers' desire to spend more time at home, and the growing selection of home fashions available to consumers. With this continued growth, the design, production, marketing, and distribution of home fashions encompasses a large potential market for exciting and rewarding careers for individuals who have expertise in textiles, design, and marketing.

In general, the home fashions industry is divided into four primary end-use categories (Yeager, 1988):

- upholstery fabrics,
- window and wall coverings,
- soft floor coverings, including area rugs, scatter rugs, and runners (room and wall-to-wall carpeting is beyond the scope of this chapter), and
- bed, bath, table, and other textile accessories and accents.

Later in this chapter, these end-use categories will be discussed in greater detail. First, a general discussion of the organization and operation of the home fashions industry and the marketing of home fashions will provide an overall context for the design, marketing, and production of these end-use products.

HOME FASHIONS AND THE TEXTILE INDUSTRY

The textile industry forms the base for the structure of the home fashions industry. The design and performance of the textiles used in home fashions play a very important role in the success of the end-use product. Indeed, for many home fashions, the design of the fabric is as important as the design of the end-use product itself. As mentioned in Chapter 3, textile companies often focus entirely on home textiles and home fashion end uses. The general organization and structure of textile companies that produce textiles primarily for the home fashions industry are the same as for those companies that produce textiles for the apparel industry (refer to Figure 3-1 for a summary of the organizational structure of the U.S. textile industry). It should be noted that many textile companies produce fabrics for both apparel and home fashions (e.g., Dan River, Milliken, Burlington, Springs Industries).

The home fashions industry is dominated by vertically integrated textile companies that produce both fabrics and home fashion end-use products. These include home fashions powerhouses such as Westpoint Pepperell, Springs Industries, Fieldcrest Cannon, Dan River, and Dundee Mills. This is because production of home fashions is often highly automated and can be accomplished very efficiently within a vertical operation. In many cases, the fabric may not need to be cut and sewn to complete the product (e.g., towels

Figure 14.1
Fieldcrest Cannon is a major producer of home textiles such as bedding and towels.

and rugs), or minimal sewing, such as sheet hemming, is performed at the textile facility. For example, a single facility of Westpoint Stevens, a division of Westpoint Pepperell, performs all production processes from cleaning cotton to creating the finished products (e.g., sheets and pillowcases) that are ready for distribution. Because of this vertical integration and automation of production, the home fashions industry has been somewhat less vulnerable to imports than apparel, although imported fabrics are a significant competitor in certain segments of the industry, particularly high-end sheeting fabrics.

LICENSING IN HOME FASHIONS

Licensing agreements involve purchasing the use of an image or design by a manufacturer for use on their products (see Chapter 2 for a complete discussion of licensing). As in the apparel industry, licensing agreements have become an important component of the home fashions industry. Licensing agreements in home fashions are classified in the same categories as apparel, including designer name licensing, character licensing, corporate licensing, nostalgia licensing, and sports licensing.

Well known ready-to-wear apparel designers have moved into the world of home fashions through licensing agreements with textile mills and home fashions manufacturers. Among the first apparel designers to license home fashions were Anne Klein, Liz Claiborne, and Laura Ashley for Burlington Domestics; Issey Miyake for Cannon; Perry Ellis for Martex; Bill Blass for Springs Industries; and Yves St. Laurent for J.P. Stevens. Although not all of these early licenses succeeded, many of them flourished. Today some of the best known designers with home fashions licensing agreements include Ralph Lauren, Laura Ashley, Jessica McClintock, Liz Claiborne, Calvin Klein, and Bill Blass. Liz Claiborne's current licensing agreement with Springs Industries, known as Liz At Home, focuses on home textiles. Eileen West has a licensing agreement with Atrium, a Valencia, Spain-based manufacturer, for a collection of flannel bedding. Leshner Mills markets the products. Home Innovations serves as Calvin Klein's exclusive licensee not only for sheets and towels but also for silverware, glassware, dinnerware, furniture, accessories, and gifts.

In addition to name designers, companies with well-known brand names are also entering into licensing agreements for home fashions. For example, Echo, known for scarfs, has a licensing agreement with Revman for a variety of home textiles. Eddie Bauer licenses with Westpoint Stevens for its sheets and pillowcases. Guess Inc., a Los Angeles jeans and sportswear manufacturer, introduced its Guess Home Collection in 1994 and operates Guess Home boutiques in New York and Beverly Hills.

Licensing is also big business for home fashions geared to children. As with apparel, licensing of cartoon and movie characters (e.g., Disney, Warner Brothers), sports teams (e.g., Dallas Cowboys), and toys (e.g., Barbie) have been very successful.

Figure 14.2
Top: Ralph Lauren licenses home fashions in addition to creating men's, women's, and children's apparel.

Bottom: Licensed products, such as Disney bedding, are big business for home fashions geared to children.

What makes these licensing agreements successful? As discussed in Chapter 2, a successful licensing agreement, whether in ready-to-wear or home fashions, depends on a well-recognized brand name with a distinct image and a licensed product that reflects that image. Successful licensed home fashion collections such as Ralph Lauren Home Collection and Guess Home Collection follow this strategy.

HOME FASHIONS DESIGN

The design phase of the home fashions industry includes textile and trim designers, who create exciting materials, and product designers, who determine the form for the final end-use product. As previously discussed, some home fashion products roll off the textile production assembly as finished products. For other types of products, the product designer works with new textiles, trims, and findings to create exciting pillows, comforters, table-top accents, and accessories. In general, designers in the home fashions industry create designs for two fashion seasons, spring/summer and fall/winter. Because fashion trends do not change as quickly for home fashions as for apparel, home fashion designs may stay on the market longer than apparel.

RESEARCH

Designers must take into account many considerations and constraints in order to successfully develop new and exciting products season after season. Inspiration can come from numerous sources when creating new shapes, textures, and color combinations. New fiber and fabric developments are also a part of the design inspiration. In addition, there are important functional needs that must be met. Performance criteria are important to the consumer. A towel must be absorbent, soft, easily laundered, and durable, as well as look attractive while displayed in the bathroom. As with apparel, fabrics used for home fashions are designed and tested for performance characteristics. Some home fashion products (e.g., rugs, upholstered furniture) must meet specific safety standards (e.g., flammability) set by law.

The designer strives to be cognizant of emerging social, political, economic and consumer trends. Anticipating and meeting customer needs are critical components of the design and production aspects of the industry. Two key elements of current home fashion trends are self-expression and individuality. These are evidenced by the increased customization of products to meet a consumer's individual wants and needs. Research is conducted regarding home fashion products and consumer trends similar to the research process for apparel products. For example, Thinsulate, an insulative material manufactured by 3M with an established name in apparel, also has attributes suited to the bedding market. However, the fiber composition needed for bedding differs from Thinsulate's specifications for apparel products. Therefore, 3M needed to conduct research and development in order to apply this fiber to a new end use in the home fashion market. "Through independent research, 3M found that consumers would be receptive to Thinsulate in bedding, and 'the consumer told us they would be willing to pay more for it'" (Rush, 1996, p. 6).

COLOR FORECASTING

As in the apparel industry, color forecasting is an important component of the home fashions industry. Some of the color forecasting services described in Chapter 5 provide research and trend forecasting for home fashions as well as for apparel products. Historically, changes in the color palette for home fashions were based on a ten-year cycle. Who can forget the pink, salmon, cerise, turquoise, and gray of the 1950s; followed by avocado and orange in the 1960s; beige, gold, and brown in the 1970s; or mauve, forest green, slate blue, gray, black and white in the 1980s? However, that ten-year color cycle appears to be accelerating as consumers are more able and willing to change their home decor and companies are providing consumers with more alternatives. Because home textile sample books might be used to market home textiles for several years, accurate color forecasting is necessary for the fashion colors to appear as up-to-date as possible. In addition, substantial lead time is needed to produce coordinated home fashion products. Therefore, on-target color forecasting is critical for success.

TEXTILE DESIGN

Textile design for home fashions includes the design of the fabric structure (e.g., weave pattern) as well as the surface design (e.g., printing, napping, glazing). Although woven fabrics are more common than other fabric structures for home fashion products, the industry has seen an increased use of knits and nonwoven fabrics, primarily for less costly products.

Textile designers for home fashions often work with computer aided design programs to develop their designs. Textile designers also create original painted artwork for fabric prints that are later scanned into a CAD system. Once the design is in the CAD system, details of the design are refined. The various colors used in the print design can be separated by computer for the printing process, since each color of the print requires a separate roller printer. Prints with a larger number of colors (13–15) are more costly to produce than prints with a few colors (1–3). The cost of developing the new print is more economical if the print can be produced in several color combinations. Therefore, several colorways or color variations are typically created for each print design. When designing a print, textile designers must take into consideration the repeat of the print so that the design can be printed effectively with a series of roller printers.

As in the apparel industry, **converters** play an important role in the production of textiles for specific home fashion end uses. These end uses include upholstery fabrics, table linens, and other fabrics that are printed or finished to improve the performance of the end-use product. For example, soil-hiding and soil-resistant finishes are often applied to fabrics used for upholstery or table linen fabrics. As with the apparel industry, most home textile print converters, such as Covington, Ametex, John Wolf, Richloom,

Figure 14.3
Soil resistant finishes are often applied to fabrics used for upholstery or table linen fabrics.

and Waverly, are based in New York and contract finishing work with a variety of finishing plants. In most cases, converters will provide original painted fabric print designs to a finishing company that will input the design into a computer system, develop fabric pigments for printing, and print and finish the fabric. For example, Waverly contracts with Cherokee Finishing Company, a division of Spartan Mills, to print and finish its upholstery fabrics.

MARKETING HOME FASHIONS

As with the apparel industry, traditional marketing processes include manufacturer showrooms, company sales representatives, trade shows, and advertising. However, the home fashions industry relies on converters and jobbers to perform marketing and distribution functions more often than does the apparel industry. As with apparel, the establishment of well-respected brand names is important in the marketing of home fashions. Consumers often rely on brand names in their decisions to purchase goods. Westpoint Stevens is well known for its Martex and Ralph Lauren brands, Fieldcrest Cannon for its Royal Velvet brand, and Burlington for Burlington House brands.

MANUFACTURER SHOWROOMS AND SALES REPRESENTATIVES

Marketing headquarters and manufacturer showrooms for most home fashions companies are located in New York City. Companies use showrooms to provide enticing visual displays of new home textiles as well as finished products for their interior design, manufacturing, and retail customers. Most companies will display new fabrics made up into end-use products to show customers how the new fabrics can be used. Coordinated ensembles of products for bed and bath, kitchen, living room, and dining areas are created and presented. Companies also distribute sample books to interior design and manufacturing customers. These sample books include swatches of home textiles that are available and pictures of finished products using the textiles.

DECORATIVE FABRIC CONVERTERS AND JOBBERS

In addition to manufacturer showrooms, converters and jobbers also play an important role in the marketing of home fashions. As mentioned earlier,

Figure 14.4
Home fashions advertisements portray inviting environments with coordinated upholstered furniture and window treatments.

converters in the home fashions industry design and sell finished textiles to jobbers, designers, and manufacturers, who use the textiles in home fashion end-use products. Some converters also produce end-use products such as bed linens and window treatments. Like manufacturers, converters create and distribute sample books and have showrooms in New York City where they display and sell their goods to jobbers as well as to interior design, manufacturing, and retailing customers.

Decorative fabric jobbers are also involved in the marketing and distribution of home textile piece goods, particularly upholstery and drapery fabrics. Traditionally, jobbers have served a warehousing and distribution function within the industry. In the past, regional jobbers would visit New York twice per year and buy large quantities of fabrics from a number of mills and converters and sell smaller quantities to interior designers, furniture manufacturers, and retail customers. Over the years, however, the jobber market has evolved into a year-round market with a number of jobbers providing nationwide distribution. Jobbers, however, continue to select colors, designs, and fabrics that best meet their customers' needs. Like manufacturers and converters, jobbers put together sample books for their customers. In recent years, the jobber market has changed as jobbers have started providing a number of services, such as importing fabrics, creating exclusive in-house fabric designs, converting fabrics, and marketing fabrics through showrooms. "All of this has blurred the distinction between manufacturer and distributor as jobbers move into areas previously reserved for mills and converters" (Green, 1990, p. 4A). In fact, as some jobbers have turned to converting, some top converters have turned to jobbing functions.

Robert Allen, one of the largest residential woven fabric jobber in the United States, serves over 60,000 accounts from its four warehouses. "According to the mills and converters that supply Robert Allen, it produces more fabric, and has more collections than any of its competitors" ("Robert Allen", 1990, p. 6A). In addition, in each fabric category (e.g., upholstery, drapery), teams of designers work to create new fabrics for their customers. Robert Allen markets its products through showrooms and showroom boutiques where finished products are shown using exclusive fabrics. In addition to fabrics, these showrooms have displays of wall coverings and finished products, such as bed coverings and draperies. Other well-known national jobbers include Fabricut, Barrow, and Kravet.

MARKETING TOOLS

As in the apparel industry, companies in the home fashions industry use a variety of marketing tools to advertise and promote their products to their customers and to the ultimate consumers. These marketing tools include

Figure 14.5
Cooperative advertising helps to provide the links in consumers' minds between brand names, end-use products, and retailers.

sample books (for home textiles), catalogs, print advertisements in trade and popular press publications, and television advertisements. Coop advertising (see Chapter 8) helps to provide the links in consumers' minds between brand names, end-use products, and retailers. Cannon textile mills and Bloomingdale's retail stores provide an example of cooperative advertising (see Figure 14-5). Electronic information will continue to expand, opening new marketing possibilities for the entire soft goods pipeline. The computer information superhighway provides immediate access for fiber, fabric, and findings suppliers; manufacturers and contractors; retailers; and consumers. For example, Karastan, a Calhoun, Georgia-based area rug company, has established a page on the World Wide Web to provide information to its dealers as well as to the ultimate consumer.

TRADE ASSOCIATIONS, TRADE SHOWS, AND TRADE PUBLICATIONS

Trade Associations. In both the ready-to-wear and the home fashions industries, trade associations focus on textiles, general categories of merchandise, and specific aspects of the industry (see Table 14-1 for a listing of selected trade associations in the home fashions industry). Textile trade associations for home fashions are the same as those for fashion apparel.

Figure 14.6
Companies cooperate with Cotton Incorporated, a trade association, to promote the use of cotton fiber for the home fashions industry.

TABLE 14-1

Selected Trade Associations for the Home Fashions Industry

American Furniture Manufacturers Association
P.O. Box 2436
High Point, NC 27261

Association of Interior Decor Specialists, Inc. (AIDS INTERNATIONAL)
2009 N. 14 Street #203
Arlington, VA 22201

Carpet and Rug Institute
P.O. Box 2048
Dalton, GA 20720

Decorative Fabrics Association (DFA)
950 3rd Avenue
New York, NY 10022

International Home Furnishings Representatives Association (IHFRA)
666 Lake Shore Drive
Chicago, IL 60611

National Association of Decorative Fabrics Distributors (NADFD)
6022 West Touhy Avenue
Chicago, IL 60648

National Association of Floor Covering Distributors (NAFCE)
13-186 Merchandise Mart
Chicago, IL 60654

National Home Fashions League, Inc. (NHFL)
107 World Trade Center
Dallas, TX 75258

National Home Furnishings Association (NHFA)
900 17th Street NW, Suite 514
Washington, DC 20006

Upholstered Furniture Action Council (UFAC)
Box 2436
High Point, NC 27261

Window Coverings Association of America
450 Skokie Boulevard
Northbrook, IL 60062

These include the American Textile Manufacturers Institute (ATMI), Cotton Incorporated, and the Wool Council (see Chapter 3 for a description of these trade associations). For example, Cotton Incorporated has been developing and promoting the use of cotton in home fashion products. Cotton Incorporated's research department develops new products that are then adopted and produced by textile mills. In recent years, Cotton Incorporated has developed cotton fabrics that could be used for upholstery, window treatments, wall coverings, table linens, and carpet (Stapleton, 1994).

Some trade associations, such as the Home Furnishings International Association and the National Home Fashions League, Incorporated, promote home furnishings or home fashions in general. Other trade associations focus on specific aspects of the industry. These trade associations, such as the Carpet and Rug Institute and the Decorative Fabrics Association, assist in conducting market research and in promoting specific end uses or areas of the industry.

Figure 14.7
Textiles are marketed to home fashions manufacturers at trade shows.

Trade Shows. In addition to housing most manufacturer showrooms for home fashions, New York City is also the home of the New York Home Textiles Market, which is held twice a year in October and March. During these market weeks, companies show samples of home textiles to jobbers, designers, manufacturers, and retailers. Textile trade shows, such as the International Fashion Fabric Exhibition (IFFE) held in New York, include some suppliers of decorative fabrics used for home fashions, although most of the exhibitors are for fabrics used in apparel and accessory production. Selected trade shows related to the home fashions industry are listed in Table 14-2.

TABLE 14-2

Selected Trade Shows for the Home Fashions Industry

Heimtextil, Germany, the world's largest trade show of fabrics and home textiles
International Home Furnishings Market
New York Home Textiles Show
New York Bed, Bath, and Linen Show
Pacific Home Fashion Fair
Peacock Alley, Dallas (luxury bed and bath linens)
US International Bed, Bath & Linen Show
World of Home Fashion: International Home Fashion Fair and Convention
(combined World of Window Coverings and Hometextil Americas shows)

Figure 14.8
The New York Home Textiles Show, held twice a year, is advertised as America's premier bed, bath, and linen show.

Figure 14.9
Trade publications provide important information to industry professionals.

Trade Publications. Trade publications are an important source of information for professionals in the home fashions industry. As with the apparel industry, some trade publications cover the entire industry, whereas others focus on specific aspects of the industry. See Table 14-3 for a listing of selected trade publications in the home fashions industry.

PRODUCTION OF HOME FASHIONS

Price, value, and quality are key features sought by home fashions consumers. These features are related to production of the product. Fast, efficient production can help to control cost factors. As discussed in Chapter 11, quality must be built into the product throughout the production processes of apparel. This is also true for home fashions. Quality assurance programs are an integral part of home fashions production facilities.

As indicated earlier, the home fashions industry includes a number of vertically integrated companies that produce not only the fabric but also the end-use product. To avoid increasing costs, some vertically integrated companies have ceased production of their own yarns. For example, "Fieldcrest Cannon expects to save money by outsourcing yarn production rather than investing in yarn facilities" (Frinton, 1996, p. 30). Some domestic apparel manufacturers turned to off-shore production as a cost-saving procedure years ago. This trend has repeated itself in the home fashions industry. In recent years, some home fashions manufacturers have elected to cease domestic production, sourcing production in other parts of the world.

As in the apparel industry, fast delivery of raw goods from suppliers coupled with quick turn-time on production help speed the product to the retailer and ultimate consumer. Continued reduction in lead time needed to produce goods will provide additional cost savings. As in the apparel industry, Quick Response strategies in the home fashions industry, including increased partnerships among segments of the industry and the use of EDI and UPC bar coding, have allowed for faster delivery of products. For example, in the area-rug business, one rug supplier, Oriental Weavers, has developed a quick-ship program called "10 Days to Success," which provides for a 10-day delivery to retailers of the company's 20 best selling machine-made rugs. Another rug supplier, Capel, has implemented a program known as Zip Ship, which promises that if an order is received by 10 a.m., any in-stock rugs will be shipped out the next business day. For custom rugs, Masland, a Mobile, Alabama area-rug supplier has implemented ZAP, a quick-delivery program that promises delivery of custom area rugs in two weeks.

END USE CATEGORIES

The home fashions industry is divided into four general end-use categories: upholstery fabrics; window and wall coverings; soft floor coverings, including

TABLE 14-3

Selected Trade Publications for the Home Fashions Industry

Bedtimes: published by International Sleep Products Association, monthly. Geared toward the mattress manufacturing industry and its suppliers, and other sleep products trades.

Decorative Home: published by Fairchild, monthly. The retailer's guide to decorative accessories and home gifts.

FDM—Furniture Design and Manufacturing: Published by Cahners Publishing Co., monthly. Articles on the furniture, bedding, and upholstering industries.

Floor Covering Weekly: Published by Hearst Business Communications, weekly. Tabloid format.

Flooring: The Magazine of Interior Surfaces: Published by Douglas Publications, monthly. Contains in-depth feature stories, as well as the latest industry new, and information on all the latest products and services in areas such as wood flooring, ceramic tile, carpet, vinyl flooring, and accessories.

Home Accents Today: Published by Cahners Business Newspapers, 8 issues per year. Merchandising and fashion news magazine of the home accent industry. It is aimed at the decorative accessory, specialty home accent, and major gift buyers shopping the major furniture markets in High Point, Dallas, Atlanta, and San Francisco; and gift markets in New York, Los Angeles, Atlanta, Dallas, and Chicago.

HFD: Previous name for Home Furnishing Network. Published by Fairchild, weekly.

HFN—Home Furnishings Network: Published by Fairchild, weekly. Ideas for retailers, wholesales, manufacturers, and suppliers, covers furniture, bedding, floor coverings, giftware and housewares.

Home Fashions Magazine: Published by Fairchild, monthly. The magazine for the home textiles retailer.

Home Furnishings Executive: Published by Pace Communications, monthly. For the home furnishings retail trade.

Home Furnishings Review: Published by the Home Furnishings International Association, monthly. Presents business information drawn from a variety of publications and other sources, digested into brief articles aimed at helping the home furnishings retailer operate a more profitable business.

Home International: Published by Fairchild, quarterly. Covers the home furnishings industry around the world.

Home Textiles Today: Published by Cahners Business Newspapers, weekly. For the marketing, merchandising, and retailing of home textile products.

Homemarket Trends: Published by Lebhar-Friedman, Inc, six times per year. Covers the home fashions industry. Includes furniture, bed and bath, table top and window treatments.

Interior Design: Published by Cahners Publishing Co., 17 issues/year. Provides information on trends and new products to the professional designer.

LBD Interior Textiles: Published by Columbia Communications, monthly. Retailing magazine for home furnishings, textiles, and bath products, including linens.

Upholstery Design & Manufacturing (UDM): Published by Cahners Publishing Company, monthly. Covers information related to the design and manufacturing of upholstery textiles and upholstered furniture.

Wallcoverings, Windows, and Interior Fashion: Published by Publishing Dynamics Inc., monthly.

Figure 14.10
Coordinated textiles and
wall paper from Daisy
Kingdom offer a com-
plete look for children's
nurseries.

area rugs, scatter rugs, and runners; and bed, bath, table, and other textile accessories and accents. Coordinated ensembles among categories have become popular. The same or coordinated textiles produced by one manufacturer might be used for upholstered furniture, window treatments, bedding, and wall coverings for an entire room. Waverly has been at the forefront of providing consumers with a coordinated, total home look by producing coordinated bed linens, bath rugs, shower curtains, laminated fabrics, lamp shades, and other products. Coordinated prints, stripes, plaids, and monochrome cotton fabrics are produced by Laura Ashley, in addition to coordinating wall paper, lamp shades, ceramic tile, and table ware. For children's nurseries, Portland, Oregon based Daisy Kingdom manufacturers completely coordinated cotton and cotton/polyester fabrics for window treatments, bedding, and apparel.

UPHOLSTERY FABRICS

Upholstery fabrics for home fashions are used primarily for sofas, love seats, chairs, and ottomans. Textiles used for **upholstery fabrics** are made from many natural and manufactured fibers. Before the development of manufactured fibers, wool, cotton, and linen were the most prevalent fibers used in upholstered home fashions. Silk has been used less frequently for uphol-

Figure 14.11
Upholstery fabrics create an important part of the atmosphere for the home.

stery, due to its cost, care requirements, and delicate structure. Manufactured fibers, particularly nylon, are commonly used in today's market. Fiber companies in the United States known for producing fibers for upholstery fabrics include BASF, Cytec, DuPont, Hoechst Celanese, and Monsanto. In recent years, olefin (also known as polypropelene or polyolefin) has made gains in the upholstery market, and cotton has regained some of its importance. Rayon blends for upholstery fabrics are experiencing growth in sales.

The performance characteristics of wool and cotton fibers are highly valued for some types of upholstered home fashions. The rising cost of these natural fibers lowered their market share in comparison to the less expensive manufactured fibers. Currently, the high-end market uses a higher percentage of natural fibers than the moderate and mass markets.

Fabric structure is another important consideration for upholstery. The durability of a fabric is affected by its fabric structure. For example, twill weaves are very durable. Whereas both pile and nonpile fabrics are used for upholstery, nonpile fabrics are preferred for heavy-use upholstered items, such as family-room sofas. Some upholstery fabrics are coated with a backing substance to enhance their end-use properties.

The price range for upholstery fabrics is broad. Some upholstery fabrics are created and sold to a high-end market segment. Jack Lenor Larsen designs and produces striking high-end fabrics that are innovative in color and texture. Over-the-counter upholstery fabrics provide a source for individuals who wish to create their own home fashions. Textile converters such as Waverly sell decorator fabrics over-the-counter to individuals as well as to manufacturers. Thus, individuals who wish to create their own home fashions have access to some of the same fabrics available in manufactured furniture.

WINDOW AND WALL COVERINGS

Window treatments consist of draperies, curtains, and fabric shades as well as decorative treatments such as valances, cornices, and swags. Curtains are typically described as "sheer, lightweight coverings that are hung without linings" (Yeager, 1988, p. 171); whereas draperies are described as "heavy, often opaque and highly patterned coverings usually hung with linings" (Yeager, 1988, p. 171). Curtains might be combined with draperies for home use, providing both decorative and functional purposes. During the day, sheer curtains can allow diffused light into a room while providing some privacy. At night, opaque draperies can be drawn for total privacy and increased warmth. In recent years, fabric valances, cornices, and swags have seen a resurgence as popular window treatments.

The fibers and fabrics used for curtains and draperies must withstand more exposure to heat and sunlight than many other textile products. Some manufactured fibers, such as nylon and polyester, withstand environmental exposure better than natural fibers, such as silk and cotton. Linen and wool, at one time quite commonly used for window coverings, are now used only occasionally. Rayon, acrylic, nylon, and polyester fibers are typically used in blends with other fibers for window treatments. The ease of care of manufactured fibers and blends combining natural with manufactured fibers is another important consideration for many consumers.

A variety of textiles is used for **wall coverings** and vertical panels and partitions. Fabric used as a wall covering can provide a cozy ambiance or an elegant distinctiveness to a room. There are various techniques for applying fabrics to wall surfaces. A tightly woven material with sturdy fabric structure will withstand the tension needed to provide a smooth fabric surface. Cotton is one of the easiest and most versatile fabrics for use as a wall covering. Luxurious visual statements can be made with velvet or moire fabrics; however these fabrics are more challenging to mount. Silk fabrics function best as wall coverings if they are first quilted or laminated to a backing fabric to stabilize the fabric.

SOFT FLOOR COVERINGS

Soft floor coverings include wall-to-wall carpeting, area rugs, runners, and scatter rugs. In this chapter, the discussion of this end-use category will focus on area floor coverings (area rugs, runners, and scatter rugs). Area floor coverings are produced in a wide variety of fibers and blends. For kitchen and bath areas, cotton, polyester, and nylon fibers are most typical. Ease of cleaning for bath and kitchen area rugs is an important consideration to the consumer. Bedroom area floor coverings might consist of natural fibers, including wool and cotton, manufactured fibers, or blends of fibers.

For other areas of the home, such as the living room, family room, and dining room, a wide variety of fibers is available. Fibers used for area floor coverings include nylon, polyester, olefin, wool, and cotton, as well as sisal, jute, and other natural plant materials. Companies in the United States that produce manufactured fibers used in carpets and rugs include DuPont Nylon Furnishings, BASF, and Hoechst Celanese.

Area floor coverings might be laid atop a hardwood floor, or atop carpeting. A variety of sizes for area rugs and runners provide many home fashions options. Scatter rugs are usually small, for example two by three feet or three by five feet. Area rugs tend to be larger, in sizes such as eight by eleven feet or eleven by fourteen feet. Runners are long in length compared to width, as they are designed for hallways or entries.

Some area floor coverings are made by machine, in a process similar to that used for carpet manufacturing. The design and texture of an area rug is often determined during the production stage by varying the colors and types of yarns used or by varying the weaving or fabrication techniques. Multicolor effects can be achieved by applying the same dye color to a yarn composed of different fibers, producing a heather effect. Improved technology in carpet and rug production has led to a greater variety of patterns and textures available to the consumer. For example, Regal Rugs has 25 yarn systems that allow the company to create a variety of multilevel surfaces, colors, and textural differences in rugs ranging from basic bath rugs to high-fashion accent rugs (Johnson, 1996).

Several other production methods are used to create hand woven, braided, hooked, crocheted, knotted, or embroidered area floor coverings. Many ethnic floor coverings are produced by hand processes. Both the ethnic design and hand processes add an exotic flavor to home fashions.

BED, BATH, TABLE, AND OTHER TEXTILE ACCESSORIES AND ACCENTS

Textile accessories and accents include:

▌ textile bedding products, including sheets and pillowcases, blankets, bedspreads, quilts, comforters, and pillows;

▌ textile products for the bath, including towels, bath rugs and mats, and shower curtains;

▌ textile accessories for tabletops, including table cloths, napkins, table runners, and placemats;

▌ textile products for the kitchen, including towels, dish cloths, hot pads, and aprons; and textile accents, such as textile wall hangings, tapestries, quilts, needlework accents, and lace accents.

The term **linens** is used to describe towels, sheets, tablecloths, napkins, and other home textiles once made almost exclusively from linen. Although currently these products are rarely made from linen, they are commonly still referred to as linens.

Bedding and Bath. Cotton has an estimated 60 percent share in the sheet industry. The dominant fabric for sheets is a fabric blend of 50 percent cotton-50 percent polyester. A number of companies also offer 100 percent cotton sheets. In recent years, wrinkle-free all-cotton sheets have become popular. However, current wrinkle-free finishes applied to the sheets diminish after multiple washings and also reduce the strength of the fabric. Several luxury producers offer linen and silk sheets.

Percale and flannel are the most typical fabric structures for sheets. Satin, sateen, and jacquard weaves are available for the specialty market. Eyelet trims, contrast piping, or scalloped edging are used as embellishments.

Besides fiber content and fabric structure, sheets are distinguished by their **thread count** and their size. Thread count refers to the total number

Figure 14.12
A variety of colors and textures adds an inviting fashion appeal to bedding and window coverings.

of "threads" or yarns in one square inch of fabric. Thread counts of 180 and 200 are the most popular among consumers. A higher thread count tends to signify a softer fabric. Total retail dollar sales in 1995 for sheets was $1.8 billion, the same as in 1994 ("Gainers, losers, new players," 1996). Sheets are available in twin, double, queen, and king sizes corresponding to standard bed sizes.

The category **top of the bed** includes comforters, duvet covers, blankets, bedspreads, dust ruffles, pillow shams, and throws. This category has been growing in recent years as consumers are striving for a coordinated look in bed/bath decoration. Bedspreads are made from a variety of fabrics and in a variety of styles, including quilted fabrics. Quilts and comforters typically are made from multicomponent fabrics and filled with down, feathers, fiberfill, or other materials.

Although most bedding is produced for adults, the infant and juvenile bedding category has grown in recent years. Licensed printed goods are spurring the market. For example, Disney Babies has licenses with Pillowtex's Beacon division, Beiderlack, Springs' Dundee, and Borden for bedding, throws, wall decorations, lamps, and matching diaper bags. Disney's "Crib in a Bag" concept offers coordinated sets including comforters, crib sheets, bumper pads, and diaper stackers (Frinton, 1995).

In the bath market, cotton is by far the dominant fiber with an estimated 95% share. Terry cloth is by far the most popular fabrication for towels. The yarns forming the loops of terry cloth are generally all cotton to enhance moisture absorbency for drying purposes. The warp and weft yarns that form the base weave structure holding the loops in place might consist of a blend of cotton with a small percentage of polyester for increased durability. When sheared on one side, the terry cloth fabric is called velour.

Towel size has become another merchandise feature. For years, towel sizes were standardized. Longer length towels became popular at luxury hotels and spas. Soon manufacturers began to offer a variety of lengths at various price points for the retail market. A variety of bath towel sizes and prices seems to be a continuing trend. A wide variety of coordinating bath mats contributes to an increase in sales in the bath category. To provide a perspective regarding the size of the bath market, total retail dollar sales in 1995 were reported as $1.45 billion for bath towels, $104 million for embellished towels, $251 million for beach towels, $540 million for bath and accent rugs, and $225 million for bath accessories ("Gainers, losers, new players," 1996). The surge in the bath market coincided with a similar increase in popularity of coordinated kitchen towels, dish cloths, mitts, and aprons.

Figure 14.13
Guess Home Collection has extended its customer base from apparel into the home fashions market with a line of bath products.

GUESS
HOME COLLECTION

Pour la Maison, Inc., 1426 South Paloma Street Los Angeles, California 90021 213.745.1500
Circle no. 11 for more information

Figure 14.14
A wide variety of fabrics
and trims provide visual
appeal for tabletop
accessories.

Textile Accessories for Tabletop and Kitchen. Textile accessories for the tabletop include table cloths, napkins, place mats, and table runners. The term **napery** is used to describe table cloths and napkins. Tabletop accessories can protect the finish of fine wood tables and can enhance the warmth and visual themes of dining rooms. Therefore a wide variety of fibers and fabrics that provide visual appeal are used in tabletop accessories. One especially important aspect of the performance of tabletop accessories is providing easy care. For example, Milliken & Company applies a soil-release finish to table linens made from Visa® fabrics to increase the performance of the fabrics. Tabletop accessories are available in a variety of sizes to fit a wide variety of shapes and sizes of tables. In accordance with labeling laws, references to "cut size" of table cloths must include the dimensions of the finished product. Textile accessories for the kitchen include towels, dish cloths, pot holders, mitts, and aprons. Similar to the design and production of other textile accessories, both appearance and performance characteristics are important determinants for fiber and fabric choices.

DISTRIBUTION AND RETAILING OF HOME FASHIONS

Home fashions constitute an important segment of the retail industry. Discount retail stores, such as Wal-Mart, Target, and Kmart, are the dominant players in retailing home fashions, with approximately 34 percent market share in home textiles. In fact, discounters account for more than half of the kitchen towel sales and nearly half of the shower curtain, mattress pad/covers, sheet/pillowcase sets, curtains/valences, and scatter rugs in the United

TABLE 14-4

Top-Selling Home Fashion Products by Retail Segment (Ranked by Market Share)

Discount Stores:
Kitchen Towels
Scatter Rugs
Shower Curtains
Curtains/Valences

Off-Price/Category Killers:
Napkins
Hand Towels
Placemats
Sheets

Chains:
Draperies
Bathroom Rugs

Sheets
Hand Towels

Department Stores:
Tablecloths
Napkins
Beach Towels
Pillow Cases

Mail Order:
Draperies
Towel Sets
Bedspreads
Curtains/Valances

States. Bed, bath, window and wall coverings, floor coverings, and uphol-stered furniture provide substantial sales for department stores. Specialty stores, including chains such as Eddie Bauer Home, Scandia Down, and Strouds, are an expanding retail segment. Off-price stores such as Bed Bath & Beyond, Pacific Linens, and Linens 'n Things are also gaining market share. Other large chains include JCPenney and Mervyn's (see Table 14-4 for top home fashion products by retail segment).

Direct mail companies such as Lands' End Coming Home, Spiegel, Pot-tery Barn, Domestications, the Linen Source, and Crate and Barrel fill another market niche. Some direct mail companies also operate retail stores. Electronic and television retailing is another merchandising approach. QVC is "the world's largest and most sophisticated electronic retailer of home fur-nishings" (McLoughlin, 1995, p. 1). The market share by retail category for each product type is shown in Table 14-5. This information helps retailers predict product-type sales distribution.

Consumers are currently updating the decor of their home environ-ments more frequently by changing the decorative fabrics used in their homes. In light of this trend, retailing of home fabrics has grown in recent years. Some stores, such as Calico Corners (headquartered in Kennett Square, Pennsylvania), focus entirely on home fabrics. For others, a greater percentage of their business is coming from home fabrics. For example, 36 percent of House of Fabrics' (headquartered in Sherman Oaks, California) business is in home fabrics, and 30 percent of Hancock Fabrics' (headquar-tered in Tupelo, Mississippi) business is in home fabrics (Pfaff, 1995). In

TABLE 14-5

Percentage of National Dollar Market Share: 1995 Forecasts

	OFF-PRICE	MAIL ORDER	CHAINS	DEPTS	DISCOUNT	ALL OTHERS
Total	4.1	11.3	16.1	16.1	34.0	18.3
Bath Towels	5.0	5.0	20.4	23.1	29.9	16.7
Bathroom Rugs	4.3	7.1	24.4	14.2	36.3	13.7
Shower Curtains	3.6	6.4	14.6	7.1	45.9	22.4
Quilts/Comforters	5.0	13.6	13.1	24.2	22.9	21.2
Bed Pillows	3.9	4.0	17.2	25.0	32.5	17.4
Sheets	5.9	5.6	23.9	23.0	30.7	10.9
Bedspreads	3.2	25.1	18.6	12.1	27.3	13.8
Mattress Pads/ Covers	2.8	8.0	14.9	15.0	42.3	17.0
Blankets	3.2	11.2	19.0	16.8	34.1	15.7
Placemats	6.1	5.3	8.4	20.6	35.4	24.2
Tablecloths	5.1	9.9	10.2	29.4	28.2	17.1
Kitchen Towels	3.7	5.1	7.6	5.7	53.0	24.8
Blinds/Shades	NA	15.2	13.3	3.4	28.4	39.7
Curtains/Valences	3.3	17.8	14.5	6.3	45.6	12.5
Scatter Rugs	4.7	5.7	12.4	7.7	47.7	21.9
Draperies	1.3	32.7	26.8	9.0	22.6	7.7

response to this growing demand for over-the-counter home fabrics, a number of home furnishing fabric suppliers, such as Waverly, Regal, Dan River, Concord Fabrics, and Spring Industries, have increased their attention to the over-the-counter home textiles business.

SOCIAL AND ENVIRONMENTAL RESPONSIBILITY

The soft goods industry thrives on change at a fast pace. This can lead to a public perception that it is an industry that encourages waste. As a society, we discard many products long before their full potential use is exhausted. In recent years, the industry has focused on social and environmental responsibility in all phases of the product use cycle. The home fashions industry has been a leader in efforts to promote **sustainable design** (also called green design), a term used to designate the "awareness of the full short and long-term consequences of any transformation of the environment" (*DesignTex*, 1995, p. 53). Sustainable design encompasses the concept that the creation, use, and discard of a product should not cause harm to the

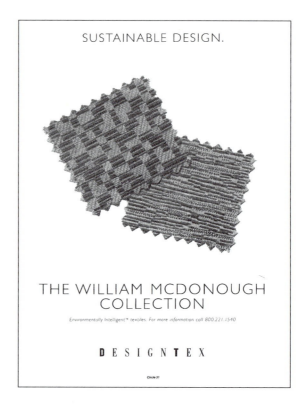

Figure 14.15
Sustainable design encompasses the concept that the creation, use, and discard of a product should not cause harm to any living system.

ecosystem. Sustainable design efforts include examples from the fiber stage through the discard stage:

▌ naturally grown fibers, such as cotton and ramie;

▌ humanely sheared, free-range sheep;

▌ yarn blended for user comfort and compostability;

▌ environmentally compatible dyes and chemicals;

▌ elimination of pollutants used in textile manufacturing;

▌ use of recycled components (e.g., fibers) in textile manufacturing;

▌ elimination of toxic vapors emitted during production or product use (such as formaldehyde on fabric wall coverings); and

▌ biodegradability or reuse of post-consumer products.

Several years ago DesignTex, based in New York City, created an environmental line of textiles that meets the sustainability guidelines (*DesignTex*, 1995). William McDonough and Michael Braungart designed a fabric collection for upholstered furniture. Their first collections utilized fabrics made from a blend of wool and ramie, both natural fibers. "This guaranteed that the fabric would be compostable and so operate in a closed loop organic lifecycle" (*DesignTex*, 1995, p. 62). Working with an independent environmental research institute in Germany and an environmental chemist, DesignTex selected dyes that used no toxins. The textile mill selected to manufacture the fabric improved its product manufacturing processes to conform to McDonough's design principles and criteria. McDonough calls this "the Second Industrial Revolution. What we're now saying is that environmental quality must be an integral part of the design of every product" (*DesignTex*, 1995, p. 65). The fabric is named Climatex Lifecycle, and is priced similarly to other high-end wool fabrics.

Rather than creating a new fabric, another approach is to recycle postconsumer materials into new products. Wellman, Inc. has been the world's largest recycler of plastic bottles, particularly soft drink bottles, since 1979. Plastic bottles are transformed into a fiber, Fortrel EcoSpun. This fiber is used for carpets and filling for pillows and comforters. "One of Wellman's most recent projects has been to team up with Carlee Corporation, a premier producer of polyester fiberfill, and create EcoFil" ("Fiberfill that is recycled," 1993, p. 40). Some users of EcoFil claim that it is superior to virgin fiberfill.

The home fashions industry provides numerous other examples of sustainable design. To provide information needed to locate recycled content products and resources, the Harris Directory offers a computer database reference that is updated every six months. Subscribers are provided with information from product manufacturers listing more than 3,500 recycled-content building materials.

The retailer may play an additional part in a product's life cycle. For consumers who have purchased a new product, some retailers offer convenient home pickup and recycle options for the discarded product. At the time a new mattress is delivered to the consumer, the old mattress might be picked up by the retailer's delivery crew and recycled.

Life-cycle evaluation of products will continue to be an important component in the home fashions industry, from both the producer's and the consumer's points of view. It may add complexity and cost to the design-manufacture-market-consume process, but sustainable design is crucial to future success in business.

Other types of social responsibility include community development efforts by local and national companies. In the home fashions industry,

> Atlanta-based Home Depot was cited for its willingness to help out after natural disasters. The 80,000-employee home improvement chain deploys teams of volunteers to help repair homes damaged by hurricanes, floods, earthquakes and other disasters. It also donates supplies, conducts on-site do-it-yourself clinics and refuses to raise prices on supplies needed during such emergencies. ("Home Depot wins community award," 1995, p. 8)

This is just one example of a company whose management is committed to donating goods and fostering community volunteer involvement by its employees.

Our global marketplace provides opportunities to support economies throughout the world. New York based Tufenkian Tibetan Carpets sells carpets made by Tibetan weavers using Tibetan wool and weaving techniques. The carpets are produced in Nepal, which neighbors Tibet, because political conditions make it impossible to export carpets from Tibet. By providing a marketing outlet for these beautiful products, the company helps ensure that traditional Tibetan carpets can continue to be produced. The weavers, both Nepalese and expatriate Tibetans, earn a livelihood with satisfactory working and living conditions, and a Montessori school for children is provided on-site. To avoid pollution of the environment, the carpet washing is not done in Nepal, since pollution controls there are inadequate. This collaboration of producer/weaver, product, and marketer provides an example of social, economic, political, and environmental responsibility.

SUMMARY

This chapter has focused on the home fashions industry, which includes four end-use categories: upholstery fabrics; window and wall coverings; soft floor coverings; and bed, bath, table, and other textile accessories and accents. The design and performance of the textiles used for home fashions play a very important role in the success of the end use. As such, the textile industry is the base for the home fashions industry, which is dominated by vertically integrated textile companies that produce both fabrics and home fashion products. Production of home fashions is often highly automated and can be accomplished very efficiently within a vertical operation. Also, the fabric may not need to be cut and sewn to complete the product, such as with towels and rugs.

Similarities, differences, and relationships between the design, production, and marketing of home fashions and the ready-two-wear industries have been discussed. An understanding of the organization and operation of the home fashions industry in the broader context of apparel fashions is important for several reasons. In recent years, the apparel and home fashions industries have become more interrelated. Apparel companies such as Ellen Tracy, Eileen West, and Guess have entered the home fashions market. Some well-known apparel designers have moved into home fashions through licensing agreements with textile mills and home fashions manufacturers. Other licensing agreements for children's home fashions include cartoon and movie characters, sports teams, and toys.

Consumer demand for home fashions has been strong. Home fashions constitute an important segment of the retail industry. Discount retailers such as Wal-Mart, Target, and Kmart are the dominant competitors in retailing home fashions. Other important home fashions merchants include department stores, specialty stores, direct mail companies, off-price retailers, and electronic retailers such as QVC. Sales of over-the-counter fabrics for the home sewing industry are on an upswing.

Market research and color forecasting are conducted prior to developing the seasonal collections. The textile and trim designers who create innovative materials and the product designers who determine the form of the final end-use product work with many considerations and constraints. There are important functional needs and performance criteria that must be met. Some products must also meet safety standards set by law. Converters play an important role in the production of textiles for home fashions. Fabrics are printed or finished to improve their performance by converters. Often the converter contracts specific finishing work with a variety of finishing plants.

The marketing of home fashions is similar to the process used in the apparel industry that includes manufacturer showrooms, company sales representatives, trade shows, and advertising. However, the home fashion industry relies on converters and jobbers to perform marketing and distribution functions more frequently than does the apparel industry. The establishment of well-respected brand names such as Royal Velvet, Martex, and Burlington House is important in the marketing of home fashions. Trade associations, trade shows, and trade publications form an important network to promote the home fashions industry.

In recent years, the industry has focused on social and environmental responsibility for all phases of the product-use cycle. The home fashions industry has been a leader in efforts to promote sustainable design, encompassing the concept that the creation, use, and discard of a product not cause harm to the ecosystem. Efforts to practice sustainable design include processes from the fiber stage through the product's discard stage. In addition, some retailers have entered the arena to provide consumers with recycling services when new products are delivered to their homes.

REFERENCES

Blackwood, Francy. (1995, April 10). Name dropping. *HFN*, p. 25, 74.

DesignTex, Inc. (1995). *Environmentally Intelligent Textiles*. (2nd ed.). (#DT052495). Charlottesville, VA: Author.

Fiberfill that is recycled. (1993, May/June). *What's New in Home Economics*, p. 40.

Frinton, Sandra. (1996, February 26.) The good news and bad. *HFN*, pp. 25, 30, 31.

Frinton, Sandra. (1995, November 20). Strength in baby bedding. *HFN*, pp. 19, 21.

Gainers, losers, new players. (1996, March 11). *HFN*, pp. 28, 32, 34, 36.

Green, John. (1990, October 1). Call them decorative fabric distributors. *HFD*, p. 4A.

The Harris Directory. (1996). [Computer diskette]. B.J. Harris. 508 Jose Street, No, 913, Santa Fe, NM 87501, 505-995-0337.

Home depot wins community award. (1995, December 4). *HFN*, p. 8.

Johnson, Sarah. (1996, March 18). Regal develops new rug yarn. *HFN*, p. 23.

McLoughlin, Bill. (1995, November 6). Home Team. *HFN*, pp. 1, 70.

Pfaff, Kimberly. (1995, August 21). Home fabric surge. *HFN*, pp. 23, 32.

Robert Allen: Cutting a wide swath. (1990, October 1). *HFD*, p. 6A.

Rush, Amy J. (1996, February 19). 3M's Thinsulate coming to bedding. *HFN*, p. 6.

Schwartz, Donna Boyle. (1995, December 4). Grand design. *HFN*, pp. 1, 58, 59.

Stapleton, Maureen A. (1994, June 20). Cotton Inc. develops new home products. *HFD*, p. 32.

Thomas, Marita. (1994, November). Home textiles eagerly eyes successful year. *Textile World*, pp. 75–80.

Williams, Alexander H. (1995, December 4). Back to basics. *HFN*, pp. 19, 23.

Yeager, Jan. (1988). *Textiles for Residential and Commercial Interiors*. NY: HarperCollins.

KEY TERMS

home fashions	**textile accessories and accents**
converters	**linens**
decorative fabric jobbers	**thread count**
upholstery fabrics	**top of the bed**
window treatments	**napery**
wall coverings	**sustainable design**
soft floor coverings	

DISCUSSION QUESTIONS

1. What are three aspects of the home fashions industry that are similar to the ready-to-wear apparel industry and three aspects that are different? Why do these similarities and differences exist?

2. Select a home fashion product (e.g., towel, rug, sheets). Outline the process used in the design, production, marketing, and distribution of the product.

3. Select a home fashion product in your home that will need replacement sometime in the future. Discuss sustainable design criteria that might be used in the selection of the replacement product and the disposal of the used textile product.

CAREER PROFILE

As with the ready-to-wear and accessories industries, the home fashion industry includes a wide variety of career possibilities, from design to production to marketing and distribution. In this field, an increasing number of states require certification by the National Council for Interior Design Qualification (NCIDQ) to use the title "Interior Designer." Certification requires education, experience, and successful completion of a qualifying examination.

INTERIOR DESIGNER OR INTERIOR DECORATING CONSULTANT,
Single-unit family-owned furniture business

Job Description
Residential interior design and retail furniture sales for individual clients. Provide layout, space planning, furniture and materials suggestions.

Typical Tasks

▌ Meet with clients in the store, handle quite a bit of furniture sales.

▌ Meet with clients in their homes, take room/space measurements, interview clients about their needs, plans, desires, and budgets.

▌ Implement plans by selling store products to clients and help locate other sources for products not sold in the store, such as window treatments and hard flooring.

What Do You Like Best About Your Job?
Meeting with the clients.

CREDITS

FIGURES

Chap. 1 opener, Fig. 3.3. Cotton Incorporated.

Figs. 1.1, 1.2, 1.3, 1.4a, 1.4b, 1.5, 1.6, 1.7, 1.8, 1.9, 1.10, 1.11, 6.5c, 6.7b, 6.9a, 6.15, 13.4. The Bettmann Archive.

Figs. 1.14a, 1.14b, 11.8. Textile/Clothing Technology Corporation [TC]^2.

Fig. 2.8. GARFIELD ©1978 Paws, Inc. Reprinted with permission of UNIVERSAL PRESS SYNDI-CATE. All rights reserved.

Figs. 3.2, 3.16, 3.17. American Textile Manufacturers Institute

Fig. 3.4. New England Tanners Club.

Fig. 3.8. American Wool Council, a division of the American Sheep Industry Association.

Fig. 3.10. Color Association of the United States.

Figs. 3.11a-c, 5.5. Pendleton Woolen Mills.

Fig. 3.14. Hoechst Celanese.

Figs. 4.2, 6.11, 6.16, 7.6, 7.9, 7.10, 7.11. Jantzen Inc.

Figs. 4.5, 7.2, 9.6, 11.3, 11.6, 11.7. Gerber Garment Technology.

Fig. 4.7. Reprinted with permission from *Apparel Industry Magazine*. ©1989.

Fig. 6.6a. Staten Island Historical Society. Staten Island, New York.

Fig. 6.6b. The Fine Arts Museums of San Francisco, Gift of Mrs. Eloise Heidland, 1982.18.1.

Fig. 6.6c. Alex Chatelain © Vogue, Conde Nast Publications Ltd.

Fig. 6.7a. Jean Morain/Editions Assouline, Paris

Fig. 6.7c. The Kobal Collection.

Fig. 6.8a. The Royal Collection © Her Majesty Queen Elizabeth II.

Fig. 6.9b. All rights reserved, The Metropolitan Museum of Art. Courtesy of Ralph Lauren.

Fig. 6.12. Gerber Garment Technology and *Bobbin®️ Magazine*. Reprinted with permission from *Bobbin®️ Magazine*. Copyright 1995 by Bobbin Blenheim Media. All rights reserved.

Fig. 6.13. Hong Tan.

Fig. 6.14. Robert Capa/Magnum Photos.

Fig. 7.3. Investronica, Inc.

Fig. 7.7. Susan Kovar/Pendleton Woolen Mills.

Figs. 7.12, 7.13. ModaCAD(R) Computer-Aided Design Systems. ©1996 ModaCAD®, Inc., Los Angeles.

Fig. 7.14. Copyright © 1994 by The New York Times Company. Reprinted by permission.

Fig. 7.16. "The Retail Product Development Model" by Gaskill, L.R. *Clothing & Textiles Research Journal*, Summer 1992. Reprinted by permission of the International Textile and Apparel Association.

Fig. 8.1. "What it takes (and pays) to sell" by Corwin, J. Blade. Reprinted with permission from *Bobbin®️ Magazine*. Copyright 1996 by Bobbin Blenheim Media. All rights reserved.

Figs. 9.1, 9.2, 9.4. InSport

Fig. 9.3. Union Special Corporation.

Fig. 9.5. Photography by Gary Weber.

Figs. 9.7, 9.8, 9.10, 11.4. Lectra Systems®.

Fig. 10.3. Maurizio Pracella.

Fig. 10.5, 10.7. © *The Oregonian*.

Fig. 10.6. Levi Strauss & Co.

Fig. 10.8. Edward Keating/NYT Pictures.

Fig. 11.9 Ellis Corporation.

Fig. 12.10. fashionmall.com.

Fig. 13.2. Bally, Inc.

Fig. 13.8. National Association of Hosiery Manufacturers.

Figs. 14.1a and 14.1b. Virgil Smithers/Fieldcrest Cannon.

Fig. 14.2a. Gary Hannabarger

Fig. 14.7. Norman Y. Lono/NYT Pictures.

Fig. 14.9. *HFN, Decorative Home, Home Textiles Today*.

TABLES

Tab. 2.2, 2.3. *Fairchild's Textile & Apparel Financial Directory 1996*, Fairchild Publications.

Tabs. 3.1, 3.5. *Daily News Record*.

Tab. 3.6. American Textile Manufacturers Institute.

Tab. 4.2. "The Fairchild 100," *Women's Wear Daily: WWD Special Report*, November 1995, Fairchild Publications.

Tab. 4.3. *Standard Industrial Classification Manual 1987*, U.S. Executive Office of the President, Office of Management and Budget.

Tab. 7.4. Reprinted with permission by *Apparel Industry Magazine*. ©1996.

Tab. 10.1. Reprinted with permission from *Bobbin® Magazine*. Copyright 1992, 1994 by Bobbin Blenheim Media. All rights reserved.

Tab. 10.4. Reprinted with permission by *Apparel Industry Magazine*. ©1992.

Tabs. 10.5, 10.6, 10.7, 11.1. Reprinted with permission by *Apparel Industry Magazine*. ©1995.

Tabs. 10.8, 10.9. Levi Strauss & Co.

Tab. 11.1. Continuing Education Subcommittee of the American Apparel Manufacturers Association Education Committee, reported in *Apparel Industry Magazine* (1995, December), p. 54.

Tab. 12.2. "Quick Response management system for the apparel industry: Definition through technologies" by Kincade, D.H. *Clothing & Textiles Research Journal*, 1995. Reprinted by permission of the International Textile and Apparel Association.

Tab. 12.3. Cheryl Jordan, Oregon State University.

Tab. 12.4 Reprinted with permission by *Apparel Industry Magazine*. ©1996.

Tab. 12.5, 12.6, 12.7. Reprinted from *STORES* Magazine © NRF Enterprises, Inc., 1995.

Tab. 12.8. "The Best Stores," Supplement to *Women's Wear Daily*, October 1994, Fairchild Publications.

Tab. 13.4, 13.5. Reprinted with permission from *Bobbin® Magazine*. Copyright 1996 by Bobbin Blenheim Media. All rights reserved.

Tab. 13.6. National Association of Hosiery Manufacturers.

Tab. 13.7. Reprinted with permission from *Bobbin® Magazine*. Copyright 1995 by Bobbin Blenheim Media. All rights reserved.

Tab. 14.4 Retail Watch '95. *HFD*, (1994, October 31), p. 40, Fairchild Publications

Tab. 14.5 Retail Watch '95. *HFD*, (1994, October 31). pp. 36-52. Fairchild Publications

ascot A long scarf worn looped at the neck.

atelier de couture Workrooms of haute couture designers and staff.

bespoke Refers to custom-made apparel, especially men's tailored apparel.

bias The diagonal cut of fabric, or 45 degrees to the length or width of the fabric, used to produce better shaping of the fabric than a straight-grain cut.

block A base pattern in the company's sample size from which a pattern for the new style is created.

blocking or boarding The application of heat to create the final shape in the finishing process for knit goods.

brand merchandise Apparel with a company label that is well-recognized by the public.

brand-name fiber Fiber sold under a specific trade name, e.g., *Lycra*® spandex.

bridge jewelry Umbrella term for several types of jewelry, including those make from silver, gold (14K, 12K, 10K), and less expensive stones; jewelry designed by artists using a variety of materials.

bundling The process of disassembling the stacked, cut fabric pieces and reassembling them grouped by garment size, color dye lot, and quantity of units ready for production.

carryover Garment styles repeated in a line from one season to the next.

chain store Retail organization that owns and operates several retail outlets that sell similar lines of merchandise in a standardized method and function under a centralized form of organizational structure.

clutch Handbag designed to be held (clutched) in the hand, but may have a strap that can be stored inside the bag.

collection A group of apparel items presented together to the buying public, usually by the high-fashion designers.

color control Color matching requirement for all like garments in the line and all their components, such as knit collars and cuffs, buttons, thread, and zippers.

color forecasting Predictions of consumers' future color preferences; research conducted by associations, color forecasting companies, and textile and apparel companies to determine color trends.

color forecasting services Companies that study and predict color trends.

colorway The variety of three or four seasonal color choices for the same solid or print fabric available for each garment style.

commercial match An acceptable color match for contractor-provided matched goods.

computer aided design (CAD) Both the hardware and software computer systems that are produced to assist with the design phase of the fabric or garment design.

computer aided design/computer aided manufacturing (CAD/CAM) The combination of computer systems that link pattern design, grading, marker making, cutting and sometimes sewing operations.

computer grading and marker making (CGMM) The computer hardware and software systems that process the pattern grading and marker making segments of the pattern for production.

computer integrated manufacturing (CIM) The "integration of various computerized processes to form a common linkage of information and manufacturing equipment to produce a finished product" (Kron, 1988, p. 52; see Chapter 11).

conglomerate Diversified company involved with significantly different lines of business.

consolidation The combining of two companies to form a new company.

contractor Company that specializes in the sewing and finishing of goods.

contractual retailer Retailer who has entered into a contractual agreement with a manufacturer, wholesaler, or other retailers in order to integrate operations and increase market impact.

convenience store Small retailers that offer fast service and convenient location.

converter Company that specializes in finishing fabrics.

coop advertising An advertising strategy in which companies share the cost of an advertisement that features all of them.

copyright Allows the copyright holder the exclusive right to use, perform, or reproduce written, pictorial, and performed work.

corporation Company established by a legal charter that outlines the scope and activity of the company. Corporations are legal entities regardless of who owns stock in the company.

cost (wholesale cost, or cost to manufacture) The total cost to manufacture a style, including materials, sundries, labor, and such auxiliary costs as freight, duty, and packaging.

costing marker The layout of the pattern pieces for the prototype used to determine the yardage required for the new style.

costume jewelry Mass-produced jewelry made from plastic, wood, brass, glass, lucite, and other less-expensive materials.

cotton gin Invented in 1794 by Eli Whitney, this machine cleans cotton seed from the cotton fibers.

counterfeit goods Products that incorporate unauthorized use of registered tradenames or trademarks.

couture A French term that literally means "high sewing," it refers to the highest-priced apparel produced in small quantities, made of high-quality fabrics utilizing considerable hand sewing techniques, and sized to fit individual clients' bodies.

couturier(ìere) Designer of haute couture.

Crafted with Pride in the USA Council Formed in 1984 to promote U.S.-made textiles and apparel.

croquis A French term that refers to a figure outline used as a basis to sketch garment design ideas. Also called a lay figure.

customs broker A person in the United States, licensed by the Customs Office, to assist apparel manufacturers in gaining customs clearance to import goods produced offshore.

cut, make, and trim (CMT) Apparel contractors who cut, make, and trim the garments for the apparel manufacturer.

cut-up trade Manufacturers who produce belts for apparel manufacturers to add to pants, skirts, and dresses.

department store Large retail establishment that departmentalizes its functions and merchandise.

die cutting A piece of metal with a sharp edge similar to a cookie cutter tooled to the exact dimensions of the shape of the pattern piece (the die). The die is positioned over the fabric to be cut, then a pressurized plate is applied to the die to cut through the fabric layers.

diffusion line Designer's less-expensive line (e.g., Armani X, DKNY).

digitizer A table embedded with sensors that relate to the X and Y coordinates (horizontal and vertical directions) that allow the shape of the pattern piece to be traced and converted to a drawing of the pattern in the computer.

direct marketing channel Marketing channel by which manufacturers sell directly to the ultimate consumer.

discount store Retail establishment that sells brand name merchandise at below traditional retail prices, including apparel in the budget/mass wholesale price zone.

distribution centers Centralized locations used by apparel companies and retailers for quality assurance, picking, packing of merchandise, and distribution to retail stores.

distribution strategy Business strategy to assure that merchandise is sold in stores that cater to the target market for which the merchandise was designed and manufactured.

dividend Corporate profits paid to stockholders; dividends are taxed as personal income.

draping A process of creating the initial garment style by molding, cutting, and pinning fabric to a mannequin.

dual or multichannel distribution Distribution strategy whereby manufacturers sell their merchandise through their own stores as well as through other retailers.

duplicate A copy of the prototype or sample style used by the sales representatives to show and sell styles in the line to retail buyers (also called sales sample).

electronic data interchange Computer-to-computer communications between companies.

empire A dress style with a raised waistline, named for Napoleon's empire and made popular by Empress Josephine of France.

export agent A person located in the country that produced the goods who assists the (U.S.) apparel manufacturer with exportation of the products.

extended marketing channel Marketing channel in which wholesalers acquire products from manufacturers and sell them to retailers or jobbers buy products from wholesalers and sell them to retailers.

Fabric and Suppliers Linkage Council (FASLINC) Formed in 1987 to establish voluntary electronic data interchange standards between textile producers and their suppliers; disbanded in 1991.

factoring The business of purchasing and collecting accounts receivable or of advancing cash on the basis of accounts receivable (1996, 2–8 Feb, The F Word, *California Apparel News*, p. 1; see chapter 9).

fallout The fabric that remains in the spaces between pattern pieces on the marker, representing the amount of fabric that is wasted.

fashion season Name given to lines or collections that correspond to seasons of the year when consumers would most likely wear the merchandise; e.g. spring, summer, fall, holiday, and resort.

fiber The basic unit in making textile yarns and fabrics.

fine jewelry Jewelry made from precious metals alone or with precious and semiprecious stones.

finish "Anything that is done to fiber, yarn, or fabric either before or after weaving or knitting to change the appearance (what you see), the hand (what you feel), and the performance (what the fabric does)" (Hollen, Sadler, Langford, & Kadolph, 1988, p. 300; see chapter 3).

fit model The live model whose body dimensions match the company's sample size and who is used to assess the fit, styling, and overall look of new prototypes.

flatknit Goods that are knit flat, as compared to goods knit in a tube (tubular knit).

flat pattern The pattern process used to make a pattern for a new style from the base block or sloper.

flexible manufacturing system (FMS) "Any departure from traditional mass production systems of apparel toward faster, smaller, more flexible production units that depend upon the coordinated efforts of minimally supervised teams of workers" (AAMA Technical Advisory Committee, 1988, as cited in Hill, 1992, p. 34; see chapter 11).

floor ready merchandise (FRM) Merchandise shipped by the manufacturer or distribution center affixed with hangtags, labels, and price information so that the retailer can immediately place the goods on the selling floor.

fourchettes Strips between the second/third, third/fourth, and fourth/fifth fingers of gloves to provide depth for the thickness of the finger.

franchise A type of contractual retail organization in which the parent company provides the franchisee with the exclusive distribution of a well-recognized brand name in a specific market area as well as assistance in running the business in return for a franchise payment.

freight forwarding company A company that moves a shipment of goods from the country where the goods were produced to the United States.

full-fashioned Goods knit with shaping along the edges to conform to the body contour.

garment dyed Apparel produced as white or colorless goods, then dyed during the finishing process.

garment specification sheet (garment spec sheet) A listing of vital information for the garment style, such as garment sketch, fabric swatch, specific fabrics for all areas including interfacings, all sundries, and construction specifications. It may also include the size specifications (dimensions).

general partnership A business arrangement in which coowners of a company share in the liability as well as the profits of the company according to the conditions of the partnership contract.

grade rules The amounts and locations of growth or reduction for pattern pieces to create the various sizes.

grading See **pattern grading**.

greige goods Fabrics that have not received finishing treatments, such as bleaching, shearing, brushing, embossing, or dyeing.

group Coordinated apparel items using a few colors and fabrics within an apparel line.

hand "The total sensation experienced when a textile is manipulated in the fingers" (Hatch, K. L. [1993]. *Textile Science*. Minneapolis: West Publishing Company, p. 44; see Chapter 6).

home fashions Textile products used for home-end uses, such as towels, bedding, draperies, and table linens, and whose styles change over time in response to fashion trends.

horizontally integrated Business strategy whereby a company focuses on a single stage of production/distribution but with varying products or services.

importer/packager Company that develops full lines of apparel with contractors in other countries and sells them to retailers as complete packages for use as private label merchandise.

initial cost estimate The preliminary estimate of the cost of a new style based on materials, sundries, labor and other such components as duty and freight.

International Ladie's Garment Worker's Union Formed in 1900, the primary union of garment workers in the women's apparel industry until 1995, when it combined with the Amalgamated Clothing and Textile Workers Union to form the Union of Needletrades, Industrial and Textile Employees (UNITE).

item house Contractor that specializes in the production of one product.

jobber An intermediary in the apparel industry who carries inventories of apparel for ready shipment to retailers.

jobber/home fashions Personnel involved in the marketing and distribution of home textile piece goods, particularly upholstery and drapery fabrics.

knock-off A facsimile of an existing garment that sells at a lower price than the original. The copy might be made in a less-expensive fabric and might have some design details modified or eliminated.

lab dip The vendor-supplied sample of the dyed-to-match product, such as fabric, zipper, button, knit collar or cuff, or thread.

last A wood, plastic, or metal mold, shaped like a foot and used to form shoes.

lay figure See *croquis*.

leased department Contractual agreement in which a retailer leases space within a large department store to run a specialty department. Typical leased departments are fine jewelry, furs, and shoes.

leveraged buyout A public corporation's stock is purchased by a group of investors who borrow money from an investment firm using the corporation's assets as collateral.

licensing An agreement in which the owner (licensor) of a particular image or design sells the right to use that image or design to another party, typically a manufacturer (licensee), for payment of royalties to the licensor.

licensor Company that has developed a well-known image (property) and sells the right to use the image to manufacturers to put on merchandise.

limited marketing channel Marketing channel in which manufacturers sell their merchandise to consumers through retailers.

limited partnership A specialized type of partnership in which a partner is liable only for the amount of capital invested in the business and any profits are shared according to the conditions of the limited partnership contract.

line One large group or several small groups of apparel items developed with a theme that links the them together.

line brochure (line catalog, or line sheet) A catalog of all the styles available in the line used to market the line to retail buyers.

line-for-line copy A garment made as an exact replica of an existing garment style, produced in a similar fabric.

linens Describes towels, sheets, tablecloths, napkins, and other home textiles once made almost exclusively from linen.

long-range forecasting Research focusing on general economic and social trends related to consumer spending patterns and the business climate.

marker A master cutting plan for the pattern pieces for a specific style.

market center Name given to cities that not only house marts and showrooms, but also have important manufacturing and retailing industries, e.g., New York, Los Angeles, Dallas, Atlanta, Chicago.

marketing Process of identifying a target market and developing appropriate strategies for product development, pricing, promotion, and distribution.

marketing channel Companies that perform the manufacturing, wholesaling, and retailing functions to get merchandise to the ultimate consumer.

market niche The blend of product type and target customer for a specific segment of the retail trade.

market research Process of providing information regarding what, where, and how much a specific group of customers want to purchase.

market week Times of the year in which retail buyers come to showrooms or exhibit halls to see the seasonal fashion lines offered by apparel companies.

mart Building or group of buildings that house showrooms in which sales representatives show apparel lines to retail buyers.

mass customization The use of computer technology to customize the garment style for the individual customer, either by individualizing the fit to the customer's measurements, or by offering individualized combinations of fabric, garment style, and size options.

mass production Type of production in which identical apparel is produced in large quantities using machines.

merchandiser In the context of this text, an apparel company employee who is responsible for planning and overseeing that the company's needs for a line are met. This person often coordinates several lines presented by the company.

merchandising Area of an apparel company that develops strategies to have the right merchandise, at the right price, at the right time, at the right locations to meet the wants and needs of the target customer.

merger Blending of one company into another company.

millinery Women's hats, and especially hat making that requires handwork.

modular manufacturing A term often used in the U.S. apparel industry to describe flexible manufacturing (Hill, 1992, p. 34; see chapter 11).

monopolistic competition Competitive situation in which many companies compete in terms of product type, but the specific products of any one company are perceived as unique by consumers.

monopoly Situation in which one company dominates the market and can thus price its goods and/or services at whatever scale it wishes.

muffler Long oblong scarf, often wool or silk, worn as an accompaniment to an overcoat.

muslin An inexpensive fabric, usually unbleached cotton, used to develop the first trial of a new garment style.

napery A term used to describe tablecloths and napkins.

national/designer brand brand name that is distributed nationally and to which consumers attach a specific image, quality level, and price.

nonstore retailer Distribution of products to consumers through means other than traditional retail stores.

off-price retailer Retailer that specializes in selling national brands or designer apparel lines at discount prices.

off-shore production Production outside the United States using production specifications provided by U.S. companies.

oligopoly Competitive situation in which a few companies dominate and essentially have control of the market making it very difficult for other companies to enter.

partnership Company owned by two or more persons; operation of partnerships are outlined in a written contract or "articles of partnership."

patent "Publicly given, exclusive right to an idea, product, or process" (Fisher & Jennings, 1991, p. 595; see Chapter 2).

pattern design system (**PDS**) A computer hardware and software system that is used by the pattern maker to create and store new garment (pattern) styles.

pattern grading Taking the production pattern pieces made in the sample size for a style and creating a set of pattern pieces for each of the sizes listed on the garment spec sheet.

power loom Automated machine used to weave cloth. Francis Cabot Lowell invented the power loom in 1813.

preliminary line sheet Catalog of styles in a line used internally by a company in the process of line development.

private corporation Type of corporation in which no public market exists for the stock in the corporation and stock has not been issued for public purchase.

private label Merchandise that includes a retailer's label on a product for which the retailer has some or full control of the manufacturing operation.

private label brand Brand name that is owned and marketed by a specific retailer for use in its stores.

production The construction process by which the materials, trims, and garment pieces are merged into a finished apparel product or accessory.

production cutting The production fabric, laid open across its entire width and many feet in length, is stacked in multiple layers with the marker resting on the top, and cut by computer or by using hand cutting machines.

production engineer A specialist who is responsible for the production pattern and/or for planning the production process, facilities, and final costing.

production marker The full size master cutting layout for all the pattern pieces for a specific style, for all the sizes specified for production.

product type the specific category or categories of apparel the company specializes in producing.

progressive bundle system Groups of a dozen (usually) garment parts placed in bundles and moved from one sewing operator to the next. Each operator performs one or several construction steps on each garment in the bundle, then passes the bundle on to the next operator.

prototype The sample garment for a new style (made in the new fabric, or made in a facsimile fabric; if made in muslin, the prototype is usually called a toile).

public corporation Type of corporation in which stock has been issued for public purchase and at least some of the shares of stock are owned by the general public.

publicity Promotional strategy whereby the company's activities are viewed as newsworthy and thus are featured or are mentioned in print, television, or other news media.

pull-down cutting The process of cutting gloves by die cutting the pieces.

pure competition Competitive situation in which there are many producers and consumers of similar products, so that price is determined by market demand.

quality assurance Area of a company that focuses on quality control issues but also takes into consideration satisfaction of consumer needs for a specific end use; standards of acceptance set forth by the contracting party (the apparel manufacturer for example) for the product being produced.

quality control Area of a company that focuses on inspecting finished products and making sure they adhere to specific quality standards.

Quick Response Comprehensive business strategy that promotes responsiveness to consumer demand, encourages business partnerships, and shortens the business cycle from raw materials to the consumer.

quirks Tiny triangular gussets in gloves at the base of the second, third, and fourth fingers.

quota Numerical limit on the number of products in specific categories that can be imported.

rack trade Manufacturers who design, produce, and market belts to retailers.

ready-to-wear (**RTW**) Apparel made with mass-production techniques using standardized sizing; sometimes referred to as "off-the-rack."

regimental stripes Fabric used for men's ties with wide and narrow stripes that were used originally to signify the various historical military regiments.

relationship merchandising A refocusing of department stores with an emphasis on presentation, customer service, and having the right products for their target market that are different than the products carried by other stores.

retailer "any business establishment that directs its marketing efforts toward the final consumer for the purpose of selling goods and services" (Lewison, 1994, p. 5; see Chapter 12).

retail store/direct market brand Brand name on merchandise that is also the name of the retail store, e.g., The Gap, L.L. Bean.

Retro The return to the fashion look of recent decades (abbreviated use of the word retrospective).

sales representative Individual who serves as the intermediary between the apparel manufacturer and the retailer, selling the apparel line to retail buyers.

sales volume Either the total number of units of a style that sold at retail or the total number of dollars consumers spent on the style.

salon de couture Haute couture designer's showroom.

sample cut A three-to-five-yard length of fabric ordered from a textile mill by the apparel manufacturer to use in making a prototype garment.

sample sewer A highly skilled technician who sews the entire prototype garment using a variety of sewing equipment and production processes similar to those used in factories.

sell through The percentage computed by the number of items sold divided by the number of items in the line the retailer purchased from the manufacturer.

sew by Also known as counter sample, a sample garment sewed by a contractor and submitted to the apparel manufacturer for approval. The sample is then used as a benchmark to compare the sewn production goods.

shopping the market Looking for new fashion trends in the retail markets that may influence the direction of an upcoming line.

short-range forecasting Researching specific fashion trends and new styles for an upcoming season and determining the level of demand and timing for these styles (also referred to as what, when, and how much to manufacture).

single-hand system A garment production method in which an individual sewer is responsible for sewing an entire garment. It is used primarily for couture or very high-priced, limited production apparel and for sewing prototypes.

size specifications The actual garment measurements at specific locations on the finished goods for each of the sizes specified for a style.

size standards Proportional increase or decrease in garment measurements for sizes produced by a ready-to-wear apparel company.

sloper A base pattern in the company's sample size used as the basis for making a pattern of the new garment style.

soft floor coverings Wall-to-wall carpet, area rugs, runners, and scatter rugs.

sole proprietorship Company owned and operated by a single individual.

source, vendor, supplier Company from which textile producers, apparel manufacturers, or retailers purchase components or products necessary in their production and distribution operations (e.g., fiber sources, fabric sources, apparel product sources).

sourcing Decision process for determining how and where textile and apparel products or their components will be produced.

specialty store Retailer establishment that focuses on a specific type of merchandise.

specification buying Retailer-initiated design and manufacture of apparel goods in which the retailer works directly with the sewing contractors (or their agents), rather than working with an apparel manufacturer to produce private label goods.

spinning mill Company that specializes in the spinning of yarn. The first spinning mill in the United States opened in 1791 by Samuel Slater.

spreading The process of unwinding the large rolls of fabric onto long, wide cutting tables, stacked layer-upon-layer, in preparation for cutting.

spreading machines Equipment designed to carry the large rolls of fabric, guided on tracks along the side edges of the cutting table, to spread the fabric smoothly and quickly.

stockholder Owner of stock or shares in a corporation; each share of stock owned by a stockholder represents a percentage of the company.

style number A number (usually four digits) assigned to each garment style that is coded to indicate the season/year for the style and other style information.

Sundries and Apparel Findings Linkage Council (SAFLINC) Formed in 1987 to establish voluntary electronic data interchange standards between apparel manufacturers and their nontextile suppliers. In 1994 it was integrated into the Quick Response Committee of the American Apparel Manufacturers Association.

supermarket Retailer establishment that carries a full line of foods and related products using a self-service strategy.

superstore Upgraded large supermarkets.

sustainable design A term used to designate the "awareness of the full short and long-term consequences of any transformation of the environment" (*Environmentally intelligent textiles,* 1995, p. 53; see Chapter 14).

swatch A small sample of the intended fabric to be used for a garment style.

table cutting The process of cutting gloves entirely by hand, on a worktable.

tagboard A heavy weight paper (also called oaktag or hard paper) used for cutting pattern pieces.

takeover The result of one company or individual gaining control of another company by buying a large enough portion of the company's shares; can be either a merger or a consolidation.

tanning The process of finishing leather, by making the skins and hides pliable and water resistant.

target customer Description of the gender, age range, lifestyle, geographic location, and price zone for the majority of the company's customers for a specific line.

tariff Tax assessed on imports.

tawning The process of finishing furs, by making the pelts pliable and water resistant.

tech drawing A drawing of the garment style as viewed flat rather than depicted three dimensionally on a fashion figure (an abbreviation of the term technical drawing). It could include drawings of close-up details of the garment.

textile accessories and accents Category of home fashions that includes textile bedding and bath products, textile kitchen products and tabletop accessories, and textile accents such as wall hangings.

Textile/Apparel Linkage Council (**TALC**) Formed in 1986 to establish voluntary electronic data interchange standards between apparel manufacturers and textile companies. In 1994 it was integrated into the Quick Response Committee of the American Apparel Manufacturers Association.

Textile/Clothing Technology Corporation (**TC**)^2 Nonprofit corporation that develops, tests, and teaches advanced apparel technology.

textile mill Company that specializes in the fabric construction stage of production (e.g., weaving, knitting).

thread count The number of yarns or "threads" in one square inch of fabric, used especially in reference to sheets in the home fashions category.

toile A French term whose literal translation means cloth; it refers to the muslin trial garment.

tolerance The stated range of acceptable dimensional measurements as a plus or minus in inches (or metric measurements) from the size specifications.

top of the bed Home fashions category that includes comforters, duvet covers, blankets, bedspreads, dust ruffles, pillow shams, and throws.

trade association Nonprofit association made up of member companies designed to research, promote, or provide educational services regarding an industry or a specific aspect of an industry.

trademark "Distinctive name, word, mark, design, or picture used by a company to identify its product" (Fisher & Jennings, 1991, p. 595; see Chapter 2).

trade show Sponsored by trade associations, apparel marts, and/or promotional companies, trade shows allow companies to promote their newest products to prospective buyers who have the opportunity to review new products from a number of companies under one roof.

trank The section of a glove that covers the palm and the face of the hand.

trend research Reading appropriate trade publications or fashion magazines to determine directions for color, fabric, and fashion.

unit production system (**UPS**) Production system in which the parts for each garment are transported on conveyors, one garment at a time, to the sewing operators who perform one or several sewing operations, then release the garment for transport to the next work station.

Universal Product Code (**UPC**) One of several barcode symbologies used for electronic identification of merchandise. A UPC number is twelve digits that identifies the manufacturer and merchandise item by stock-keeping unit.

upholstery fabrics Fabrics used primarily for sofas, love seats, chairs, and ottomans.

usage The number of yards (yardage) of fabric(s) required to make the garment style. It usually refers to the most economical layout, which uses the least amount of fabric.

vendor *See* **source**, **vendor**, **supplier**

vendor-managed retail inventory Programs in which retail sales/stockout data are reviewed by the manufacturer and replenishments are ordered as often as required.

vendor marking Hangtags, labels, and price information affixed to merchandise by the vendor (manufacturer).

vertical integration or vertical marketing channel Business strategy in which a company handles several steps in production and/or distribution.

Voluntary Inter-Industry Communications Standards Committee (VICS) Formed in 1986 to gain agreement among retailers and producers on common standards of communication, including the use of Universal Product Code system and electronic data interchange formats.

wall coverings Fabrics used to cover walls, vertical panels, and partitions.

warehouse retailer Retailer who reduces operating expenses and offers goods at discount prices by combining showroom, warehouse, and retail operations together.

window treatments Draperies, curtains, and fabric shades, as well as decorative treatments such as valances, cornices, and swags.

work-in-process (WIP) The quantity of goods in the process of assembly in the sewing factory at a given time.

wholesale price The price of the style that the retailer will pay the apparel manufacturer for the goods. The price is based on the manufacturer's cost to produce the style plus the manufacturer's profit.

yarn Collection of fibers or filaments laid or twisted together to form a continuous strand strong enough for use in fabrics.

zeitgeist The social spirit of the time of a popular culture during a specific time frame.

Standard Industrial Classification
(SIC), 71
stockholders, 36
store ownership groups, 335
stores
types of, 333–334
strike off, 165
style number, 171
style selection, 189–190
Sundries and Apparel Findings Linkage
Council (SAFLINC), 26
supermarket retailing, 339–340
superstore, 339
sustainable design, 415–418
swatch, 79, 166, 193
sweatshops, 9, 286–287

takeover, 40
Talbots 366, 372
tanning process, 69–70
Target, 17, 87, 113, 205, 337, 413
target costing, 187
target customer, 137, 211
definition of, 137
profile of, 137–138
tariff, 228, 276
tawning process, 70–71
technical drawing, 165–166
television retailing, 343, 414
terms of agreement
order placement, 194
textile(s), 62
definition of, 62
development, 10, 13, 16
end uses of, 65–66
textile accessories, 413
Textile/Apparel Linkage Council
(TALC), 26
Textile/Clothing Technology
Corporation (TC)², 20–22,
25, 198
member benefits, 22
mission, 21

textile design, 84–85, 90, 165, 378,
397–398
textile industry
environmental issues in, 91–92
structure of, 63–65
textile mill, 16, 65, 80–84, 88
textile technology, 17, 90–91
textile testing, 86–87
Thinsulate, 396
thread count, 411–412
throwster, 65
toile, 167
tolerance, 255
top of the bed, 412
trade associations, 133
accessories, 360
apparel, 14, 120–121, 140
home fashions, 401–402
retailing, 344
textile, 16, 74–77, 78–79, 401
trade laws, 52–53, 54, 286
trademarks, 49–51
definition, 49
in textiles, 77–78
trade publications, 11, 24, 74, 122, 143,
344, 359, 404–405, 406
trade shows, 217–218, 360, 403
textile, 144–145
Triangle Shirtwaist Co., 10
trunk show, 238

Union of Needletrades, Industrial and
Textile Employees, 21, 25
United States Shoe Corporation, 362
unit production system (UPS), 303–305
universal product code (UPC),
326–328, 405
unlimited liability, 32, 35
upholstery fabrics, 407–409
usage, 186–187

vending machine, 343
vendor, 248, 251

vendor–managed retail inventory,
330–331
vendor marking, 325
vertical integration, 65, 80, 323, 393
VF Corporation, 331
Victoria's Secret, 113
Vionnet, Madeleine, 13, 167–168
visual merchandising, 237
Vogue 11, 139
Voluntary Inter–Industry
Communications Standards
Committee (VICS), 22, 26
Vuitton, Louis, 382

Wal–Mart, 17, 18, 45, 200, 288,
337, 413
wall coverings, 409
Wannamaker's, 8
warehouse retailer, 341
Westpoint Pepperell, 393, 394
window treatments, 409
Whitney, Eli, 5
wholesale price, 190–191
wholesale price zones, 111–112
wool, 68
processing, 68
Wool Bureau, Inc., 50, 74, 75
Women's Wear Daily, 11, 24, 124, 139,
236, 280, 344
work-in-process, 303, 304
World Wide Web, 401
Worth, Charles Frederick, 103
Wrangler, 112

yarn
definition of, 62
filament, 62, 72
spun, 62

zeitgeist 162